¡CHICANA POWER!

CW00520690

CHICANA MATTERS SERIES, DEENA J. GONZÁLEZ
AND ANTONIA CASTAÑEDA, EDITORS

Chicana Matters Series focuses on one of the largest population groups in the United States today, documenting the lives, values, philosophies, and artistry of contemporary Chicanas. Books in this series may be richly diverse, reflecting the experiences of Chicanas themselves, and incorporating a broad spectrum of topics and fields of inquiry. Cumulatively, the books represent the leading knowledge and scholarship in a significant and growing field of research and, along with the literary works, art, and activism of Chicanas, underscore their significance in the history and culture of the United States.

¡CHICANA POWER!

Contested Histories of Feminism

in the Chicano Movement

MAYLEI BLACKWELL

UNIVERSITY OF TEXAS PRESS   *Austin*

Copyright © 2011 by the University of Texas Press
All rights reserved
Printed in the United States of America
Third paperback printing, 2012

Requests for permission to reproduce material from this work should be sent to:
Permissions
University of Texas Press
P.O. Box 7819
Austin, TX 78713-7819
www.utexas.edu/utpress/about/bpermission.html

♾ The paper used in this book meets the minimum requirements of
ANSI/NISO Z39.48-1992 (R1997) (Permanence of Paper).

Earlier versions of chapter 3 were published as "Bearing Bandoleras: Transfigurative Liberation and the Iconography of la Nueva Chicana," in *Beyond the Frame: Women of Color and Visual Representations*, eds. Neferti X. M. Tadiar and Angela Y. Davis (New York: Palgrave, 2005), 171–196, reprinted with permission of Palgrave Macmillan, and "Contested Histories: la Hijas de Cuauhtémoc, Chicana Feminisms and Print Culture in the Chicano Movement, 1968–1973," in *Chicana Feminisms: A Critical Reader*, eds. Gabriela Arredondo, Aída Hurtado, Norma Klahn, Olga Nájera-Ramírez, and Patricia Zavella (Durham, NC: Duke University Press, 2003), 59–89, reprinted with permission.

LIBRARY OF CONGRESS CATALOGING-IN-PUBLICATION DATA

Blackwell, Maylei, 1969–
¡Chicana power! : contested histories of feminism in the Chicano movement / by Maylei Blackwell. — 1st ed.
    p.   cm. — (Chicana matters series)
Includes bibliographical references and index.
ISBN 978-0-292-72588-1 (cloth : alk. paper) —
ISBN 978-0-292-72690-1 (pbk. : alk. paper)
1. Mexican American women.   2. Feminism—United States.   3. Women political activists—United States.   I. Title.
E184.M5B55   2011
305.48′86872073—dc22   2011006831

CONTENTS

ACKNOWLEDGMENTS

I was taught in the Cherokee way to believe that stories have power: the power to inspire, the power to heal, the power to transform, the power to incite new possibilities, in fact, to create new worlds. I learned to be an oral historian by witnessing the stories of my family. I became a holder of stories, listening to the narratives that wove me into generations across the long march, relocation days, and the time before creating an umbilicus to those who dreamt me into being. I also grew up, like many sons and daughters of migrants, with my father in a distant land (Thailand, to be precise). Stories of him connected me across continents, linking me to a sense of belonging that formed an amulet of protection for my heart in the context where my difference and the color of my skin made me a target of racism.

The stories at the center of this book have power. When I first started hearing these stories, I was a waitress, a student, and an activist. As a young, woman of color feminist, these stories connected me to a genealogy and a knowledge that the battles we were fighting others had fought before us. Now twenty years later, they connect me to a hope that others will be inspired and transformed by these new stories.

What you are holding in your hands is the result of a journey twenty years in the making. Along the way many, many have offered their insights, their labor, their inspiration, and their encouragement. First and foremost I thank Anna NietoGomez for her enduring work in formulating Chicana feminist theory and practice, for her uncompromised view of social justice and her courage in articulating early on the inseparability of race, class, and gender oppressions. I thank her for sharing her story, for the many conversations that now span decades, and for all the care she took in reading the manuscript cover to cover. I also thank the many others who shared their stories and critical reflections with me, especially Leticia Hernández, Sylvia Castillo, Corinne Sánchez, Cecelia Quijano, Martha Cotera, Keta Miranda, Betita Martinez, Elma Barrera, Gloria Guardiola, and Yolanda Birdwell. I acknowledge those activists such as Norma Owens and Cindy Honesto, who are not present to tell their story, but whose stories are central to this history.

At California State University, Long Beach, Sherna Gluck inspired me with her critical mind and fierce sense of justice. Our conversations on feminist historiography and oral history have continued off and on for twenty years. I also thank Norma Chinchilla, Sharon Sievers, Kathryn MacMahon, Federico Sánchez (who taught the first Chicano History class I attended),

Chanzo Nettles, Rex Gilliland, Adrienne Carrier, Alicia Nevarez, and the Students for Peace and Justice. I met Dr. Antonia Castañeda and Dr. Vicki Ruiz in 1992 in Chicago at an OAH panel and even as an undergraduate, they received with me warmth and have offered their support and tireless encouragement throughout the many years of this project. The community formed by all the activists and scholars of Mujeres Activas en Letras y Cambio Social have supported my development as a scholar and this book since its inception.

At UC Santa Cruz, I thank Angela Davis, who served as my advisor throughout my doctoral training in the History of Consciousness Department. She so firmly believed in me that I had to relinquish my own self-doubt and figure out how to try to live up to her expectations of me. I thank her for continuing to walk and weave a path of activism and scholarship and encouraging us to bring our social justice concerns centrally into our intellectual labor, instead of doing activism "on the side." I would like to thank Patricia Zavella for her grounded vision of Chicana feminisms as well as her dedication to her students, myself included, who she has mentored for over ten years. In 1997, I was told by my Qualifying Exam committee that I would pass the exam on one condition. As I held my breath, they told me that they would pass me only if I agreed to publish the material as a book manuscript. So in some sense, I am finally passing my qualifying exam. I thank the amazing community of scholars who trained me including Sonia Alvarez, Rosa Linda Fregoso, and Jonathan Fox. Thank you to Norma Klahn and Pedro Castillo for their work in creating the intellectual space provided by the Chicano/Latino Resource Center at UCSC as well as those who forged critical dialogues Latin American and Latino Studies at UCSC. I thank Guillermo Delgado, Donna Harraway, Nancy Chen, Olga Nájera Ramirez, Aída Hurtado, Jim Clifford, Neferti Tadiar, and Rosie Cabrera. I was lucky to be able to study with Chicana feminist historian Emma Pérez as a visiting professor and thank her for pushing us to move beyond established paradigms and to create new epistemologies in the archaeology of Chicana feminisms.

I am grateful for research funding and support I received from the Pre-Doctoral Scholars Program of the California State University Office of the Chancellor, the Chicano/Latino Research Center at UC Santa Cruz for summer research funding and the opportunity to present my research for the first time, the History of Consciousness Department, the Women's Studies Dissertation at the University of California, Santa Barbara, the Summer Faculty Research Grant at Loyola Marymount University, and the Career Enhancement Fellowship of the Woodrow Wilson National Foundation. I thank Norma Alarcón, who served as my mentor for the UC President's Postdoctoral Fellowship Program, as well as Kimberly M. Adkinson and Sheila O'Rourke. At

UCLA, this research was generously supported by the Institute for American Cultures, the Chicano Studies Research Center, the Committee on Research of the Academic Senate, the Chancellor's Office for Faculty Diversity, and Reynaldo Macias in his role as the Acting Dean of Social Sciences.

Along the way I made many, many friends, supporters, and critics that helped shape this project. While academic writing is a solitary process that can be isolating, the journey of this book was a community-making process. I have been honored to be part of several critical intellectual/political community spaces along the way, as I learned to tell this story. The Research Cluster for the Study of Women of Color in Conflict and Collaboration helped me survive and thrive in graduate school. I would like to thank Keta Miranda, Luz Calvo, Deborah Vargas, Michelle Habell Pallán, JoAnne Barker, Catriona Rueda Esquibel, Laura Kuo, Nancy San Martin, Kale Fajardo, Darshan Campos, J. Kehaulani Kauanui, M.R. Daniel, Andy Smith, and Isabel Vélez. Julian Blecker, Sergio de la Mora, Sherrie Tucker, Ivelisse Rivera, and Phil Rodriguez also offered community and *amistad* during my time in Santa Cruz. I was also deeply touched by the friendship of Gloría Anzaldúa who encouraged me to write and taught me that walking along the ocean's edge, communing with Yemayá, and writing dates with friends are key to a writer's life.

Many lent their ears, eyes, hearts, and minds to giving feedback. I would like to especially thank Vicki Ruiz, Horacio Roque Ramirez, Gloria Cuádraz, Sherna Gluck, Teresa Barnett, Andreana Clay, Clarissa Rojas, Jeanne Scheper, Nancy Mirabal, Jennifer Guglielmo, Tiffany Ann Lopez, and Leisette Rodriguez. With all my heart, I thank the brilliant and talented members of the LOUD Collective, a Women of Color Writing Group, for the nourishment (food, ideas, writing, and community), especially Jody Kim, Arlene Keizer, Jayna Brown, Victoria Bomberry, Erica Edwards, Aisha Finch, Tiffany Willoboughy Herard, Caroline Streeter, Deb Vargas, and most especially Grace Hong, a dedicated friend, colleague, and comrade. Many others offered support along the way. I thank Devra Weber, Richard Martinez, Nadine Naber, Inés Hernández-Ávila, Renya Ramirez, Denise Segura, Mariana Pérez Oscana, Elisa Huerta, Cynthia Orozco, Chandra Mohanty, Beverly Guy-Sheftall, Jacqui Alexander, and Alma López for the beautiful artwork on the cover.

At UCLA, Mignon Moore, Purnima Mankekar, Sandra Hale, Rafael Pérez Torres, Vilma Ortiz, and Mishuana Goeman made sure I was on the right path and listened to my ideas as they unfolded into this book. My colleagues in the César E. Chávez Department of Chicana and Chicano Studies have offered their support and created a vibrant space for student learning, scholarly production and social engagement at UCLA. I have had the pleasure to teach many students who shaped this project with their ideas, questions, and preoccupations. I have also been honored to mentor many young scholars, some who have traveled with me as I worked on different parts of this book and several who have provided research assistance. I would like to especially thank Janyce Cardenas, Eowyn Williamson, Yamisette Westerband, Lidia Galisia, Monica de la Torre, and especially Rosie Bermudez, intrepid research assistant and all around homegirl.

I would especially like to thank the editors of the Chicana Matters Series, Deena González and Antonia Castañeda, as well as Theresa May for handling this project with care and attention. Many friendships outside of the academy sustained me when my spirits sagged or when I could not see the end of the road. Thank you to Josephine Ramos, Persephone Gonzalez, Delia Meraz, Alice Hom, Susana Moreno, Iyatunde Dixon, Queen Hollins, Odilia Romero, Lola de la Riva, Osa Hidalgo de la Riva, tatiana de la tierra, Olga García Echeverría, and the delightful and talented members of the Tongue Fisters whose mix of poetry, good food, and friendship helped me recover from writing trauma. Spirit and healing were central to this journey. I offer my gratitude to the medicine people Eagle Woman and Running Wolf and the community of Gadohi Usquanigodi for bringing me home to the Tsalagi way. I thank the Sanctuary Sangha at Manzanita Village along with Caitriona Reed and Michelle Benzamin Miki and many others in the community of healers including Cathy, Micki, Laura, and Cat.

Finally, my family inspired this journey and sustained me at each step. Thank you to Marya Blackwell, Stephanie Holand, Gary Blackwell, Alphonce Brown, Rubi Fregoso, Jose Legaspi, Luna Yareli, and Cosme Queztal for their love and support.

¡CHICANA POWER!

THE TELLING IS POLITICAL

THIS BOOK DOCUMENTS how a generation of Chicana activists of the 1960s and 1970s created a multifaceted vision of liberation that continues to reverberate today as contemporary activists, artists, and intellectuals, both grassroots and academic, struggle for, revise, and rework the political legacy of Chicana feminism they inspired. *¡Chicana Power!* illuminates how Chicana organizers were influenced not only by the awakening of racial consciousness and cultural renewal generated by the Chicano movement but also by the struggles over gender and sexuality within it, which together ultimately produced a new Chicana political identity. Based on the culmination of many years of archival research and the rich oral histories I conducted with the pioneering Chicana activist and theorist Anna NietoGomez and the members of the Hijas de Cuauhtémoc, one of the first and arguably most influential Latina feminist organizations, this book builds an analysis of the interplay of social and political factors that gave rise to Chicana feminism within the regional and national development of the Chicano movement in the late 1960s and 1970s.[1] Excavating the local histories of Chicana political organizing in Southern California, I examine how NietoGomez and the Hijas de Cuauhtémoc forged an autonomous space for women's political participation and challenged the gendered confines of Chicano cultural nationalism within campus and community politics and later in the formation of the field of Chicana studies.[2] This project builds a critical genealogy of the Hijas de Cuauhtémoc, who, along with other early Chicana feminists, are historically significant because this group of young women was one of the first to mobilize Chicanas around the gendered and sexual experience of racial and economic marginalization. Further, their elaboration of an early analysis of the interrelated nature of gender, racial, sexual, and class power—a hallmark of women of color feminism—provides us with a lasting and important political legacy for combating multiple oppressions and creating multi-issue organizations even today.[3] In fact, many of the theoretical innovations attributed to women of color feminisms of the 1980s, such as the concept of intersectionality or interventions regarding multiple subjectivity ascribed to the postmodern turn in feminist theory, in fact have their roots in the political views of women of color activists in social movements of the 1960s and 1970s.

Coming together to address the repudiation of women's leadership and the marginalization of women's issues in the Chicano student movement, this group began organizing in 1968 and published one of the first Chicana newspapers in 1971. *Las Hijas de Cuauhtémoc* was named for the Mexican feminist organization that demanded women's civil and political rights and an end to the Díaz dictatorship at the turn of the twentieth century.[4] Reclaiming an alternative tradition of women's resistance, the Hijas de Cuauhtémoc shifted the gendered political terrain as well as the historical imaginary of the Chicano movement by deploying what I call "retrofitted memory." I use the concept of retrofitted memory to theorize how new gendered political identities are produced *through* history and how those historical narratives engender new contestatory identities and political practices.

RETROFITTED MEMORY: NEW STRUCTURES OF REMEMBRANCE

Retrofitted memory is a form of countermemory that uses fragments of older histories that have been disjunctured by colonial practices of organizing historical knowledge or by masculinist renderings of history that disappear women's political involvement in order to create space for women in historical traditions that erase them. It draws from other Chicano cultural practices, such as the *rasquache* aesthetic, or customizing of cars, that use older parts (or what is spit out as junk in global capitalist forms of production and waste) to refine existing bodies or frameworks.[5] By drawing from both discarded and suppressed forms of knowledge, retrofitted memory creates new forms of consciousness customized to embodied material realities, political visions, and creative desires for societal transformation.

Retrofitted memory assumes that the project of hegemony is never complete and must be constantly resolidified and renarrated in history. It is precisely within the gaps, interstices, silences, and crevices of the uneven narratives of domination that possibilities lie for fracturing dominant narratives and creating spaces for new historical subjects to emerge. Fragments of historical knowledge and memory are not merely recuperated, then, but retrofitted into new forms of political subjectivity that may draw from one historical or geographic context to be refashioned in another. For emergent political subjects, retrofitted memory creates alternative registers of meaning and authority, both moral and political.

¡Chicana Power! not only recovers histories that have been erased and excavates new feminist genealogies of resistance; it also transforms the ways we understand these historical narratives and the political nature of the knowledge practices that produce them. More than a book of history, this historiographic intervention asks us to consider why, despite the clear emergence of Chicana feminism throughout the late 1960s and 1970s, the history of Chicana feminisms *in* the movement is still largely an untold story? Histories of the Chicano and feminist movements have failed to fully record the vital forms of Chicana political consciousness and organizing that existed in this period. As the first book-length study of women in the Chicano movement, this project contributes to the growing scholarship that is beginning to historicize Chicana activism of the second half of the twentieth century.[6] It extends a conversation about the roots of Chicana feminism in Mexico, primarily women's involvement in the radical tradition of anarchism and socialism, which has informed labor and civil rights movements by Latinas/os north of the border. While there are many other sources of Chicana feminist consciousness and organizing projects that need to be more fully documented, the story of Anna NietoGomez and members of Las Hijas de Cuauhtémoc is a significant thread in the multilayered struggle around gender and sexuality in *el movimiento*. Although they were a small organization, their impact as one of the first organizations to explicitly call for and theorize Chicana feminism was paramount. Their ideas informed the terrain of struggle across movement sectors, reached into gendered discussions in other regions, and gave other women and men who believed in gender equity within the broader project of Chicano liberation a vehicle for speaking out. While their work was vital within the student movement, they were also part of a broader mobilization of movement women in the greater Los Angeles region that included the East Los Angeles Chicana Welfare Rights Organization and the Comisión Femenil Mexicana Nacional.

While this history bursts with telling, it has also been a challenging one to tell because it makes us reconsider the limited (and limiting) conventions of writing history. Drawing on Foucault's notion of genealogy, I examine the social movement spaces in which Chicana feminist knowledges were produced as well as the "mechanics of erasure" that have obscured them.[7] This means looking at the conditions in which a story/history is told, interrogating the erasures, and listening to the gaps and interstices to reveal the workings of power, as suggested by the Haitian scholar Michel-Rolph Trouillot's two sides of historicity. He argues that we engage "simultaneously in the sociohistorical process and in narrative constructions about that process."[8] Further, he argues:

> What matters most are the process and conditions of production of such narratives. Only a focus on that process can uncover the ways in which the two sides of historicity intertwine in a particular context. Only through the overlap can we discover the differential exercise of power that makes some narratives possible and silences others.[9]

Rather than an expansive history of the participation of all women in the Chicano movement, *¡Chicana Power!* is guided by the strategy of genealogy in its in-depth excavation of historical knowledge produced by Chicana activists like the Hijas de Cuauhtémoc, which can serve as an alternative analytics through which to understand both Chicano and feminist histories. By focusing on what I call the mechanics of erasure in historical writings, this study attempts to undermine, instead of replicate, the power relations and regime of truth that hold these mechanics in place. It is not enough to say, "The women were there, too." To subvert the ideologies of these official histories, we must overturn the epistemological register that licenses them.

Because the add-and-stir method is not sufficient, this project proposes an alternative historiographic framework for understanding women's social movements. Illustrating that history is more than just a narrative of the past, it examines how memory circulates in popular culture and produces and maintains political identities and the boundaries of what is politically possible today.

While other Chicano movement histories give a sweeping, epic portrayal of a political movement and link historical significance to the problematic of why movements emerge and decline, this narrative is organized around historicizing the genesis of feminist consciousness and understanding gender and sexual politics during the Chicano movement. It locates the contributions of the Hijas de Cuauhtémoc within the development of Chicana feminism in relation to other organizations and contextualizes their interventions in regional, cross-regional, and national developments. And it reveals the unprecedented shifts in gendered consciousness and political subjectivity that resulted from women's participation in the Chicano movement.

PRELUDE

The architecture of this book builds on the historical importance of the women I interviewed and the knowledge collectively produced in their oral histories.

I begin to introduce them to you here in this prelude so that through their stories you can hear the distortions in the historical record. As in music, this prelude functions as more than just an introduction to the historical record. It sets the soundscape and signals the major riffs and musical samples of those narratives of the Chicano movement. It signals to you, the reader, how the knowledge and contestatory histories generated by these women's voices challenge us to think not only about who has been erased, but why. Elucidating the political investments of "telling" history, this prelude presents the testimonial strategy of life story that shifts established epistemologies and the historical paradigms that have dominated sixties social movement histories.

The telling of this history begins at a kitchen table over a cup of steaming *canela* (cinnamon tea) in the Norwalk apartment of Anna NietoGomez in April 1991. Before we settled deeply into her history, Anna moved to the sink to wash dishes while being interviewed, so we propped the recorder on the windowsill. With her hands in hot, soapy water, her story began to unfold. I dried the dishes and listened. Our interview was the first she had granted since the movement days.

When I arrived at Anna's kitchen table, to my surprise, she began to interview *me*. She asked many questions, beginning with why I was still in school. As a full-time student with a double major and a minor who worked as a waitress full-time (I was on the six-year plan), I had to admit I had not really thought of graduating. My time was consumed with activism against U.S. intervention in Central America, Students for Peace and Justice, the women of color feminist coalition, and civil disobedience at ACT UP demonstrations protesting the fact that the county had only five beds for HIV/AIDS patients as the health crisis became a pandemic. After listening to me patiently, Anna impressed on me the need to move on from California State University, Long Beach, based on her experience as a student activist there twenty years earlier. She told me that many women of her generation, despite being advocates for education, did not complete their studies because, in addition to the hostile university climate, their purpose became activism instead of education. I began to see the broader arch of social justice work through the invisible legacy of those who had struggled to open the way to the university. The cost of this invisibility was discovering with disbelief that as women of color student activists we were struggling with some of the same issues, despite the groundbreaking work of the Hijas de Cuauhtémoc more than two decades earlier. This lent new urgency to my oral history project.

After that day in April I spent the next month interviewing Anna, indexing our interviews, and returning with more questions. We conducted more than ten hours of recorded oral history during this first round of interviews. And we spent much more time talking over tea or sitting on the ground in front of her file cabinets pouring over movement documents. From there a relationship began that has spanned two decades. What we could not have anticipated was how the power of being witnessed helped Anna on a path of healing and how listening to her story changed me in ways that were immediate and immeasurable. Within a year of meeting Anna I completed my coursework, graduated, and applied to Ph.D. programs. Over the next decade I went on to interview other members of the Hijas de Cuauhtémoc and women active in the Chicano student movement.[10] This story interweaves the rich oral histories of Chicana activists and organizers and is deeply rooted in the oral history of Anna NietoGomez.

The group of Chicanas whose lives are at the center of this project were born between 1946 and 1952 and form part of a postwar Mexican American generation. Many of their families were displaced by the massive waves of migration brought on by the Mexican Revolution or were shaped by labor histories and the busts and booms of U.S. capitalism that have circumscribed the life chances of Mexicanas/os in the United States. Yet, over time, their families had all located to the greater Los Angeles area to the neighborhoods of Boyle Heights, San Bernardino, Long Beach, Hawaiian Gardens, and Lakewood, among other places.[11] Shaped by cyclical labor and structural displacement, their working-class families labored in the railroad and aircraft industries, among others, or ran small businesses.

Many histories of women of color are often told through, and thus structured by, the historiographic practices that have created silences about them. In contrast, this prelude provides the context to understand how these histories are contested and how the telling of history is political.[12] It situates the Hijas de Cuauhtémoc as knowledge producers who give us new tools to "read" the structures of telling that have produced silences about early Chicana feminisms.

LAS HIJAS DE CUAUHTÉMOC

We recognize that we are oppressed as Raza and as women. We believe that the struggle is not with the male but with the existing system of oppression. But the Chicano must also be educated to the problems and oppression of La Chicana so that he may not be used as a tool to divide by keeping man against woman.
"OUR PHILOSOPHY," LAS HIJAS DE CUAUHTÉMOC (1971)

As one of the first explicitly feminist Chicana political groups in the Chicano movement, the Hijas de Cuauhtémoc emerged within the ranks of the

United Mexican American Students (UMAS) at California State University, Long Beach, in 1968. After the historic 1969 *Plan de Santa Barbara* UMAS, along with other youth organizations and student groups, united under the name el Movimiento Estudiantil Chicano de Aztlán (MEChA). From 1968 to 1971 Chicana activists at Long Beach State met as an informal group under such names as Las Mujeres de Longo and Las Chicanas de Aztlán.[13] As Chicana student activists they were asked by movement leaders to meet with new female members to educate them politically because male leaders had concluded that the women lacked the appropriate skills in political analysis. Ironically, the focus of these educational meetings quickly shifted from imparting political knowledge to addressing issues that were emerging from the women's experience in the movement. Eventually these meetings provided a vehicle for discussing internal sexual politics, as well as a space for naming the issues affecting working-class Chicanas that were not being addressed in Chicano student movement organizations. Chicana activists began to speak about the conditions of their lives; to analyze how they were positioned by multiple and interlocking oppressions of race, class, and gender; and to understand the collective issues faced by women entering the university for the first time.

A growing critique emerged that centered on the gap between the movement's rhetoric on equal rights and the ways in which women were treated not as equal social and political actors but as secretaries and cooks. Although women were the backbone of the student movement, providing much of the labor, they were not seen as public leaders and yet they rarely stayed in their designated place. From the very inception of the Chicano student movement in the late 1960s, there were Chicana leaders, both formal and informal and specific women's agendas. The role of women and gender ideology were hotly debated—a fact that has been left out of most movement histories. This erasure normalizes a masculine hegemony within the Chicano movement that was much more contested at the time.

It was a dispute regarding the nomination of Anna NietoGomez for the presidency of MEChA that transformed the informal women's discussion group into an autonomous women's organization. Many women, however, continued as members of MEChA, engaging in what Latin American feminists have called *double militancia*, or double activism. Although NietoGomez was democratically elected by the many students with whom she worked, her leadership was consistently undermined by a few male leaders of MEChA who stated openly that they did not want to be represented by a woman. They criticized Chicanas who demanded that women's rights be respected, arguing that they were playing into the dominant culture's attempt to divide the movement. Ironically, however, it was actually the chauvinism, discrimination, and sexual harassment of those male leaders that in part led to the rise of feminism among Chicanas in the youth movement. Women throughout the Chicano movement were no longer willing to tolerate internal organizational practices and masculinist political culture, which were exclusionary, undemocratic, and unfair. They fought the suppression of women's leadership and the sexual politics and double standards they experienced by holding their comrades accountable, organizing women's caucuses, and, after much negotiation, forming their own organizations.

Along with their campus-based activism, members of the women's group worked cooperatively with community groups such as the Long Beach Raza Center, Católicos por la Raza, the United Farm Workers (UFW) boycott, a Hawaiian Gardens' community group, and a Norwalk *mutualista* (mutual aid) society and with incarcerated Chicanas/os or those recently released from prison (*pintas/pintos*). Their local campus and community organizing was linked to other Chicana organizing in Texas, New Mexico, and Colorado, as well as in San Diego/Tijuana, the San Francisco Bay Area, and the Central Valley of California.

Working together, Chicana activists in the greater Los Angeles area organized the first regional Chicana conference, held at Cal State Los Angeles on May 8, 1971. An estimated 250 Chicanas gathered to formulate agendas for the national conference scheduled for later that month.[14] Enough successful fund-raisers were organized to send a Southern California delegation, many of whom were Hijas de Cuauhtémoc members, to the May 28–30 Conferencia de Mujeres por la Raza, held in Houston, Texas, at the YWCA. It was decided at the Houston conference that the *Hijas de Cuauhtémoc* newspaper would be published nationally.[15]

Unfortunately, this vision of a national Chicana newspaper was not realized. The conference ended in a walkout that characterized the tensions that surrounded Chicana feminism at the time.[16] Las Hijas de Cuauhtémoc overcame the feelings of disappointment, and some members went on to found the first Chicana feminist scholarly journal, *Encuentro Femenil*, in 1973.

Hijas de Cuauhtémoc and *Encuentro Femenil* created a vital Chicana feminist print culture in which new political identities, discourses, and strategies were constructed and debated. This print culture forged a Chicana feminist counterpublic that opened up spaces for Chicana dialogue across regions, social movement sectors, activist generations, and social differences. Moreover, it provided a space for women to contest the limiting masculinist politics embedded in the gendered project of Chicano nationalism that articulated the subject-citizen of Aztlán as male. While not all sectors of the Chicano movement espoused nationalism as a political strategy, it was the primary ideological and political project that united several divergent political movements, especially within youth organizing and the student movement. This book pays particular attention to the gendered project of Chicano nationalism and how gender issues and women were figured in other ideological threads that made up the broader philosophical weave of the Chicano movement.

While this book is not the history of all women in the Chicano movement or even the full story of the emergence of all forms of Chicana feminisms, it accesses a genealogy of Chicana feminism articulated through community making, collective mobilization, and creative reimagining. By tracing this significant group of activists and telling the story of the emergence of this strain of Chicana *feminismo*, I hope to lay the groundwork for uncovering many other untold stories of individuals, organizations, and political formations that will add to our understanding of a political tradition of Chicana feminism. Such stories might include women who articulated a spectrum of Chicana feminist ideas in mixed organizations, women who did not necessarily call themselves feminists, and a number of men who struggled to include gender and sexual justice in the broader agenda of liberation. This telling is an invitation and a call to action to continue the historical excavation and analysis, to chart the underground stories, and to develop a better understanding of the actors who have already been recognized. More than a chronological span of dates and an ordering of facts, these archaeologies of memory not only tell a different story but also engage in a different mode of telling.

THE ARCHIVE AND THE REPERTOIRE OF ORAL HISTORY

This book draws on two different ways of knowing and telling. One site of knowledge production is the alternative archive—what I call Chicana print cultures—that forged a Chicana counterpublic during the 1960s and 1970s. In addition to this rich archive, there is a vast body of living memory and embodied knowledge that Diana Taylor refers to as a nonarchival system of transfer she calls the repertoire, "a form of knowing as well as a system of storing and transmitting knowledge."[17] Taylor distinguishes the repertoire from archival memory that functions across time and space because "archival memory succeeds in separating the source of 'knowledge' from the knower—in time and/or space"—and can be recaptured years later by a researcher. She argues, "The repertoire, on the other hand, enacts embodied memory: performances, gestures, orality, movement, dance, singing—in short, all those acts usually thought of as ephemeral, non-reproducible knowledge. The repertoire requires presence: people participate in the production and reproduction of knowledge by 'being there,' being a part of the transmission."[18]

I approach oral history as a memory performance and part of the repertoire because it "both keeps and transforms choreographies of meaning." Taylor's notion of repertoire, as embodied knowledge/practice, is useful for understanding oral history as a form of "embodied memory, because it is live, and exceeds the archive's ability to capture it."[19] Critically, Taylor argues that like the archive, the repertoire is also mediated. The use of oral history is also a mediated process of dissemination rather than a direct representation of the subaltern, disrupting what Gayatri Spivak calls an alibi of authenticity.[20] Like practioners of performance studies, oral historians represent and discuss these transmissions through writing or via the archive.

Unlike performance studies, in oral history the "oral" is burdened by the "history," which bears the traces of the weightiness of officiality, rules of evidence, and the pressures of positivism. Perhaps oral history is a hybrid that fits somewhere in between the archive and the repertoire, depending on how the narrator narrates, how the listener listens, and how the researcher wields the apparatus of objectivity that records or captures this performance. Ultimately, it may come down to how much we listen to the embodied practice of memory and the shifting conditions under which knowledge can be shared rather than reduce that memory performance only to a transcript to be studied. Exceeding the archive in its embodied enactment of memory, oral history can be reduced to an object of the archive if we understand it only as textual evidence or a primary source of history because the archival apparatus frames the object of knowledge as well as the ways it is knowable.[21]

I am attracted to Taylor's beautiful conceptualization of the repertoire because it represents the gestures, tones, and sighs—the literal performance of memory, how narrators rock themselves when they talk of difficult memories, how we stop the tape when tears flow. The repertoire reflects the many conversations that occur "off tape" that create an embodied knowledge that I reference in my telling here but that do not fit easily into the realm of documentary evidence since that knowledge and way of knowing is not textual (and its traces do not appear in the transcripts). In this way oral history as performance is part of the repertoire (and its transcript belongs to the archive).

An added dimension of the word *repertoire* is that it is used by social movement scholars to refer to the range of strategies and tactics that social movement actors use to create and contest meaning, power, and representation. I argue that memory is also part of the repertoire of the excluded, politically marginalized, and specifically the colonized. The central role of imagination and a cultural life-world created beyond the reach of the state has been documented by historians such as Emma Pérez in her theorization of the decolonial imaginary and Robin D. G. Kelley's attention to the black radical imagination.[22] Part of the repertoire of resistance to colonialism, injustice, and oppression is what I am calling retrofitted memory. It is a radical act of re-membering, becoming whole in ways that honor alternative or non-normative ways of being.[23] I call attention to how exclusionary historical narratives do not merely *represent* historical realities but help to produce those realities by enforcing the boundaries of legitimate political memory and then subjectivities they authorize. Structures of remembrance construct an archive of knowledge as well as a Chicana/o structure of feeling that narrate belonging and create a sense of legacy that shapes the horizon of political possibilities. Re-membering is a vital act in creating political subjectivity, and Chicana feminists have developed a significant repertoire of remembrance.[24] Their strategies include re-membering themselves in time and place, being whole under erasure, creating new terrains of memory in which to forge a vision of a history in which Chicanas and their communities have a central role in creating a better world. Oral history is part of this repertoire of remembrance and shares a political tradition with Latin American *testimonio*. It is never the same twice, it is specific to time and place, and it relies on the alchemy between oral historian and narrator.

ORGANIZATION OF THE BOOK

Archaeology seeks to uncover discursive practices by unmasking them.
EMMA PÉREZ, *THE DECOLONIAL IMAGINARY*

Chapter 1 disentangles various historiographies to interrogate how Chicana feminist genealogies have been rendered silent through the existing modes of telling history. Following Pérez, I use Foucault's archaeology of knowledge to understand the ways in which Chicanas have been omitted from the social histories of the Chicano and women's movements. Pérez argues "that for historians, revitalizing Foucault's archaeology, the precursor to his genealogical method, can help us examine where in the discourse the gaps, the interstitial moments of history, reappear to be seen or heard as that third space."[25] For this reason, I dedicate a chapter to investigating the mechanics of erasure that make Chicanas "eccentric subjects" to their own history.[26]

Within second wave feminist historiography, the failure to read, interpret, and analyze the multiple sources, sites, and practices of women of color feminisms has obscured and overwritten these diverse feminist traditions. Chicano movement historiography often denies the historical importance of women's autonomous agency within the movement because it periodizes the emergence of Chicana feminism within the decline of el movimiento Chicano and situates Chicana organizing and feminism as occurring "after" the height of the Chicano movement, usually during the 1980s. Others have gone even further to suggest that feminism and struggles over sexuality are among the reasons for the demobilization of the Chicano movement.[27] The additive logic where questions of gender or sexuality are added on only peripherally (and at a later point) fails to depict accurately the complexity of these interwoven struggles and replicates the hierarchy of oppressions, which continues in movement histories that rely on a singular lens of analysis based on race. Thus the primacy of race and narratives that center and naturalize male dominance remain the dominant historical and theoretical models we use to teach in the field of Chicana/o Studies, thereby institutionalizing this erasure of early Chicana feminisms in the curriculum. Both historical narratives and typologies of feminism still struggle to uproot similar issues surrounding how the category of gender is seen as an unmarked racial category (read: "white"), reflecting what I call the politics of periodization, a historiographic device that erases the historical agency of Chicanas or women of color in social transformation by consistently depicting their role or their importance as occurring *after* the "real revolution."

Chapter 2 focuses on the gendered, racial, and class experiences of young Chicanas in the late 1960s as they entered college in large numbers for the first time in U.S. history. It explores the gendered expectations and norms that were constructed through the political scripts emanating from Chicano nationalism, which often measured a woman's dedication to the movement by her loyalty to male leaders. Because family was used as both a guiding metaphor and a mobilizing strategy of Chicano politics, political familialism often played a role in reinforcing patriarchal structures as an unspoken organizing principle. Women involved in the movement participated in constructing, contesting, and negotiating this set of gendered norms.

Chapter 3, through a close textual analysis of archival documents, illustrates that Chicano nationalism was not just a political project of racial/ethnic pride but a gendered project as well. It theorizes the concept of retrofitted memory by exploring how the Hijas de Cuauhtémoc of the 1960s and 1970s chose their name as a way to reclaim an earlier Mexican feminist political tradition. While building political legitimacy within Chicano nationalism, ultimately the Hijas de Cuauhtémoc not only moved between Mexican and Chicano nationalist imaginaries, but also beyond them. In addition, this chapter maps the iconography of la Nueva Chicana through the rich array of photographs and images published in movement newspapers between 1969 and 1976, paying close attention to the representational struggles waged around gender roles and leadership.

Chapter 4 examines the formation of a Chicana print community across regions, social movement actors, and activist generations. Early Chicana feminists not only engendered movement print culture; they built an alternative print community in which they articulated a new Chicana feminist political imaginary and social subjectivity. The subaltern counterpublic constituted by Chicana feminist print culture is a crucial site of historical inquiry and provides a window onto the development of Chicana feminist ideology, discourse, and political praxis in a way that accounts for how ideas traveled locally as well as circulated nationally.[28] Further, I argue that this political pedagogy became an underlying impulse for the practice of anthologizing that was central to early women of color feminisms.

Chapter 5 examines the cross-regional tensions and collaborations among Chicana feminists who converged on the historic 1971 Conferencia de Mujeres por la Raza, the first-ever national gathering of Chicanas, which attracted six hundred participants from over twenty-three states. The resolutions passed at the conference were revolutionary and centered on issues of employment discrimination and racism, gender oppression, abortion, birth control, child care, Chicana political leadership, sexuality, motherhood, economic justice, and reproductive and educational rights, as well as the repressive role of the Catholic Church and a condemnation of the Vietnam War. This conference is often seen as the height of early Chicana feminism. Yet it was marked by deep tensions over the role women's issues would play in movement agendas and what the primary struggle and mode of organizing of a Chicana movement should be. Drawing from archival research and oral histories with organizers and participants from both sides of the split that led to a walkout, I map the political fault lines that fractured early Chicana feminism. I use the 1971 Houston conference as a genealogical map of the growing number of Chicana feminist organizations and the causes of this political conflict and its reverberations and historical implications. I demonstrate how the conflicts at the Houston conference were the result of differences within regional political cultures, gendered movement discourses, and organizational tactics that ultimately disrupted the development of a national Chicana movement in the 1970s.

Chapter 6 follows the narrative thread of organizing and maps out the various political trajectories members of the Hijas de Cuauhtémoc created as their activism moved beyond campus organizing throughout the 1970s. It elucidates how the Hijas de Cuauhtémoc, inspired by third world liberation struggles, ultimately moved beyond narrow forms of nationalism to form coalitions with other women of color in the United States and to help build community organizations in the greater Los Angeles area that focused on welfare rights, employment, health, and ending violence.

CHAPTER ONE

SPINNING THE RECORD:
HISTORICAL WRITING AND RIGHTING

The historian's political project, then, is to write a history that decolonizes otherness.
EMMA PÉREZ, *THE DECOLONIAL IMAGINARY*

HISTORIES OF THE PRESENT are often complicated by sedimented narratives that structure absences in the historical record and our historical memory.[1] This chapter examines the sanctioned histories and historiographic practices of the U.S. women's movement and Chicano movement and charts a different kind of telling through an oral history project with members of the Hijas de Cuauhtémoc. Not only do their oral histories, critical memories, and movement narratives chronicle an untold story of the women involved in the Chicano movement, but they also contest the mode in which the history of this era has been told and challenge us to transform existing paradigms of historical knowledge. This unsanctioned history powerfully reveals how the telling of social movement histories is a project that shapes identity formations and the maintenance of political boundaries in our current context.

This chapter interrogates how women of color feminist genealogies are rendered silent by dominant forms of historiographic practice and proposes an alternative method of registering such genealogies. Despite clear historical evidence of Chicana activism and the emergence of Chicana feminism as early as 1968, many Chicano movement histories claim that Chicanas did not articulate their own agenda until the 1980s, thereby historicizing the emergence of Chicana feminism within the decline of el movimiento Chicano. Feminist historiography of the second wave women's movement is equally distorted, focusing almost exclusively on small, East Coast, largely middle-class, white women's consciousness-raising groups, thereby ignoring the participation of women of color in the women's movement. This narrow view of the origins of feminism also ignores other diverse political formations that gave rise to women of color feminisms outside of that movement. Instead this project recovers histories of multiple feminist insurgencies and theorizes multiply insurgent forms of feminist practice.

The forms of analysis and narrative strategies employed by the narrators whose stories appear in this work have provided the means by which to transform the systems of knowledge and undermine the mechanics of erasure that have written them out of history. The oral histories recuperate subjugated knowledges and uncover genealogies of resistance, and they transform the landscape of meaning and discursive fields in which that knowledge is produced. Through this process I have learned not only to listen to the oral histories that have been narrated to me but also to listen to the *way* that they are told. Working against the mode in which testimonios and oral histories are often read, I invite readers to see this work, not as a set of "consuming stories," but as a set of interventions that invite multiple reading and interpretive strategies.[2]

While subjugated knowledges are produced by dominant modes of producing historicity,[3] Patricia Hill Collins argues that the subjugation of knowledge occurs not only in classification and hierarchization, as Foucault claims, but also by those who control what she calls "knowledge validation procedures."[4] Historical narratives produce the subjects they name in historical, popular, and institutional memory. My project is inherently involved not only in recovering histories but also in historiography—what I will call the conditions of enunciability: the methods and tools of historical inquiry that constitute political modes of "telling" in historical writing and the ways these conventions constitute a political practice.[5]

DISMANTLING DOMINANT NARRATIVES: DECENTERING HEGEMONIC FEMINIST HISTORIOGRAPHY

It is not surprising that the most interesting attempts to define feminism have come from scholars whose work has been the history of feminism; that they do not agree whether feminism is a revolutionary, evolutionary, a movement, a process, or a state of mind should not discourage us. . . . We need to expand our sense of what feminism is, and has been, in order to write effectively its history.
SHARON SIEVERS, "SIX (OR MORE) FEMINISTS IN
SEARCH OF A HISTORIAN"

Despite ample critique of the universalizing historical narrative of the women's liberation movement, historians of U.S. feminism have only recently begun to revise the historiography of the second wave of women's organizing in a manner that recognizes and accounts for the multiple feminist insurgencies of women of color and the multiple sources and practices of this consciousness.[6] Feminists have recognized the role of history in the production of political identities and thus the stakes in a feminist historiography. For example, Sara Evans argues, "One cannot build a future without a sense of the past. Movements require history because history provides an explanation for oppression. And it impels action by offering a vision of a transformative future. Both the nature of that vision and the strategies for achieving it are rooted in historical understanding."[7] We cannot understand our feminist futures without a better understanding of the multiple origins of our feminist pasts.

I began this project in 1991 as a member of an oral history collective based at California State University, Long Beach, that focused on rethinking the historiography of the second wave feminist movement collectively, in our seminars and meetings, and individually, through our own oral history projects.[8] Led by Sherna Gluck, we conducted oral histories with members of women's organizations largely based in the greater Los Angeles area, including Johnnie Tillmon, founder of the ANC Mothers Anonymous of Watts; the Hijas de Cuauhtémoc of Long Beach; Asian Sisters in Los Angeles; and women involved in the American Indian Movement who developed a women's arm of AIM, Women of All Red Nations (WARN). These oral history projects revealed an urgent need to decenter the dominant narrative of what the Chicana feminist theorist Chela Sandoval has called "hegemonic feminism" because that paradigm obscures as many histories as it elucidates.[9] Further, these collaborative conversations identified the need to look at sources of feminist consciousness and activism in multiple locations, including antipoverty grassroots community organizing, racially specific movements (civil rights, sovereignty), third world solidarity movements and the organizing efforts of working class women, women of color, and lesbians.

We called attention to the need for a model of history that could document the multiple feminisms produced by women who have been marginalized along economic, racial, and sexual lines. We challenged the hegemonic narrative of second wave feminist historiography as too narrow and also critiqued as insufficient the ways in which scholars attempted to add on women of color to the liberal, Marxist, radical typology. Further, we joined historians such as Vicki Ruiz and Ellen DuBois in thinking about the effect of East Coast regionalism on our understanding of the women's movement, which, when it did not completely erase women of color, produced a black/white binary that failed to see other diverse sources of feminist consciousness during the 1960s and 1970s.[10]

PERIODIZATION AND THE LIMITATIONS
OF THE WAVES MODEL

The history of feminism in the United States has been conceptualized through a falsely universalized construct of femininity based on white middle-class women that has been periodized into two waves of activism. First wave feminism is historically marked by the feminist struggle for suffrage; it acknowledges the ways that women's suffrage emerged from women's involvement in the movement for the abolition of slavery but conceptually understands feminism through gender as the sole category of analysis and centers almost exclusively on white women's experience.[11] This historical depiction of the first wave of feminism often underplays the contribution of black women such as Sojourner Truth, Maria Stewart, Harriet Tubman, Ida Wells Barnett, and Anna Julia Cooper to the development of feminist discourse and strategy in the struggle against slavery from which the women's suffrage movement developed. Further, this periodization fails to account for diverse women of color feminisms that have emerged from a different set of daily lived conditions that were articulated by Mexicana labor organizers, Puerto Rican women in the independence movement, Asian women immigrant trade unionists, and black women in the club movement, for example.[12] Indeed, the institutional, organizational, and philosophical relationship between these movements and the campaign for suffrage is consistently mischaracterized through a historiography in which women's issues are cleaved from the gender politics of citizenship, labor, independence, sovereignty, and human dignity as imagined by women of color organizers. For example, the periodization of women's movements in the United States overlooks diverse sources of women of color feminism and activism such as Tejana feminists in the League of United Latin American Citizens (LULAC) in the 1930s, feminist black nationalists in the Garveyite movement, and black labor activism by women such as Nannie Burroughs and Maggie Wallace, who helped to establish the National Association of Wage Earners in 1920, or Mary McCleod Bethune, who sought to organize black female domestic and factory workers.[13]

In her important study, *Living for the Revolution*, Kimberly Springer argues that black feminist organizations in the 1960s and 1970s were the first to use feminist theory to advance the work of previous black women's organizations. Through oral histories with Chicana feminists, there is a corollary trend in that organizations such as the Hijas de Cuauhtémoc were among the first of many in the 1960s and 1970s to produce theory based on naming and conceptualizing how Chicanas experience multiple oppression in between the two national cultures of Mexico and the United States. Yet, as I explore later in this book, this group of feminists took up their identity as Chicana feminists by connecting to a genealogy of Mexican feminism on both sides of the border that had reformist as well as socialist and anarchist roots. Thus, in addition to paying attention to how women of color feminisms challenge the dominant narrative of periodization embodied by the wave model, we must give our critical attention to how women of color feminisms are different from each other and develop from different genealogies and traditions of political struggle and cross different borders and diasporas.

Similarly, the second wave women's movement is periodized and constructed through a narrative of 1960s radical politics in which feminism is seen to emerge out of both the black civil rights movement and the New Left.[14] Even women of color who were involved in the women's movement such as Patricia Bell Scott and Helen Zia critique the homogenization and the whitewashing of the women's liberation movement, which is a process of historicizing, not a historical process.[15] Janet R. Jakobsen argues that this is a way for hegemonic feminism to project its exclusionary histories as being resolved in the past and to continually reenact this erasure through the process of periodization.[16] Because of this erasure within the waves paradigm, women of color second wave feminist consciousness is often narrativized as happening in the 1980s. Fortunately, scholars have begun to locate different genealogies and other sources of women of color, working-class, and lesbian feminist consciousness such as the welfare rights and antipoverty organizing of the 1963 ANC Mothers of Watts or, as Rosalyn Baxandall has documented, organizations like the Mt. Vernon/New Rochelle Group, founded in 1960, and Mothers Alone Working (MAW), founded in 1965. These cases expand the scope of our historical understanding of where and how feminist consciousness and practice emerged in the postwar period and challenge us to think beyond the ways in which the dominant narrative of the second wave has overshadowed Other forms of feminisms.[17]

Finally, some scholars have removed women of color feminisms from the second wave altogether, instead marking their emergence as the beginning of the third wave of feminism in the United States. While women of color feminisms are critical to third wave feminist theory and praxis, it is a mistake to erase them from the second wave because they are central to understanding the complexity of this period. To put them only in the third wave is to adopt the "add-on" method and understand these feminist traditions as emerging only in response to the racism of the feminism movement, which recenters hegemonic feminism instead of providing an understanding of the diverse historical impulses that gave rise to women of color feminisms.[18] Further, by erasing women of color in the second wave we miss the ways in which, Springer argues, women of color organizations contributed to "broadening the scope of the women's movement by challenging Eurocentric and classist interpretations of women's issues."[19] Despite the fact that most feminists acknowledge that the 1981 publication of *This Bridge Called My Back*, edited by Cherríe Moraga and Gloria Anzaldúa, marks a shift in feminist consciousness, feminist historians have just begun to revise their singular narrative of feminism's history or their conception of a unified and exclusive subject of feminism.[20]

BAIT AND SWITCH: WOMEN OF COLOR AS "IMPORTANT" BUT NOT PRESENT

Because most histories of the second wave have been written with an East Coast bias, their engagement with race tends to be imagined as a white/black dichotomy.[21] The dominant origins narrative of the women's liberation movement is drawn from how white women developed their political consciousness of women's oppression while working in the civil rights movement. The problem with this "bait and switch" move is that it acknowledges the importance of women of color in the emergence of feminist consciousness but then elaborates the history of feminism and generates historical paradigms of feminism as if white women were the only historical actors.

The narrative classically cites "strong" black women as the source of white women's consciousness, continuing a narrow scope of white, educated, middle-class women instead of broadening the scope of understanding to the complex forms of gender consciousness and roots of feminism within that generation of black women's activism.[22] Further, we can see how this narrative, almost exclusively based on white women's critique of sexism in the civil rights movement, misses other forms of feminist consciousness that were later developed by participants.[23] To illustrate, many studies of the origins of feminism include white women's critique of sexism, illustrated best by the statement, "Sex and Caste: A Kind of Memo," developed by Casey Hayden and Mary King within the Student Non-Violent Coordinating Committee (SNCC) in 1965, challenging male superiority and an unequal gendered division of labor within the organization and society's institutions.[24] Most studies then develop a singular trajectory from there instead of including the multiple forms of feminism that emerged from a diversity of women's involvement in the civil rights movement such as the emergence of black women's feminist agenda in the founding of the Black Women's Alliance in SNCC in

1968, which quickly became the Third World Women's Alliance (TWWA) after Puerto Rican women joined the organization.[25] What this narrow view excludes is the diverse forms of feminist consciousness developed by participants and, moreover, a critical genealogy of women of color feminisms.

Alice Echols's *Daring to Be Bad* discusses at various points why black women did not join radical white feminist groups. However, her narrative remains centered on white women's experience of radical feminism.[26] For example, Echols writes:

> Of course, from the early days of the movement there were black women like Florence Kennedy, Frances Beale, Cellestine Ware, and Patricia Robinson who tried to show the connections between racism and male dominance. But most politically active black women, even if they critiqued the black movement for sexism, chose not to become involved in the feminist struggle. Efforts to generate a black feminist movement, which date back to 1973 with the founding of the short-lived National Black Feminist Organization, were less than successful.[27]

Echols's version of radical feminism produces unified historical subjects rather than historicizing the many political trajectories that joined in building this strain of feminism. Not until the epilogue does she include a brief two-page discussion of the role women of color played in the movement.

Even after continued critique among historians of women of color feminisms, the add-and-stir method continues to be employed. In *The World Split Open*, Ruth Rosen claims that although second wave feminism began with white women dealing with issues that applied to them, "it didn't take long for racial and ethnic minorities to reinvent feminism for themselves."[28] The refusal to decenter the dominant underlying assumption creates a hegemonic narrative in which the (white) women's movement is historicized as the original and primary feminism that is copied by others.[29] The failure to fully decenter the hegemonic narrative causes several temporal slippages in Rosen's texts. Although she recognizes the development of multiple feminisms, she refers to them as "new" populations of women despite the long history of indigenous, African, Latino, and Asian peoples in what is now the United States. Rosen does document many black and Chicana feminist events in the chronology that begins her book, but the most substantive discussion of women of color feminisms follows her section on "postfeminists," or the third wave.

LOCATING THE MULTIPLE FEMINIST INSURGENCIES
OF WOMEN OF COLOR

*The difficulty we have constructing this more complicated story is not
merely a failure to deal with the specifics of race and class; the difficulty
is also, I believe, in how we see history and politics — in an underlying
focus on linear order and symmetry which makes us wary, fearing that
layering multiple and asymmetrical stories will only result in chaos with
no women's history or women's story to tell, that political community
is a product of homogeneity, and that exploring too fully our differences
will leaves us void of any common ground on which to build a collective
struggle. These are the ideas/assumptions, which I want to encourage
us to think past.*
ELSA BARKLEY BROWN, "WHAT HAS HAPPENED HERE"

Inspired by black popular art forms such as cooking jambalaya, quilting, and
jazz, Elsa Barkley Brown reminds us not to search for uniformity and singu-
larity but rather embrace multivocality and unevenness in creating new historiographic models.[30] With this in mind, I propose a new historiographic
framework that theorizes the multiple feminist insurgencies of women of
color by looking beyond "the" women's liberation movement as the only
site that produced "real" feminisms. A theory and methodology of multiple
feminist insurgencies maps the multisited emergence of women of color as
a historical political formation and requires historians to look toward other
social movements and other, unexpected, social locations for feminist roots
and practices. Because this method entails a more complete analysis of race,
class, gender, and sexuality, it could be the basis for producing new forms of
feminist historical knowledge.

Women of color political subjectivities have gone largely unhistoricized
because they often occurred *between* various and distinct social movements.
Modes of historical inquiry have not developed a method for registering
women of color as multiply constituted political subjects because they rely on
(and constitute) monolithic narratives of unitary political subjects. Critically,
my historiographic model elucidates women of color as multiply constituted
political subjects, naming feminist subjects who were multiply insurgent and
those who struggled on numerous fronts to confront multiple oppressions.
An example might be an Asian American woman who develops her feminism in the antiwar movement, goes on to work in the Third World Liberation Front where she confronts homophobia and heterosexism, and begins

doing early lesbian of color organizing.[31] In addition to addressing the ways in which the dominant narrative produces hegemonic feminism by erasing feminist identities that are multiply constituted, this model allows us to recognize the diverse origins and independent struggles of feminist agendas that emerged from different political traditions both within the given chronology of second wave feminism and outside it. This broader understanding of feminist consciousness and practice will allow us to rewrite limiting typologies that universalize white middle-class experience.

MULTIPLE ORIGINS, AUTONOMOUS (OR SEPARATE) TRADITIONS

One of the most limiting consequences of the dominant narrative of second wave historiography is that it obscures the multiple forms of feminism, the diversity of struggles from which they emerge, and the breadth of agendas they produced. Two important studies document the multiple origins of feminisms within the second wave. Becky Thompson, in *A Promise and a Way of Life*, has argued that there are multiple feminist traditions with separate origins that influenced each other.[32] And Benita Roth's *Separate Roads to Feminism* argues that the second wave was actually composed of multiple feminisms "that were organizationally distinct and organized around racial lines."[33]

I have argued that one of the reasons that women of color are not being registered in existing social movement history and historiographic frameworks is due to a failure to see the multiple strands of intervention and contribution that led to the formation of a U.S. women of color political identity.[34] An alternative mapping of this genealogy includes three interrelated but distinct historical processes, or sites of political consciousness, that form the basis for understanding the multiple feminist insurgencies of women of color. The first site of emergence is the rich variety of racially specific feminist projects that overlapped and converged with movements for racial justice throughout the sixties and seventies. These are what Angela Davis has called "the gender struggles we encountered as we mounted our radical opposition to racism."[35] Many historians have located women of color as political subjects through their feminist critiques of black nationalism, Chicano nationalism, or general challenges to sexism within the multiple movements in which women of color were active.[36] This activism and feminist consciousness draws from a long tradition of grassroots, community, and antipoverty organizing, as illustrated by the early welfare rights movement and other movements based on nationalism, communism, self-help, and mutual aid and service organizations.[37] Further, these political traditions grounded in communities of color and lesbian and gay communities are based on different lived experience.[38]

The second site is the diverse forms of consciousness that women of color activists developed as they traveled in the early women's liberation movement, what Barbara Noda has referred to as "low riding in the women's movement."[39] Sandoval theorized the modes of differential and oppositional consciousness that this low riding has produced. While women of color did articulate their forms of feminism in relation to an antiracist critique of white feminism, it would be a dangerous assumption to historicize women of color feminisms from the limited interpretation that sees *Bridge* only in relation to that critique. This kind of thinking does not acknowledge earlier genealogies of women of color feminisms and fails to understand the fuller epistemological project of the anthology.

While women of color feminist consciousness did emerge from a critique of sexism in nationalist and civil rights organizations and an antiracist critique of women's liberation, a third site of emergence, usually dropped out of the false historical narrative historicizing women of color feminism in the 1980s, is the forms of gendered solidarity born out of U.S. third world liberation struggles. The category "third world women," which came into use decades earlier, was based on women's solidarity built by activists in coalitional political projects who created new organizations such as the Third World Women's Alliance (1970).[40] This emergence of third world women feminism, as a political subjectivity, was facilitated by new political identities and visions of liberation in third world solidarity that inspired political projects among racially and economically marginalized communities in the United States. Recuperating this genealogy of U.S. third world feminism relies on recovering the importance of a transnational imaginary produced by critiques of U.S. imperialism in constructing this U.S.-specific racial and political formation. People of color in the United States began to understand their common struggle with third world liberation as they theorized their position as "internal colonies" that had been exploited in the development of U.S. capitalism and imperialism.[41] This transnational form of solidarity was localized among female activists and facilitated a form of solidarity with historically racialized communities in the United States as well as with emergent third world diasporas. So while many forms of women of color feminisms did arise from critiques of nationalism within the black, Chicano, and Puerto Rican movements, there was an equally strong strain of internationalism in those movements based on a critique of capitalism and imperialism that has not yet been fully historicized. As a constructed political identity that functioned as more than a coalition of "identity" constituencies, historically third world women localized transnational forms of solidarity with women's concerns in a way that facilitated not only a cross-racial and cross-community linking of struggles but also a new gendered racial formation in the United States.[42]

HIDDEN GENDER INSURGENCIES: DECENTERING THE UNITARY SUBJECT OF FEMINISMS AND THE SINGULAR FIELD OF INTERPRETATION

Framing feminist history through the single axis of gender not only misses the women of color feminists active in women's organizations; it also overlooks those formal and informal women's groups that existed within the American Indian Movement, the antiwar movement, the Chicano and Black Power movements, the Asian American and student movements, community and welfare rights organizations, nationalist movements, and the New Left. Women's participation in these movements transformed them, sparking the need for a multifaceted analysis of the interconnectedness of forms of oppression. These actors often incited internal gender and feminist insurgencies (many named, others strategically not named) that were modes of feminist analysis and political action that form a genealogical strand of what is now recognized as women of color feminisms. Historians of feminism or women's movements need to understand that the contextual meaning of the word *feminism* is highly differentiated and often problematic. The assumption that there has been no early history of women of color feminisms because organizers or movements have not used the word *feminist* erases almost every feminist labor organizer, party activist, and community organizer, and, in fact, much of the history of feminism.

Hidden gender insurgencies, or submerged feminist insurgencies, are vital practices within feminism that often go unrecognized.[43] At the heart of this issue is the Gramscian notion that political consciousness is formed out of daily lived conditions.[44] For example, in the 1970s American Indian women in WARN took up those issues that affected them most, such as alcoholism and violence against women, land and treaty struggles, and their connection to the environment and women's health.[45] Whether or not these concerns are shared by other feminists or are even seen as feminist demands by others, these political priorities and women's struggle to address them predate mainstream feminisms' relatively recent attention to them. Further, they incorporate a critique of gendered relations of power through an analysis of each feminist's social and historical location. When I refer to "hidden gender insurgencies," I do not mean that multiple insurgent forms of feminist consciousness are a secret or that they occur only within the interior spaces of a community or solely within the realm of women. Hidden gender insurgencies call attention to how the social analyst and researcher is a positioned subject whose field of visibility and codes of intelligibility are informed by that positionality. How researchers are positioned in relation to their subjects may affect how they decode meanings and what analytical frameworks they rely on. While we can learn new codes and ways of seeing, we must also remind ourselves of the role of situated knowledges and partial perspectives in our work.[46]

Increasingly, historical and cultural studies scholarship is acknowledging the diverse roots, locations, and traditions of feminist consciousness.[47] Angela Davis's work, *Blues Legacies and Black Feminism*, is illustrative. Her analysis is an inquiry into "unacknowledged traditions of feminist consciousness," which she studies through the lives, musical forms, lyrics, and performative codes of blues women to understand the "hints of feminist attitudes [that] emerge from their music through fissures of patriarchal discourse." Davis explores forms of social consciousness, and the songs she analyzes provide a "rich terrain for examining a historical feminist consciousness that reflected the lives of working-class black communities."[48] She finds that issues like violence against women, sexuality, and women's agency were publicly discussed in subversive ways that predate second wave feminism by twenty to thirty years. Davis also challenges ideas about gay liberation and queer histories, thus tying women of color political activists to struggles for queer liberation.

My argument regarding multiple feminist insurgencies, and hidden gender insurgencies, is not that we should see feminism everywhere but rather that we must dismantle narrow definitions and understandings of feminism, which are linked to the narrow ways in which feminisms have been historicized. This is especially vital when we consider the ways in which historical narratives are constructed and knowledge is produced and the implications for feminist epistemologies and practices. If we see how multiple historical sites and social locations have produced a diversity of unnamed feminist traditions and we understand how these insurgent forms of feminism were influenced by their own conditions of possibility, then, as subjects of history, we must understand the key role their partial and fragmented historical tellings has on our own history.[49]

MULTIPLY INSURGENT FEMINISMS

Many feminist practices of women of color, lesbians, and working-class women are not clearly registered in dominant frames because they involve political subjects who have multiple identities and who most often engage in multi-issue organizing or work on several political fronts, not all of which put gender at the center. Further, many of these forms of feminist consciousness were produced by being in between movements and coalitions. These particular practices have produced new forms of analysis and new political identities that are often not registered in feminist epistemologies based on rigid typologies such as Liberal, Socialist, or Radical.

Much ink has been spilled on theorizing the multiple identities that led to multisited, intersectional understandings of feminism produced by women of color, lesbians, and organized working-class women. Known as the "ampersand problem," women of color are political actors whose feminist political analysis is based on an understanding of the simultaneity of forms of oppression. Accordingly, their movement building and political praxis tend not to privilege one oppression over another but rather has fought for them to be seen as interconnected. Women of color activists occupied diverse political locations in the 1960s and 1970s where they attempted to name, theorize, and dismantle the way their lives were circumscribed by multiple systems of oppressions. One of the first scholarly publications to elucidate multiple oppressions was Frances Beal's "Double Jeopardy: To Be Black and Female," published in 1970. Several publications followed, but they often interpreted identity as a mathematical equation that placed various forms of discrimination in an additive formulation, making it seem that these forms of oppression were discrete phenomena that happened in isolation from one another, as opposed to overlapping or occurring simultaneously.

I want to call attention to how Chicana feminists also forged a collective identity based on a critical understanding of the intersecting nature of these oppressions, impressing on us the need to understand the parallel development of various women of color feminisms. Further, it is vital to acknowledge the social movement roots of concepts like intersectionality and multiple subjectivities, the core theoretical claims of women of color feminisms, as these ideas move into the often convoluted channels of academia, law, and policy.[50]

TYPOLOGIES

In 1991 Chela Sandoval theorized a differential consciousness that, like the gears of a car, shift tactically among various ideologies as the organization of power within particular sites of resistance requires. Sandoval claimed:

> What U.S. third world feminism demands is a new subjectivity, a political revision that denies any one ideology as the final answer, while instead posit-

ing a tactical subjectivity with the capacity to recenter depending upon the kinds of oppression to be confronted. This is what the shift from hegemonic oppositional theory and practice to a U.S. third world theory and method of oppositional consciousness requires.[51]

Whereas Sandoval's analysis names only the hegemonic gears of feminist typologies that she aims to destabilize (by rewriting them), I would like to emphasize the multiple locations in which women of color feminist subjects emerge in order to enact shifts in consciousness and strategy outside of those named in feminist typologies and to confront the multiple systems of oppression that change over time. A theory of multiple feminist insurgencies leaves spaces open for contestation, conflict, and internal diversity and accounts for submerged histories of subaltern feminisms not likely to be registered in feminist epistemologies regulated by rigid, narrow typologies. Moreover, I would suggest that a multiple insurgencies model is not only an analytical framework for interpreting social movement histories and interrogating the politics of historiography; it also serves as a basis for theorizing and producing new forms of feminist knowledge and epistemology. A multiple insurgencies model functions as a porous theoretical apparatus that is a critical epistemological practice. It is not only concerned with excavating histories and producing new knowledge but also is attentive to how that knowledge is produced and questions the politics surrounding existing modes of knowing and systems (archives) of knowledge.

A history based on the multiple insurgencies of women of color could account for the ways in which the emergence of this political identity was forged through vitally necessary acts of solidarity, shared survival strategies, dialogue, conflict, and negotiation that occurred in multiple and diverse social movement spaces. This requires us to complicate our notions of social movements and political subjectivities in order to see the multiple sites of contestation, production of political knowledge, and registers of meaning that women of color navigated in order to formulate new theories and politicized identities to constitute themselves as political subjects. This includes subjects with multiple identities as well as subjects who are multiply insurgent, meaning their organizing tends to take on the following characteristics: (1) multiple issues or struggles in one movement, (2) an intersectional understanding of power and oppression, and (3) the tendency to work in and between movements.

CHICANO MOVEMENT HISTORIOGRAPHY:
CHALLENGING THE "GREAT MAN" NARRATIVE
AND THE POLITICS OF PERIODIZATION

Historians' neglect of women has been a function of their ideas about historical significance. Their categories and periodization have been masculine by definition, for they have defined significance primarily by power. ROSAURA SÁNCHEZ, "THE HISTORY OF CHICANAS"

As suggested by Sánchez, historians' understanding of historical significance is shaped primarily by their understanding of power as a top-down unilateral force rather than a multisited force that flows in a capillary fashion.[52] In Marxist and poststructuralist currents, Chicana feminist historians understand power as multisited, occurring in dominant society as well as the family, the community, and movement organizations. Telling the history of the Chicano movement has not only erased women's early participation; it has produced a masculine hegemony within those narratives, reinscribing dominant gender relations that were widely debated at the time. By examining the contested histories of gender and feminism in the Chicano movement, this study opens a path to telling the histories of women's mass involvement and their role in changing our notions of Chicana/o politics in ways that have not been fully acknowledged or documented.

While the Chicano movement developed from a multitude of community-based political and civil rights struggles (ranging from agricultural and industrial labor, migration, access to education, and political representation to the Vietnam War, racism and discrimination, land grant struggles, and local control of community institutions), its historiography has been organized around a cosmology of male heroes that reifies the "great man" narrative and interpretive structure.[53] The figures of Reies López Tijerina, Rodolfo "Corky" Gonzales, José Angel Gutiérrez, and César Chávez have eclipsed a fuller historical understanding of these social movements, especially women's participation.[54] While these leaders' contributions are indeed important, the way in which they have been historicized has produced a monolithic portrayal of the Chicano movement. The history is organized around epic male heroes rather than the multisited local community and labor struggles that coalesced into a national movement. This mode of telling Chicano movement history does a disservice to the historical memory of the majority of its participants and obscures the fact that the collective action and daily acts of courage of thousands of everyday people changed the tide of history. A history of Chicana feminism in the movement necessarily crosses social movement sectors and deploys a different organizational logic, one that challenges the narrative so influenced by the imperatives of institutional history that is structured around telling the histories of institutions such as labor unions, social service organizations, and political organizations. It is not so much that Chicanas were not critical actors and leaders in the Chicano movement but that the conceptual frames social movement scholars have used have made them unintelligible or invisible.

The mechanics of erasure within established models of Chicano historiography include the politics of periodization, the *vendida* (sellout) logic, temporal slippages, and a narrative structure that reduces multivariant movement organizing to a single analytical lens. This single lens flattens our understanding of Chicana and Chicano political actors, portraying them as unified subjects whose motivations for political action can be understood only through race or class.[55] Other simultaneous and intersecting oppressions are added on to movement narratives in a linear fashion, never decentering the primacy of race (as unmarked masculinity) as a unitary category within historiographic practice.

Chicano movement history has used a temporal linearity that locates women's and feminists' interventions outside of movement histories instead of including them in a larger agenda for social justice integral to the legacy of the Chicano movement. To fully understand the contested histories of gender and sexuality in the Chicano movement we must interrogate the politics behind the linear temporal schema that consistently "adds on" Chicana feminist interventions, periodizing them within the logic of decline (or sometime part of the cause of the end) of el movimiento.

This temporal linearity has enacted a narrative structure that hierarchizes "primary" oppressions and then enumerates subsequent "additions" that critique but do not necessarily change, or even complicate, histories that designate one oppression as primary. This space of the "and then . . ." silences difference and reproduces a hierarchization of oppressions within social movement historiographies that marginalizes some people (i.e., women of color and gays and lesbians) and perpetually represents them as secondary. If marginalized peoples get added on to the end of a linear trajectory of history, the dominant narrative is neither complicated nor destabilized, and its concepts and ways of knowing remain entrenched. Further, it denies us the opportunity to understand how movements developed sophisticated analytical tools to name complex political subjects who function amid multiple oppressions, who have developed multiple subjectivities, and who live and create these structures in the hybrid and often violent space of the borderlands.[56]

Examples of how Chicana feminism has been added on to the historiographies of the Chicano movement include two principal texts that chronicle its history. In earlier versions of Rodolfo Acuña's *Occupied America*, which has served as the standard (textbook) historical narrative of Chicano Studies, the section "A Challenge to Male Domination" was located "historically" (linearly) in the Hispanic (read: sold out) 1980s chapter. Adding on feminism *after* the movement reflects the politics of periodization, a historiographic device that denies Chicanas or women of color historical agency in social transformation by consistently depicting their role or importance as occurring after the "real revolution" or period of social change. Fortunately, Acuña's later editions include a much wider spectrum of women's involvement in the Chicano movement, reflecting a deepening awareness of the importance of women and a shift in the field of Chicana and Chicano Studies. Carlos Muñoz's *Youth, Identity, Power* remains one of the only book-length studies dealing with the Chicano student movement.[57] The two-sentence discussion of sexism in the movement is located in a section titled "The Decline of the Student Movement," indicating an underlying assumption that women's involvement in the movement and critiques regarding sexism represent a division that signaled "decline" rather than contribution to strengthening the movement and broadening its vision of social change.

Within the Chicano student movement, Muñoz claims, "the various stances on sexism became another reason for division within MEChA, with many women deciding to spend their energy on the development of their own feminist organizations."[58] This claim is not historically accurate because Chicana feminists who emerged out of the movement did not leave it to organize as women but most often engaged in a form of double-time activism. There were varied strategies, but the predominant practice for women's organizations that emerged from MEChA or Chicano movement organizations was to function as a caucus, or if they did form autonomous organizations they engaged in what Latin American women on the left called double militancia.[59] This strategy created parallel autonomous women's spaces to construct shared feminist visions, identities, and political strategies while the majority of activists remained within Chicano Movement organizations in order to transform the organizations from within.

OF MALINCHES, *AGRINGADAS*, AND OTHER TRAITOROUS TALES: UPROOTING THE VENDIDA LOGIC

Much of the Chicano movement's rejection of feminism has been overdetermined by what I call the vendida logic. The vendida logic was a silencing mechanism used against dissident Chicana activists that labeled them as divisive or as sellouts to the movement due to their desire to include Chicana

rights within the movement. The vendida logic had several dominant variations that still reverberate in Chicano movement historiography. The four rhetorical axes that it operates on are (1) Race (feminists were *agringadas*, or race
traitors); (2) Ideological Purity (feminists were sellouts dividing the movement from the primary struggle that they, as members of the movement, did
not have the right to shape and articulate); (3) Sexual (feminists were sexual
deviants or lesbians); and (4) Culturalist (feminists were inauthentic/outside
of/antagonistic to Chicano culture). Seemingly ignorant of the feminist history of Latin America and the ways that Chicana feminists took their inspiration from early-twentieth-century Mexican feminism and women's revolutionary participation, historians continue the vendida logic by claiming, for
example, that Chicana feminists "were influenced by ideas foreign to their
community—namely bourgeois feminist ideology."[60] Despite historical evidence to the contrary, these narratives reduce all forms of feminism to its
liberal bourgeoisie form, and often reduce feminist beliefs and agendas to
stereotypes.

During the 1970s and 1980s an early Chicana feminist chronicler and La
Raza Unida Party (RUP) member, Martha Cotera, penned foundational historical texts that began a counter-telling of Chicana feminism, *Diosa y Hembra* (1976) and *The Chicana Feminist* (1977). Other early collections of feminist histories include *Essays on la Mujer*, edited by Rosaura Sánchez and
Rosa Martinez Cruz in 1977, Magdalena Mora and Adelaida Del Castillo's
Mexican Women in the United States, published in 1980. Three case studies of
women in the Chicano student movement were published in the late 1970s
and early 1980s by Sonia López, Adelaida Del Castillo, and Patricia Hernandez.[61] Even some of these early histories were influenced by this vendida
logic, including defensive claims that the women in their study put "la raza
primero." This practice abdicates a historical tradition of Mexicana and Chicana feminisms and participates in the good woman/bad woman dichotomy
used against those who stray from the patriarchal fold. Hernandez's study examines how women who engage in *la política* were seen as untraditional; yet
she writes, "The Chicana activist is not just a 'women's libber.' She charges
United States society with racism as well as sexism. She constitutes an integral part of her people's struggle against discrimination, low-paying jobs and
inadequate housing and education."[62] Hernandez's claim illustrates the imperative of the vendida logic as well as the danger of reducing feminism to the
single lens of gender at the exclusion of struggles against racial and economic
discrimination.

Although there is little historical evidence in the archival research and oral
histories with Chicana women activists that the women's liberation move-

ment influenced the *formation* of early Chicana feminist identities, the insidiousness of the vendida logic is that everyone was so busy claiming they were not Anglo-cized feminists that it made it seem like there were many women in the Chicano movement who were.[63] While these problems are a product of the historical context in which these histories were produced, they did circumscribe the way women's lives could be narrated in early movement histories. Because the logic of antifeminism was so pervasive, early studies often replicate unilinear and homogenizing narratives that depict Chicanas moving from their supposed static, monolithic experience of traditional culture to activism. What this misses is the multisited struggle of early women of color feminism in which different forms of political consciousness emerged side by side, in tandem, and often in conflict with one another.

Other mechanics of erasure attempt to locate Chicana feminist interventions as emerging solely in the space of the university instead of drawing on the long tradition of gender and feminist community-based activism. This move plays on the false dichotomy between "the" community as the site of authenticity and the academy (read: middle class or sold out) and dismisses the university as a critical historical site for the transformation of the relations of power/knowledge. Finally, there is a reticence to deal with sexism and homophobia in the field of Chicana and Chicano Studies because these issues are seen as "resolved." This tendency has resulted in interesting temporal slippages within Chicano Studies curricula where texts by Cherríe Moraga and Gloria Anzaldúa, vital and critical voices in the field, have been used to stand in for the emergence of feminism in the movement. Scholars have actually told me that a history of gender, sexuality, or feminism in the Chicano movement is no longer necessary because we have Moraga and Anzaldúa. The irony is that what these authors said in the 1980s was impossible to say in most movement spaces so they turned to creating new poetic revolutions to express their radical visions. Their path to social criticism and politics through creative writing and the essayist tradition was a result of their multisited struggle against exclusion as Chicanas, women, and lesbians in several social movements. My argument is that we need all these histories and genealogies of the contested histories of gender and sexuality in Chicana/o and Latina/o communities in order to transform these exclusions.

The shifts we have seen in the field of Chicana and Chicano Studies are the hard-won gains of many Chicana feminist and lesbian activists and critics who have actively worked to dismantle (hetero)sexism and gender oppression in political organizations, in their writings, and in scholarly associations like the National Association for Chicano Studies (NACS) and Mujeres Activas en Letras y Cambio Social (MALCS) since the late 1970s and early 1980s.[64] Their

activism within NACS even inspired the organization to change its name—
to the National Association for Chicana and Chicano Studies (NACCS)—in
order to mark the inclusion of women.[65]

Yet even these challenges have been met with reactionary retreat, as can
be seen in the retrograde argument posed by Ignacio M. García that seems
to be calling for the "good old days" of male dominance in the field of Chicano Studies. Instead of seeing *El Plan de Santa Barbara*, the 1969 founding
document of Chicano Studies, as a living document or legacy, he discusses the
supposed decline of the field by drawing a linear narrative between the *Plan*
and the contemporary major challenge to Chicano Studies, which he sees as
Chicana Studies scholarship. Not surprisingly, García's understanding of the
Chicano Movement lacks a historical analysis of the struggles of gender and
sexuality. His assessment of the Chicana feminist contribution to the field
reads:

> Because they are critical of the ideological premises of the Chicano Move-
> ment, they reject much of what came out of it. They believe that the concepts
> of community and family much extolled by early Chicano intellectuals are
> sexist and seek to limit their non-domestic growth. . . . Some Chicana femi-
> nists have, however, not limited themselves to attacking Chicanos, but have
> been extremely critical of Chicanas who do not follow their brand of femi-
> nism. Their adversarial approach has created divisions in a number of institu-
> tions, particularly those in California. While they see themselves as victims,
> they are in fact quite influential in their programs and in NACS. The lesbian
> Chicana scholars have even gone as far as promoting the idea that homosexu-
> ality is an integral part of Chicano culture.[66]

As García's narrow argument illustrates, it is not simply a question of different
schools of thought but a battle over who has the right to represent Chicana/o
history and cultures.

Only recently have Chicano historians such as Ernesto Chávez, in his study
of four Los Angeles Chicano movement organizations, critically examined
the question of identity, the ideological underpinnings of Chicano cultural
nationalism as a political platform, and the ways in which it "privileged males
and marginalized females."[67] Chicana historian Lorena Oropeza investigated
the nature of Chicano resistance to the Vietnam War as a fundamental break
in the strategy of integration and accommodation by earlier Mexican American generations. Documenting subtle forms of solidarity and consciousness
of other colonized people of color, Oropeza incorporates the shift in the
meaning of Chicano masculinity from one based on military service to one

more oriented toward community. Acknowledging the importance of gender, George Mariscal also pushes back on the notion that the Chicano movement was monolithic or even ideologically unified around nationalism by calling attention to internationalist tendencies in the context of the Vietnam War. He argues that the Chicano movement was "a diffuse movement cross-cut by regional, gender, and class issues." He continues, "The Movimiento (also known as La Causa or La Movida) was a mass mobilization dedicated to a wide range of social projects, from ethnic separatism to socialist internationalism, from electoral politics to institutional reform and even armed insurrection."[68]

Instead of seeing the Chicano movement as one monolithic entity that subsumes regional and other internal differences, these studies increasingly help us to see the regional and local struggles that loosely coalesced on the national level. As historians of the Chicano movement are reaching consensus on how diverse sectors of the movement unified around the rejection of the liberal path to political integration, they are also increasingly coming to acknowledge gender and, to a lesser degree, sexuality as key analytical axes from which to understand Chicano politics. In order to see women's political agency within the Chicano movement, we must shift our gaze away from hero narratives and look more closely at localized political spaces so that we can put women back into a history they had a role in shaping. Although many have criticized the male-dominated narratives of the Chicano movement, new histories of women and feminist activism have begun to emerge.[69]

NEW CHICANA HISTORIOGRAPHY

Putting women at the center of analysis does not simply mean that we now include subjects that were formerly excluded. Rather, the inclusion of women's experience will fundamentally alter the way in which . . . history is written.

YOLANDA BROYLES-GONZÁLEZ, "TOWARD A RE-VISION OF CHICANA/O THEATER HISTORY"

Chicano movement historians have used colonialism, class, and race as the lenses of analysis through which to interpret history. Chicana feminist historians such as Vicki Ruiz, Emma Pérez, Antonia Castañeda, Deena González, Yolanda Leyva, Cynthia Orozco, Lorena Oropeza, Miroslava Chávez-García, and Lydia Otero ask us to consider how broadening the scope of our analysis to include genders and sexualities might shift our understanding of people of Mexican descent in the United States. Chicana historians have worked to reinvigorate methodological questions of voice, agency, and silence and an understanding of how to read the gaps in dominant and exclusionary subaltern histories.[70] By using gender and sexuality as lenses to understand racial and economic oppression and the Chicano condition, Chicana feminist historians have read against the grain of the colonial archive.[71] They have not only interrogated how knowledge is produced, by areas of the discipline such as the West and the borderlands, but they have also mapped an alternative history of the major movements of nineteenth-century Chicano history.[72] Questioning the appropriateness of divisions such as America/Latin America, Pérez and Ruiz have drawn from the roots of Chicana feminism outside the borders of what is now the United States and in the diasporic experience of women of Mexican descent. In addition, along with other women of color feminist historians, Chicanas have furthered an intersectional approach to understanding the simultaneous and multifaceted impact of economic, racial/ethnic, and national origin status on shaping gendered and sexual historical processes.

The richness of women's participation in the Chicano movement in its vibrant spectrum of gender consciousness, and with its attendant tensions, is a story that is finally being more fully explored. Historicizing women's experience in Chicano movement organizations has produced startling fresh perspectives on political stories and ideological formations we thought we knew. In three recent studies the inclusion of gender and sexuality as an analytical lens has not only added new historical knowledge but also shifted the paradigms through which we understand leadership, the role of collectivity in cultural production, and new forms of gendered consciousness and female solidarity. These studies document how women's experience of the movement were qualitatively different and how gendered political demands emerged out of three Chicano movement organizations that did not include gender or women's rights as part of their political agendas.

Dolores Delgado Bernal's study of women's participation and leadership in the 1968 high school walkouts in East Los Angeles, known as the Blowouts, led to a reconceptualization of leadership in the Chicano Movement. Despite the fact that she was told that there were no female leaders in the 1968 Blowouts, Delgado Bernal notes, "In distinct ways and to varying degrees, the women I interviewed participated in these different dimensions of leadership. Their participation was vital to the Blowouts, yet because a traditional leadership paradigm does not acknowledge the importance of those who participate in organizing, developing consciousness, and networking, their leadership remains unrecognized and unappreciated by most historians."[73] Delgado Bernal found that if we shift the paradigm of leadership based on individual leaders, we get a broader vision of leadership, and the historical and pivotal roles that women have played in Chicano movements become visible.

Yolanda Broyles-González's groundbreaking study of women in El Teatro Campesino also questioned the ways in which Chicano Movement histories are "text-centered, chronological, and male-centered." She questioned "the classism and sexism that informs the production of knowledge [that] made it unnecessary to approach those [women] ensemble members for an oral history" and spent ten years gathering testimonies and transcribing interviews with participants.[74] In addition to her discovery of new forms of documentary evidence, her method involving participant observation followed the ways in which the creative production process shifted the epistemic register, allowing her to document the collective process of artistic authorship and production the Teatro Campesino women used to create theater and new forms of community. In addition to this generative collaborative process, Broyles-González documented the roles of women in the history of Chicano theater during movement times, the impact of male dominance on the organization, and the way in which women negotiated these limitations by creating alternative pathways.

Dionne Espinoza's oral history with female members of the East Los Angeles chapter of the Brown Berets documented new forms of gender consciousness and female solidarity as members participated in the Blowouts, attended the Youth Liberation Conference and Poor People's March on Washington, and organized protests against police brutality. The women grew increasingly conscious of the gendered division of movement labor as they worked on *La Causa*, the organization's newspaper, and provided the organizational backbone during the arrests of the L.A. 13 (who were charged with conspiracy after the walkouts) and the Biltmore 6 cases (when members were charged with property destruction during a talk given by then-Governor Ronald Reagan). Eventually, the women broke with the Berets and formed las Adelitas de Aztlán to protest the ways their labor was appropriated and went unrecognized in running the Free Clinic in East Los Angeles, which was directed by Gloria Arellanes. Based on the new forms of female solidarity that las Adelitas crafted in their call to action through *una familia de hermanas* (a family of sisters), Espinoza critically examined the reworking of nationalist discursive frames as well as new forms of gendered consciousness that she calls feminist nationalism.[75]

All three studies focus on movement organizations or events that have been well documented in previous studies, but the use of women's oral histories with rank-and-file members instead of the top-down approach produced dramatically different interpretations of that history and new conceptual frameworks for analyzing Chicana politics. This demonstrates that as we look away from the great man narrative, we can see collective processes of organization and different forms of political and artistic collaboration, as well as women's communities and spaces within the movement and what I have called hidden gender insurgencies. Chicanas are critical to document because they created new political identities, solidarities, forms of consciousness, and artistic modes of production, and, most important, because they show how Chicana organizing in the 1960s and 1970s, whether in mixed organizations or women's groups, created new ways of being political and organizing in ways that empowered others.[76]

After many years during which the field was populated largely by biographies and autobiographies of male Chicano leaders, new work by women who were active in the politics and the arts of the movement is starting to appear. Among these is a collection of the writings of Enriqueta Longeaux y Vásquez from the New Mexico land grant newspaper, *El Grito del Norte*, edited by Lorena Oropeza and Dionne Espinoza.[77] In addition, women's participation in the Mexican American Youth Association (MAYO) and the Chicano third party, La Raza Unida, has been documented in a collection of interviews by José Angel Gutiérrez, Michelle Meléndez, and Sonia Adriana Noyola.[78] Laura E. Garcia, Sandra M. Gutierrez, and Felicitas Nuñez have collected the memories, excerpts, and seven short plays produced by the San Diego–based Chicana theater group, Teatro de las Chicanas.[79] And Yolanda Alaniz, with her collaborator Megan Cornish, was able to document the critical role of Raza women on the left, documenting the organization MUJER in the state of Washington as well as new forms of Chicana grassroots leadership and mobilization in the Northwest.[80]

I recover this emerging alternative historiography to situate the rich genealogies of early Chicana feminisms and help to excavate a Chicana feminist epistemology. In this oral history project Chicana print cultures serve as a historiographic countercanon to map the genealogies of Chicana feminist resistance that began as a critical political formation within the Chicano movement. This alternative print practice includes a rich essayist tradition practiced by the early Chicana feminists Enriqueta Longeaux y Vasquez, Anna Nieto-Gomez, Betita Martinez, and Francisca Flores, who penned incisive editorial pieces that have been built on by later generations of Chicana scholars.

SPINNING THE HISTORICAL RECORD: ORAL HISTORIAN AS DJ

When I began this research in 1991 I embarked on a quest to turn up the volume on the stories of gender and sexuality that have been dubbed out of the Chicano historical record. Through this journey I found that being an oral historian is like being a DJ. As one digs through the old crates of records (historical archives) to find missing stories, the songs (narrative grooves, if you will) must be selected and their elements remixed to produce new meanings. Oral historians spin the historical record by sampling new voices and cutting and mixing the established soundscape to allow listeners to hear something different, even in grooves they thought they knew.

While this metaphor refers to the interpretive process, it also has methodological implications. For example, as oral historian/DJ I learned to listen in multiple registers as the activist women I interviewed narrated themselves and the histories of the Chicano movement by shifting between the individual and the collective "I." Listening for shifts in the narrator's voice and position is part of understanding their strategy of narration. The act of *testimonio*, of bearing witness, creates a political intervention through narration. Understanding the multiple registers complicates the feminist adage that the political is not only personal, but it is also multiple and mediated.

This book draws from a Chicana feminist intellectual tradition and an epistemological approach known as theories of the flesh—a theory-making practice that grounds knowledge making in lived experience and the realm of everyday life.[81] My methodology blends the life history approach developed by feminist oral historians/ethnographers and Latin American testimonio.[82] Working at the intersection of these methodologies allows me to hold the individual "I" of women's life histories in productive tension with the collective "I" of testimonio and social movement narrative. I draw from these traditions to foreground the importance of oral history, life narrative, auto-ethnography, and other forms of oral narrative deployed by women of color to produce politically and socially engaged histories of (in)migration, political mobilization, and community making.[83] Women of color activists have used testimony and autobiographical writing to ensure that their voices and contribution to the radical social movements of the 1960s will be included in the historical record.[84] My methodological approach understands that oral history's importance lies not only in the corrective it offers to masculinist and Eurocentric histories but also in the epistemological shift it can enact by inviting new voices into our interpretive and analytical reflections.[85]

In an oral history project engaged with social or political movements, what is articulated in the realm of the personal in the individual life history is given meaning in and through the collective.[86] These differential modes of telling that shift between the individual's story and the collective story of social movements means the oral historian as DJ listens in at least two registers and can learn to hear the multiple modes of the personal and collective.

The individual act of self-narration is a memory performance and a political strategy that calls our attention to memory as a powerful tool of political resistance.[87] Therein lies a rich site for listening, interpretation, and critical understanding. Historically in writings about othered or subaltern groups the meanings surrounding the ethnic/racial, gendered, sexual, or classed categories have colluded to create monolithic, static, and often essentialized representations. Narrators negotiate the complexities of their individual and collective memories through this "burden of representation" that many marginalized peoples navigate. For example, during points in her interviews Anna NietoGomez would reassert that she was articulating a singular voice, claiming that she was speaking only for herself as a strategy to move away from this totalizing view. In an explicit maneuver to break out of stereotypical representation, she made it a point to discuss the wide spectrum of Chicana experiences, as well as her individual story within that realm, as an act of representational agency.

Listening in multiple registers is crucial with dissident voices that may have been unpopular or even censured at the time. It requires listening for the revolution within the revolution or the nondominant groove in the song. In this context testimonio changes the nature of representation and narration, breaking open simplistic understandings of the binary subject/object, researcher/researched, because it includes the narrator's negotiation of her own means of representation.

Another example of listening on different registers is how the DJ synchs knowledge from multiple sources. While testifying and crafting public histories, women's activism often blurs the personal and the political to produce new forms of historical knowledge and new political possibilities. The shift between public and private knowledge introduces intimacies and personal details into the public record. A different epistemology is produced by the way all these interviews happened in the private realm of the narrator's (and occasionally my own) home, where public facts mix with the intimate and random details as we searched in spare bedrooms, under beds, or in garages and closets for movement documents and photos. Being a DJ historian requires listening at the public and private register and while stories may be spoken but not publicly aired, it allows for a layering of both epistemologies and blending of meanings.

Through personal reflection on sexual politics and the gendered organization of power a different way of knowing or new epistemologies are introduced into the (warped) historical record. What and who are excluded, silenced, and marginalized in movement politics and narratives is part of the DJ's challenge in navigating multiple knowledges, some of which are or have been forbidden.

Chisme, or gossip, can be understood as an alternative archive that records underground or unofficial histories that counter the male-dominated history of the movement. On the other hand, rumor and gossip were used against strong female leaders to target their sexuality as "deviant" because they challenged traditional gender roles and power inequalities. Frequently, women who challenged sexism or sexist politics were labeled lesbians. Merely being a feminist meant that you would be called a lesbian, and lesbian baiting was a powerful silencing weapon.[88] As DJ/oral historian, I see this as a layering of memory tracks, a layering of that which is spoken and that which has been silenced, recalling the way Yolanda Leyva theorizes listening to the silences.[89]

Sexuality profoundly shapes the telling of these contested histories. The silencing of women's diverse sexualities in the movement is another form of subjugated knowledge. One of the members of the organization who died before I began interviewing came out as a lesbian many years after her involvement with the group.[90] How do I tell her story when she was not out during the movement and without knowing how she would like to be remembered? Already we are missing a vital part of history. Her invisibility potentially has an impact on hundreds of young lesbian, gay, bisexual, transgender, and queer Chicanas and Chicanos and other people of color who are looking for a way to see themselves historically in the struggle of their communities. Often queer activists have been or are lead organizers of labor-, class-, and race-based movements (even many gender movements) but have not been recognized in their wholeness or remembered in this way. These tensions are not resolved here narratively but form part of these contested and contesting histories.

Instead of using oral history like any other archival source, my work more deeply engages with and is influenced by feminist ethnography and the theorizing of memory in oral history and cultural studies.[91] This is an oral history project that produces a different way of knowing and telling history that requires a shift in epistemology rather than a mere methodological orientation. "Shared authority," as many practitioners of oral history refer to it, opens the space for a multivocality in the text and for interpretive differences and partial knowledges to emerge. It calls into question the ways in which memory shapes lived experience. In my theorization of retrofitted memory I complicate the category of experience by considering how political events are remembered and misremembered, by exploring how trauma shapes memory, and by illustrating how political subjectivities are constructed through the ways in which we are called to remember.

Like DJs, oral historians are not dispassionate. We engage the apparatus of representation by sampling and circulating our mixes, which are then trans-

formed by the way the listeners (readers) participate through their own interpretations, call-ins, and shout-outs that make DJing a technology of exchange. Such an approach allows for a reconsideration of Gayatri Spivak's
provocative question, "Can the Subaltern Speak?," which opened up a space
of interrogation around oral history calling into question methodologies
of knowledge retrieval. Howard Winant discusses this intervention in productive ways for thinking about oral history: "Spivak critiques the romantic
notion that the colonized Other is simply the revolutionary mirror-image
of the Western Self, that it represents a coherent and unitary subject position which speaks with the clear and transparent 'voice of the oppressed.'"[92]
Rather than romanticize the subaltern, I use Spivak's question to understand
how "dominant discursive fields . . . constitute subaltern subjects, define their
modalities of expression, and structure the positions from which they speak
and are heard."[93] The question, can the subaltern speak? reminds us that the
subaltern can and does speak, in multiple, sometimes contradictory registers.
Yet the question illustrates the fiction of the speaking subject and makes us
ponder not if the subaltern speaks but if the subaltern can be heard within
the current circuits of power and international political economy.[94] The subaltern is made intelligible in part because he is mediated by two notions of
representation.

The first kind of representation is the "speaking for" mode of political representation, and the second type is the "re-presentation" of art or philosophy.[95] Illustrating the power behind representation, Spivak demonstrates
how the functions of representation, "between a proxy and a portrait," are
operative in political representation. She argues that in order to represent by
proxy, one is necessarily representing by depiction.[96]

Using the DJ tactic, I have observed a third mode of representation in relation to the question, can the subaltern speak? This mode is informed by how
narrators make specific interventions into how scholars represent them and
produce knowledge about themselves in what Angie Chabram-Dernersesian
calls auto-ethnography.[97] This third mode of representation—represent'n'—
is an enunciative practice of hip-hop culture, used by African American, Chicano, and other youth. When a caller calls in to a DJ on the radio, he or she
is "located" as represent'n' through a sense of place or social belonging. She
will often say, "This is Claudia represent'n' El Monte [or East Los, La Puente,
Santa Ana, or Long Beach]." When someone speaks herself into being or
speaks her truth (from the vantage point of that place), others respond: represent. In Chicano oldies shows place is transformed, space becomes territo-
rialized differently, and distances collapse or are bridged through the affective
work that is performed by nostalgia. The radio shows have the ability to cre-

ate relations (family, friends, community) through the affective work across geographic separations, caused by loved ones traveling long distances to look for work, the harvest patterns of migrant field work, and especially by the mass incarceration of young people of color, Chicano men, and, increasingly, women. The Art Laboe radio show is a classic illustration of such affective power. In the oldies call-in show places such as San Leandro, Fresno, Arizona, and Los Angeles are constituted through the circulation of words and assist in creating a radiographic rendering of social space by making a mobile and shifting map—a social and political geography. As a researcher and oral historian who is positioned as the "younger generation" by the narrators she interviews, another DJ tactic is the intergenerational sampling of oldies into new rhymes in which the layering of memory and time helps each generation make meaning and claim their place in narrative grooves that have been passed down. This seems ever more critical as changing technologies have led to an increasing array of the layers of musical time for younger and younger audiences.

The third mode of representation, represent'n', is not about speaking for (proxy) but speaking from: it performs an embodied knowledge of location or a situated knowledge.[98] It does not operate outside power relations or the problematics of representation but shifts our ear to hear differently when the subaltern takes the mic and speaks. When the radio DJ answers or hails the listener-become-speaker, the caller becomes a subject in the process of enunciation who is not speaking for the whole community but speaking from a specific location. This, at its root, includes an analysis of the politics of location and processes of collective self-enunciation. Internal to this mode of represent'n' is the notion that all representation is mediated by power, capital, and agency.

The third mode of representation is critical to rethinking ethnographic representation, shared authority, memory, and experience. DJ strategies allow me to shift the mode of representation in a manner that challenges our assumptions of romantic voices of the silenced speaking, or what I have called "consuming stories."[99] Testimonio and oral history are often received by "consuming" the supposedly pure Other or subaltern through supposedly unmediated narrative instead of considering the politics of production and political economy involved in the narrative and the political strategies of the narrators.[100] My incorporation of DJ tactics into oral history methodology allows me to make apparent my role as oral historian in cutting, mixing, and sampling the narratives and demonstrating the constructed nature of the enterprise. It also invites you the reader to listen differently.

CHICANA INSURGENCIES: STORIES OF TRANSFORMATION, YOUTH REBELLION, AND CHICANA CAMPUS ORGANIZING

IN GREATER LOS ANGELES, the Chicano movement of the 1960s and 1970s were heady days filled with personal, communal, political, and social change. The transformations were stunning for those who were involved as they began to learn about the farmworkers' struggle, the ins and outs of political organizing, the right to quality education, and the historical legacy of their people in the Southwest, or Aztlán. While there was a romantic quality to being involved in a community of resistance, many young people joined the Chicano student movement in order to confront the new forms of race, gender, and class discrimination they experienced in educational institutions as they collectively entered universities for the first time. This chapter documents the experiences of this generation and illustrates how the alienation they felt as they entered university pushed them toward social justice activism and educational advocacy. Many became active in the larger Chicano student movement as a survival strategy, finding a political home on campus with deep links to the communities from which they came. Yet it was the contradictions Chicana activists found in the particular ways that "home" was constituted that compelled them to address the issues of gender and sexual power that were not originally part of the Chicano movement agenda.

While they were the first generation of Chicanas to enter college in historically significant numbers, many did not complete their studies. Their grades were frequently sacrificed to the movement as they provided the organizational backbone to campus and community organizations while simultaneously forming the first groups on behalf of themselves as Chicanas. Racial hostility, sexual politics, and a lack of reproductive health care and guidance were just some of the issues with which these Chicanas grappled as they tried to find their own voice and perspective on campuses and in the Chicano movement.[1]

This chapter brings activist women's lives to the forefront, revealing a layer of movement history that uncovers the "internalities of power" in the Chicano movement from the perspective of those involved.[2] Without their rich life narratives and analyses, we could miss the complex and multisited formation of Chicana feminist consciousness and fail to see the hidden transcripts of gendered insurgencies within the political mobilizations, marches, and battles that are usually told as heroic stories.[3] This approach tells more intimate and nuanced stories of gender, race, and sexuality and the ways these forms of power were negotiated in the local spaces of the movement and in the dominant society. Focusing on both the broader histories of social movement genealogies and on a gendered social history of organizing allows for a deeper historical understanding of how newfound friendships became survival networks and *comadrazgo* engendered new forms of female solidarity, ultimately leading to new forms of collective Chicana consciousness.[4]

Coming together in 1968 at California State University, Long Beach (then known as Long Beach State College), las Chicanas de Aztlán, an informal rap group of Chicana student activists, began to name how the racial and economic oppression and educational inequality had gendered and sexual dimensions that influenced their lives as Chicanas but were not addressed by the Chicano student movement. The group formalized and began to organize and run consciousness-raising and solidarity-building sessions for Chicanas on campus as well as for incoming female freshmen. This led them to create a philosophy of sisterhood, Hermanidad, and to publish a Chicana feminist newspaper, *Hijas de Cuauhtémoc*, a name they became known by after the newspaper's first issue. In addition to addressing the structural and cultural roots of oppression, the group's efforts to bring gender equality and liberatory ethics to relationships, sexuality, power, women's status, labor and leadership, familial bonds, and organizational structures resulted in enduring historical changes for that generation of Chicanas.

HISTORICAL ROOTS OF CHICANA INSURGENCY

Expansions and depressions in the U.S. economy and the need for low-wage labor have historically shaped the waves of Mexican immigration and U.S. immigration policy. During the era of the Great Depression, spanning the years from 1920 to World War II, over 500,000 people of Mexican descent, the majority of whom were U.S. citizens, were either deported or repatriated. Historians estimate that just "during the period of 1930–1939, Mexicans constituted 46.3 percent of all people deported from the United States. Yet, Mexicans comprised less than 1 percent of the total U.S. population. . . . [As] the depression worsened, repatriation, deportation and voluntary or induced departures spread their ominous shadow across the entire United States. Trains, cars, trucks, and buses streamed southward from every corner of the land."[5] Yet in order to address the labor shortage caused by World War II the United States imported nearly 220,000 braceros to keep agricultural production and the wartime economy running. During the period 1953–1965, when the economy declined after the postwar boom, Operation Wetback was instituted, and again Mexicanos found themselves unwelcome.

During the 1920s and 1930s Mexican children residing in the United States and Mexican American students suffered deplorable conditions in education, including segregated schools that often severely punished the use of Spanish and pushed students toward vocational and domestic skills to provide an unskilled labor pool. Unlike other models of American immigration based on European assimilation, Mexican American youth of the second, third, and fourth generations were not incorporated into an upwardly mobile college-going population but were proletarianized and often even criminalized as illustrated by two highly publicized incidents: the Sleepy Lagoon trial (1942) in which a dozen Mexican American youths were tried and convicted of murder in a racially biased and error-laden trial (the conviction was later overturned) and the World War II–era Zoot Suit Riots in which sailors and soldiers on leave in Los Angeles violently assaulted "zoot suiters," who were for the most part Mexican American, African American, and Filipino youth. The local press lauded the actions of the servicemen for upholding proper American masculinity while characterizing the youth as violent criminals and decrying the excess of fabric in the zoot suit as unpatriotic during wartime. While portrayed as socially deviant and in "excess" of their productive role as workers by the dominant culture, many Chicanos of the 1960s viewed the pachuco as a symbol of resistance, celebrating his style and subaltern masculinity. What has been overlooked, until Catherine Ramírez's study, *The Women in the Zoot Suit*, is the role women played in the zoot suit culture and the cultural and gendered politics of Chicano nationalism.[6]

In the postwar era the policies affecting Mexican American youth were, if not replaced, at least accompanied by the gains of the civil rights movement and the increased access to higher education provided by the G.I. Bill. For returning Chicano veterans, the G.I. Bill provided access to vocational training, which allowed them to obtain jobs in more established industries as well as access to the working and middle classes by offering low-cost loans to finance the purchase of homes. Some veterans sought the security and improvement of life chances for their families by sending their children to college, due to the G.I. Bills of 1944, 1952, and 1966,[7] in their search for the ever elusive

American dream. Yet even as this generation continued to build a political voice through historic forums such as the League of United Latin American Citizens, founded in 1929, and the Latino civil rights organization El Congreso de Pueblos de Hablan Española, the Chicano generation was born out of the rejection of liberalism as they grew impatient waiting for the benefits of political integration and gradual change championed by previous generations in the face of continued racial and economic hostility.[8]

All the members of the Hijas de Cuauhtémoc were born between the years 1946 and 1952. Those I interviewed located themselves at least in the second-generation experience, although a few could trace their family genealogies back to the 1600s, recalling the saying, "We never crossed the border, the border crossed us." (See figure I.1.) While their family histories are shaped by the displacement of the Mexican Revolution, labor migrations, picking cotton in Texas or agricultural work in California, fleeing racism, finding better work opportunities, and marriage to other Chicanas/os, Mexicanas/os or Puertorriqueñas/os, over time, all settled in the greater Los Angeles area.[9] While all stressed education as a means of collective self-improvement, many families were not completely supportive of their *daughters* attending college. Women in this generation were the first in their families to receive access to higher education.

The 1964 Civil Rights Act authorized passage of the 1965 Higher Education Act, which had broad impact on opening up equal opportunity for low-income and minority students in higher education.[10] As a result, by the late 1960s a small but growing number of Mexican American students were attending colleges across the Southwest.[11] In fact, the education scholar Patricia Gándara documents this trend, finding that financial aid and higher education recruitment programs, like the National Defense Education Act (NDEA) of 1958 and the Higher Education Act of 1965, led to the largest increase of low-income students and students of color in history. By 1975 their numbers peaked and have not been matched since.[12]

While the transition to college was an important historical development, many Chicanas faced extreme difficulties negotiating the new social world of the university, which was layered over and mediated by older expectations of family and community. Chicana activism emerged from these changing circumstances. Although some of these young women's lives had been circumscribed by traditional notions of family, patriarchy, and Catholicism, at college a wide range of life experiences informed them and contributed to their political vision and activism.

DECONSTRUCTING THE IDEAL CHICANA: CONTESTED
TRADITIONS AND GENDERED POLITICAL SCRIPTS

The oral histories of the Hijas de Cuauhtémoc reveal that while several members came from "traditional" (conventionally gendered) backgrounds, many others drew their sense of political agency and gender identity from other community-based "traditions" of female strength and resistance. As descendants of female labor organizers, political party activists, railroad workers, and women who managed family households on scarce resources, most Chicana activists I interviewed stated that it was their mothers, *abuelas* (grandmothers), or *tías* (aunts) who served as their role models. This suggests that Chicana feminism emerged not only from the gendered contradictions of the movement, as scholars have suggested, but also from how gendered movement discourses, based on an idealized nationalist recovery of cultural "tradition," did not resonate with many Chicanas' lived experiences. The construction of gender for women in the movement was based on what Alma García has called the "Ideal Chicana," an ideal that "glorified Chicanas as strong, long-suffering women who had endured and kept Chicano culture and family intact."[13] The Ideal Chicana prescribed the gender norms of many movement organizational practices. Not only was family used as both a metaphor and a mobilizing strategy, but ideologies of political familialism, which often left patriarchal structures unquestioned, played a role in naturalizing male supremacy and reinforcing women's marginalization.[14] In response, movement women began to construct, contest, and negotiate these gendered roles and relationships.

The oral histories conducted for this study illustrate that activist women were raised in a diversity of gendered formations that range from conventional gender expectations to what some have called "protofeminist" working-class attitudes and a mix and contradiction of all these views. Instead of measuring women's strength and refusal to conform to conventional confining gender roles against dominant norms of European American femininity, I argue that we must place them within a critical genealogy of women's resistance that has emerged from the experiences of women of color. Such a formulation allows us to see how feminism has emerged from diverse experiences, including labor participation, migration, and conditions of racial exclusion and poverty. In the tradition of Angela Davis's work, which locates early working-class black feminisms in the hidden transcripts of blues songs and performers of the 1930s and 1940s, I want to claim the forms of feminism that spring out of daily life, not just "precursors" or protofeminisms, but working-class forms of feminist consciousness.[15]

The Hijas de Cuauhtémoc developed their own Chicana *feminismos* (feminisms) by reclaiming and retrofitting the memory of early-twentieth-century Mexican feminists who demanded educational, wage, and political equality, as well as the legacies of feminist activists who were part of a long genealogy of socialism and anarchism in Mexico and the U.S./Mexico borderlands. If we assume that Chicana feminism emerged historically only from the Chicano movement, we fail to recognize other rich traditions such as Mexican women's labor activism in the United States.[16] Their actions and theories were born out of a long history of Chicana and Latina labor organizing and radicalism that is illustrated in the early writings of Lucy Parsons. Born Lucía Eldine Gonzalez in Texas in 1854 of mixed-race ancestry (black, Native American, and Mexican), Lucy Parsons went on to help organize the 1886 march of 80,000 workers that launched a day-long general strike on what would come to be known as the first May Day.[17] Demanding an eight-hour day, the march shut down the city of Chicago. In 1905 Parsons participated in the founding of the International Workers of the World (IWW), and she continued to organize in Chicago, leading hunger strikes and demonstrations, for which she was repeatedly arrested. She wrote for two radical newspapers, the *Liberator* and the anarchist publication the *Alarm*.[18]

Other female labor and community organizers played a key role in founding the first Latino civil rights organization, El Congreso de Pueblos de Hablan Española, and demanded the inclusion of women's rights in the first Latino civil rights agenda. Guatemalan-born Luisa Moreno (see figure I.2) immigrated to New York in 1928 and, despite her elite background, ended up sewing in a sweatshop in Spanish Harlem. There she began to organize a Latina garment workers' union to fight the deplorable working conditions. Moreno joined the Congress of Industrial Organizations (CIO), and by 1938 she became a representative for the United Cannery, Agricultural, Packing, and Allied Workers of America (UCAPAWA) for which she organized a successful strike of pecan shellers with local organizers such as Emma Tenayuca, who had been organizing in San Antonio, Texas, since the early 1930s. In 1939 Moreno, along with other activists such as the prominent Los Angeles–based Josefina Fierro de Bright (see figure I.3 p. 126), organized the first national meeting of El Congreso de Pueblos de Hablan Española (the Congress of Spanish-Speaking People), which drew between 1,000 and 1,500 activists from 128 organizations.[19] Critically, both Moreno and Fierro de Bright fought for the inclusion of women's rights in the national Latino civil rights agenda. Their position is detailed in a resolution passed at the second national convention of El Congreso that argued that Mexican women suffer from a double oppression and resolved to form a women's committee to "support and work for women's equality, so that they may receive equal wages, enjoy the same rights as men in social, economic, and civil liberties."[20]

Born in Mexicali, Mexico, Fierro de Bright represents the long legacy of Mexican women's activism as both her grandmother and mother were ardent supporters of the political leader Juan Flores Magón and the Partido Liberal Mexicano. Fierro de Bright began organizing in East Los Angeles against "factories and shops that would sell to Mexicanos but refused to hire them."[21] At the age of eighteen she became a lead organizer of El Congreso. Although Moreno is often credited with organizing the first conference, the Chicana historian Vicki L. Ruiz asserts that Fierro de Bright was instrumental in "buoying the day to day operations of the fragile southern California chapters."[22] Under Moreno and Fierro de Bright's leadership, El Congreso recruited over 80,000 members. Like Moreno, Fierro de Bright was red-baited for her activism and her connections to the Communist Party, until she and her husband decided to leave the United States.[23]

Another notable Chicana activist, Emma Tenayuca, who at the age of sixteen, in 1934, belonged to a ladies auxiliary of LULAC, participated in her first labor strike in San Antonio and in the next three years became active in organizing two locals of the International Ladies' Garment Workers Union. Tenayuca became a leader of the Workers' Alliance of America, a national federation of unemployed workers' organizations in San Antonio where she came in direct contact with workers from the garment, cigar, and pecan shelling industries. In late January 1938, when 2,000 pecan shellers decided to strike, they asked Tenayuca to be their strike representative.[24] Six thousand to 10,000 strikers faced tear gas and billy clubs; 1,000 strikers, including Tenayuca, were arrested by San Antonio police in an effort to quell the strike. In 1939 Tenayuca became the chair of the Texas Communist Party.[25]

Manuela Solis Sager, a lifelong activist, began organizing garment and agricultural workers in Laredo, Texas, between 1932 and 1933. Solis Sager was also a member of the Communist Party and "was active in struggles to end the Vietnam War, to free Angela Davis, and for immigrant rights."[26] She provided an important generational link by staying in San Antonio and participating in the Chicano and women's movements, electoral politics, and the movement to end U.S. imperialism.[27] Although the rise of the New Left in the 1960s is often tied to the activism of red diaper babies, there needs to be further historical study of the role that Mexicans in the United States played in left politics throughout the twentieth century, with special attention to women's participation and how it shaped future generations of activists.[28]

This legacy of women's activism, which often combined gender justice and the fight against capitalist exploitation, is a legacy of leftist organizing and working-class radicalism that vividly illustrates the interconnection between the economic, racial, and gendered oppression of Mexican women in the United States. Feminist activists in the Chicano movement drew on the history and experience of women's resistance to dominant cultural formations and institutions as well as female activists of the Mexican American generation in Los Angeles such as those involved in the Community Service Organization (CSO) and the grassroots effort to get Edward Royal elected.[29] Yet what distinguishes them as a political generation is that they collectively named, theorized, and built a political praxis to confront oppression in student, community, and labor organizing, in the cultural arts, in educational and scholarly associations, and in their homes.

While the Chicano movement has been understood as a cultural, political, and generational shift (from Mexican American to Chicano), what has not been well documented is how Chicana feminist activists in the 1960s and 1970s collectively named, theorized, and created a politics around intersecting oppressions that were unique to their political generation. The life histories of activist women tell this important story and simultaneously provide insight into both the psychic/subjective and the structural/social changes involved. Rather than coming to the movement and "finding themselves" as women, their consciousness and political action often derived from the contradictions between their life experiences as women and the movement scripts that constructed the Ideal Chicana.[30]

While the Ideal Chicana was based on the rebirth and rediscovery of cultural narratives, this process constructed, as much as represented, cultural norms through the patriarchal organization of power. Alma García has argued that "Chicana feminists challenged traditional gender roles because they limited their participation and acceptance within the Chicano movement."[31] As much as the conditions they found in the movement, Chicanas' activism was born out of the everyday strength of women at the center of familial and community life whose sensibilities drew from a structure of feeling or commonsense beliefs about more egalitarian gendered roles based on a long legacy of working-class women's labor participation, activism, and, in some cases, radicalism.

Although the lives of some of the women I interviewed had been circumscribed by patriarchy and Catholicism, there were diverse life experiences. Some stated that they shared a sense of injustice around "traditional" gender roles as girls, but few had taken action to challenge these injustices in their families while growing up. Anna NietoGomez challenged patriarchal norms as a girl because, she explains, she was exposed to traditions of both patriarchy and women's independence. Born in 1946 in San Bernardino, California, NietoGomez is a third-generation Chicana on her mother's side, while her father's side of the family has roots in New Mexico that can be traced to the 1600s. NietoGomez's parents were born in New Mexico but met in California, and she is the eldest of three children. Due to severe asthma, between the ages of three and seven she lived with her maternal and paternal grandparents in San Bernardino and Bakersfield, California, respectively.

Her first direct action protest took place years before she entered college. Even as a girl she had developed ideas about women's position in the family. When she disliked the way her grandpa Gomez treated her grandma Maria, she negotiated a change of behavior by going on a meal strike. She describes the incident this way:

> Another important thing to me was that my grandma did not eat at the same table as my grandpa. He ate by *himself* like a patrón, and for whatever reason, I don't know where I got it, I thought that it was wrong. She would cook dinner or breakfast or lunch, and we were allowed to eat at the same table as my grandpa, but my grandma would not eat at that table until everyone was finished—like a servant, like she wasn't family—so that didn't seem right to me since neither my father nor my other grandfather treated their wives this way. Dinner would not begin until the wife sat at the table.
>
> When my grandpa called me to come and eat, I was on the couch with my brother, who wanted to go eat, but I told him he couldn't. I had decided . . . that we weren't going to go eat until my grandma ate at the table with us. I remember my grandfather saying [in a deep booming voice], "Anna, come to eat." I said, "No." And he goes [again in a deep voice], "No? You can't tell me no. Come to eat." My brother wanted to eat, but I yanked him down and said, "We're not eating until my grandma eats with us." And he [grandpa] goes, "You are telling me what to do?" And I said, "We're not going to eat until my grandma eats at the same table."
>
> And he smiled and said, "Doña Maria, come and sit down." She sat down and ate with us from that time on, and this made me very happy.[32]

NietoGomez explains that there was a diversity of experiences among the women in her own family, illuminating a basic idea that she emphasized many times throughout our interviews: the experiences and backgrounds of Chicanas are not monolithic. Continually deconstructing the idea of a singular or Ideal Chicana experience, NietoGomez took her cues about gendered expectations from her mother and her father. Her mother had graduated from high school and began working for the Santa Fe Railroad in 1944, at the age of eighteen.

NietoGomez's father taught her the importance of independence because he felt that women should be taught how to manage on their own—a perspective he developed while watching his mother fight for survival as a single mom. She also credits her father for teaching her how to cook and sew and for teaching her mother how to build a house and fix the car.

Chicana activists drew on diverse life experiences to inform their politics. Sylvia Castillo, born in 1952, resided with her family in Pico Rivera (a working-class neighborhood of Southeast Los Angeles) until her father took a job in the aerospace industry and the family moved to Lakewood, becoming among the first to integrate that largely all-white neighborhood. Before her participation in the Chicano student movement, Castillo was a politically conscious high school student who came to political organizing through her family's union involvement and her mother's activism in the Democratic Party. She explains:

> My mother had climbed the rungs of the Democratic Party and was doing organizing work for the UAW [United Auto Workers]. At sixteen I had exposure to the Chicano movement because in 1966 my mother had started working with César Chávez through the UAW. The UAW Local 148 was the union sector that represented the aircraft workers of which my father was part, and my uncle was a union steward. My mother was a liaison for the auxiliary to the UFWOC [United Farmworkers Organizing Committee]. At that time, the UFWOC brought together a coalition of unions to do the support [and build] economic infrastructure so that the boycott could happen. So I would travel periodically up to Delano taking clothes and food that we would have organized here in Long Beach and we would hang out . . . at the union hall called the 40 Acres where the Filipino and Chicano/Mexicano workers would come together on Friday nights. We would be there to deliver the food and participate in the fellowship and food, and there would be *teatro* and music.[33]

Other members of the Hijas de Cuauhtémoc were raised with more conventional gendered expectations or by families with more conservative political views. Sonia López's foundational 1977 study of Chicana student activists states, "To the Chicano Student Movement came many young women who were away from home for the first time, and who were still imbued with the traditions of the familia. . . . Chicana women made important decisions about the conflicts between traditional cultural roles and new revolutionary roles."[34] For example, Leticia Hernández was not politically involved before she went to college, as her family enforced conservative gender roles and political views. Hernández, born in 1952, grew up with her first-generation mother and grandmother and her second-generation father in the East Los Angeles housing project Pico Gardens. After attending Catholic grade school, Hernández transferred to the public school system, where her actions and behavior were under constant surveillance by her father, who forbade her participation in the 1968 Chicano student walkouts.

> In the beginning, at college, people talked of the Chicano power and the movimiento. I didn't think I should get involved because I was there to go to school. I was the first to graduate from high school in my family. My last year in high school during, well, of course, in Lincoln High School and Garfield and at Roosevelt we had a lot of riots and I was always too afraid to join because my dad would kill me if I had gotten caught. People were being threatened with "if you participate you won't graduate." My father insisted that I be home by three o'clock, so there were no extracurricular activities, and walking to and from Roosevelt High School I had to make it in half an hour. I had to be home by three-thirty, come hell or high water. No matter how cute you wanted to look in your high heels I had to be home in half an hour. So there was this real tight rein around me. So I was very sheltered. My parents were also very conservative; they talked about César Chávez as being a Communist.[35]

Sharing the experience of many Chicanas, Hernández narrates how at college she encountered the dual process of confronting new forms of racism and racialization while experiencing new gender expectations and relatively more independence as a woman.

Corinne Sánchez, a third-generation Chicana who transferred from San Bernardino City College to Cal State Long Beach in 1968, where she became a student leader, describes how she was raised with the notion that her first duty as a woman was to be a mother and have children.

> It was a real conflict for us, our generation of women, to be socially educated and oriented to being traditional and now faced with doing everything in opposition to that. We really were rejected by our families, by our own men and even the men of our generation men who were involved with the same causes.[36]

When Chicanas joined the movement they brought diverse gendered histories that informed how they navigated a political terrain checkered with the gendered political scripts of the Chicano movement and the intense sexual politics of the 1960s as well as newfound freedoms and autonomy.

FROM BARRIO TO UNIVERSITY: THE PROMISE AND CHALLENGE OF THE COLLEGE EXPERIENCE FOR CHICANAS IN THE LATE 1960S

In order for Chicanas to even begin to control her destiny, she must have access to higher education. For without an education, she will still continue to be at the mercy of the Anglo system of injustice.
CINDY HONESTO, *HIJAS DE CUAUHTÉMOC*, 1971

The members of the Hijas de Cuauhtémoc whom I interviewed began college between 1967 and 1970. They all describe intense isolation and alienation stemming from the fact that there were few Chicanas/os or Latinas/os on campus, let alone other people of color. While the new racial consciousness on campuses did provide them with an analysis of their experience as well as new communities of support, there were gendered aspects of college life and simultaneous racialized, gendered, and classed-based experiences that their male counterparts did not share. The new radical campus politics did not incorporate a gendered analysis of racial oppression or educational experiences. Many activists in this political generation were left on their own to name and challenge the racialized gender discrimination and gendered racism they faced. Their shared effort to make visible the multiple and simultaneous nature of oppressions would become a key theoretical node of women of color feminisms.

NietoGomez recalls that there were only three Chicanas among the students who started the United Mexican American Students (UMAS) organization in 1967 at what was then Long Beach State College. Chicano power and student movement politics were both a refuge against isolation and a mode of survival. NietoGomez and Corinne Sánchez were among the first Hijas de Cuauhtémoc members to enter college. Their work in movement politics focused heavily on Chicano recruitment, and they served as counselors, Educational Opportunity Program (EOP) advisers, and peer mentors to prevent dropouts. In addition to their community and campus activism and their academic work, this generation laid the intellectual, institutional, and political foundation for the discipline of Chicana and Chicano Studies.

In the mid- to late 1960s, as Mexican American youth went to college in unprecedented numbers, they found campus environments that were a radical departure from what anyone in their families or communities had experi-

enced. The transition to college was not just a watershed personal development for this generation; it was an important historical development that
changed what it meant to be a Mexican American woman living in the United
States. It was not, however, without significant challenges. It was in her role
as EOP counselor that NietoGomez developed a greater sense of political
consciousness about women's oppression.

> If you ask me, the number one problem in retention of the Chicanos who
> were on campus was guilt, you know? It was a form of survivor guilt. Every-
> body talked about the fact that they only had to share the bathroom with one
> person or that they had the bathroom all to themselves. Their standard of
> living had risen drastically [in the dorms], and yet their parents' or their fami-
> lies' standard of living was still, you know, low. They felt great guilt about
> that disparity. On the one hand they enjoyed and they really liked school, but
> on the other they felt like they had abandoned their families, and they needed
> to work that out for themselves.

There were also gendered differences. NietoGomez recalls, "The men felt
guilty about not contributing economically to their families; the women felt
guilty and selfish for not helping their families economically, not helping their
mother's raise their siblings, or not beginning to have families of their own
with all the social pressures that existed." She notes that there was a lot of
new social freedom for some Chicanas: "Education gave them freedom. They
didn't have to cook for the entire family or brothers. They could devote their
whole lives to study and work."[37]

Although their achievement represented the hopes and dreams of the generations before them and the aspirations of their families, some young women
did not receive full support from their families because educational attain-
ment also entailed breaking out of conventional gender roles. Leticia Hernández's testimony describes some of the contradictions of being the first to
go to college.

> My family stressed the importance of education. We were very poor, at times,
> trying to scrape enough money together for rent. The family of five lived in
> a one-bedroom house. My grandmother never taught me to sew because she
> didn't want me to spend my life sewing in factories. They wanted me to have
> opportunities outside of factory work.[38]

When I asked if her parents were excited for her and supportive of the opportunity to attend college, she said:

> My parents were . . . god, I guess they were torn with yes they wanted me to
> go to college but no they didn't want me to go so far away, by myself. They
> thought that I shouldn't be living by myself and that I probably wasn't. . . .
> My parents held conservative social views, and my behavior was regulated by
> the confinements of not being seen as a questionable woman. They felt I was
> too young and [being on my own] was seen as if I was out there whoring.

In addition to negotiating these contradictions, the transition from the barrio
to campus was so radical that many Chicanas either dropped out within the
first year or never managed to finish their degrees due to their activism, which
put collective survival before individual academic success. Many who did not
possess the coping strategies or cultural capital to negotiate their way around
the institutions of higher education found political work and collective organizing crucial to their survival. Hernández continues:

> So campus was a totally different experience, dealing with activists, the
> dorms, etc. The EOP program did not train students. For example, the first
> day of school, I missed my first class because nobody told me that the bells
> did not ring. It went down hill from there. . . . I felt out of place in college. I
> gained close to one hundred pounds because I could not deal with the stress.
> I did not know how to deal with being outside of my environment. In order
> to shield myself from that, I gained a lot of weight. I partied a lot.
>
> The only haven was the movement, which I became very involved with. I
> marched a lot . . . to Delano, on Vons, crushing grapes at the grocery store,
> going to East L.A. to talk to kids about going to college. I was really busy
> preaching education but not doing it, following through for myself. . . . I was
> so busy with activism that I did not do well. . . . I organized Ballet Folklorico
> at Cal State Long Beach, which took my attention after working on the Hijas
> de Cuauhtémoc and UMAS. But everyone dealt with this differently. I be-
> came involved in Chicano power. Another Chicana I knew became a disco
> queen. At the time the main goal for women in college was to get married to
> a college-educated man.[39]

INVISIBILITY BLUES

NietoGomez described the deep alienation she felt as one of the first Chicanas to step onto a college campus in the late 1960s. She described feeling lost
in lecture classes of 250 people and how professors would literally ignore
her when she raised her hand or walk away from her while she was talking to

them. Chicanos and Chicanas were made to feel invisible—literally, ethnically, and culturally unintelligible.

> I was going through an identity crisis because nobody knew what a Chicano was, and it seemed like every day someone asked me, "What are you?" I had never been questioned about my identity before. I came from a segregated town. I mean, that was always a given, you know, that was just always a given [that we were Chicanos]. Every day people would ask, "Well, what are you? You're so strange looking." [I began to wonder] why are they asking me that over and over, "Are you Polynesian? Are you Guamanin? Are you Indonesian? Are you Filipino?" God, you know, I'd look at the map at how far away some of these places were, and I would try to imagine what those people look like. It bothered me a lot, so much that when I would get up in the morning I would look in the mirror and ask myself, "What are you? Why doesn't anybody know you're Chicano? The whole world used to know what you were. Why don't they know now?"

When NietoGomez finally did encounter another student from her community, she found that he was trying to survive this new environment by trying to "pass," or fit into the dominant culture of the university, even if it meant denying where he came from.

> There was a boy who I had dated who had also gone to Long Beach before me. He was on a baseball scholarship. In San Bernardino we were good friends, and he'd come to my house and he had eaten with my family. One day I saw him at the college, and he was rushing a fraternity so he was surrounded by these blonde, blue-eyed women in ponytails in some kind of uniform who were rushing a sorority. When I saw him I told him, "I'm so happy to see you." He looked at me, and he turned around and turned his back to me. [It was devastating] because I had not seen anybody I'd known since arriving at Cal State Long Beach. It was so big, and you may not see the same person for weeks. Nobody would talk to you, and I could go through weeks without anybody talking to me. I was just really, totally alienated.
>
> When he was with these blond girls he was denying that he knew me; he was ashamed of me. He was pretending that he wasn't Mexican, and I just got so angry, I stepped back and kicked him in the butt and walked away. When I did that, then he went chasing after me: "Anna, Anna, I'm sorry. I'm sorry." I said, "How could you do that to me? I haven't seen somebody I've known since I've been here." He says, "Anna, this means so much to me. Don't spoil it, don't spoil it," so I walked away.

Like many in her cohort, NietoGomez's isolation, homesickness, and invisibility led to depression. Finding others like her on campus helped her survive, and the movement provided a haven.

> I remember one time it was after class and I had another one so I had to wait fifteen minutes. I looked up and this guy was carrying this poster, like a sign, you know, like when they picket and stuff. . . . He was a Chicano, and on this poster were these words, and I didn't know the words. So I sounded it out—chi-ca-no—"Chicano!" Oh my god! I had never seen it written—it was only an oral word, something I heard in my community. I was raised that we were Chicanos, but I had never seen it written in black and white. I was so ecstatic because I felt so alone. I jumped up and I called, "Are you a Chicano?" And he goes, "Yeah man." I go, "I'm a Chicana! I'm a Chicana! Isn't that wonderful?" It was like I had found someone from Mars, so he told me that we were having a meeting sometime that week, down the hill in the EOP building, and to come. I said, "You mean there's more Chicanos here?" and he says, "Yeah."
>
> I went to my first UMAS meeting, in these rickety old bungalows painted institutional green all the way down the hill. I remember walking in and there were about twelve or fifteen Chicanos—mostly guys, some girls—and I remember my eyes just going around the little room looking at them, soaking them all in so I could remember them until I died, you know? I was just so happy to see them, and then we started talking and we were all going through the same experiences. My experience was not unusual. They also didn't know anybody; nobody would talk to them; they didn't know what they were doing there; they felt so isolated, so alone, and so we decided that we would meet and do things together.[40]

Many of the students encountered new forms of racism while integrating with white students. Some of these experiences occurred in the public sphere, but some took place in much closer proximity to the student apartments and dormitory halls. Hernández narrates the conditions that moved her from the sidelines to the center of political activity.

> Because they didn't have enough men in the off-campus dorms, they put all these minority kids on the third floor of the men's wing. We felt that they had discriminated against us because the people who were in those dormitories were the wealthier kids, the snobbish kind, I mean. I remember they had put one of us into a room with this *gabacha* [slang for "white girl"] roommate. Irma had gotten into her room, and she was there on the first day arranging

her room when this white girl comes in with skis in one hand and a beach bag in the other hand. She turns around and looks at the room, looks at these three Mexicans in her room, and throws down the skis and the bag in disgust and says, "What are you doing in my room?"[41]

When Irma explained that she was her roommate, the woman insisted that she could not be and stormed out of the room. NietoGomez had a similar experience. Upon meeting her new roommate, she made her a welcome dinner. From that point on the roommate expected her to cook and clean for her. Because many of the women had grown up in all-Chicano communities or with African Americans, they had never faced this kind of blatant racism. Cecelia Quijano, a leader of the 1968 walkouts in Huntington Park, attended Upward Bound with many of the Hijas de Cuauhtémoc members the summer before she entered UCLA. She described her first days on campus this way:

It was very frightening for me, I had never been away from home. . . . So I wasn't with my parents and my brothers and sisters. It was very scary. I really didn't know what to do with myself when I got there. As a matter of fact, I remember that like the first week of school, I was going into a library where you could put headphones on and listen to music. We were not savvy enough to start study groups or that kind of thing. There were a lot of us just kind of wandering around, trying to figure out what we were supposed to do. A student came up to me, you know, this white guy, and he, you know, called me some names.

When I asked what he called her, she replied:

He called me a stupid Mexican bitch. Yeah. And I was like [pause] oh, you know, I flipped him off and told him fuck you, but it really shook me. Because, I thought, man, this is the real thing. People really don't like you. I [think that's when] I understood the concept of discrimination. I understood what racism was.[42]

Despite and because of these challenges, many women who became Chicano student movement activists developed strategies for surviving in the university and supporting each other. Hernández recalls her shift in consciousness:

[At first it seemed to me that] UMAS only wanted to indoctrinate the new students who had no political consciousness, those who had not been involved in the walkouts, [but] the things that the people in UMAS were say-

ing began to make sense after a few days in college. . . . It was the first time
I had blatant discrimination . . . to my face. This made us understand what
UMAS was saying . . . all the discrimination and negative experiences I suf-
fered from people in power. I began to realize why teachers did certain
things. . . . I saw things differently; I became active in UMAS. . . . My parents
thought that I had changed and that the movement people were communists.
They were beside themselves because I held these views. They didn't like what
I was doing. . . . Once I moved out I never went back.[43]

CHICANO STUDENT MOVEMENT ORGANIZING

The Chicano student movement had been simmering since the mid-1960s. It
gained momentum in the East L.A. Blowouts, the mobilization around the
persecution of the organizers of the Blowouts, the L.A. 13, led by Hoover's
FBI in collaboration with the Los Angeles Sheriff and Police Departments,
as well as the 1969 Denver Youth Liberation Conference.[44] The movement
formalized its agenda in the 1969 *Plan de Santa Barbara*, drafted at the Chicano Coordinating Council on Higher Education (CCCHE) conference at
the University of California, Santa Barbara. This was the founding convention
of el Movimiento Estudiantil Chicano de Aztlán, marking the shift away from
UMAS, the Mexican American Youth Organization (MAYO), and Mexican-
American Students (MAS) and a place to put *El Plan Espiritual de Aztlán* into
action through a twofold program of commitment to students and community members.

By the late sixties the UMAS chapter at Cal State Long Beach included
women, and several were among the core activists in the informal leadership of the organization.[45] The mostly all-male leadership felt that "women
had less political knowledge than themselves and that women need to raise
their consciousness. The veteran Chicanas were in charge of this education."[46]
These political education groups provided a forum for movement women to
meet among themselves, sharing ideas and discussing issues. These meetings
eventually became the political vehicle for the first informal support group, las
Chicanas de Aztlán, known informally as *las mujeres de longo*. Formed in 1968
in Long Beach, the group became strong advocates for Chicanas and saw it as
their mutual responsibility to provide support and encouragement to other
Chicanas. Through firsthand knowledge and investigations into the roots of
Chicana dropouts, the group discovered some of the major reasons that universities were unable to retain Chicanas.

As the Chicano movement sought to gain civil and political rights, articulated through ethnic pride, it was also a defining moment in the con-

struction and definition of racialized gender roles. Chicano youth militancy was rooted in challenging the exclusionary nature and ideological project of educational institutions. Eventually their experiences with racism in higher education and the lack of response from institutions transformed the liberal aspiration of access and inclusion to a more radical vision of social change that saw education as part of the struggle for liberation and sought alternative institutions, curricula, and pedagogies. The Chicano Movement and the mass youth movement of the 1960s and 1970s produced a generational political shift even for those not directly involved. Political mobilization informed and inspired young Chicanas to define their role as *mujeres en lucha* (women in struggle) and, in turn, reshaped their roles as women of the world, as partners, mothers, and daughters, revolutionizing the web of relationships that situate social actors and members of their communities.

Women activists learned to name the structures of exclusion and inequality they faced and how to negotiate complex relationships of power within and outside their community. Familial bonds, female friendships, and relationships with political comrades were the sites through which they gained new forms of consciousness, named inequitable power relations, and strived to create new forms of solidarity, as well as a different organizational culture. Many of the activist women I interviewed created new forms of community and belonging, new structures of feeling and meaning, and new types of consciousness and solidarity.[47] Their participation in campus and community political organizations and larger social movement mobilizations created new networks, consciousness, identities, and, ultimately, new forms of both interconnectedness and autonomy as women.[48] Further, they began to theorize their experience and collective knowledge in print, thereby transforming structures of knowledge/power that reproduce social relations.

RAZA RECRUITMENT AND THE GENDERED POLITICS OF RETENTION

As early UMAS members, Corinne Sánchez and Anna NietoGomez, along with several other student activists, were involved in organizing the first Dia de la Raza recruitment day at Long Beach State University on October 12, 1968. As a result, the number of Chicanos on campus tripled the next year. Not only had Chicana/o activists tripled their numbers on campus, but they were able to secure a trailer to serve as the organization's office as well as a phone and work-study students to help with administrative tasks. They also helped organize events with nationally recognized speakers such as Corky Gonzales from the Crusade for Justice in Denver, Colorado, and Armando

Rodriguez, who was director of the Commission on Spanish-Speaking Affairs in Washington, D.C.[49]

While the women were extremely active in recruitment events that brought Chicana/o high school students to the university, they were disheartened to find that only one-third of new college recruits were women, and over half of those women dropped out before their junior year. In fact, the informal support group of activist women that later became the Hijas de Cuauhtémoc narrate their political origins as emerging out of an effort to solve this problem.

> Las Mujeres decided to investigate the low retention rate of Chicanas in higher education. They discovered two important facts related to the dropout rate of Chicanas on college campus. First, Chicanas did not fail because of academic deficiencies; in fact, Chicanas reflected high grade point average overall. Second, nebulous support from faculty, peer group, and counselors, as well as from the family, provided little psychological reinforcement for the Chicana to stay in college.[50]

The group found that Chicanas suffered guilt at not contributing to the household income of their families and social pressures to get married. A silent factor that contributed to dropout rates was unplanned pregnancy and lack of access to birth control. In the complex context of the sexual revolution many Chicanas were faced with the contradiction between new freedoms and expectations and continued gender inequality and the sexual double standard.

Gender and sexual power relations circumscribed the working conditions of the movement, the learning conditions at college, and the ways in which Chicanas were seen as young women. Without the cultural capital to negotiate this new institutional space, many Chicanos relied heavily on programs such as EOP. Yet the lack of support was insidious for young women because the precise places where they could look for support and guidance were undermined by the ways they were often sexualized or endured sexual harassment. EOP counselors were seen as mentors and guides, but as Leticia Hernández describes, this often led to abuse of power: "The EOP counselors were peer counselors, but the guys picked up on the girls; it was a big joke in retrospect. At the time, they thought that they were trying to help, but they were really trying to get them in bed, especially at Long Beach State."[51] NietoGomez reflected on her role as a counselor and how she came to political consciousness of Chicana oppression.

> The pill was not yet widely available, so for women the number one reason for dropping out was pregnancy either by the guys on the campus or by their

old boyfriends in the community who didn't want them to go on to college. As a counselor, the kids called on me for all kinds of problems. I think being the EOP counselor is what raised my consciousness in that it's really being a social worker, and you get involved in the basic issues the students were experiencing. The memories that had stayed in my mind aren't like daily memories but the most sensational or traumatic ones that I experienced. So that's what I'll share, but I just want to make sure to tell you that they weren't necessarily typical, but they were like the first time I had ever encountered such problems.

One is [pause] girls [pause] committing self-abortions calling me from an emergency hospital on their deathbeds, you know, because they had tried to perform an abortion with a coke bottle or with a hanger. They'd either call me from the hospital or from the dorm and I'd have to [pause] be involved in getting the ambulance, getting them to the hospital. Instead of telling their parents, I would be the person they were calling for help. I'd be there holding their hand and—I had never heard of an abortion. I didn't know what an abortion was when I—These girls evidently knew about it and I couldn't understand what in the world would drive them to put a coke bottle in their vaginas. Where did they hear all this information about using a hanger? [pause] I think that's why I was, well, those memories are always going to be there, and they were [pause] tiny little girls you know.

I often felt it was a curse for a Chicana to be cute and beautiful because it left her very vulnerable because being cute and beautiful does not necessarily mean you have control over your life or especially your body at that time. There was no birth control, there were no legal abortions. I thought, what a waste. What an absolute crime that here these girls felt they couldn't go home pregnant. It was like if they would go home and be stoned to death. It was just ultimately not something they could do. They knew they had a future there, you know? They just didn't want to let go of it, so they did this very desperate act and it ruined them, you know, psychologically. That was very traumatic for me. That didn't make sense, and I was trying to keep kids in school.

I realized for the women the number one problem was they didn't have control of their bodies. That was the reason for dropping out, because they usually had the highest grade point average coming in, and they kept that grade point average higher than the Chicanos who stayed in college. I tried to let students know that there was a safe way. We would see what we could do to help them, and they had counselors to help them work this out because there was no [reproductive health] counseling available.[52]

Issues surrounding reproductive health care were very charged. Not only was abortion viewed negatively, but Latinas have had a history of being experimented on without their knowledge or consent, and Mexicanas in Los Angeles were facing forced sterilization because of racist medical practices as well as monolingual staffing.[53]

THE EMERGENCE OF FEMINISM IN THE CHICANO STUDENT MOVEMENT

More elaborate than other framing documents of the Chicano movement, *El Plan de Santa Barbara* was written in 1969 and united former Chicano student and youth groups under the name el Movimiento Estudiantil Chicano de Aztlán (MEChA). Written in the new spirit of nationalism embodied in *El Plan Espiritual de Aztlán*, *El Plan de Santa Barbara* laid out a blueprint for education. Although activist women like Anna NietoGomez participated in creating this collective document, its version of Chicanismo was articulated through culturally mediated concepts of masculinity such as brotherhood, familialism, and *carnalismo* (brotherhood). It read, in part:

> The student movement is more than a political movement, it is cultural and social as well. The spirit of MEChA must be one of "hermandad" and cultural awareness. MEChA must bring to the mind of every young Chicano that the liberation of his people from prejudice and oppression is in his hands. . . . MEChA, then, is more than a name; it is a spirit of unity, of brotherhood, and a resolve to undertake a struggle for liberation in a society were justice is but a word. MEChA is a means to an end.

Details of organizational life, coalition building, leadership, education, recruitment, and the role students had in the "barrios" and "colonias" were also spelled out in this document.

> It is important that every Chicano student on campus be made to feel that he has a place on that campus and that he has a feeling of familia with his Chicano brothers. . . . Above all the feeling of hermandad must prevail so that the organization is more to the members than just a club or a clique. MEChA must be a learning and fulfilling experience that develops dedication and commitment.[54]

Although detailed plans were delineated, the structure of organization, leadership, and decision making were not mentioned. This led to problems for the women at Cal State Long Beach who moved into the leadership of UMAS and MEChA in the late 1960s. By repudiating democratically elected female leaders, the informal masculinist discourse circulating in the movement culture became political practice.

According to female student activists in Southern California, women's marginalization in the Chicano student movement in the late 1960s occurred on at least three levels. First, women often were not seen as the real political subjects of the movement but as auxiliary members. As a result, they were relegated to supporting roles, reinforcing the gendered division of labor. During meetings their ideas were often dismissed on the basis of their gender, marginalizing them in the political and decision-making process. Second, women were discouraged from taking leadership roles and were sometimes outright undermined when they were elected to them. Third, women felt that the sexual politics of the movement were counterproductive to their full participation and treated them as sexual objects instead of encouraging the recognition of their full humanity and creating organizational structures in which they could be fully realized as part of their people's struggle for liberation.

TALKING LIKE A HEAVY: ON BEING HEARD, POLITICAL SPEECH, AND MOVEMENT CULTURE

A "heavy" was a leader and a capable strategist, although not necessarily an elected organizational leader or office holder. They were student leaders in their own right. Inversely, office holders were not necessarily considered heavies. Consequently, women who were elected officers, such as secretaries or treasurers, remained outside the strategic meetings of these individuals. These meetings took place outside the formal structure of the organization, and membership was generally not aware of them.
ADELAIDA R. DEL CASTILLO, "MEXICAN WOMEN IN ORGANIZATION"

Informal leadership structures in some student movement organizations had implications for women's participation. For example, Leticia Hernández described the decision makers of MEChA:

MEChA was a large group but there were only a few people involved in the executive team. A small number of people would stay up until all hours of the night deciding policy, etc. . . . The other members were not involved. The meetings would start off big but when things really got underway only the same small group remained making decisions. It took a lot of staying power, time and energy to stay there until the end. I felt that things were drawn out as a strategy to wear down the opposition and new ideas.[55]

One key roadblock to women's effective participation in the early days of the Chicano student movement was the issue of voice. A depiction shared by many women was the dismissive attitudes they encountered within UMAS and MEChA. Several mentioned, for example, that when a woman brought up an idea in a meeting, it would go unrecognized. Then a guy might bring up essentially the same idea, and his resolution would be discussed, engaged, and passed.[56] Leticia Hernández explains:

At meetings the men in the organization would not involve the women. When women would make suggestions the men would ridicule the ideas and talk for hours, then another guy would suggest the same idea, and because it was a guy who offered the idea, it would be agreed to. The women were never given credit for their input.[57]

Women had to adopt different strategies to be heard. This, coupled with the fact that women were relegated to secretarial and other support roles, signified to women that although they often provided the backbone of the organizational labor, their ideas, voices, and leadership were not recognized.

Chicana student activists increasingly felt their political vision and voice were devalued in political organizing meetings, and some became aware of the informal power structure of movement heavies that women had little access to outside of being someone's girlfriend. Politicized speech had its own language in the movement. At the time this language was largely reserved for men, except for the few occasions when women adopted these codes and the vernacular of el movimiento. Women began adopting what was seen as the masculinized speech of the street and other codes of movement culture because language was viewed as a site of authenticity. Rejecting the policing of the language purists on either side of the border, Chicana/o youth adopted caló, the Chicano streetwise blend of Spanish and English, as movimiento vernacular in Los Angeles.[58]

The political speech of the movement was gendered, as was the vernacular movimiento culture, meetings, and rallies. The culture of political meetings was largely the culture of the "vatos," or street warriors, reflecting the way the youth movement idealized the street warrior as a form of resistance, though it was also, incidentally, a subaltern form of masculinity. One strategy movement women used to enter into movement culture was to appropriate the language of heavies. While several of the activists cursed with regularity, others, like NietoGomez, stated that even though they had never never cursed before, these words gave them power.

> Learning to cuss was empowering for me as a woman in UMAS. I had never cussed before this. . . . The words gave me power. When the women would speak, the men would act as if they didn't hear anything. Finally, I spoke out and said, "I think that idea is fucked." The room was silent. Someone asked me what I had said, and I repeated myself. From then on, I gained respect and room to speak by cussing. It was empowering. Corinne tried it also. The guys then dialogued with us. That made us equal. The guys from East L.A. [the epicenter of Chicano youth rebellion in Los Angeles], cussed a lot, and the other guys joined in because it was like a status language. It was the language of the heavies, and Corinne and I became one of the heavies. . . . Corinne and I were the workhorses. Sometimes in the middle of the night, while working, we discussed the use of cussing and philosophized. We talked about devaluing ourselves by cussing to get respect but concluded that we would not receive recognition if we didn't continue cussing. I came to enjoy it because it permitted me to do things that were not allowed in the past.[59]

As much as political skills, one's membership and commitment were often measured by standards of cultural authenticity that were largely mapped on to subaltern forms or masculinized. This tried the patience of many female activists who felt they were measured by posturing instead of substantive contributions. Female leaders attempted to adapt to these codes as best as they could, while others felt quite comfortable using the language of the street. When NietoGomez ran for office under the slogan, "Vote for a Heavy Vice President! Vote for Anna Nieto Gomez!"[60] While the movement embraced carnalismo as a way to create solidarity, it also led to the creation of a social movement culture based on masculinized codes, behaviors, and modes of organizing, thereby creating and reinforcing political philosophies and practices that had gendered implications for how the movement organized and who it validated as organizers and leaders.[61]

WHO CLEANS THE HOUSE OF REVOLUTION? GENDERED DIVISION OF LABOR IN THE MOVEMENT

When something must be done there is always a Chicana there to do the work. "It is her place and duty to stand behind and back up her Macho!" This is the attitude of a great many heavies. . . . If the

Chicanas were not in these organizations, who would do the work? If all Chicanas boycotted typing, filing, and all her duties as a female, what would happen? What would have happened during the last student elections, if the Chicanas had not worked like dogs on the campaign, speeches, and platforms while the heavies were out getting loaded? . . . Chicanos take the credit for the suggestions, the work, and even the pride of Chicana product. They take the credit without even a thank you to the workers.[62] NANCY NIETO, *HIJAS DE CUAUHTÉMOC*, 1971

In her article in the first issue of *Hijas de Cuauhtémoc*, Nancy Nieto critiques the gendered division of labor, which she frames through the Marxian formula of the workers having a sense of ownership of their own labor and its value. She asks the men in her organization how they can take credit for women's work without any form of recognition, without even a thank you. Using the metaphor "Plumas Planchadas," Cherríe Moraga captures how much of the work of organizing Chicano resistance was dependent on women's labor while simultaneously making it invisible. This practice denies the importance of women's work in creating change and organizing community.[63] Making the role of women in the Chicano movement visible, Moraga calls attention to the fact that much cultural recovery and celebration was made possible by the labor of women who made sure that Aztec warriors and *danzantes* (dancers) had their regalia, or, symbolically, their feathers, ironed.

Increasingly, many female organizers in the Chicano Movement felt that the gendered division of political work was a reflection not only of male privilege but also of the ways in which Chicanas were disregarded as real political actors and relegated to the kitchens and mimeographing rooms of the movement. Chicanas were in charge of developing, typing up, and mimeographing position papers; doing all the fund-raising, cooking, and organizing events; doing the office work, the cleanup work, and the majority of the organizational tasks. Although this labor was pivotal to the actual functioning of the political movement, it was seen as women's work and therefore devalued.[64]

Leticia Hernández said that women sought partnership in student movement politics, but when they ventured outside of predetermined and subservient roles they came under fire for being "lesbians" or were defeminized, thus illustrating the ideological linkage between political labor, organizing tasks, gender, and sexuality.

We didn't want to be defeminized but just wanted to do what we could to get our people where they needed to go. Some of the women who were involved experienced a lot of harassment, and many were going through the same things on different campuses in different organizations. They wanted the women to be silent, in the background, making tortillas, stuffing envelopes, typing, cleaning up after people. . . . If women played these roles, there was no tension. . . . The problem in the movement was that guys expected the women to be like their mothers at home. They did not take notice that they were in a social activist context.

When I asked if she thought those were the roles their mothers played, if those gendered roles and expectations were in fact learned in the home, she replied:

No. [One guy's] mother was vocal and took charge, but men in the movement had their ideas of what women should do—that is, be barefoot, pregnant, tied to the kitchen stove. The men felt that they should be the ones to make the statements and they should be the ones to write the papers and that the women should be the ones to type the papers and women should be the ones who serve the coffee on the side and make everything nice and comfy for them when they come home from the "war." . . . Even though they were involved, they were expected to be doing backroom, subservient things, to think and say what the men say.[65]

Hernández's answer reveals the level to which "tradition" was mobilized for the benefit of a few and legitimated by the ideological and gendered project of Chicano nationalism. It also reflects the shifting roles and demands of masculinity for working-class Chicanos upon entering the university. Historically valued as men based on their physical labor, young Chicano men of this generation had to renegotiate both class- and gender-based expectations of masculinity. The measure of a man, historically, for working-class men of color was the calluses on their laboring hands. How did they retain their masculinity and have the "soft hands" of those who do not earn a living by manual labor? Were the sometimes virile forms of nationalism or masculine ideals based on the stereotype of the *vato loco* that circulated in the movement efforts to negotiate this shifting terrain of working-class masculinity? Sexual politics may have been an alternative way of confirming their masculinity in a heteropatriarchal model.[66]

DECONSTRUCTING "DEEP MACHO HANGUPS": SEXUAL
POLITICS WITHIN THE CHICANO STUDENT MOVEMENT

*Another aspect of the MACHO attitude is their lack of respect for
Chicanas. They play their games, plotting girl against girl for their own
benefit (both women and men play this very unrevolutionary game).
They use the movement and Chicanismo to take her into bed. And
when she refuses, she is a vendida because she is not looking after
the welfare of her men. How much lower can Chicanos go, to use
the movimiento for their own ends?*
NANCY NIETO, *HIJAS DE CUAUHTÉMOC*, 1971

Las Chicanas de Aztlán at Cal State Long Beach began to develop a critique
of the sexual politics of the movement, which included the idea that commitment to the revolution was measured by how "down" you were to a revolutionary man. While sexual discovery and experimentation were not uncom-
mon in campus life, what I am foregrounding are sexual politics in which the
parameters of women's status and commitment to the cause were measured
by their sexual availability to movement men. While it was only some men
who abused their status as leaders for sexual gain, the sexual objectification
and harassment of women was fairly widespread and shaped movement political practice and culture.

Activist Chicanas critiqued the fact that women were sexualized within
movement spaces, seen as sexual objects instead of political comrades. Their
treatment by male counterparts ranged from relatively harmless notions of
revolutionary sweethearts to more dangerous working and organizing conditions. Activist women became critical of the ways young women faced a
form of sexual initiation into the movement whereby men, under the guise of
mentorship and political education, would initiate sexual relationships with
incoming freshmen woman. This practice was so prevalent across campuses
in Southern California that when activists gathered for the first Chicana regional conference of Los Angeles in 1971, it turned from a workshop on political education into a discussion and critique of sexual politics.[67] Once Chicanas broke the silence surrounding these practices and began a process of
collectively raising consciousness around their experiences, they knowingly
warned others of this practice, which they called having your pants "radical-
ized" off. Another form of sexual politics involved the notion of male pre-
rogative whereby being "down for the revolution," Chicanas were expected
to make themselves sexually available to movement men. Sexual politics were
also manifested in the ways in which older women (sometimes former girl-

friends of leaders) were politically undermined when, after falling out of sexual/political favor, their position and voice in the organization were less respected. In *Hijas de Cuauhtémoc*, women called their male counterparts to task for what they saw as an informal political strategy to undermine the power of more experienced Chicanas by playing them off younger (or less politically seasoned) women through sexual relations with their male antagonists. These sexual politics relied on classical patriarchal female competition and created conditions that made female solidarity both necessary and increasingly difficult. A final example of the movement's sexual politics has to do with the ways in which women who stepped outside of normative gender roles to provide leadership in the organization or challenged sexual politics in the movement were portrayed as sexually immoral or deviant and often labeled as dykes or lesbians.

Leticia Hernández illuminates how sexual politics occurred on several levels in movement organizations.

> The women felt that they were being used as far as sexuality within the movement. A lot of sexual double standards. It's a whole difference between men and women, too, you know. Girls go to college young, naive, maybe they fall in love with someone, and so they go to bed with somebody and think that this guy is going to marry them. He's going to do her for a couple of weeks or maybe a couple of months and then drop her, you know. He has no intention of marrying her or anybody else. This would happen to women; they would pick up the pieces, and it would happen again and they'd get a reputation, or else if they didn't go to bed with the guys the men thought the women who don't are lesbians, or that women are holding out for some reason, that they want to be men. This was a difficult position for women to be in within this kind of organizing. There was no winning in this kind of situation. The men would talk of liberation and freedom only when they wanted to get you in bed, but they didn't really believe these ideas.[68]

To combat this predicament women took collective action and began to document it in *Hijas de Cuauhtémoc* so they could inform other women and develop a shared analysis.[69]

REVOLUTION IN THE MORNING, OR FALLING IN LOVE CHICANO-STYLE

In the midst of a generational shift around cultural and political values, Chicanas found themselves immersed in the contradictions of the sexual revolution, where new sexual freedoms were explored in the context of continued inequality for women. Women of color reflections on this period paint a more complicated portrait of the so-called sexual revolution. Many activist young women of this era not only shared a sense of political urgency but also the coming-of-age experience of falling in love, "making it" for the first time, and negotiating romantic involvements with fellow activists. The connection between love and politics was drawn out by one of the members who had been dating her boyfriend from East Los Angeles for four years. During this courtship they became engaged. Yet it was not until the night before the Chicano Moratorium that they made love for the first time. "We made it for the first time, and I gave him myself because we really believed the revolution would come in the morning," she said.

Compounding the complexity of shifting sexual attitudes, these negotiations occurred in a context in which there was limited access to women's reproductive health care. Abortion was illegal until 1973, and the burden of responsibility, combined with silence about such issues, fell on the shoulders of women.

Strikingly, many more of the memories of major movement landmarks and turning points were narrated to me not as stories of falling in love but as ones in which young Chicanas engaged in political work with a community of resistance faced sexual harassment from fellow activists. Sylvia Castillo's story of coming to consciousness and becoming politically involved as a high school student was mixed with learning how not to be taken advantage of and serves as a telling example of what young women faced while trying to find their grounding in the movement.

My introduction to Cal State Long Beach happened in January 1970 through my organizing work with the United Farm Workers around the grape boycott. I had met some of the Cal State Long Beach MEChA leadership when I was seventeen, and I was organizing with the UFW boycott committee for the Long Beach/San Pedro area, and at that time they were more interested in the fact that I was "jail bait" and trying to figure out if I would be game to date any of them.

They invited my sister and me to come to an Upward Bound meeting that was hosted at the MEChA trailer. I was seventeen then, so my sister would have been fourteen. It was January. So we attended a meeting, and it was the one during which they were taking young people to the Chicano Moratorium march that was happening in East L.A. It was just a common custom that the college guys got first crack at the youngest and the finest who were being recruited to college. I hadn't even been recruited to college yet, and I was already falling on that recruitment conveyer belt.

After the February moratorium march, Castillo continued to be involved in local movement politics by attending the court hearings for those arrested at the Católicos por la Raza protest at St. Basil's Church. But because she didn't drive, she caught a ride with one of the male student leaders. She rejected his sexual advances, even after he offered her drugs and alcohol, but recalled, "He felt very entitled, and one day he told me that his nuts were hard and I had to do something about it. I remember going to my high school teacher because I couldn't figure out how to deal with unwanted attention."

When the opportunity arose to travel to Denver to attend the Chicano Youth Liberation Conference, Castillo was excited. But, like her other early political experiences, this one would be rife with sexual harassment and intimidation. Her parents allowed her to attend the conference with the agreement that she stay with an aunt in Denver.

> [The student leader] had told my mother he had his eye on me. We had already gone to several events so I knew his intentions. I decided I'd ask my cousin to come with me, Janice Contreras, who went to Franklin High, and we planned to stay at my auntie Olga's house in Denver. So when we get to Denver the first day of the conference, the most amazing experience for me was sitting in an auditorium of this kind of huge old 1930s building with cathedral ceilings that must have been like twenty feet from the ground. There was a stage in front and the *bandera mexicana* and this big banner with the Aztec stylized icon that says "Somos Aztlan" and another red and black banner of Che Guevara's image. I remember the first speaker was Corky [Gonzalez], and it was very agitational. Every time he would pause they would do "Chicano Power! Chicano Power!" I remember being way in the back and having to stand, but I would say that there was like a thousand people in that room, and Brown Berets and Black Berets could be seen dotting this sea of brown faces. The guys were wearing ponchos, and the women were wearing peasant dresses made of white, jeans, and adelita boots, and there were black braids everywhere. There were signs that people had that showed where they were from. California, New Mexico, Tejas. I remember there was one lonely sign that said "Alaska."

Later at the conference, at the end of the day, Castillo had lost track of her cousin and found herself alone with the same guy who had been pursuing

her. While talking together, he suddenly became physical, and when she rejected his sexual advances, he quickly turned on her, saying, "Fuck you, get
your own ride." Castillo continues, "So I called my aunt up because he was
saying, 'No, I can't take you, you're going to have to spend the night here
with everybody else.' So he was setting up a situation so he could vamp. I got
my cousin. I called my aunt, who came and picked us up." Castillo and her
cousin ended up missing one whole day of the conference because her aunt
was upset and kept them at home, worried for their safety. Castillo pleaded
with her aunt, "Don't you realize this is the start of the revolution? You gotta
let me go back."[70]

While unwanted sexual advances shaped activist women's experiences of
the watershed moments of the Chicano Movement, back on campus female
activists began to name these prevalent practices. Nancy Nieto's article,
"Macho Attitudes," calls out the sexual politics as well as the sexual division
of labor in the movement.

> When a freshman male comes to MEChA, he is approached and welcomed.
> But he is taught by observation that the Chicanas are only useful in areas of
> clerical and sexual activities. . . . Deep macho hang-ups are the reasons for the
> Chicanos having certain beliefs [such] as: "Men are supposed to be leaders, to
> fight and to protect." When these Chicanos see their women becoming edu-
> cated, they jump back! When their women stand up for themselves and really
> begin to contribute to the movement, they react and shout, "Women's lib,
> women's lib!"[71]

As their political consciousness grew, Chicanas began to forge new forms
of solidarity with other women. It was becoming clearer and clearer that they
were not experiencing isolated incidents. Sexual politics enacted by a few men
in the movement conflated women's political loyalty with whether or not
they would sleep with men in the movement, thereby undermining the solidarity among women, especially those who had been there long enough to see
the pattern. The good woman/bad woman dichotomy was operative in this
brand of sexual politics that both relied on and reinforced heteronormative
and patriarchal power.[72] López found:

> The Chicanas who voiced their discontent with the organizations and with
> male leadership were often labeled as "women's libbers" and "lesbians." This
> served to isolate and discredit them, a method practiced both covertly and
> overtly. . . . [I]n practice the men continued to be the *jefes* in decision making
> policies and political direction. Chicanas who belonged to Chicana groups

FIGURE 2.1. Political Cartoon, *Hijas de Cuauhtémoc*, unpublished issue.
Courtesy of Sylvia Castillo.

came to be seen as a clique by those Chicanas who were not involved in any
kind of Chicana awareness process. This division, more often than not, was
used by those men who felt their *machismo* threatened, pitting one group
against the other. This situation often created a breakdown of communication among women in the organizations. It hindered their working together
as compañeras.[73]

Strong women were discredited with accusations of being "sexually per-
verse or promiscuous," and the emergence of Chicana feminism was silenced
through lesbian baiting.[74] Ironically, for the most part, many (if not most) of
the Hijas de Cuauhtémoc were struggling merely to stand by their men but as

equal partners in the struggles against oppression. Their critique and ensuing formation of Chicana feminist consciousness was often locked into a male/female binary as they had not yet developed a critique of the power and politics that exist between women.

CHINGÓN POLITICS: WOMEN'S POLITICAL LEADERSHIP AND THE CONSTRUCTION OF GENDERED FORMS OF EMPOWERMENT

I ran for president and won. There was a silent attempted coup to drive me out. [My opponent] thought that if he could drive me out even though I won, he would demoralize me out. Statewide, I was the only woman among all the student presidents at that time.
ANNA NIETOGOMEZ

Chingón politics demonstrates what bell hooks calls "the effects of equating freedom with manhood, of sexualizing liberation."[75] Characterized by a narrow view of nationalism and a culture of domination, chingón politics, according to Elizabeth (Betita) Martinez, advocates for culture uncritically and defines concepts and styles of leadership in a patriarchal way.[76] Del Castillo's study found:

> Leadership role models being unmistakably male, both within the general Chicano Movement and the student sector of the movement, presented problems for women who actually filled these roles. Generally, women students were expected by their male peers to involve themselves actively but in subordination. . . . A case in point involved a university where the formation and development of UMAS was largely attributable to female leadership. When the organization sponsored a conference featuring as a guest speaker Rodolfo "Corky" Gonzales, of Denver's Crusade for Justice, opinions concerning female leaders surfaced. It was considered improper and embarrassing for a national leader to come on campus and see that the organization's leadership was female. Consequently, the organization decided that only males would be the visible representatives for the occasion. . . . At another state college, the election of its first female UMAS chairperson caused the derision of that organization's male membership in other campus UMAS groups.[77]

While many Chicanas joined the student movement to confront the cultural and institutional racism and class bias they found upon entering college and the political arena, some found discrimination in the movement itself.

The movement was not sufficiently addressing the very real, material needs of women or the way gender intersected with race and class.[78] When Chicanas began to discuss these issues among themselves, some women began to express them publicly and attempt to move into leadership positions to better represent the needs of Chicanos. No one foresaw that the negative response to women's organizing would create deep cleavages within the student movement at Cal State Long Beach.

Corinne Sánchez and Sylvia Castillo say that the great resistance of men to Anna NietoGomez's presidency was a significant catalyst for women to begin organizing. Democratically elected president of MEChA, NietoGomez won wide support from the student body, which recognized her leadership capacity and had gotten to know her when she was an early EOP peer counselor.[79] Despite her election, much of the informal male leadership ("heavies") attempted to maintain control by holding meetings without NietoGomez and her supporters. Even though NietoGomez served as vice president of UMAS, her presidency the following year was plagued by internal politics. Although she had several male allies, several men with power in the organization explicitly stated that they did not want to be represented by a woman.

As an EOP counselor, NietoGomez advocated for students within the larger Chicano community. In fact, her unhappiness with the movement's lack of concern for student issues informed her decision to run for the presidency. At the time she never guessed that winning the election would cause such outrage.

> I was interested in social issues and students, and the guy who I was running against was interested in power. He was not interested in students but in his own political gain. So I confronted him by telling him that I would run against him. We saw the purpose of the movement differently. He held the philosophy that the ends justified the means. He told me, "I know you're running for president just to give the appearance of there being a choice." I told him, "No. I'm running because I don't want you as president and I believe that the students should come first, and that's why I'm running." He told me I didn't have a chance in the world.

After she won the election, she found that resistance to female leadership was not confined to this social movement location. NietoGomez explains:

> I would go to all these meetings and these conferences, and the dudes really felt that my being nominated as president indicated how wimpy the male leadership must have been in the student organization [at Long Beach].

They saw it as more of a flaw than a progressive step. This was in 1969. They overtly expressed their prejudice and disapproval of my being president, so I had to really numb myself to that kind of ridicule and lack of acceptance.[80]

Several of the women I interviewed mentioned supportive male comrades. Although women in other sectors of the movement faced sexism, it seems to have been especially virulent in the youth and student sectors of the larger movement. One self-defined rank-and-file member remarks:

The older women, Corinne and Anna, they were doing senior-level work, but the guys, well . . . Anna was the first [woman] president of MEChA in '69–'70. . . . [Her opponent] had his male ego hurt because he didn't win the election, and he was always undermining her. He was calling meetings be-hind her back. The guys were doing stuff on their own and leaving her out of it. Really, only a few people opposed Anna's leadership, but they weren't the most powerful within the group, the leadership. We were upset. There were so many people who felt Anna could do a good job. It was okay if she was vice president, secretary, or treasurer, but her being the chairperson of the or-ganization was too much. The guys wanted to be in control of everything all the time. They couldn't blame anybody but themselves; they underestimated Anna. . . . They gave her a rough time, undermining her, trying to hold meet-ings without her and then implement their own ideas.[81]

This kind of ridicule and harassment did not have a devastating impact only on NietoGomez and local campus politics; it also had reverberations for other women in the Los Angeles Chicano student movement who considered seeking leadership roles. For example, Keta Miranda, a student at Los Ange-les City College (LACC), describes how hearing about NietoGomez's presi-dency at Long Beach State influenced her when, in 1970, she heard that the chair of MEChA, Richard Martinez, was leaving LACC:

He was leaving school. The women of MEChA thought that I should be the chair. . . . I had been a member of MEChA since '68, so they figured I had a record of commitment and that I understood all the politics of the Chicano. [It seemed as if there was no clear] traditional male leadership of MEChA, and since that hadn't come about, that's when the women thought I should be the chair. . . . Then I didn't know whether I should run or not—or whether I should just withdraw my name or not. That is when it became the most confusing for me.

MACHETE Page 3

PICTORIAL

Chicanas
on the move

Keta Miranda
ASB Councilwoman of Minority Affairs

Rebecca Fajardo
MECHA Secretary

Mimi Leder
MECHA Representative to SDS

Sandra Ornelas
Machete Campus Editor

Esther Inclan
Secretary, MECHA Chairman

Debbie Miranda
Secretary, ICC Chairman

Women still powerless

Rosa Martinez
Machete Correspondent (SFVS)
"Whatever women do they must do twice as well as men to be thought of half as good. Luckily this is not difficult."
— Whitton

Vital Statistics
Statistics are for the most part boring, but in this case they may lend some credibility to the fact that women, although numerically a majority, in fact are a minority group.

feminism is not limited to the U.S. alone. Mexico did not have a single woman delegate in the Senate until 1963; and Brazil has only one woman in 326 member Chamber of Deputies. Venezuela has only 5 women in 184 members of Con-

Third World people. A change that will include women on the principals of equality.

The amount of power women could exercise in the struggle for peace and liberation could be staggering. Their po-

FIGURE 2.2. Keta Miranda, *El MACHETE* 2:1 (October 2, 1969): 3. Courtesy of LACC.

Miranda discussed the issue with people in the larger political communities of Students for a Democratic Society and MEChA. During these discussions someone asked Miranda if she had heard that a Chicana had become president of MEChA in Long Beach. She recalls:

> So right there I was always fascinated with Anna Nieto. Not knowing her, I tried to find out. At that time in L.A. we had MEChA Central. I was a MEChA Central representative, and we were a sort of policy-making group. I was asking a lot of people at that time if they knew anything that was happening in Long Beach, trying to find out, then I heard the rumors—a lot of rumors about Anna. So I remembered the first time her name ever came up, then after that, like I said, it was just rumor, rumor, rumor, rumor.

When asked what kind of rumors, she replied:

> One was that she held a MEChA meeting after she was elected and that the guys challenged her leadership and they were trying to disrupt the meeting.

The way the rumor went was that she called one of the guys out [by saying], "Look, either you are going to stay in this meeting or you are going to get out. Or you'll be moved out." [I even heard that] she actually sucker punched some dude, bam! Then there was the one, of course, that she was lesbian and that the whole caucus, all the women were lesbians. I didn't really buy that one, but somehow I wanted to believe she sucker punched that dude.[82]

In addition to verbal harassment, several of the Chicana student activists at Cal State Long Beach mentioned other silencing mechanisms.[83] For example, in a theatrical display, Anna NietoGomez was hung in effigy outside the MEChA trailer by members of the campus teatro group, who were also MEChA members. They held a procession and mock burial for Chicana student movement leaders where coffins were placed in front of tombstones with the names Anna NietoGomez, Corinne Sánchez, and Norma Owens on them.[84] NietoGomez explains:

I was not the first Chicana MEChA chairperson. The first Chicana MEChA chairperson was—her name was Christine Rodriguez, I believe—and she was at UCI [University of California, Irvine]—I was the most visible because I traveled up and down all over kingdom come and creation. I got a lot of respect, but also I got a lot of hateful prejudice, *a lot* of hateful prejudice. On my campus, [the guy who lost the election] plotted with others to hang an effigy of me outside the MEChA office and had the [campus] teatro [group] do a funeral, a mass for me. . . . [Another male leader] was the priest who buried me, the Hijas de Cuauhtémoc, Norma [Owens], and Corinne [Sánchez]. It's strange. I didn't feel hurt or angry but just numb. The political nucleus had been won over.

Within UMAS and MEChA, the more women gained independence in the organization, the more contested and bitter the struggles became. For example, when I asked NietoGomez how she dealt with the backlash, she replied:

It was a very hard year for me because I had to continually numb myself in order to cope with the prejudice and the rejection and still be able to function and do what I believe in a place that I didn't feel safe, you know, didn't feel safe at all. I too was becoming a young woman, and I had to numb my feelings, my sexual feelings, my emotional feelings, my need to be with friends, [all the things a normal young woman feels]. I had to numb all of those things because those were things that would make me vulnerable and make me a target. Any false move would open up a window where they could hurt me, and so I really numbed myself. It took me years to get over that numbing because that was my way of defending myself. [Pause] And a lot of what I did was just [to] become a self-righteous person . . . because I just truly believed that what I was doing was right.[85]

Conceding that this coping strategy probably did not gain her allies, Nieto-Gomez said she survived by seeking support from movement people off campus: "I would look outside of the student movement and look for normalcy, and I was seeing women and men acting in normal ways supporting what I was doing and that's what kept me going." Other women avoided assuming leadership roles because of the hardships and rumors women leaders faced. I asked Miranda, "So did you run for president?" She said, "No, I decided not to." When I asked if it was because of what she had heard about this experience, she reflected:

I think that was a big influence. It was frightening, and by then there were rumors in MEChA as to what would happen if I became chair—that I would be attacked; that there would be some kind of meeting to disqualify MEChA, to make MEChA no longer exist on campus either through campus politics or MEChA Central to say that the organization wasn't functioning. Then also the rumors about my own personal life, [about] my own sexual activities, [and it] had just gotten way out [of hand].[86]

CHICANA LEADERSHIP AND THE ART OF EMPOWERING OTHERS

We [women] have practiced a different kind of leadership, a leadership that empowers others, not a hierarchical kind of leadership.
ROSIE CASTRO OF THE TEXAS LA RAZA UNIDA PARTY,
QUOTED IN MARTINEZ, "CHINGÓN POLITICS DIE HARD"

Rosie Castro's speech, which was delivered at a Chicano movement activists' reunion in the late 1990s, is a commentary on the differential notions of leadership among Chicanas and Chicanos. Many women activists conceptualized leadership in terms of collective community empowerment rather than the power of one individual.[87]

As is richly illustrated by Dolores Delgado Bernal in her study of Chicanas in the East Los Angeles Blowouts, the struggle over women's leadership in the Chicano student movement was not just a struggle over representation or only about men or women; it was also about what kind of leadership was practiced and whether it empowered an individual or a group. Drawing from studies of working-class women's mobilization that observed that grassroots female leaders do not distinguish between the tasks of organizing and those of leadership, Delgado Bernal reconceptualized the meaning of leadership by identifying five activities that she considered dimensions of grassroots leadership.[88] These activities were "networking, organizing, developing consciousness, holding an elected or appointed office and acting as an official or unofficial spokesperson."[89]

Delgado Bernal's work not only shifts our thinking on leadership in the Chicano movement but also allows us to examine the implication of the ways la familia stood as a metaphor for both the movement and la Raza as a whole. The family is a social structure, which historically sustained communities and individuals, as well as a political form of nation building or a mode of imagining community. Yet as a political organizing strategy its embedded patriarchal power structures and forms of social organization often went unchallenged.

Many models of leadership were informed by what Maxine Baca Zinn has called political familialism, a fusing of cultural and political forms of resistance that mobilized whole families as an organizing strategy in Chicano Movement organizations and actions, including the UFW, the mobilization in Crystal City that led to the formation of La Raza Unida Party, and the Crusade for Justice in Denver. Baca Zinn quotes Rodolfo "Corky" Gonzales's conception that Chicano nationalism emerges from "la familia chicana." "What are the common denominators that unite the people? The key common denominator is nationalism. . . . [N]ationalism becomes La familia. Nationalism comes first out of the family." She goes on:

> Total family participation results in changes in the relative position of men and women. Such changes have hurled Chicanas out of the traditional subordinate roles. It would be inaccurate to conclude that male dominance has disappeared, but the political activism of the women of La Raza has weakened the patriarchal patterns. Political familialism has disrupted the sex role stability of Chicano families.[90]

Using the patriarchal heteronormative family as the model of leadership has significantly shaped the Chicano movement and the politics of memory and the structures through which movimiento history is told.[91] The dangers of a discourse of national liberation that leaves unexamined the privileging of men as the true subject of the revolution is that it draws on culturally specific reinscriptions of patriarchal and heterosexist power relations to mobilize political actors by stating that the revolution serves and calls on every man, woman, and child—in that order. Political familism both reinforced and disrupted the patriarchal arrangement of la familia, but as a political imaginary la familia was not fully reimagined in the Chicano movement, nor was its patriarchal anchoring dislodged. Rosa Linda Fregoso cautions against the romance of familia and describes how early Chicana activists were silenced through the "overinvestment in the mythology of family loyalty and solidarity" and how this overinvestment "hindered development of a systematic analysis of the underside of familism."[92]

FORGING HERMAN(I)DAD: NEW STRATEGIES AND NEW SOLIDARITIES IN THE MOBILIZATION OF WOMEN IN THE CHICANO STUDENT MOVEMENT

We believe that the struggle is not with the male but the existing system of oppression. But the Chicano must also be educated to the problems and oppression of La Chicana so that he may not be used as a tool to divide by keeping man against women.
"OUR PHILOSOPHY," *HIJAS DE CUAUHTÉMOC*, 1971

The women's group eventually became a vehicle through which to voice complaints about the contradictions between the civil rights discourse and the way women were treated in the organization. What the women "wanted, in essence, was some accountability from the men . . . that they be consistent with their ideology because the women weren't treated with respect."[93] López, in her study of Chicanas in the student movement, observes, "Chicanas saw the need to organize Chicana groups due to the inconsistencies between the liberation rhetoric of the Movement and the reality as it existed for Chicanas within the Movement—that of being exploited by their own people for their labor and sexuality."[94] The group at Cal State Long Beach became a site for women within the movement to organize collectively based on their own experiences as young, working-class Chicanas around issues that were not being addressed in the student movement.

Rap and study groups were part of the student movement's consciousness-raising efforts. Corinne Sánchez recalls:

I just remember Anna. She was the leader. . . . [S]he was *our* leader. She just started bringing rap groups together, and that was real popular then. It just grew to a very powerful group in the sense that we were being heard more than the men outside Long Beach State. It's not that we started off as a rap group; it just evolved from our involvement. In other words, we were attending protest marches . . . we were in the forefront. We were going to conferences throughout the state.[95]

One of the distinctions between this group and other women who may have experienced similar conditions within the Chicano student movement is that they took collective action in order to confront the specificity of the gendered racism they faced. They collectively challenged the oppressive conditions for Chicanos in a racist society but also the conditions for women both within and outside the movement. Their sense of urgency, which focused on helping Chicanas survive in universities, initiated the transformation from a support group to an advocacy group. A member of a slightly younger generation of women activists recalls an intervention between veteran organizers and incoming Chicana freshmen that she felt was a turning point. The meeting began with the purpose of finding ways for the women to support one another on campuses, but the conversation quickly turned to the question of sexual politics and women's solidarity. Sylvia Castillo narrates how this meeting, although uncomfortable at times, produced a new philosophy of Chicana solidarity.

I remember going to a meeting off-campus. It was at Leticia and Martha Lopez and Anna's apartment on Orange Avenue. I remember going there with my cousin Janice who also had started college with me. There might have been about fifteen to twenty women there who had just started college. I remember this kind of vividly. It was the first time that I met Sara Estrella and Martha Lopez and Leticia and Cindy Honesto. It was the fall of '70. It was presented as an opportunity for us to get together because we're all trying to struggle to get into school and/or stay in school, and this was an opportunity to be sister-like.

I was definitely a freshman when I attended this meeting. I remember the central question was that, you know, we were some of the first women to come on campus and that it was in all of our best interest to help one another stay in school and that there were some obstacles that were going to confront us. The discussion began around, well, some of the men already beginning to—well, the bottom line was that some of the men who were in relationships with some of the sophomores were beginning to hone in on some of the freshmen. So the sophomore women were having a conversation with us, and the end result was, you know, "We really have to put together some kind of pact because we are feeling very threatened because now you guys are new meat. Last year we were freshmen, and that's how we ended up with the guys that we're with. These guys are in MEChA and we're dating them and you should just know that so that we don't want you to get caught up in anything." And then some girls who were there took the position, "All bets are off, man. We're on campus, and you can't legislate or determine who I date."

I remember we also talked about the ways that guys would use the younger women to do their homework or research or type their papers and that that was messed up. Not everyone in the room was really on board. You know, some were, like, "Well, that's my business if I want to do that for my boyfriend and that's nobody's business but my own." Those themes resonated with me [given her experience with the men on campus the previous summer at the Denver Youth Liberation Conference]. We were having to deal with transitioning to a campus and then having to talk about how these guys were already taking [advantage] and then hearing how some women did not even get that they were being used.

[It was uncomfortable because] the conversation quickly moved off of what we need to stay in school like birth control classes to . . . how, well, there was one girl who apparently was dating someone's boyfriend. The boyfriend had gone outside of the relationship with this woman, and the woman was in the room. That's how the issue became sisterhood and commitment to one another came up. We talked about how we couldn't be seeing other people's men and [pause] it was really uncomfortable. I remember, you know, we talked about making a commitment not to do that to one another.[96]

According to Castillo, the philosophy of hermanidad was the "result of a series of discussions that had been going on with the freshman class of Chicanas who were at Cal State Long Beach," and the more veteran organizers like "Anna NietoGomez who was present as the convener of [the meeting] through her role as an EOP adviser or instructor. So the philosophy was a reflection of those discussions. Our philosophy was la hermanidad, and even that term was very controversial because it wasn't really a word. We kind of made it up."[97]

Much of the debate over hermanidad revolved around how to make the concept of *hermandad*, or brotherhood, relevant for women to create a specific form of solidarity and sisterhood. Hernández reflects on changing or feminizing the word:

I had a big problem with *hermanidad* being a word because I was a real Spanish-language purist, and I got into a real wrangle with Anna about

FIGURE 2.3. Hijas de Cuauhtémoc house meeting, from left to right: Cindy Honesto, Sylvia Castillo, Sonia Lopez, unknown, Martha Lopez. Photo courtesy of Sylvia Castillo.

this. It was about this time that I kind of . . . well, I couldn't see their point. To me, it was a wrong word to use. I mean it was not correct. The correct word was *hermandad*, and I was stuck on that, and they wanted *hermanidad* because supposedly this made it sound feminist. I told them it made them sound stupid. They were trying to tell me that we can create our own language, but I've never really bought into that, especially at that time.[98]

Hernández's discomfort about the creation of new words to articulate new political ideas illustrates the tension surrounding tradition. Must one stay true to it, or can it be used as a point of departure to create new political possibilities? Despite their disagreements, the group did create a new political philosophy of Chicana sisterhood and solidarity. The text of "Our Philosophy" began this way: "The goal for the Hijas is to involve women in the struggle of her people by identifying and dealing with the problems of La Chicana." Hermanidad began to name gendered racism and the way patriarchal power divided women. Asserting that "all Chicanas should look at each other as sisters not as rivals," the platform sought to establish a political program for Chicanas. It called for counseling and support in the areas of finance, education, sex, legal matters, and medical care. There was a call to action for Chicanas to work together to identify how perceived cultural values impeded social change. They called for a "political education program to be established for Chicanas by Chicanas." The power of this call to hermanidad is that it saw women as vital and necessary agents of social change, and it named the specificity of oppression and the issues facing them. They demanded, "Political ideology must be developed in order to prepare and support her [la Chicana] in the struggle of her people." The Basic Beliefs were outlined as follows:

1. There is little unity among Chicanas in the Movement. In order to strive to build a stronger bond, we hope to promote "La Hermanidad" concept in organizing Chicanas.

2. We recognize that the oldest example of divide and conquer has been to promote competition and envy among our women and men. This has made our movement very vulnerable and weak. Therefore, we feel that the following values must always be in mind when organizing Chicanas.

   a. First, we recognize that knowledge is a source of power and control. Therefore, we must constantly be transferring our knowledge to others. At the same time, we must always be seeking knowledge.

   b. Second, in order to reduce clique rivalry, strong communication must be built and constantly reinforced among all Chicanas.

   c. Third, all accomplishments should be recognized as for the people.

3. We recognize that we are oppressed as Raza and as women. We believe that the struggle is not with the male but the existing system of oppression. But the Chicano must also be educated to the problems and oppression of La Chicana so that he may not be used as a tool to divide by keeping man against women.

4. Any Man or Woman who condones or accepts the oppression of the Chicana and transfers this value to the Children, works only to destroy the revolution. For if we condone the oppression of our own people, we are not better than our oppressor.

5. As Chicanas striving for change in the movement, our only gauge for success is our ability to change also, to meet the needs to our people.

As Hermanas, we have a responsibility to help each other in problems that are common among all of us.[99]

While conceptualizing a new philosophy of female solidarity was vital to Chicana student mobilization everywhere, in this one social movement location, the creation of a new word, *hermanidad*, illustrates the creation of a more inclusive political tradition that would inform many generations of women in Chicano organizations to come. Demanding that their presence and the specificity of women's experience and oppression be registered is a debate that continued. Decades later the struggle for the inclusion of the /a in Chicano/a or the word *Chicana* in the National Association for Chicana and Chicano Studies, for example, represents women's struggle to not only represent their differently gendered experiences, but their ability to cut and mix cultural traditions to create feminist innovations.

The informal rap groups of 1968 and 1969 became a mobilized group in 1970. In addition to the group that formed at Long Beach State, las Chicanas de Aztlán at San Diego State University and Concilio Mujeres at San Francisco State University, for example, formed for similar reasons. Between 1970 and 1972 Chicana groups formed at Fresno State College, Cal State Los Angeles, and Stanford University.[100] These young women organized themselves to address their common political needs in relation to women in the movement, the community, and the university. They began a dialogue with other Chicanas that facilitated a shift in consciousness and the articulation of an explicitly Chicana gendered political identity.

DOUBLE MILITANCIA

In our movement we must work overtime on the question of the women's role. Women have to work on separate projects or services very pertinent for changes for las mujeres. This work will be done . . . to realize that in the struggle for liberation of a people, we must count the other half of the work force — women.
[KETA MIRANDA], "EL MOVIMIENTO AND THE CHICANA," LA RAZA MAGAZINE, 1971 [101]

Despite the critique of the day that asserted that feminism was part of the dominant culture's attempt to divide the movement, a specifically Chicana agenda and *ideologically* diverse forms of Chicana feminism were created from within the ranks of the Chicano movement. For example, the Cal State Los

Angeles CFM chapter's goals included visiting penal institutions, constructing a dormitory for Chicanas "who face hostility and resistance to the furthering of their education in their home environment," and fomenting leadership of women in the student movement. Over forty women gathered to decide on four resolutions: a "woman's right to self-determination in order to be free to make decisions affecting her own body," the need to establish links with other women's organizations throughout the world, the need to ensure resources for Chicanas at the state and federal level, and that the group become a Comisión Femenil Mexicana chapter.[102] This Chicana student organization also found resistance on campus. "MECHA, the one prominent Chicano organization on campus, felt that its power was being threatened. Because of previous attempts to establish Chicana organizations that failed, the leaders of MECHA felt that the Comisión had to be tolerated rather than accepted, until it would burn itself out and vanish into oblivion, just as the others had, such as VELA and Chicana Forum."[103]

At Long Beach State the Chicana group was never really a "separate" organization from MEChA; the women worked in both groups, engaging in double-time activism, which was common among Chicana activists. Because their political needs were not being addressed in MEChA, they organized on their own behalf. Yet they also remained in MEChA, often carrying out the day-to-day work that keeps an organization running. In a 1971 newspaper interview, Sylvia Castillo addressed the issue of the organization's independence from MEChA this way: "No. Our goal is to involve the Chicana with the struggle of her people by identifying and dealing with the problems of the Chicana." Later in the article she continued, "The organization is part of the Chicano movement specializing in Chicana needs across the nation. We also have the distinction of publishing the only Chicana newspaper in the nation."[104] In fact, NietoGomez said that she saw their work as part of the mission of MEChA, and the Chicana group often did fund-raising for *El Alacrán*, the MEChA newspaper.[105]

Within Latin American women's movements double militancia (double activism) is a historic strategy of revolutionary and leftist women who developed forms of gendered critiques that were not being addressed by their comrades.[106] Their double militancia spawned a region-wide debate on the need to be autonomous as women's organizations and be merely women's auxiliaries that functioned to incorporate women in the struggle and carry out the party line. Other social movements have also found it is important for women to have their own space to develop their own voice, leadership, and new forms of analysis.

Understanding that these Chicana groups were not separate or separatist is crucial for historical accuracy, because the emergence of Chicana feminisms is often narrated as occurring outside of and after the Chicano Movement rather than within it. They functioned as a parallel counter public within the movement as Chicana activists multiplied the subjects enlisted in the Chicano Movement's project of liberation.

RETROFITTED MEMORY: CHICANA HISTORICAL SUBJECTIVITIES BETWEEN AND BEYOND NATIONALIST IMAGINARIES

Memory does not become the repository of registering suppressed histories, albeit critically, but of reconstructing the moral frameworks of historical discourse to interrogate the present as living history.
HENRY GIROUX, "INSURGENT MULTICULTURALISM
AND THE PROMISE OF PEDAGOGY"

AFTER 1971 LAS Chicanas de Aztlán became known by the name of their newspaper, the *Hijas de Cuauhtémoc*, named in tribute to Mexican feminist organizations that worked for women's political rights, education, and an end to the dictatorship of Porfirio Díaz at the turn of the twentieth century. The Hijas de Cuauhtémoc created the space for Chicana political agency, not only through political organizing, but also by disarticulating the confining masculinist codes of the Chicano nationalist imaginary and by reimagining a historical subjectivity based on counternarratives of feminist history. This form of countermemory, or what I theorize as retrofitted memory, provides an analytical framework for understanding the production of new political subjectivities within narratives of the past. Retrofitted memory laid the foundation for the historical subjectivity of Chicana feministas by retrofitting cultural narratives that were constructed by the emergent project of Chicano nationalism, specifically, reworking gender norms inscribed in those narratives.

It was on the terrain of history and representation where the struggle of gender, culture, and political subjectivity (who was a revolutionary and why) was waged. To illustrate these struggles over meaning I look to visual cultural history of la Nueva Chicana within the politicized iconography of movement media including posters, newspapers, political pamphlets, photos, and film. Reading both the formal and ideological aspect of images, my rendering explores the way that Chicana activists shifted how they were portrayed on the terrain of history and within the pedagogy of nationalism.[1] The gendered struggles over the iconography of nationalism have significance when we see visual tropes not just as "representations" of what already existed in Chicano culture but rather as political and cultural practices that played a constitutive role in the domain of culture. Finally, I map the visual struggle around icons such as the Soldadera (female revolutionary soldier) to illustrate the cultural work that these reclaimed historical narratives and images performed in creating new spaces.[2]

ON NATIONALISM

The Chicano movement of the late 1960s and early 1970s was motivated by several ideological strands of which Chicano cultural nationalism was a dominant one. Chicano nationalism, as an ideological platform, was defined at the 1969 Denver Youth Liberation Conference, where over one thousand participants worked on passing resolutions embodied in the manifesto *El Plan Espiritual de Aztlán*.[3] This stated ideological hegemony was not without contestations, especially from those who subscribed to a more Marxist-oriented analysis that critiqued cultural nationalism as insufficient to transform the class-based structural inequalities that plagued the majority of Chicanos living in the United States. Another, internationalist current understood the Chicano condition in terms of coloniality and linked its vision of liberation to other third world struggles for decolonization.[4] That being said, cultural nationalism still informed the cultural politics of many Marxists and internationalists, as well as organizations that did not identify as nationalist. The backlash against Chicana organizing was tied in part to how Chicano cultural nationalism was not just an ideology of cultural pride and unity but also a gendered construction that mediated how gender roles and expectations were played out in the political practices of the Chicano student movement.[5]

Alma García argues that "one source of ideological disagreement between Chicana feminism and cultural nationalist ideology was cultural survival, which was often posited as an obstacle to the redefinition of gender roles."[6] Initially cultural nationalism was meant to resist the historical inaccuracies of white supremacy and to provide the rich ground for cultural renewal and innovation to flourish. It provided a common ground and political grammar to unify disparate regions, identities, and social locations. The following reflection from the 1969 *Chicano Student Movement* newspaper illustrates this point.

> Cultural nationalism gives the Chicano the relevancy that Anglo brainwashing has destroyed, by filling the incredible vacuum created by the struggle of

the dominant but irrelevant value system of the majority against that of the minority. In our case, cultural nationalism becomes a tool which we use to organize our oppressed Chicano communities. By throwing out most of the garbage and lies that have been perpetrated on us, we construct another set of values that are more relevant to our needs. We teach our children about Joaquin Murrieta, not Robin Hood, about Zapata, not Kit Carson. We learn about the Mayan and Aztec empires. We rewrite the history of the Southwest. Thus we talk of cultural nationalism as the road for freedom and he who denies this road denies himself and necessarily denies the survival of our people. Como dice en *el plan espiritual de Aztlán*: "Por la Raza todo, fuera de la Raza NADA."[7]

Departing from the intention of this unifying vision, cultural nationalism also served as a regulatory apparatus to discipline deviant subjects who do not fit within those boundaries, especially in relation to sexuality, gender, and, often, race (i.e., who was seen as truly Chicano [enough]).[8]

The interpretive struggle over the meaning within nationalism is still heard today in academic debates. On the one hand, several activists criticize the reduction of all the complexities and contradictions of the ideological strands of the Chicano Movement to cultural nationalism. On the other hand, among the women activists I interview, there is a strong critique of nationalism. Over the years I have come to understand their responses as more than a critique of the limitations of nationalism as an analytical frame for understanding Chicano oppression and a plan for liberation. It also includes a critique of the way nationalism was wielded to justify certain behaviors and underwrite an exclusionary or narrow political culture within the movement. What activists are problematizing is not just a philosophy or ideology but how it served to justify sexism, the policing of identity, and the exclusion of diversity.

Discussion of the Chicano movement often freezes the discourse as nationalists versus feminists, when of course the categorical distinction was not that neat. Critically, what my conversations with Chicana activists reveal is that often a critique of nationalism stands in for the kinds of behaviors this discourse authorized. In other words, embedded in the critique is a challenge to the ways in which culturalist arguments were used to support and give historical weight to male dominance, supremacy, and sexual politics. While other ideological leanings, Marxism, for example, may have been sexist, nationalism is often a shorthand way of saying sexist, which speaks to the ways in which nationalism was used to legitimate male dominance in cultural and political terms. Ultimately, we can understand nationalism as a signifying practice of political meaning-making rather than strictly as a narrowly defined ideology.

Thus the Chicana feminist critique of nationalism should be understood as a critique both of the ideology and of the way the cultural logic of nationalism was used to legitimate the patriarchal abuse of power and authoritarianism. This elliptical nature and layered meaning of Chicano cultural nationalism for Chicana feminists can be seen as an internal shorthand and perhaps explains why very few Chicano scholars have fully taken up the feminist critique of nationalism.[9]

Many feminists argued against nationalism because it replicated patriarchal power structures and cultural norms through an approximation of a patriarchal logic that saw only men as the head of family, and by extension as leaders of *la familia de la raza* (the movement) and of the nation. This was reinforced by the revolutionary rhetoric through an unspoken hierarchy of power. Elucidating the underlying logic of why those who challenged patriarchy were consistently inscribed as outside or against the Chicano nation, Fregoso argues, "Not only did the masculinist equation of family with nation inhibit feminist critiques of la familia, but the rigid binaries of 'them' versus 'us' fostered by Chicano nationalists meant that any insurgent voices within the movement had to be positioned outside the familism romance, on the side of the colonialist enemies of the Chicano nation."[10] Some activists created what Pérez called a feminism–in–nationalism or Espinoza called feminist nationalism, while others worked to retrofit nationalism toward racial, gender, and class liberation, searching for models that moved beyond the masculinist confines of nationalism.

Perhaps signaling what Fanon pointed to as a stage within national liberation, the young activists involved in the Hijas de Cuauhtémoc named the limitations of nationalism as it was conceptualized and put into political practice at the time.[11] Postcolonial and transnational feminist criticism came also to understand third world and decolonial nationalism as a project of the bourgeoisie to create national unity under which they would create new relations of rule and, ultimately, a discourse reinforced by European constructs of modernity. Ella Shohat, for example, argues, "Third world secular nationalism, including its feminist wing, meanwhile, have often adopted the modernizing agenda drawn from Eurocentric 'progressive' discourses, venerating a modernity ironically made possible, as it were, on the backs of working class men and women."[12] In "supporting agendas of modernity," Inderpal Grewal and Caren Kaplan point out, "feminists misrecognize and fail to resist Western hegemonies."[13]

On the other hand, some posit the critique of nationalism as purely an academic endeavor that is by extension elitist and bourgeois, arguing instead that nationalism is an ideology that is embraced by the working class, the community, and activists.[14] This flies in the face of many working-class and community-based organizers who work across national and racial lines and contradicts the understanding that historically nationalism has been an intellectual project of the middle classes that seeks to build narratives of national unity that often then serve to suppress or manage difference. My project here is not to resolve this complex, now multigenerational debate on nationalism but to historicize correctly the multistranded and multivocal relationship of many early Chicana feminists with nationalism.

Chicano cultural nationalism was forged through the recuperation or rediscovery of a historical legacy suppressed by colonization. More than an act of reclamation, it was the production of a Chicano identity. If we understand how the formation of a Chicano identity was crafted through narratives of labor history, migration, and resistance to colonization, then it is vital for us to also understand that identities are not fixed in the past and merely recovered through historical memory. Pivotal to this project was the public acknowledgment of indigenous roots, developed through a historical consciousness, which was embodied in the concept of Aztlán. This concept invoked an ahistorical notion of the collective unconscious that was spatialized in a historical imaginary of the Southwest.[15] Remembrance of preconquest narratives of place helped to forge racial and cultural pride, but it was also criticized at the time because women are made invisible through this construction of nationalist patrimony that universalizes masculine subjects through the category "Chicano," encoding a gendered mode of remembrance.[16]

While there is compelling political potential within nationalism to reclaim precolonial narratives and a sense of place, especially for those whose histories have been held captive by U.S. hegemony, nationalist history, and white supremacy, we need a more critical analysis of both the problems in this formulation and the kinds of power relationships it continues to authorize. As much a project of recovery and racial pride, Chicano cultural nationalism also had the potential to be racially regulating and left unexamined has a racial politics that can promote exclusion. Processes of decolonization are often facilitated through the reclamation of a precolonial past as consistent with the opening passage of *El Plan*:

> In the spirit of a new people that is conscious not only of its proud historical heritage but also of the brutal 'gringo' invasions of our territories, *we*, the Chicano inhabitants and civilizers of the northern land of Aztlán from whence came our forefathers, reclaiming the land of their birth and conse-

crating the determination of our people in the sun, *declare*, that the call of our blood is our power, our responsibility, and our inevitable destiny.[17]

A sense of belonging, place, and time is inscribed in *El Plan*. However, the imperializing tone in the way Aztlán is conceived lays over the homelands of other sovereign indigenous nations, and the claim that Chicanos are "civilizers" of this territory with a biological destiny should be problematized. Angie Chabram-Dernersesian offers an important critique of the way early movement documents function as "blueprints for containing ethnic difference . . . where la raza: Méxicanos, Españoles, Latinos, Hispanos, and Chicanos; Yaquis, Tarahumaras, Chamulas, Zapotecs, mestizos and indios are all the same because of . . . [an] authenticating universal discourse of the Chicano." Further, she argues that mestizaje, as a gendered discourse that manages racial and ethnic differences is a nationalist narrative of unification that has functioned to consolidate the Mexican authoritarian state project historically.[18] Ernesto Chávez argues, "Mexican nationalism became a Chicano nationalism created to confront the inequalities in American society during the Vietnam era," calling our attention to residual cultures. Yet we must also be aware of the political residue embedded in those narratives. Mexican nationalism, for example, has celebrated a glorious indigenous past while denying an indigenous present by promoting Vasconcelos's notion of mestizaje, which was a racial project of whitening aimed at deindianizing indigenous peoples.[19]

MASCULINITY, NATIONHOOD, AND NARRATIVES OF RESISTANCE, OR CAN MACHISMO BE REVOLUTIONARY?

For Chicanos machismo is not so much the expression of male pride as it is the political expression of an ethnic identity that transcends gender.
ARMANDO RENDÓN, *CHICANO MANIFESTO*, 1971

The Chicano movement constructed a specific kind of masculinity—a subaltern masculinity. It recalled and built on the tradition of the social bandit of the U.S.-Mexico border, praised in many corridos and regional oral traditions, and the pachuco of the 1930s and 1940s as visible symbols of cultural autonomy and resistance.[20] Outlaw masculinities such as the pinto or cholo served as revolutionary prototypes. Part of Chicano working-class heritage, these figures survived brutalization at the hands of the U.S. state, police, and Border Patrol and resisted and survived outside of or autonomous from the structure that sought to subdue them. Thus they became figures of resistance representing self-determination, masculinity, and Chicano-ness (or people-hood). Perhaps best epitomized by Corky Gonzales, an award-winning boxer, this movement icon's self-determined, heterosexual masculinity was a model for young militant Chicano men.

Subaltern masculinity was idealized and deployed as a mechanism to decolonize Mexicano/Chicano people, configuring part of a larger construction of gender in the movement that was established in the domain of "tradition." Further, once these constructions of masculinity had been established as inherited tradition, they enabled the transformation of a historically specific configuration of race, class, and gender into a seemingly timeless ideal through an interlocking definition of manhood, peoplehood, self-determination, and the reclamation of working-class ideals. This "tradition" of masculinity countered the way racism denied men of color the right to be men under patriarchal norms; asserting "machismo" then became a pathway to resist the gendered implications of white supremacy.[21]

In his 1985 work Alfredo Mirandé delineates the two views of "machismo"—as pathological and as compensation for colonization. In his conclusion, titled "Machismo and Decolonization," he mediates between these two views to state that the internalization of imposed stereotypes of masculinity and the excessive demonstration of that masculinity are intertwined.

> To the contrary, if colonized people are to be decolonized, it becomes imperative that they take an active part in demythicizing [*sic*] their experiences and in redefining themselves and their culture. Part of this process entails recognition of machismo as an important component of the culture, not simply a negative and pathological force, as many social scientists would have us believe, but as a positive force that has served to resist cultural genocide. Machismo is ultimately a symbol of the resistance of Chicanos to colonial control, both cultural and physical. It symbolizes the pride, dignity, and tenacity of the Chicano people as they have resisted the onslaught of economic, political, and cultural control. It symbolizes, most importantly, resistance to acculturation and assimilation into Anglo society. If the term is associated with the male and with masculinity, it is not because he has more actively resisted acculturation and assimilation, but perhaps because his resistance has been more visible and manifest.[22]

Further, the conflation of peoplehood with a kind of manhood that came to stand in for nation was a linchpin that was used to legitimate exclusionary practices and enact the patriarchal assumption that men should lead nations, families, and the movement. In Armando Rendón's 1971 *Chicano Manifesto*, this particular construction of Chicano masculinity is seen not just as gender ideology but as political practice.

> The essence of machismo, of being macho, is as much a symbolic principle of the Chicano revolt as it is a guideline for the conduct of family life, male-female relationships, and personal self-esteem. . . . The Chicano revolt is a manifestation of Mexican Americans exerting their manhood and woman-hood against the Anglo society. Macho, in other words, can no longer relate merely to manhood but must relate to nationhood as well.[23]

The marshaling of machismo as a revolutionary strategy relied on notions of male pride in being responsible for the family by providing strength and pro-tection and being the breadwinner.

Chicano cultural nationalism created a contradictory position for women. They were seen simultaneously as the bearers of tradition, culture, and family—which became politicized ideals in nationalist thinking—and the unspoken subjects of a discourse of political rights. It also engendered constructions of idealized femininity largely by conflating a conservative cultural construct of "tradition" with a particular version of family. La familia functioned as an allegory of Raza and as a structuring metaphor for the Chicano movement as a whole. While familial structures have been crucial for collective survival, this view of family was seen as the foundational unit of revolutionary cul-ture: the nationalist premise that the nation needed every man, woman, and child—in that order. Women's roles within the Chicano movement were cir-cumscribed by these proscriptions that were rigidly framed around the patri-archal, heterosexual family (also known as heteropatriarchy) as the organizing principle. This cultural reinscription of the virgin/whore, good woman/bad woman dichotomy is part of the family melodrama of nationalism through which these binaries function to regulate and police women's sexuality. In the nationalist version of the script, patriarchal roles are inscribed on women through figures such as the Virgin of Guadalupe and la Malinche.[24] The com-plex psychology of conquest was notoriously portrayed in gendered, sexual, and racial terms by Octavio Paz in *The Labyrinth of Solitude*, in which he por-trayed the supposed lack of self-worth in the Mexican national character as a result of being "hijos de la Chingada," sons of the (raped) fucked mother. In the Chicano movement, Chicana feminists began a critical excavation of Malintzín Tenépal and a reclaiming of her as a historical woman of tremen-dous influence and limited choices.[25] Norma Alarcón draws out the link to women's role in the symbolic economy of the nation: "It is worthwhile to

remember that the historical founding moment of the construction of mes-
tiza(o) subjectivity entails the rejection and denial of the dark Indian Mother
as Indian, which has compelled women often to collude in silence against
themselves, and to actually deny the Indian position even as that position is
visually stylized and represented in the making of the fatherland."[26]

In her important 1974 article, "Chicanas and El Movimiento," Adaljiza
Sosa-Riddell provides an analysis of how machismo is a myth imposed by
colonizers or neocolonizers that Chicanos have been goaded into emulat-
ing.[27] Historically racist stereotypes in the dominant culture conflate the word
machismo (originally a code of male conduct and responsibility under patriarchy) with all forms of misogyny that defines sexism as a Latino, working-
class problem and makes invisible the hegemonic project of everyday male
supremacy in the dominant culture.

Anna NietoGomez offered a telling analysis, signifying her understanding
that masculinity was constructed through movement discourses:

> Looking back, I see that these guys were trying out idealized roles of man-
> hood so everything was exaggerated. Working in the community helped me
> out because I got to work with men who seemed more normal. I worked at
> the Norwalk Senior Citizen Center [started as a mutualista group], which
> was all Chicanos, and they fund-raised the money for the first Hijas de
> Cuauhtémoc publication. I saw their male identity as being comfortable and
> part of who they were. Back on campus it seemed the guys were role-playing
> the exaggerated stereotypical macho and forced women to play out their pas-
> sive role . . . which was a very rigid thing, instead of being yourself. If these
> guys deviated from this hyper macho role, they were criticized for being
> wimps or Anglocized because Anglo men were stereotyped as weak. . . .
> [T]hey were seen as too concerned with themselves and neglecting the group
> and never standing up for what they believed in.[28]

NietoGomez's reflection gives us insight into how the effects of a virile
form of masculinist nationalism were felt more detrimentally among student
and youth sectors of the movement. If fact, this observation was made at
the 1969 Corazón de Aztlán symposium at UCLA featuring a wide array
of movement women. *La Raza* reported on the symposium, commenting
that the "panelists alone would give us the impression that liberated Chicanas are generally over 30." Even though the symposium was organized by
youths, "the generality that could be drawn from this is that the older Chicanas are living liberation, while the younger ones are still planning to move
toward it."[29]

Women activists in the Black Power movement dealt with the question of how to challenge sexism in a context in which black men had been "emasculated" by historical relations of capitalist racial domination.[30] Puerto Rican women involved in national liberation and community empowerment movements also confronted this challenge. In fact, women in the New York chapter of the Puerto Rican Young Lords party organized themselves and presented a series of demands to the central organizing committee that included the demand for more women in leadership roles and for a change in the organization's ten-point program. The revision of the ten-point plan changed the language that claimed that machismo was revolutionary to read that machismo could never be revolutionary and that true revolution included men and women and all members of the community.[31]

RETROFITTED MEMORY: SHIFTING THE GENDERED PROJECT OF CULTURAL NATIONALISM

Or is quite different practice entailed—not the rediscovery but the production of identity. Not an identity grounded in the archaeology, but in the re-telling of the past?
STUART HALL, "CULTURAL IDENTITY AND DIASPORA"

Cultural nationalist identities were forged through historical narratives, but, as Stuart Hall's crucial intervention reminds us, these identities are not fixed in the past and merely recovered through historical memory.[32] Rather, political identities are constructed through the narratives of the past and *produced* through the positioning of the subject in relation to those narratives. Hall states:

> Far from being grounded in a mere "recovery" of the past, which is waiting to be found, and which, when found, will secure our sense of ourselves into eternity, identities are the names we give to the different ways we are positioned by, and position ourselves within, the narratives of the past.[33]

Chicano nationalism was not just a discourse of cultural pride; it was also a discourse that produced gendered ideologies that shaped movement ideas about political leadership, the roles of men and women, and the sexual division of political labor. Chicana activists in the student movement contested the ways in which their participation in the political realm was circumscribed by their representation in the symbolic realm as mothers of the nation, bearers of culture, or sites of authenticity, those for whom the struggle is waged, revolutionary sweethearts, and martyrs of the struggle.

More than their conventional political work, the work of engendering the political culture of el movimiento Chicano, helped activist women find historical and political agency through retrofitted memory. One of the most significant interventions of the Hijas de Cuauhtémoc was to shift the historical imaginary and site of political agency away from the mythic terrain of Aztlán to the participation of women in the Mexican Revolution. By crafting an identity through this alternative sense of women's role in the Mexican Revolution, the women of the Hijas de Cuauhtémoc complicated static meanings of gender within Chicano nationalism, multiplied the forms of gendered subjectivity available to activist women, and, most important, created a new historical imaginary, which authorized an autonomous female political agency. By basing their agency on the historical traditions of Mexican "feminist foremothers," Chicanas contested how cultural icons—la Malinche, la Virgen, la Adelita—served as conservative proscriptions for women's behavior that enforced dominant patriarchal gender ideology.

By moving from the mythic terrain of Aztlán into a political historical consciousness, the Hijas were able to disrupt the gendered ideologies embedded in nationalist symbols. George Lipsitz argues that

> myth and folklore are not enough. It is the oppressions of history—of gender, of race, and of class—that make aggrieved populations suspicious of dominant narratives [of history]. . . . Storytelling that leaves history to the oppressor, that imagines a world of desire detached from the world of necessity, cannot challenge the hegemony of dominant discourse. But story-telling that . . . employs the insights and passions of myth and folklore in the service of revising history, can be a powerful tool of contestation.[34]

Lipsitz suggests another mode of remembrance, that of countermemory, which, unlike myth, does not detach itself from a larger historical context. As Lipsitz defines it, "Countermemory forces revision of existing histories by supplying new perspectives about the past. Countermemory focuses on localized experiences with oppression, using them to reframe and refocus dominant narratives purporting to represent universal experience."[35] This construction of countermemory is evident in the work of groups like Mujeres de Longo, Chicanas de Aztlán, and, later, Las Hijas de Cuauhtémoc, who forged movement spaces for Chicanas by building a new political subjectivity that linked their own struggles for education and political rights to those of their foremothers.

As suggested by Alarcón, to move beyond merely breaking with nationalism requires "revision and appropriation of cherished metaphysical beliefs."[36] The Hijas de Cuauhtémoc worked to reframe masculinist discourses of the movement on several levels. First, Chicano nationalism utilized Aztec (Mexica) imagery and the concept of Aztlán to narrate a Chicano indigeneity and reclaim a sense of belonging. Aztlán served as a decolonizing imaginary to signify homeland and served as a mode of historical consciousness and a precolonial sense of place about the U.S. Southwest. Taking the name Hijas de Cuauhtémoc helped this group of Chicanas align themselves historically and politically with a decolonial imaginary. It located them within a genealogy of resistance by invoking Cuauhtémoc, the last Aztec emperor, who resisted the colonial military occupation of Tenochitlán and even was said to have plotted rebellions after his surrender and subsequent torture. The act of taking on the name Hijas de Cuauhtémoc had the effect of subverting the silencing mechanism or Malinche complex deployed by Chicano nationalists who felt that a women's agenda in the movement was divisive. By resignifying women's role in nationalist culture to take on the anticolonial struggle that Cuauhtémoc symbolized (instead of the vendida or traitor role that Malinche came to mean), the Hijas de Cuauhtémoc carved out a space for Chicana political subjectivity within the movement. More than using memory merely to add women to existing movement narratives (i.e., Aztec princesses or revolutionary sweethearts), the Hijas de Cuauhtémoc shifted the historical terrain of struggle by retrofitting new narratives that engendered the project of liberation. Moreover, their retrofitted memory created new forms of Chicana feminist political subjectivity and refigured gendered forms of representation, which they circulated via their newspaper.

By locating themselves within an untold feminist history of the Mexican Revolution, these women shifted the political possibilities for women in the movement. This new sense of historical memory inspired their commitment to the emancipation of all Chicano/Mexicano people, which required a struggle for social, economic, racial, and gender justice. The publication of their newspaper was coupled with galvanized political activities on campuses and in the communities. The production of a new political identity for Chicana feminists involved not merely reclaiming historical narratives to reflect women's political identities but also producing them.

Retrofitted memory is a practice whereby social actors read the interstices, gaps, and silences of existing historical narratives in order to retrofit, rework, and refashion older narratives to create new historical openings, political possibilities, and genealogies of resistance. Drawing on alternative histories, the Combahee River Collective, a black feminist group in Boston established as a local chapter of the National Black Feminist Organization (NBFO) in 1973, also used retrofitted memory to locate their multiply insurgent feminist project. They rooted their feminist interventions in the revolutionary legacies of historical events to legitimate their feminist claims within larger race-based movements and to contest the erasure of diverse forms of feminism by the feminist movement. The Combahee River Collective, for example, also had grown tired of the gender and sexual repression in the various civil rights, Black Power, and Marxist organizations and used retrofitted memory to re-fashion a legacy to address multiple oppressions. The group was named after a 1863 guerrilla action led by Harriet Tubman that liberated more than 750 enslaved Africans. The collective's widely anthologized 1977 statement draws this connection to a historical imaginary: "Before looking to the recent de-velopment of Black feminism we would like to affirm that we find our origins in the historical reality of Afro-American women's continuous life-and-death struggle for survival and liberation."[37]

Emma Pérez's concept, feminism-in-nationalism, theorized how Mexica-nas and Chicanas who have been afforded little space in nationalist imaginar-ies work in the interstices and gaps to change the way they are symbolically represented by the nation.[38] By using this feminism-in-nationalism, or third space feminism strategy, the Hijas de Cuauhtémoc forged a space for dialogue on women's issues within the Chicano movement by changing the gendered political modes of movement organizing and resignifying the narratives of nationalism. Their reclamation of earlier feminists and female political leaders was a way to constitute a historical tradition, gain political legitimacy within Chicano nationalism, and, most important, create a new historical imaginary, which authorized an autonomous female political agency.

THE DAUGHTERS OF REVOLUTION: ON DECOLONIZING MEMORY AND FORGING FEMINIST LEGACY

For the Hijas de Cuauhtémoc, an evolving sense of Chicana identity and po-litical subjectivity was consolidated by an incidental historical finding that changed their lives. Although the Long Beach group of Chicanas had been meeting informally through the late 1960s, they did not become known as the Hijas de Cuauhtémoc until NietoGomez discovered a Mexican feminist historical legacy in the library one day.[39] Taking this genealogical strand, they began to weave a historical legacy that animated their own emergent feminista political convictions. Influenced by aspects of Mexican history that had been lost or suppressed, they forged a feminist historical countermemory that drew on a legacy of Mexicanas who had struggled for the right to education and a history of radicalism.

NietoGomez describes her feelings about finding this information:

Even though I was in the library, it was like I had been in a cave and someone had put the light in the candle and I realized how important it was to read about your own kind, your own women of your own culture, of your own historical heritage doing the things that you were doing to kind of reaffirm and validate that you're not a strange, alien person, that what you're doing is normal and . . . not only normal, but a part of your history. So I Xeroxed and just passed it on and passed it on. We even had a meeting at my house. We read it word for word like it was gold. We talked about how it felt to read about Mexican women who had organized as a group and who were advocating for women's rights. I don't know how much . . . more difficult it would have been for our self-validation if we hadn't read that we had sisters before us who had done that. So then they became our models; our heroes—to carry on the tradition—so that's why we used their name in the newspaper.[40]

The women formed a study group and instead of collapsing under the attacks that they were agringadas (whitewashed), malinches (sellouts), or divisive influences, they were empowered by their historical knowledge and decided to circulate this information. According to NietoGomez, "It made it more a national issue as opposed to an individual issue, which made us feel less selfish because it took us a while to feel comfortable talking about ourselves as women and women's problems because they were always being minimized and diminished; they were always being viewed as something that was petty."[41]

The Hijas de Cuauhtémoc felt they had rekindled the fires and could now pass on the message of the importance of women's education. It authorized them to organize around the immediate survival of Chicanas on campus and to work on a feminist political project that was indeed part of a retrofitted nationalist tradition. While it seemed appropriate for the young activists to take the name of an organization that had also fought to gain equal rights for women, what they did not know at the time was that they also shared histories of migration, discrimination, and perseverance. Mexican anthropologist Manuel Gamio's historically rich life stories of Mexican migrants contains an example of this shared genealogy. Between 1926 and 1927 Gamio interviewed Señora Flores de Andrade of El Paso, one of the original members of the first Hijas de Cuauhtémoc. Her life story documents experiences that illustrate how these young Chicanas had come full circle into a long history of Mexican women's political involvement and migration.

Señora Flores de Andrade established El Club Hijas de Cuauhtémoc in the early 1900s in Chihuahua in collaboration with the Partido Liberal Mexicano (PLM). Gamio interviewed her after the revolution, in El Paso, about

her trafficking of arms, supplies, and medicines, her safe house for political
dissidents, and the spread of political propaganda associated with the Flores
Magón brothers.[42] Señora Flores de Andrade grew up on a hacienda in Chihuahua and was cared for by her grandparents, who died when she was thirteen. Her life of relative independence and comfort was quickly transformed
by her political convictions. Her grandparents left her an inheritance that represented a fifth of all their landholdings in Chihuahua. Against the advice of
her sister and aunt, she broke from feudalistic tradition by declaring that all
the peasants who worked the land now owned it. Dividing the land equally
among them, she also declared them owners of the grains and seeds, agricultural equipment, and farm animals. In the story of her life, she discusses how
she maintained her political convictions and activities, even though they contributed to her impoverishment.

> Then I decided to go to the city of Chihuahua and there, even though I was
> a widow with six children, I began to struggle for liberal ideals, organiz-
> ing a women's club called the Hijas de Cuauhtémoc. It was a semi-secret
> society that worked with the liberal party of the Flores Magón brothers in
> order to combat the dictatorship of don Porfirio Díaz. We were able to estab-
> lish branches of this women's club in all parts of the state through intense
> propaganda.
>   My political activities caused members of my family to become very
> angry, especially on the part of my aunt, who was like a mother to me. For
> this reason, I became more and more impoverished until I arrived at misery.
> Four bitter years passed in Chihuahua in which I suffered for the bare neces-
> sities on one hand, and struggling for the defense of my ideals on the other.
> My relatives told me not to involve myself in the struggle of the people, be-
> cause nothing good would come of it. Even if the town crucified me, I was
> going to continue to fight for the cause I considered just.
>   My economic situation in Chihuahua became so grave that I had to accept
> donations of money that were offered to me as charity by the rich people in
> the capital of the state who knew me and my family. My aunt helped a little,
> but I preferred that she gave me nothing because she continued to scold me
> and cause me to suffer. There were rich people that cut me off or that, in one
> way or another, suggested that I become their lover. They offered money and
> comforts, but I would have preferred anything before sacrificing and prosti-
> tuting myself in this way.
>   Finally, after being in Chihuahua for four years, I decided to come to El
> Paso, Texas. First, to see if I could better my economic situation, and sec-
> ond, to continue struggling in that region of liberal ideals. That is to say, in

order to conspire against the dictatorship of don Porfirio. I came to El Paso in 1906, with my children and with the comrade Mendoza, who came to participate in propaganda work. I put my children in the Sacred Heart of Jesus School, a Catholic institution, where they treated me well and cared for my children.

In 1909, a group of comrades founded a liberal women's club in El Paso. They named me president of said group and a little later, I began to direct the propaganda work in El Paso and Ciudad Juárez. For that time, my house was converted into a center of the conspiracy against the dictator. They charged me with getting funds, clothing, medicine—and even ammunition and arms together to begin the revolutionary movement because the uprisings had already begun in many places.[43]

Another Hijas de Cuauhtémoc club was founded in Mexico City in 1910, comprising mostly middle-class women who marched in protest against the Díaz dictatorship at the beginning of the revolution, on September 11, 1910. They got a thousand Mexican women to sign a petition asking for Díaz's resignation, which finally caused his wife to advise his withdrawal.[44] They continued to organize, and a suffragist sentiment solidified early in the revolution that led to several hundred women signing a letter to interim President Francisco León de la Barra requesting women's suffrage by pointing out that since the 1857 Constitution made no mention of the sex of voters they were not in fact barred from voting. Declaring it time that Mexican women's educational and political rights be recognized, a manifesto of the Cuauhtémoc feminist league called for political enfranchisement and the full emancipation of Mexican women in "economic, physical, intellectual and moral struggles."[45]

Foreshadowing the importance of Chicana feminist print cultures in the 1960s, Juana Belén Gutiérrez de Mendoza was a journalist who began to edit the newspaper *La Voz de Ocampo* in 1901 and went on to found the magazine *Vesper*, in which she published declarations and revolutionary manifestos—for which she was incarcerated. During her time in jail, the Mexico City Hijas de Cuauhtémoc was founded. According to the Mexican feminist historian Ana Lau Jaiven:

> During her stay in jail, Juana Belén met Inés Malváez and Elisa Acuña Rossetti. The three, interested in the problems of women, decided that it was possible to articulate the revolutionary struggle with the struggle of women to gain civil and political rights. They constituted themselves into la Sociedad Hijas de Cuauhtémoc, and later converted into la Sociedad Regeneración y

Concordia, whose program consisted in bettering the life conditions of indigenous people and agricultural and urban workers; overcoming the challenges for women in the economic, political, moral and intellectual planes, as well as the struggle to gain equal rights.[46]

Shirlene Soto has documented other early feminist organizations, such as Admiradoras de Juárez (1904), Sociedad Protectora de la Mujer (1904), Hijas de Anáhuac (1907), one of the first women's revolutionary organizations founded by textile workers, Amigas del Pueblo (1911), and Regeneración y Concordia (1911). Another leader of the Hijas de Cuauhtémoc of Mexico City, Dolores Jimenez y Muro, was a PLM and Liga Feminista member. She called attention to women's role in bringing an end to political corruption and penned their feminist slogan, "Es tiempo de que las mujeres mexiano reconozcan que sus derechos y obligaciones van más allá del hogar [It is time that Mexican women recognize that their rights and obligations go much farther than just the home]." For her leadership and role in organizing the September 11 demonstration, Dolores Jimenez y Muro was imprisoned.[47]

In addition to agitating against Díaz, the Hijas de Cuauhtémoc worked for women's suffrage and advocated for women's right to education. *El Tiempo Illustrado*, one of the newspapers at the time that carried news about women, featured a picture of eighteen arrested members of the group on May 28, 1911 (figure 3.1).[48] Other members of the club, such as Julia Nava de Ruisánchez, Inés Malváez, and Juana Gutiérrez de Mendoza, continued to work for women's suffrage. Their efforts were part of women's active role in the revolution, and as a movement for women's emancipation gained force in Mexico, revolutionary leaders began to support the cause of women's rights.

The tradition of Mexicana/Chicana feminist print culture and revolutionary activism also reached north of the border through the work of Sara Estela Ramírez and the Villarreal sisters. One of the first histories written about Ramírez was by the Chicano movement activist Inés Hernández Ávila.[49] Born in Villa de Progresso, Coahuila, Mexico, Ramírez relocated to Laredo, Texas, in 1898 and supported the Magón brothers and the PLM from its inception in 1901, even participating in La Junta, a group responsible for the organization's early development.[50] In 1904 when the Magón brothers fled Mexico, Ramírez housed the Magón brothers, in addition to other Magonistas including Juana Belén Gutiérrez de Mendoza, and Elisa Acuña Rossetti. Her home in Laredo also served as the headquarters of the organization.[51]

Known for her poetry, Ramírez also wrote for two Spanish-language newspapers in South Texas between 1908 and 1910, *El Democrática Fronterizo* and *La Crónica*, writing articles in support of the working class and many mutual

FIGURE 3.1. Women's Antireelection Club, Hijas de Cuauhtémoc, meeting at the home of Francisco I. Madero, Mexico City, 1911. Photo courtesy of la Fototeca Nacional del Instituto Nacional de Antropología e Historia de México.

aid societies such as Sociedad de Obreros and Igualdad y Progreso. She was active in Regeneración y Concordia, a women's rights organization that "like the Hijas De Cuauhtémoc . . . combined feminist demands for equality with comprehensive political reform issues. Its goals were to better the lot of indigenous races, the peasantry and urban proletariat."[52] As an activist, journalist, and PLM member, Ramírez was aligned with other women who worked for these causes, namely, Dolores Jimenez y Muro, Juana Belén Gutiérrez de Mendoza, and Elisa Acuña Rossetti, and this generation of women, Pérez argues, "endorsed an (inter)nationalist revolution, but by advocating their own agenda, the women wrote and spoke third space feminism."[53]

This group of third space feminist intellectuals also included Teresa and Andrea Villarreal who in 1910 published *La Mujer Moderna*, "a San Antonio based newspaper that championed the emancipation of women."[54] Along with the El Paso weekly *Voz de la Mujer*, published by Isidra T. de Cárdenas, *La Mujer Moderna* promoted women's emancipation as well as Mexican revolutionary politics. The sisters were originally from Coahuila and fled to San Antonio to avoid persecution by the Porfirio Díaz regime.[55] Together they raised funds and organized with Leona Vicario and worked directly with the Liberal Union of Mexican Women, as well as the San Antonio–based organization Regeneración, which "called for the liberation of women as a crucial outcome of the Mexican revolution."[56] Teresa served as president of the organization, and the group issued a women's statement that read, "It is now time for woman to become independent and for men to stop considering themselves the center of the universe and to stop oppressing her and to give her in daily life the position of comrade and companion that corresponds to her."[57] The following year witnessed the 1911 Primer Congreso Mexicanista, which brought together Tejano educational, labor, and civil rights activists with writers, journalists, and mutual aid societies. The gathering resulted in the formation of two organizations: the Gran Liga Mexicanista de Beneficencia y Protección (Great Mexican League of Benefit and Protection) and the Liga Femenil Mexicanista (Mexicanist Feminine League), both of which took the motto "Por la Raza y para la Raza."

IMAGED COMMUNITIES: REPRESENTATION AND BELONGING TO THE IMAGINED COMMUNITY OF THE NATION

Benedict Anderson's influential work articulates a conceptualization of the nation as an imagined community and explores how the nation is constituted through print communities.[58] I have refashioned Anderson's notion of imagined communities to include "image(d) communities" to call attention to the role the circulation of images in Chicano movement print media played in the formation of political community. Photos, images, art, photojournalism, and collage produced the larger imagined community that linked activists through visual images. The visual culture imaged collective self-representation and depicted the struggles that were occurring within organizations and movement culture across the country. The concept "image(d) communities" names how Chicanas/activists produced visual images and new symbols as a political practice and collective conversation of reimagining historical subjectivity across temporal and spatial borders.[59]

With both word and image, the Hijas de Cuauhtémoc engaged in what Kobena Mercer describes as critical dialogism, "the potential to overturn the binaristic relations of hegemonic boundary maintenance by multiplying critical dialogues within particular communities and between the various constituencies that make up the 'imagined community' of the nation."[60] Their political and symbolic work broke down the unitary concept of the citizen-subject of Aztlán as male, thereby diversifying and multiplying the subjects of resistance enlisted in a Chicana/o project of liberation. The distribution, production, and circulation of print texts in the form of political pamphlets and

newspapers were critical to the formation of a Chicano historical consciousness, and the images embedded in this vibrant print culture were also key to
creating image(d) communities that enlisted new political subjects into Chicana subjectivity. Moreover, as I explore further in chapter 4, the circulation
of images was a powerful constitutive practice in forming Chicana counterpublics whereby members of this alternative discursive space produced and
were interpolated by alternative subjective registers of Chicana feminisms.

The reverberations of Chicana feminist iconography can be traced from
the circulation of visual images within print cultures to forging new image(d)
communities through wider networks of conversation and collaboration, such
as the production of the "Chicana Feminist Slide Show" that Anna Nieto-
Gomez developed as part of her Chicana Studies curriculum, to the transformation of that material into a script written by NietoGomez for Sylvia Morales's 1976 film, *La Chicana*. These reverberations cross time, as evidenced in
the resurfacing of movimiento images by Chicana feminist visual artists today.

VISUALITY AND SOCIAL MOVEMENTS

Emphasizing the image(d) community that was constituted through the circulation of images, I would like to use the 1967 Chicano historical epic, *Yo
Soy Joaquín*, written by Rodolfo "Corky" Gonzales, founder of the civil rights
organization Crusade for Justice in Denver, Colorado, as an establishing shot
to explore the visual tropes specific to the Chicano nationalist imaginary. This
text was widely read and performed at rallies and by teatro groups as the self-
proclaimed "epic of the Mexican American people."[61] Rather than focus on
the written text itself, which other Chicano scholars have done,[62] I want to examine the way gender was deployed in the visual images that accompany the
text to illustrate the way the iconography of nationalism operated during this
period. The images printed in *Yo Soy Joaquín* circulated widely in movement
print culture through mass distribution and photocopying, and they were extremely popular among activists because they articulated in poetic form the
emerging ideology of Chicano cultural nationalism. The introduction to the
1972 edition speaks to this broad circulation:

> Since 1967, the Crusade for Justice has published in mimeographed, photo-
> copied, and printed editions, over 100,000 copies which have been given
> away or sold. . . . *I am Joaquín* has been reproduced by numerous Chicano
> Press newspapers, which print 10,000 to 20,000 copy editions. . . . [I]t has
> been copied and reproduced by student groups, farm workers organizations,
> teachers, barrio groups, professionals and workers (all sectors of Aztlán).

The images in *Yo Soy Joaquín* depict how revolutionary male prototypes were signified over and over until they became archetypes of Chicano nationalism, visually encoding the political subjectivity of the movement as male. Other visual tropes of the revolutionary male hero and the familia as allegory for the movement established the dominant mode of address and representational strategy of the Chicano movement. The images depict the creation of movement archetypes through icons of the pachuco, the stoic worker, or the romanticized revolutionary, which came to constitute a field of subject positions where la Raza (the people), the "heroes" of the people, and the national subject were viewed as male. This visual field marginalized women's political subjectivity to that of the suffering witnesses to historic oppression, the bearers of pain and cultural survival, revolutionary mothers or supporters/helpmates to revolutionary male leaders. Based on her analysis of the filmic version of *Yo Soy Joaquín*, the Chicana feminist cultural theorist Rosa Linda Fregoso argues that these images posit

> a "collective" cultural identity that is singularly male-centered. Multiple identities are subsumed into a collectivity whose narrative voice is enacted in this historical male subject, Joaquín. The males who inform Chicano cultural identity have names (Cuauhtémoc, Moctezuma, Juan Diego, and so on), but the females are nameless abstractions. Indeed, as opposed to appearing as historical subjects, women are positioned as the metaphors for the emotive side of Chicano collective cultural identity, as "faithful" wives or "suffering" Mexican mothers.[63]

The cover of *Yo Soy Joaquín* illustrates the reclamation of subaltern masculinities—pachucos, cholos, homeboys—working-class young men as the privileged site of political subjectivity. The book features images of Brown Berets from what I call the "Che Guevara Low Shot" because low shots valorize the young militant man as revolutionary subject/hero. It shows the masculinized pride of la Raza (and resonates with other masculine images of resistance, such as the Black Panthers). The poem that accompanied the image reads, "Here I stand. Poor in money, arrogant with pride, bold with machismo, rich in courage."[64] Another photo depicts the family as the structuring metaphor for la Raza and for the movement as a whole. Visually, the man is centered and the photograph's formal and gendered composition elucidates the hierarchy of power, even though one of the women who is visually on the margins is Dolores Huerta, illustrating the power of these visual tropes that place men at the center of movimiento photos as "fathers" of la familia de Aztlán.[65]

The way the retelling of the epic past is staged in the text functions to establish male lineage and revolutionary legacy within the Chicano movement through masculinist notions of historical subjectivity. These roots are inscribed on the bodies of the man sitting below a portrait of Benito Juárez. The framing device of Juárez delineates male lineage and ancestral struggle. The images of women in *Yo Soy Joaquín* echo many of the ideological sentiments forwarded by the movement. Women are represented as martyrs, virgins, or mothers. Women are literally (and visually martyred as) the bearers of the pain of injustice and figured as mothers of the people, with accompanying text reading, "I shed tears of anguish as I see my children." The suffering mother archetype is depicted instead of images of women in the movement, many of whom were mothers, who engaged in community and labor organizing, demanded child care, developed a new form of feminist consciousness in the United States, and engaged in collective action while balancing their family lives.[66]

The dominant mode of address and representational strategy of the Chicano movement was enacted through the idealization of the people and the construction of "heroes" of the people. Movement archetypes, such as the pachuco, the stoic worker, or the romanticized revolutionary, constituted a field of subject positions. More than just "representations" of what already existed within Chicano culture, these visual tropes were political and cultural practices that played a constitutive role in the domain of culture. Establishing the dominant mode of address, the iconography of nationalism was gendered through the visual tropes of the revolutionary male hero and the familia as allegory in the Chicano movement. Decoupling the nationalist and hetero-patriarchal underpinnings of family, cultural theorist Richard T. Rodriguez argues that "if minority nationalisms endeavor to liberate their purported constituencies from the subordinating forces of the state, they must relinquish their dependency on exclusionary kinship relations."[67]

BEYOND THE REVOLUTIONARY (M)OTHER

Perhaps the most enduring image in the symbolic economy of nationalism is what I call the Revolutionary (m)Other. These images represent the way in which women are figured as part of the revolution and defined by their role as reproducers of the nation. For example, the Revolutionary (m)Other images in the Chicano movement classic *Yo Soy Joaquín* are accompanied by the text, "I must fight and win this struggle for my sons." The image of the Revolutionary (m)Other is common in national liberation struggles that seek to locate women's revolutionary agency within motherhood. To figure women and their participation in the revolutionary process, women were represented not just as mothers of the nation but as mothers of a new nation bearing arms of revolutionary struggle. The image of the Revolutionary (m)Other depicts a woman with a machine gun over one shoulder as she cradles and nurses a baby at her breast, such as those featured on billboards in Cuba or on the Nicaraguan Women's Revolutionary organization (AMNLAE) posters. They protect the revolution while they bear the new nation. The image of Revolutionary (m)Others epitomizes the way women's bodies stand in for the nation metaphorically and reveal the contradictions and complicities between colonialism and nationalism's deployment of women's bodies in the (post)colonial project. Scholars have commented on these contradictions. For example:

> Often made to metaphorize the nation, the image of the revolutionary woman carrying a bomb or waving a flag was celebrated precisely because her precarious position within the revolution called attention to its fissures. Thus, the same Third Worldist discourse that valorized the revolutionary female figure has also condemned Third World feminists as "traitors to the nation" in response to their critique of the masculinist narration of the nation.[68]

BEARING BANDOLERAS: THE TRANSFIGURATIVE LIBERATION OF ICONS

Movement iconography served as a terrain of struggle over the signification or meaning of women's political agency in the Chicano movement. Icons such as the Soldadera call into question fissures that are located at the crossroads of the bandoleras women bear symbolically and politically. Chicana women leaders and feminists reclaimed counternarratives of revolutionary women and the image of the Soldadera through the lens of Chicana resistance. In the first issue of their newspaper, the Hijas de Cuauhtémoc began to resignify the image of the Soldadera through historical narratives to produce a revolutionary historical agency.[69] They began to etch a proud, newly reclaimed mythopoetic epic of history located firmly in nationalism, which imaged women *como las reinas y madres de nuestra nación* (queens and mothers of our nation).[70] In an article on women's history in Mexico, student activist and member of the Hijas de Cuauhtémoc, Martha López, wrote about "La Mexicana" and women in the Mexican Revolution. Her story elucidates the rich historical consciousness and connections this group used to forge both a national imaginary of Raza women and a tradition that authorized a space for themselves vis-à-vis their detractors, who claimed that women's autonomous organizing was anti-Raza/Chicano.[71]

The figure of the Soldadera, although a seemingly politicized image, also functioned as a conservative model of the role Chicanas were expected to play in the movement. As noted by Vicki Ruiz, who points out the limitations of this figure for women's agency, la Soldadera was construed as a foot soldier of the movement who would follow the party line and carry out orders on the ground level.[72] La Soldadera was seen as a loyal camp follower or as a woman who "stands by her man" to provide comfort to the revolutionary hero. Also in circulation was the figure of la Adelita, which conjured up an image of the revolutionary sweetheart whose role was to inspire and support her compañeros.

The Soldadera had many kinds of signifying possibilities and was a site of struggle over the role of women in the movement in many competing narratives. La Adelita, representing the revolutionary sweetheart, circulated in movement culture and more broadly within Chicano popular culture and was airbrushed on customized cars and tattooed on backs and arms.[73] The most iconic representation is a color painting of a woman on one knee, holding a rifle, her abundant chest crossed with bandoleras. This image is highly sexualized as the center of the image depicts erect nipples, seductively tossed hair, and half-opened lips.[74] Some images of the Soldadera featured the self-abnegating foot soldiers of the movement who did the reproductive work. In either case women were represented through their erotic or reproductive labor, while the nationalist project and Chicano pride were projected on their bodies.

Instead of just reclaiming women's participation in the movement and illustrating female icons, I want to complicate our understanding of the cultural work of political iconography and read the struggle surrounding these icons as visual negotiations of political subjectivity, forms of political participation, and the way spaces of belonging were negotiated. To anchor this discussion, I turn to a popular Chicano movement photo (figure 3.2) as a point of departure to chart how dominant visual tropes within Chicano movement print culture helped to produce and maintain gendered political scripts about the terms of women's political participation. In turn, Chicana activists engaged political icons and politicized iconography in order to negotiate their own political agency and (re)figure themselves within movement iconography by creating new images of women's revolutionary participation.

This photograph first appeared in the *Chicano Student Movement* newspaper in 1969 and was republished in numerous places, including the first issue of *La Raza*, where it was advertised as a political poster. It marks one point where Chicana feminists reclaimed narratives of women's participation in the Mexican Revolution of 1910 as a way to negotiate a different political agency within the masculinist registers of Chicano nationalism.

FIGURE 3.2. Hilda Reyes. *Chicano Student Movement 2:2* (August 1969): 3.

In the photo the figure of the young woman, a member of the Brown Berets, captures the contradictions and contestations surrounding the Soldadera and the position of women within both narratives and movement practices of Chicano nationalism. She is politically and visually present in the movement, but her gaze is turned away, deflected. The photograph frames her in a medium shot; the top of her head reaches out of the frame. Because her head is turned, her gaze laterally oblique, the viewer's focus is pulled to the center of her body—her *corazón, pecho*—bearing bandoleras. The crossed bandoleras represent an intersection—simultaneously symbolizing her revolutionary commitment and invoking the complex ways women and women's bodies are made to stand in for the nation, in both historic projects of nation building and numerous revolutionary struggles.

The photograph was taken in the late 1960s at the Fiesta de los Barrios at Lincoln High School and published in the 1969 *Chicano Student Newspaper*, which documented the historic East Los Angeles Blowouts where students demanded an end to racist education. Taken by the activist, photographer, and editor Raul Ruiz, it is a grainy black-and-white image of Hilda Reyes that circulated widely in *La Raza* and as a poster. It is a powerful movement document because, while the context of the rally is evident, the focus of the image is on one actor. The quality of realism is also reliant on the seemingly unstaged nature of the image. In documentary fashion it claims to represent and document a moment in political history innocent of staging; the woman seems unaware that her photo is being taken. There is a young man in the background to the woman's left whose body is partially beyond the frame. He seems to be propositioning or attempting to talk with the woman, who appears to be ignoring him. She is at a political rally, perhaps listening to a speaker. Another woman in the background gazes directly into the camera.

In most reproductions of the photo the man and the background have been cropped out. The cropping can be read several ways. It is cutting the central image away from the context in which it was taken. Within feminista reclaimings of this image, the cropping may suggest that we center our attention on women's revolutionary participation. Yet, just as in most movement histories, the background of the lived working and organizing conditions of women in the movement, or even their stories, have been cropped out. This framing calls attention to the constructed nature of all representation and the multitude of factors that shape how we see historic events.

In the photo the woman bears the bandoleras (signifier of both present and historic revolutions) across her heart and in that way is represented both as a documentary image of an activist at a political event and a symbol of it. The imagery of women simultaneously in combat gear, with the accoutrements of war or revolution, featuring the breast of the nation metaphorically, has been used in other anti-imperialist movements for national liberation before and after the height of the Chicano movement.

The figure of the Soldadera and her manifestation in the image of this young Brown Beret activist also calls attention to the fissures of the nation Aztlán and the manner in which it engenders its subject/citizens. U.S. nationalist and racial justice movements articulated their discursive project of decolonization and anti-imperialism most often through an ideological alignment with third world liberation movements where masculinist nationalism was manifest through a construction of a specific revolutionary masculinity, à la Che Guevara.[75]

The image in this 1969 photograph has continued to circulate nearly four decades later as a compelling tribute to Chicana Power on T-shirts and stickers, in a book dedicated to historical writings of Chicana feminism, and even on the cover of a Chicano oldies album (Figure 3.3).[76] As much as this image represents a site of contestation and negotiation of women's political subjectivity and agency within the Chicano movement, it also represents a continued struggle over popular memory and identity formation. It calls our attention to the ways in which women and Chicana feminism are the eccentric subjects of Chicano movement narratives, because the narrative of male dominance is continually recycled, instead of representing the complicated ways

FIGURE 3.3. CD cover, *Chicano Power: Latin Rock* Soul Jazz Records Ltd. Courtesy of Soul Jazz Records, London, UK.

in which women participated, transformed, and provided leadership in the movement. As a mediation of the representations of women's widespread participation in the Chicano movement, the continued circulation of this image also invokes the empowering message of Chicana resistance, as well as a mode of retrofitted memory where retrofitted icons create a structure of remembrance within the movimiento narratives that honor Chicana resistance (see Figure 3.6).

The historic development of an iconography of la Nueva Chicana can be seen in the ways in which women's agency and political subjectivities were not only constituted by movement imaging practices but also by how Chicana feminists refigured themselves in the circulation and production of their own images. The iconography of the New Chicana reworked the gendered nationalist constructions of the Adelita, la Revolucionaria, and other figures. Deploying different frames of reference and modes of address in its visual strategies, these representational practices show us how Chicana activists shifted nationalist representational registers and figured themselves as new historical subjects. For example, an excerpt from the introduction by one of the editors of *Encuentro Femenil* describes how Chicanas looked with initial enthusiasm for images of women but were disappointed at how limited they were.

> At best she would be referred to mystically as "la India," the bulwark of the family, or she would be referred to romantically as "la Adelita," "la Soldadera" of the movement. La mujer either had a baby in her arms or a rifle in her hand or both. But few dealt with the identity of la mujer in the family, or even knew who was "la Adelita."[77]

Chicana feminists established discursive and visual spaces in which to negotiate alternative subjectivities by reworking the icons and cultural narratives of the Chicano movement. This tradition "of working simultaneously within and against dominant cultural" structures has been expanded and theorized by the cultural critic Yvonne Yarbro-Bejarano in her study of the representational strategies deployed by Chicana lesbians.[78] In theorizing the "cultural specificity of the lesbianization of the heterosexual icons of popular culture" in Latina cultural production, she calls upon what Amalia Mesa-Baines calls "the transfigurative liberation of the icon."[79]

Nationalist symbols operated in a system of signification and meaning in this ideological and historical context. If we look at this as an early attempt to resignify gender, sexuality, and race, then the symbols themselves can be seen as points of contestation. This explains the constant reworking of the nation from the margins to signify who belongs and under what conditions and the boundaries of social and political agency for the national subject. Within the gendered/sexual economy of cultural nationalist meaning, the seams of its gendered construction had been sutured onto the fabric of the historical imaginary and popularized through cultural nationalist discourse as popular memory. The work of the Hijas de Cuauhtémoc, along with many other Chicana feminists, was, then, to rework and resignify symbols and icons of female agency, thereby opening up new possibilities for women's participation and leadership by creating an alternative feminist apparatus of interpellation that changes the hailing mechanism of the Chicana/o subject.[80]

Artists like Yolanda Lopez, Ester Hernandez, and, more recently, Alma López all rework the signifying possibilities for la Virgen de Guadalupe around women's agency, resistance, and sexuality.[81] Chicana lesbian feminist artists have been especially active in creating new signifying possibilities for female icons, expanding the range of meanings to include even the figure of the Virgin as a matrix of power and desire or the vulva. This form of cultural work is a kind of retrofitted memory because it changes the relationship Chicanas have as historical subjects to the sexed and gendered narratives of the past. Early and continuing acts of resignification articulated a kind of feminism within nationalism that revealed and disrupted the virgin/whore dichotomy and engendered the very symbols of national liberation. Articulating new modes of representation within movement iconography, political discourse, and historical memory played a constitutive role in engendering a space for Chicanas in the movement and opened the way for new political possibilities. In fact, Catrióna Rueda Esquibel argues, "in the four decades since *el movimiento*, both straight and queer Chicanas 'reinvented' nationalist mythologies to better portray the participation of women and of gays and lesbians, in spite of obstacles."[82]

The cultural production and political practice of the Hijas de Cuauhtémoc involved working in and through a nationalist discursive terrain to rework the narratives of nation to create new possibilities for Chicana feminist subjectivity. This politics of disidentification did not reproduce the same national symbols but engaged in resignifying figures such as Cuauhtémoc in order to create or recall a women's decolonial and revolutionary legacy. In earlier writings, I used the term *politics of disidentification* to describe how they disidentify with the sexist gendered/sexual politics underwriting nationalist representation while resignifying them.[83] Jose Muñoz much more fully theorized disidentification to be "descriptive of the survival strategies the minority subject practices in order to negotiate a phobic majoritarian public sphere that continuously elides or punishes the existence of subjects who do not conform to the phantasm of normative citizenship."[84] Critically, Muñoz also includes the kind of ambivalence that disidentificatory politics produced. While the Hijas de Cuauhtémoc formed around strategies of feminism-in-nationalism, they moved between both the Mexican and the Chicano nationalist imaginary, and eventually beyond them.

THE ICONOGRAPHY OF LA NUEVA CHICANA

I want to now turn my gaze to the ways Chicanas represented and refigured themselves through the circulation and production of their own images in the late 1960s and 1970s. For even when Chicanas did not produce the images, the way they chose to use them in their publications, circulate them within their existing print communities, and negotiate the terms on which they would constitute an image(d) community reveal a great deal about the development of both Chicana cultural practice and subject formation. The production of a politicized historical subjectivity of the "New Chicana" was created, in part, through the images that circulated in newspapers, political pamphlets, photos, and film media.[85] The Chicano art critic Tomás Ybarro-Frausto discusses the transformative role of new cultural productions and their circulation in public cultures, which he argues opens up new social spaces and oppositional publics.[86]

In addition to taking on the name of an earlier Mexican feminist organization, *Hijas de Cuauhtémoc* began transforming the figure of the Soldadera by reclaiming it through the publication of archival photos and reappropriating nationalist iconography. One way the Hijas de Cuauhtémoc reworked nationalist imagery was on the cover page of one of their newspaper editions, which features a drawing of a woman with a machete in her hand (Figure 3.4). In the image the eagle overshadows the woman as she uses her machete to cut herself free, in a metaphor for oppression. This illustrates the signifying practice of disidentification staged on the terrain of nationalism whereby its principal symbols are deployed in a manner that leaves room for alternative readings. H. Villa, the artist who drew the image, was a prisoner who sent his artwork to the women of Las Hijas de Cuauhtémoc with the express purpose that it would be used in their newspaper. Figures I.6 and I.7 also illustrate how Mexican and Chicana nationalist iconography was used by Chicana organizations like the Chicana Welfare Rights Organization, whose reclamation of the eagle eating a serpent on a cactus carried the slogan, "Causa de los Pobres" (Cause of the Poor), or how *Encuentro Femenil* used a similar image of a different woman emerging from the net of oppression without the eagle, wielding a larger machete, an image drawn by Pat Portrera Crary (see Figure I.6).

Beyond the photos of la Soldadera, other images throughout the Chicano movement press began to position women as revolutionary subjects. For example, in an image from *La Raza* (which several of the women wrote for), a Chicana activist is viewed over her shoulder as she reads a newspaper with a huge masthead declaring, "Mujer Como Revolucionaria" (Figure 3.5). This image accompanies the manifestos and position papers produced at the Los Angeles Chicana Regional Conference, which was a preparatory conference for the first-ever national Chicana conference in Houston in 1971. This image changes the dominant tropes in the pedagogy of nationalism to suggest that this revolucionaria has her own sense of political agency and is gaining knowledge about herself as a political subject, mirroring the position of the imagined reader.

In *Hijas de Cuauhtémoc*, one of the most revealing visual patterns is the photo collage, which included photos taken at conferences and events and created a collective Chicana subject of resistance. In Chicana newspapers, as well as a good number of Chicano community papers, the photojournalism

FIGURE 3.4. *Hijas de Cuauhtémoc* 1, front cover art. H. Villa, artist.

illustrates that women represented themselves differently. Along with many Chicano student and community newspapers with a homegrown, or do-it-yourself, style, they put themselves into the narrative of revolution, but instead of using singular low shot images, they used photo collage to create a sense of sisterhood and collaboration, visually representing the forms of female solidarity that they sought to create in their political work. The different use of visuality and images of revolutionary participation created a different mode of address in Chicano movement visual culture, which enlisted or hailed women into the project of liberation on their own terms. This new iconography encouraged women's participation and created new forms of politi-

FIGURE 3.5. "La Mujer como Revolucionaria," Regional Chicana Conference. *La Raza Magazine*, 1971.

cal subjectivity based on a historical consciousness of women's participation in the Mexican Revolution.

Several of the images in women's newspapers also dialogically rework and engender some of the visual tropes that establish male revolutionary patrimony in the Chicano movement. In the report from the Chicana Regional Conference, there is an image that references how women (re)imaged themselves into the legacy of struggle. This shot uses a framing device similar to the Benito Juárez photo mentioned above. Yet this image begins to disrupt the male lineage of nationalist patrimony, by depicting a Chicana Brown Beret as the revolutionary descendant of Che Guevara as she sits below his larger-than-life poster. Along with many other Chicana and Chicano publications where women worked on staff, *Hijas de Cuauhtémoc* offered many other images of women who were dialogically engaged and that resignified other popularized images of women's passivity. Specifically, the image of the Martyr was invoked by women wearing rebozos on their heads but (re)presented in positions on the verge of action—often appearing as if they carried arms or some weapon of resistance under their rebozos.

These images map the migration from suffering, submission, and passivity to active subjects of history and politics. They constituted the emergence of la Nueva Chicana and were common figures in the visual and discursive struggle Chicana feminists engaged in as they created new images, reworked older more traditional representations, and used innovative designs to create new subjectivity. The mode of photo layout and collage—almost like a family album—in the movement newspapers, are illustrative of how Chicanas image themselves collectively. The sequence of images shows the historic development of an iconography of the New Chicana and traces the ways in which women's agency and political subjectivities were constituted in a new image(d) community of Chicana feminists. By tracing the development of New Chicana iconographic practices, we can see how the images of the movement martyr, the revolutionary (m)Other, the Soldadera, and the revolucionaria shift the nationalist representational regime by multiplying the possible subject positions and options for women in the movement.

CONTINUED MOVEMENT, RESURFACING ICONS, AND THE POLITICS OF RE-MEMBERING AND FORGETTING

The photo of the woman bearing bandoleras discussed in this chapter continues to circulate, not just in Chicana/o Studies, but also in popular culture, music, and political culture. But what happens in the circulation and migration of this image? Because movement histories are sites of contemporary identity construction and maintenance, we must be attentive to how modes of remembrance are structured by gender, sexuality, and relations of power in ways that are bound by the historical conjunctures that produce them. Because the "movement" is often constructed as a monolithic and unitary narrative of origins in which the often-bitter struggles of gender and sexuality are forgotten, when it is invoked in an act of remembrance these same structures of gender are reenacted. At other times there are powerful reworkings of these images that create a kind of Chicana feminist retrofitted memory as seen in the Oakland-based graphic artist Favianna Rodriguez's piece *Xicana Power: ¡Viva la Xicana!*

When these images circulate in popular culture, they often come to stand in for the movement and in this instance women in the movement. They are images that evoke powerful narratives that have traveled through time, and they testify to the pull and power of Chicano nationalism. Historically they have erased the mass participation of women in radical movements of the 1960s and 1970s as well as the simultaneous struggles surrounding gender and sexuality that women engaged in while in those movements. The activist, scholar, and historian Angela Y. Davis has written a critical reflection of the ways in which her own image is associated with a kind of black nationalism

FIGURE 3.6. "Xicana Power." Artwork by Favianna Rodriguez, 1999. Courtesy of Favianna Rodriguez.

that she herself contested: "What I am trying to suggest is that contemporary representations of nationalism in African-American and diasporic popular culture are far too frequently reifications of a very complex and contradictory project that had an emancipatory moment leading beyond itself." Suggesting that we explore the "suppressed moments of the history of sixties nationalisms," Davis calls upon the still revolutionary potential of the images, icons, and narratives of the sixties and seventies as they circulate in popular culture when they accurately portray the complexity of those political traditions and legacies. "Young people with 'nationalist' proclivities ought, at least, to have the opportunity to choose which tradition of nationalism they will embrace. How will they position themselves en masse in defense of women's rights and in defense of gay rights if they are not aware of the historical precedents for such positionings?"[87] In recovering the suppressed feminist history of the Chicano movement, the visual terrain is a critical aspect of understanding the role, political work, and legacy of Chicanas in the movement. The visual terrain is critical because if history is knowable only through representation, we can also study representation as a site of historicity and a place in which historical subjectivities were imaged and imagined.

FIGURE I.1. Right from center: Antonia Pichardo, great-grandmother of Anna NietoGomez. Center: Francisca Pichardo de Perez, great-aunt of Anna NietoGomez. Photo taken in Carthage, New Mexico, October 1912. Courtesy of Anna NietoGomez.

FIGURE I.2. Luisa Moreno walking down the street in Mexico. Stanford University, Special Collections.

FIGURE I.3. Josefina Fierro de Bright, Los Angeles, 1940. Stanford University, Special Collections.

FIGURE I.4. Anna NietoGomez, 1977. Photo by Vanessa Nieto Gomez. Courtesy of Anna NietoGomez.

FIGURE 1.5. Anna NietoGomez speaking at a conference, 1973. Courtesy of Anna NietoGomez.

FIGURE 1.6. Front cover of *Encuentro Femenil* 1:1 (1973).

FIGURE 1.7. La Causa de los Pobres, Chicana Welfare Rights Organization. Courtesy of Anna NietoGomez.

FIGURE 1.8. Young Chicanas participating in the Blow Outs. Courtesy of Devra Weber.

FIGURE 1.9. Brown Berets in formation. Courtesy of Devra Weber.

FIGURE I.10. UFW women marching. Courtesy of Devra Weber.

FIGURE I.11. "Brown Is Beautiful," Antiwar Protest August 29, 1970, National Chicano Moratorium.

FIGURE I.12. Garfield High School and, later, Long Beach State student Elvia Arguelles at 1970 Chicano Moratorium (bottom right). Courtesy of Devra Weber.

FIGURE 1.13. Chicana protester. Courtesy of Devra Weber.

FIGURE 1.14. Chicana protesting. Courtesy of Devra Weber.

FIGURE 1.15. Photo of (from left to right) unknown, Gloria Steinem, Cilia Teresa, and Elma Barrera. Courtesy of Elma Barrera.

FIGURE 1.16. "Support Anna Nieto Gomez." © Barbara Carrasco, cover of UCLA's *La Gente*. Courtesy of Barbara Carrasco.

FIGURE I.17. Newspaper table, La Conferencia de Mujeres por la Raza, May 1971. Courtesy of Anna NietoGomez.

FIGURE I.18. La Conferencia de Mujeres por la Raza, May 1971. Courtesy of Anna NietoGomez.

ENGENDERING PRINT CULTURES AND CHICANA FEMINIST COUNTERPUBLICS IN THE CHICANO MOVEMENT

THE PUBLICATION OF *Hijas de Cuauhtémoc* heralded a critical historical moment in the development of Chicana feminist theories and practices. This publication was among the first in the nation dedicated to a Chicana feminist vision, marking a gendered shift in the print culture of the Chicano movement and signaling the growth of Chicana feminist communities locally and translocally. It was an articulation of Chicana feminist political, poetic, and historical vision that had been circulating beneath the surface of the movement. The newspaper theorized and editorialized new forms of feminismo and began to name the interconnections of class, gender, and race through an innovative mixed-genre format that was equal parts journalism, poetry, photography, art, social critique, recovered women's history, and political manifesto.[1] It engaged economic and social issues, political consciousness, Mexicana/Chicana history, campus and community struggles, and Chicana political developments and gave many young activists a voice to express their political insights and visions.

This chapter analyzes print culture as a strategic site of intervention and contestation for women in the Chicano Movement.[2] It explores how members like Anna NietoGomez, Corinne Sánchez, and Martha López extended the reach of *Hijas de Cuauhtémoc*, when they went on to help found and edit *Encuentro Femenil*, the first Chicana feminist journal dedicated to scholarship and activism in 1973. Exploring the text, circulation, and function of *Hijas de Cuauhtémoc* and *Encuentro Femenil*, this chapter examines the formation of a Chicana print community across regions, social movement sectors, activist generations, and social differences. Through print-mediated exchange, new identities, regional and ideological differences, strategies, theories, and practices were debated and discussed in campus and community meetings and at local and national conferences. These ideas were then shared and transformed as editorials, articles, conference proceedings, reports, movement debates, and political position papers, which traveled widely through the process of republication.[3]

I argue that these print mediated discussions not only built new critical interpretive communities; they, along with caucuses and conferences, constituted a Chicana counterpublic.[4] Nancy Fraser conceptualizes counterpublics as parallel discursive arenas where those excluded from dominant discourses "invent and circulate counter discourses, so as to formulate oppositional interpretations of their identities, interests, and needs."[5] Fraser reformulated the notion of the public sphere articulated by Jürgen Habermas in *The Structural Transformation of the Public Sphere*, by arguing that counterpublics contest the "exclusionary norms of the 'official bourgeois public sphere,' elaborating alternative styles of political behavior and alternative norms of public speech."[6] Critically, Fraser located the formation of subaltern counterpublics within new social movements and relied on critical historiographies to inform her understanding of these political processes. Fraser defines the importance of counterpublics by stating "that members of subordinated groups—women, workers, people of color, and lesbians and gays—have repeatedly found it advantageous to constitute alternative counterpublics."[7] My argument develops by tracing the genealogy of Chicana counterpublics and their critical work in making Chicana feminist formations visible in diverse locations, thereby legitimating women's ideas translocally and helping to build cross-regional coalitions.

Although the *Hijas de Cuauhtémoc* newspaper was short-lived—all three issues were published in 1971—the spaces it opened in movement print culture for dialogue on Chicana issues were pivotal.[8] As a critical site of historical inquiry, the Chicana print communities constituted by the circulation of these publications, along with other movement publications, serve as a vantage point to understand the development of Chicana feminist ideology, discourse, and political praxis in a way that accounts for how ideas traveled locally and nationally. Movement print culture functioned as a mediating space where new ideas, theories, and political claims were constructed, negotiated and contested.

The Chicana feminist historian Martha Cotera chronicles the development of Chicana feminist print communities through publications such as *Regeneración, Encuentro Femenil, Hijas de Cuauhtémoc, La Comadre, Fuego de Aztlán, Imagenes de la Chicana, Hembra, Tejidos, La Cosecha* [*De Colores*], and *Hojas Poéticas*, as well as the popular journals *La Luz, Nuestro,* and *El Caracol,* which often featured feminist writings.[9] While a few community publications regularly featured stories on Chicana feminism (such as *Regeneración* and *El Grito del Norte* of New Mexico) and some student movement papers had special issues on women (such as CSUN's *El Popo Femenil* and UC Berkeley's *El Grito*), *Hijas de Cuauhtémoc* was one of the few newspapers in the early years dedicated to Chicanas.[10] Focusing on histories of Mexican feminist activism, women in the movement, and community organizing around key issues such as welfare, employment, and prison, the paper offered an analysis of gender in the racialized and working-class context of Chicanas' lives.[11]

In New Mexico, longtime civil rights activist and former SNCC member, Elizabeth (Betita) Martinez, edited the movement magazine *El Grito del Norte*, along with many other activists in the New Mexican land grant movement, including Enriqueta Longeaux y Vasquez.[12] The longtime activist Francisca Flores and Ramona Morín of the women's auxiliary of G.I. Forum founded the community-based newsletter *La Carta Editorial* in 1963 to report on political activities. Flores, who was a member of the Sleepy Lagoon Defense Committee as a young woman, changed *La Carta Editorial* to magazine format in 1970 and renamed it *Regeneración*.[13] *Regeneración* was known for its news stories on women's organizing in the movement and in the community, op-ed pieces that critiqued the sexism of the Chicano movement, and articles on Chicana history, poetry, and legislation affecting the lives of Chicanas. Chicana print communities documented the submerged but parallel development of Chicana consciousness in women's workshops, caucuses, and auxiliaries. At times these often subversive spaces incited gender insurgencies or the development of strategy and were often effective at transforming an organization from within. At other times these spaces allowed women to develop autonomous political spaces within the Chicano Movement, increasing the organizational density and the ability of the movement to deal with the multiple issues, sources of oppression, and myriad experiences of Chicanas and Chicanos living in the United States. One rich example is Mujeres por la Raza (MPLR), founded in Crystal City in 1970 by women active in La Raza Unida, the Chicano third party. Chicana print communities not only circulated news of what occurred in women's caucus of mixed-gender organizations or conferences; they helped develop continuity between meetings, bridged geographic distances, and continued conversations between meetings.

Weaving the organizational history of the Hijas de Cuauhtémoc and its members between 1968 and 1974 into a larger historical analysis of the emergence of Chicana feminisms, this chapter illustrates the transformation of Chicana consciousness as the newspaper expanded its readership and imagined political community, from local campus politics to community-based organizations to regional and then national audiences. It explores each issue and traces the developments of the newspaper until it was announced as the national voice and print vehicle of Chicana feminists at the first Chicana conference in 1971. In addition, the chapter traces how Chicana print communities developed through the publication of *Encuentro Femenil* in 1973–1974 as early Chicana feminists linked political developments within social movements to intellectual and political debate, forging some of the first Chicana Studies scholarship. It illustrates how Chicana feminist intellectual and journalistic traditions emerged in tandem with community-based organizations. The scope of the chapter tracks shifts in print community strategies through the mid- to late 1970s and traces the legacy of those strategies in alternative print communities that forged a political project through the technology of anthologizing by women of color in the 1970s and 1980s. This epistemological and writing tradition, called "theories of the flesh," named how multiple forms of oppression were experienced and how these experiences could serve as new sites of solidarity and even new desires as epitomized by *This Bridge Called My Back: Writings by Radical Women of Color*, edited by Cherríe Moraga and Gloria Anzaldúa in 1981. Moreover, knowledge production has been intimately tied to the experience of being excluded from multiple social movements and, as Chela Sandoval has theorized, included shifting in and between ideologies to create a differential form of oppositional consciousness for U.S. third world feminism.[14] Others retrofitted those ideologies from within the interstices of class, race, or nation with a gender and sexual analysis, creating what Emma Pérez has called third space feminism.[15] Still others blended all the political traditions they were excluded from to create a hybrid form of what Anzaldúa called mestiza consciousness.[16]

CHICANA PRINT CULTURE: GENDERING IMAGINED COMMUNITIES OF THE NATION

Benedict Anderson's influential conceptualization of nation as an imagined community has been effectively taken up to produce new insights about social movements and communities of resistance. Reconfiguring this formulation for the historical specificity of anticolonial nationalisms, Partha Chatterjee, a historian involved in the Subaltern Studies Group, maintains that it is not through conflict with the state but in the cultural realm that prefigures this struggle where decolonizing nationalist imaginaries are constituted.[17] He argues that anticolonial nationalism creates a domain of sovereignty in colonial society and that this domain is produced through "an entire institutional network of printing presses, publishing houses, newspapers, [and] magazines . . . created . . . outside the purview of the state . . . through which the new language [of nationalist liberation] . . . is given shape."[18]

Whereas other third world movements for national liberation aimed to overthrow the colonial state, the Chicano movement contested state power and its violence, discrimination, and lack of channels of representation.[19] Chicano cultural nationalism was a form of decolonizing nationalism where the circulation of print media in the form of student and community newspapers, political pamphlets, and movement magazines played a formative role. The formation of Chicana and Chicano print communities coincided with the movimiento imperative to create alternative knowledge, parallel institutions, and cultural formations.[20]

While Chatterjee illustrates how domains of cultural and social sovereignty are vital spaces of articulating an anticolonial political imaginary, questions of gender, race, and sexuality have historically been overlooked in theories of (anticolonial) nationalism. Emma Pérez's work on "sexing the decolonial imaginary" gives us tools to understand the complex ways in which questions of gender and sexuality are embedded in the processes of articulating political subjectivity and the project of decolonization.[21] The *Hijas de Cuauhtémoc* newspaper broke down the unitary concept of the citizen-subject of Aztlán as male, thereby diversifying and multiplying the subjects of resistance enlisted in the Chicana/o project of liberation.

Along with many other publications from California, New Mexico, and Texas, the gendered print community constituted by means of the circulation of *Hijas de Cuauhtémoc* was vital to the creation of Chicana feminist movement networks and alliances. Through the late 1960s and early 1970s, new forms of print media and newspapers emerged to get out the word about the ongoing struggles of the Chicano movement. Chicana activists participated in these modes of print communication and began to create new ones, ultimately forming a parallel Chicana counterpublic that multiplied the spaces of participation for women and gendered analysis.[22] Members of the Hijas de Cuauhtémoc recall the critical role of print communities in the political work of consciousness raising. It was common for each campus and/or community organization to have some form of publication and study group or political education program. Through movement print culture and the exchange of reading materials, each group knew what the other groups were doing and thinking. This was crucial to the ideological development of Chicana/o political community and the constitution of a shared political imaginary. Anna NietoGomez recalls, "We exposed each other to new ideas, networked, and dialogued about refining ideology. We did this through dialogue with different campus institutions: UCLA history, Cal State L.A. history with Marxist tendencies, UC San Diego's third world perspective. Paulo Freire was a model, as was Frantz Fanon's *Wretched of the Earth*."[23]

This endeavor is illustrated by the proliferation of Chicano newspapers, artistic magazines such as *Con Safos* and *ChismeArte*, and community-based publications, many of which came together as the Chicano Press Association (CPA). The CPA emerged during the late 1960s as the number of independent Chicano newspapers increased greatly and served to link a wide variety of publications throughout the nation. Although without a central office, officers, or an official membership, this loose federation of Chicano newspapers came together to fight the ways in which the Chicano community was constantly ignored in the mainstream press, with a few notable exceptions, including the *Los Angeles Times* reporter Ruben Salazar, who was killed during the Chicano Moratorium by a deputy of the Los Angeles County Sheriff's Department. The first CPA conference was held in early 1968 in Albuquerque, New Mexico, where over fifty Chicano newspapers were represented. This coalition of underground Chicano press included *La Raza, El Grito del Norte, El Gallo, Inside Eastside, Chicano Student Movement, El Malcriado, Compass, Infierno, Lado, El Paisano, La Voz Mexicana, Los Muertos Hablan, Revolución, El Popo, El Machete,* and *La Hormiga,* in addition to others that went in and out of print. According to Raul Ruiz, "If you published a newspaper and you were Chicano and you printed the names and addresses of the other newspapers then you simply became a member."[24]

All the women involved in the Hijas de Cuauhtémoc drew from their experience writing for Chicano student movement newspapers such as Long Beach State's *El Alacrán* or from working for community newspapers and magazines such as *La Raza,* the premier movement newspaper in Southern California. NietoGomez described the explosive events of the moment and the imperative to "get the word out": "A lot of things were going on in L.A. at the time: the East L.A. Blowouts, picketing, the Biltmore Seven, and there was *La Raza* community newspaper. . . . As part of a stated political agenda of linking campus to community, they would ask the college students to get involved and work on the newspaper at night. I would go to community meetings and then write up a report for the newspaper the next day. It was very exciting, and I learned a lot."[25]

CONFERENCES AND COUNTERPUBLICS

The practice of publishing conference proceedings and continuing debates in print served not only as an important mode of circulation but also as a mode of contestation. This is exemplified in the circulation of the infamous statement from the 1969 Denver Youth Liberation Conference, organized by Rodolfo "Corky" Gonzales and the Crusade for Justice, declaring that it was the consensus of the Chicana caucus that "the Chicana does not want to be liberated." While many consider the conference where *El Plan Espiritual de Aztlán* was adopted a defining moment of the Chicano movement, "Chicana activists raised the issue of the traditional role of the Chicana in the movement, and how it limited her capabilities and her development."[26] The representative of the caucus, when it was time to present the workshop report to the full conference, stated, "It was the consensus of the group that the Chicana woman does not want to be liberated." Some activists who were at the caucus meeting were shocked to hear this proclamation at the final plenary because, contrary to the statement, at the meeting of the women's caucus strategies for gaining fuller participation for women within the movement were widely discussed.[27] This statement illustrates the contested and contestatory nature of Chicana feminism and the difficulty of articulating a new kind of Chicana political subject within the confines of an emergent, masculinist nationalism. The declaration on the floor of the Denver Youth Liberation Conference also points to what I call hidden gender insurgencies, where subversive spaces were constituted in the movement's organizational structures, largely through women's caucuses, which kept the focus on the question of the inequality of women. When direct confrontation on women's issues was not tactically possible and not politically strategic, many demands were negotiated below the surface of public movement spaces.

Enriqueta Longeaux y Vasquez published a 1969 article in *El Grito del Norte* in response to this incident, which was widely reprinted.

> While attending a Raza conference in Colorado this year, I went to one of the workshops that were being held to discuss the role of the Chicana woman. When the time came for the women to make the presentation to the full conference, the only thing that the workshop representative said was this: "It was the consensus of the group that the Chicana does not want to be liberated." As a woman who has been faced with having to live as a member of the "Mexican-American" minority as a breadwinner and a mother raising children, living in housing projects and having much concern for other humans leading to much community involvement, this was quite a blow. I could have cried.[28]

Sonia López, in her study of Chicanas in the student movement, observes, "This outcome can be viewed in two ways: either the majority of Chicanas attending the conference did not see or understand the contradiction of the sexual roles between Chicanas and Chicanos, or they simply did not want to alienate the men."[29] Beatríz Pesquera, who attended the caucus meeting, discussed how this statement functioned as a distancing mechanism from the largely white and middle-class women's liberation movement. Pesquera, in contrast, recalled that the conference was one of the first events where Chicanos from across the country got together en masse and even at the beginning Chicanas were there to formulate their own political vision and discuss how to eradicate barriers to their participation in the struggle for Chicana liberation.

Betita Martinez recalls the conference as "pulsating with energy, music, and chants. [It was pure] excitement all these people together. It was very positive! The thing I remember most, however, is this women's workshop where [there were] 50 to 70 women together, [all] Chicanas! On the one hand, women were doing the work. They were often in the leadership; they had a lot of the ideas, and at the same time they were often consistently expected to make the food, to do typing, clerical work." While the women's caucus agreed to equality between men and women, they rejected the idea of creating a separate organization, and the consensus that the "Chicana does not want to be liberated" was an effort to signal that solidarity. But, Martinez argues, "that was as much a rejection of the women's liberation movement of those years, which was seen as, and in many ways was, overwhelmingly middle-class and Anglo women, white women, who did not understand racist oppression, did not understand oppression of people half of whom are male."[30] Although the results and representation of what occurred at the workshop were contradictory to the experience of the women who attended it, this meeting served as the basis for the continued work of Chicanas in women's caucuses.

Even two years later, in the 1971 publication of the newspaper, dialogue on the issues women initiated at the conference continued. The immediate response that was issued by Longeaux y Vasquez, originally printed in *El Grito del Norte* (1969), was widely reprinted in forums such as Robin Morgan's *Sisterhood Is Powerful* (1970) and the first issue of *Hijas de Cuauhtémoc* (1971), which also included a response by Anna NietoGomez titled "Chicanas Identify!"

This statement implies that any problems that a Chicana speaks of are not her problems but Anglo ideas and therefore threatens her people, La Raza. To take it a step further, it implies that the Chicana has no right to spend time on problems she faces because unique problems of a special group are disruptive to the unity of the movement. This is not and cannot be true. . . . Being compared to Anglo women has been the greatest injustice and the strongest device used to keep Chicanas quiet. . . . No Chicana who has worked in the movement deserved to be compared with any Anglo woman or Gay Liberation. These comparisons are divisive and threatening to the strength of the movement.[31]

The infamous statement at the Denver Youth Liberation Conference can be seen in part as a reaction to the vendida logic. The irony of the antifeminist rhetoric of the statement is that the caucus itself advanced a position that called for the emancipation of Chicanas. Yet activists were so busy defending themselves against the charges that feminism was whitewashed or lesbian that they did not always disrupt the underlying heteropatriarchal assumptions of those charges. Dialogue was initiated immediately and taken up around the country. The practice of publishing conference proceedings, debates, and conflicts was crucial to crafting venues that promoted critically needed conversations about women's struggles. Chicana print culture constructed interpretive communities, which served as spaces to build and discuss not only different political positions but also the multiple political and regional meanings of Chicana identities. The fact that contending perspectives and controversial pieces were included in the publication of the Hijas newspaper illustrates that Chicana print communities were not unified discursive fields but sites of construction and contestation.

Efforts to distinguish and distance Chicana feminism from the Anglo women's movement continued after the 1969 Denver Youth Liberation Conference. Echoing the idea of double militancia, NietoGomez wrote, "If the Anglo women's movement (AWM) saw itself as an independent force for social change, Las Femenisitas [*sic*] see their fight against sexual oppression as part of the struggle of her people."[32] *Hijas de Cuauhtémoc* published a lengthy analysis of the differences between the two movements, and many other writers reflected on these differences, including Martha Cotera in her essays "Feminism as We See It," "Among the Feminists: Racist and Classist Issues," and, later, "Feminism, the Chicana and Anglo Versions: An Historical Analysis."[33] Cotera writes, "Any feelings or sympathy toward feminism must have its force directed inward and its expression structured con consciencia de nuestras necesidades y apsiraciones [with a consciousness of our needs and aspirations]. It cannot be a contrary separatist course or be directed by non-Chicano terminology or leadership."[34] Such examples demonstrate that Chicana feminism—in its community and academic forms—has developed as part of a larger project of liberation of Chicana and Chicano communities, not outside it.

BUILDING COALITIONS AND TRANSLOCAL STRATEGIES

The translocal strategy and technology of republication helped to forge a new political subjectivity of la Nueva Chicana through critical dialogues that constructed multiple meanings, locations, and practices.[35] The kind of translocalism I am identifying here more precisely involves how actors who are often multiply marginalized create linkages with social actors across locales in order to build new affiliations and solidarities and create imagined political communities. *Hijas de Cuauhtémoc*, along with other publications, provided a forum for Chicanas to dialogue across regions and social movement sectors, which was crucial to the formation of a Chicana counterpublic. *Hijas de Cuauhtémoc* ran articles by Chicanas around the country, including Rosita Morales's "La mujer todavía impotente," originally published in Spanish in Houston's *Papel Chicano*. The republication of articles circulated diverse Chicana political ideas in a multitude of places, formats, and modes that crossed regional political traditions and was an important translocal strategy to formulate shared political demands. In fact, a primary mode of translocal dialogue happened when local community papers would reprint articles from across regions and across different social movements, as exemplified by the reprinting of an *Hijas de Cuauhtémoc* article by a local women's movement paper in Eugene, Oregon, as well as in *El Young Lord*, the newspaper of a chapter of the Young Lords Party.[36] These discussions, discursive formations, and strategies traveled and were transformed by differing geographic and political communities through the process of republication.

This mode of circulation and the emergence of a translocal Chicana feminist counterpublic is described by the Tejana activist Martha Cotera, who, reflecting back on the movement, acknowledged the impact of California Chicana feminist writings for Tejanas organizing in La Raza Unida Party (RUP). Speaking of Anna NietoGomez, Cotera states, "Well, you know, it was Anna's articles that always got us what we wanted from the men [in Texas]."[37] Revealing a tactic used in local struggles to press for their demands, Cotera recalls that Tejana activists would draw upon the most forthright feminist writings from California as a strategy to represent their call for women's leadership, in keeping with other national developments. This tactic also played upon underlying regional differences in the Chicano movement at a time when Chicana feminist dialogues navigated ideological differences over how to organize suitable strategies for different political contexts and regional variations.[38] Not only was this tool used to increase pressure for women's demands in different regional contexts, but it served to spread ideas across geographic regions.

This strategy also fortified feminist political convictions and forged solidarity for activists whose ideas were often forcefully challenged in the beginning. In the student movement it gave women a place to move in and through, and sometimes outside of, nationalist discourse and created a space where sexism within the movement could be challenged. The students involved in the Hijas de Cuauhtémoc endured a great amount of harassment, scorn, and criticism: NietoGomez was hung in effigy, and other leaders of the organization were buried in a mock burial. All the women I interviewed described the ostracism they encountered regardless of whether they defined themselves as feministas. Their detractors made a range of claims, including that they were on an "Anglo bourgeoisie trip," were *agringadas* (Anglo-cized)," or "malinches." In relation to these forms of silencing, Pesquera and Segura write:

> Chicanas who deviated from a nationalist political stance were subjected to negative sanctions including being labeled vendida [sell-outs], or agabachadas [white identified]. . . . Once labeled thus, they became subject to marginalization within Chicano Movement organizations.[39]

Citing Martha Cotera's observation that "[being called a feminist] was a good enough reason for not listening to some of the most active women in the community," Pesquera and Segura argue that "such social and political sanctions discouraged women from articulating feminist issues," resulting in what I have been calling the vendida logic, where activists felt compelled to adopt an antifeminist discourse in order to be taken seriously. Feminist baiting was most often articulated as lesbian baiting, revealing the patriarchal doubling that polices gender and sexuality.

Due to criticism and sometimes outright harassment Chicana feminists faced in the movement, print communities were fundamental in forging an alternative Chicana public sphere by reconfiguring movement spaces, not operating outside them. Chicana activists in California keenly watched the developments in Tejas and followed developments through the movement press. Of specific interest were the women activists such as Luz Gutiérrez and Virginia Muzquiz, who helped to found La Raza Unida Party on January 17, 1970. Other Chicana activists, including Ino Álvarez, Evey Chapa, and Martha Cotera, who were central in the local organizing committees and ran as candidates, helped formalize women's presence in the party by forming Mujeres por la Raza (MPLR).[40] "When RUP held its first state convention in San Antonio in October 1971, women comprised 31 of the 104 delegates, likely a result of the caucus's actions."[41] In an article in *Caracol* magazine, Evey Chapa argued that mujeres have always been active in La Raza Unida Party, doing much of the work necessary for the creation of an alternative third political party. As a member of the MPLR, she helped draft the RUP platform, which guaranteed equal rights for all women and included provisions on the political education and recruitment of women to increase their presence in decision making.[42] Women also participated in the leadership of the RUP.

Virginia Musquiz became national chair from 1972 to 1974, and Maria Elena Martinez was state chair from 1976 to 1978. The Mujeres por la Raza Unida began to hold their own conferences beginning in 1973.

REGIONAL ORGANIZING AND
LAS HIJAS DE CUAUHTÉMOC

Although the first issue of the newspaper was primarily concerned with Chicanas at Cal State Long Beach, the publication strategy of *Hijas de Cuauhtémoc* coincided with their growing presence in regional organizing.[43] The second issue was published as a regional organizing tool leading up to the Los Angeles Chicana Educational Conference, which was preparatory to the first national Chicana conference, La Conferencia de Mujeres por la Raza, to be held in Houston in May 1971. While there had been one women's conference, the Corazón de Aztlán symposium held at UCLA on November 25, 1969, featuring Alicia Hernández and Susan Racho (MEChA de UCLA), Gerry Gonzalez (Crusade for Sustained Justice), Enriqueta Longeaux y Vasquez and Betita Martinez (from New Mexico), and Dolores Huerta (UFW), the Hijas membership realized there was little contact or communication in California between Chicanas.[44] As a remedy to this situation, they joined with the Chicana group at CSU Los Angeles to organize the Chicana Educational Conference and invited "Chicanas from the high schools, the community, the Pinta [prison] and the colleges." When 250 Chicanas attended, they realized that the newspaper needed to move beyond campus and become broader in scope in order to mobilize statewide communication. This marked a shift in the role of the newspaper as it became a regional forum for Chicanas, and the subsequent issue was planned to present the results from the Southern California conference to the National Conference. The third issue reported that the May regional conference was organized around five workshops and began with performances by las Adelitas and Teatro de las Chicanas, a poetry reading of "Yo soy Chicana de Aztlán" by Sara Estrella, and an hour-long lecture titled "History of La Mexicana." The published proceedings of the conference included reports from the following workshops: Philosophy of La Chicana Nueva; Chicanas in Education; La Chicana y la Comunidad (including welfare rights, child care, and consumer education); Chicana and Communication (which strategized around the need for a common statewide newspaper, the collection and distribution of Chicana literatures, and regional financial support for the statewide paper); and Political Education of La Chicana (which touched on the issues of Chicanas/Chicanos and the war, Chicanos in a capitalist society, and the ideology of the movement).[45] The conference ended with a session that compiled all the ideas from the workshops and formulated them into a platform for the National conference. It was followed by a dance at which the Fabulous Sounds played.[46]

The Hijas de Cuauhtémoc pooled their earnings to publish their third issue and held several fund-raising activities to pay for their trip to the Conferencia de Mujeres por la Raza in Houston. Community members donated station wagons to transport the women from Los Angeles to Houston. They struggled to gather resources, but finally some twelve women, ranging in age from eighteen to twenty-five, from CSU Long Beach, CSU Los Angeles, and Los Angeles City College piled into the station wagons and began their long journey across the desert. For many it was the first odyssey away from home alone.

The Hijas de Cuauhtémoc and other representatives from the Los Angeles regional conference prepared to participate in the national conference by developing a regional platform. They came armed with the newspaper, which contained the ideas and resolutions of the regional meeting, in addition to their five-point plan of "Hermanidad." The gendered print community the Hijas de Cuauhtémoc were constructing had been getting larger with each issue, so by the first day of the 1971 Houston conference, when Chicanas from all over the country met, they passed a resolution naming *Hijas de Cuauhtémoc* the national paper for Chicana activists through which they planned to forge a national Chicana organization.

BUILDING A CHICANA COUNTERPUBLIC: *ENCUENTRO FEMENIL* AND COMMUNITY-BASED ORGANIZING

While no issues of *Hijas de Cuauhtémoc* were published after 1971, the political project of its members continued through the formation of the first journal of Chicana scholarship, *Encuentro Femenil*, published in spring 1973. The preface to the first volume states:

> Hijas de Cuauhtémoc is a feminist group with the education of Raza women as their primary goal. Fully aware that feminism should not be viewed as any type of disadvantage, but rather as a means of recognizing one's full and total capabilities, the HIJAS founded the "ENCUENTRO FEMENIL" Journal, which now has evolved into a totally independent publication. Realizing that our struggle is racial as well as sexual, we, as Raza women, could in no way fight for feminism without it being an effort on behalf of our people. Through ENCUENTRO FEMENIL, we would like to see the efforts of enlightened women bring about positive alternatives for change.

The journal's editorial staff included Hijas de Cuauhtémoc members Anna NietoGomez, Martha López, and Corinne Sánchez, as well as the Los Angeles–area activists Adelaida R. Del Castillo and Francine Holcom. Other Hijas members who collaborated on photography or public relations included Cindy Honesto and Norma J. Owen. Del Castillo recalled her participation this way:

> In 1969 I became an UMAS-MEChA member at the University of California, Los Angeles. . . . [I]n 1971, I left school and worked with a group of Chicana feminists who published *Encuentro Femenil* in 1973 and 1974. For myself, as for many others, experiences such as these initiated valuable insight into racism and sexism in this country and contributed to the effective political direction of the growing activism of the Chicano Movement.[47]

Continuing to use print to create a counterpublic, the journal served as an important space for autonomous Chicana cultural production and the emergence of Chicana feminist scholarship that was deeply embedded in community-based Chicana organizing. For example, Del Castillo's essay, "Malintzín Tenépal: A Preliminary Look into a New Perspective" (1974), published in the second issue, was one of the first to demystify la Malinche as a symbol of female betrayal. The first issue contains an interview with Alicia Escalante, an East Los Angeles leader in organizing poor women's movements (Madres por Justicia), an article written by Anna NietoGomez outlining the plan for a Chicana Studies program, and articles dedicated to labor issues and Chicana feminist thinking.[48]

This period also witnessed the growth of Chicana community and political organizations as a result of the pioneering efforts of a few activists who built the foundation throughout the 1960s as well as the War on Poverty.[49] The publication of *Encuentro Femenil* not only documented the political mobilization of Chicanas; it fostered new forms of Chicana political solidarity and participation. Organizations that emerged in this period included the Chicana Welfare Rights Organization, founded by Alicia Escalante in 1967, and the Comisión Femenil Mexicana Nacional, founded by Francisca Flores and Simmie Romero at the Women's Workshop of the Mexican American National Issues Conference in 1970. Campus and community alliances were forged the next year when a Comisión Femenil Mexicana chapter was established on the campus of California State College, Los Angeles.[50] Chicanas mobilized across the country, and many new organizations began to form, including the National Chicana Political Caucus, MARA (a Chicana prison organization at the California Institute for Women), the formation of a Chicana caucus at the 1970 Chicano Coordinating Council on Higher Education

(CCCHE) meeting in San Diego, and finally the women's caucus of La Raza Unida Party in Texas in 1973.

COMMUNITY ORGANIZING AND THE EMERGENCE OF CHICANA FEMINIST SCHOLARSHIP

Chicana public spheres were forged and expanded by linking community and political organizations and Chicana print. Anna NietoGomez formed alliances with the longtime labor activist Francisca Flores, publisher of *Regeneración* and founder of Comisión Femenil Mexicana, which opened the Chicana Service Action Center in East L.A. She also began working closely with Alicia Escalante, who founded the Chicana Welfare Rights Organization.

Alicia Escalante, born in El Paso, Texas, grew up knowing poverty.[51] At the age of ten she relocated with her mother to Los Angeles, where she had her first experience with the welfare system. Recalling the harsh treatment that her mother received from the "Anglo" social worker, Escalante explained, "Her whole attitude towards my mother was one of hostility. I sensed prejudice; I sensed that she could have done something more than to give her tokens. And I hated her for stripping my mother of her pride, who was kind, good, struggling to survive."[52]

Living in a housing project from 1958 through 1968, Escalante was forced by economic necessity to go on and off welfare various times while she raised her children as a single mother. Through her negative experiences with public assistance while seeking care for her daughter's health problems, Escalante began attending protests against then-Governor Ronald Reagan's Medi-Cal cutbacks.[53] Along with other welfare mothers Escalante founded the East Los Angeles Welfare Rights Organization in 1967.[54] She attributes the founding of the organization to the negative experiences women in her community faced and the insights she gained by attending Los Angeles chapter meetings of the National Welfare Rights Organization (NWRO) run by the longtime welfare activist Johnnie Tillmon. The NWRO had fought against Medi-Cal cutbacks in California that had seriously affected her family. Escalante also recalled:

> In addition, there was always the problem of assigned social workers not informing welfare recipients of their legal rights. The NWRO inspired me to organize our neighbors and friends in the barrio who were also affected by the cutbacks, but who were unaware of their rights as recipients.[55]

Founded by George Wiley in 1965, the NWRO leadership was male, although African American women formed the base of the organization.[56] Like many local chapters of the NWRO, the Los Angeles chapter was led by women who had begun organizing in 1961 as the ANC (Aid to Needy Children) Mothers in the Watts area of Los Angeles years before the national organization was founded.[57] Although the East L.A. Welfare Rights Organization (ELAWRO) had its early beginnings with the NWRO, the organization quickly split with its national counterpart. Escalante asserts that the Chicano Movement had considerable influence over the organization: "We chose to place more emphasis on the special needs and problems of the Chicano communities. It was for this reason that a break was made from the national organization. Though basically the same goals were kept, the operation of the Chicana Welfare Rights Organization had been more in keeping with our culture and tradition."[58]

Escalante secured office space for the organization, and welfare mothers themselves ran the office on a volunteer basis. The structure of the organization was described as a "familia," and if the organization was in need of funds the women would sell tamales and menudo. The mission of the ELAWRO was to inform Chicana welfare mothers of their rights, and they advocated for the translation of welfare forms into Spanish. In addition, the organization fought to establish new welfare offices in Spanish-speaking communities and demanded that the Department of Social Services hire bilingual and bicultural social workers. Advocates attempted to remove obstacles to communication between the welfare system and the people it was attempting to serve. The women began to familiarize themselves with the policies and regulations of the welfare system and to learn how to navigate the bureaucracy on local, state, and federal levels, which were often not in communication with each other—to the detriment of welfare recipients. Escalante explained their tactics involving advocacy, research, and mobilization:

> Whenever there were discrepancies at the local level, we documented them and brought it to the attention of the administrators. We would ask to meet with the director of welfare and if he tried to avoid meeting with us, we would go to the county board of supervisors. We would write politicians concerning issues like the Talmadge law, or pilot projects affecting large communities. We would undertake surveys and conduct research. And if we had to, we would take the county to court. We tried to pursue an issue until it was resolved.[59]

The Talmadge Amendment to the Social Security Act of 1973 would have required mothers on public assistance with children over six years of age to register with the state employment office and report every two weeks until they found a job, but, as usual, it proved shortsighted and had no child care provisions. The organization critiqued the idea of forced labor and articulated the right of mothers to be with their young children. NietoGomez was a member of the Chicana Welfare Rights Organization, and her alliance with Escalante is documented in their collaborative publication, "Canto de Alicia," based on Escalante's testimony on welfare abuses, as well as her article, "Madres por Justicia!!" both published in *Encuentro Femenil*. In order to help mobilize the opposition to the Talmadge Amendment, NietoGomez published an article titled, "What Is the Talmadge Amendment?" in *Regeneración*. Francisca Flores's "A Reaction to the Discussions on the Talmadge Amendment to the Social Security Act" in *Regeneración* was reprinted in *Encuentro Femenil*. Because of her long history as a labor activist, Flores encouraged the ELAWRO to reframe its resistance to the amendment, away from the right of welfare mothers to stay at home with their children to a broader conceptualization of the rights of all workers to have adequate child care and a living wage for working mothers.[60] Escalante and the board members and Advisory Committee of the ELAWRO published a response in which they took issue with Flores's comments and defended their focus on welfare mothers: "In fact, it is the Welfare mother and her family who has practically been 'singled out' by the system as a target for elimination from the Welfare rolls. . . . The main issue here is obviously the right of those on government aid to be able to check and prohibit any encroachments the government might make, in exchange for the aid, on these individual's civil liberties."[61] In addition to the demands Flores suggested (child care, increased minimum wage, and increased job opportunities), the Chicana Welfare Rights Organization called for meaningful training, a civil service requirement to allow welfare recipients to become county employees, compensatory stipends for bilingual workers, a community children's center that would be bicultural and bilingual, and the participation of welfare recipients on the State Social Welfare Board.[62] We can see through this collaboration among community organizers and activist writers and scholars how the early Chicana print community worked in tandem with community-based struggles, serving both as a form of community pedagogy and as a Chicana feminist politics of knowledge production, debate, and distribution.

The ELAWRO had accomplished many things by 1974. Their efforts opened up entry-level positions for welfare recipients in the welfare system, and they participated in the hiring of new social workers. New welfare offices were built in the heart of the barrio and were staffed by bilingual and bicultural social workers and staff. The organization fought diligently against the Talmadge Amendment, though with little success, and a Supreme Court ruling in 1974 declared that the welfare system no longer had to translate the documents into Spanish.

A critical link between the older generation of Mexican American women activists of the 1940s and 1950s and the emergence of a younger generation of Chicana activists in the 1960s and 1970s was Francisca Flores. Coming of age in San Diego during the period of the Mexican Revolution, Flores met many veterans of the revolution and exiled Mexican leftists, labor activists, and socialists during an extended stay at the sanitarium as she recovered from tuberculosis during her teenage and young adult years.[63]

Following her release from the sanitarium in 1939, Flores moved to Los Angeles, where she became active in leftist political organizations such as El Congreso de Pueblos de Hablan Española (the Spanish-Speaking Peoples Congress), the Mexican American labor and civil rights organization founded in 1938 by Josefina Fierro de Bright, Bert Corona, and Luisa Moreno. In addition to her previously mentioned involvement with the Sleepy Lagoon Defense Committee, she aided Carey McWilliams with his early publication, *North from Mexico* (1949). Flores worked on the campaigns to elect Edward Roybal to the Los Angeles City Council in the late 1940s and to the U.S. Congress in 1963 through her involvement with the Eastside Democratic Club. In addition, she was one of cofounders of the Mexican American Political Association (MAPA) in 1960.[64]

Within Chicana/o print communities in Los Angeles, Flores's work as a writer, publisher, and organizer was generative. She first worked on *Carta Perales*, an eastside news journal later titled *Carta Editorial*, which was published between 1963 and 1969. From 1968 to 1975 Flores served as editor of the Chicano movement magazine *Regeneración* (1970–1975), known as a vital forum for reporting the discrimination and police brutality that exploded on the eastside streets following the famous 1970 Chicano Moratorium and the death of Ruben Salazar and for its political analysis and consistent commitment to Chicana rights.[65]

During the mid-1960s Flores was involved with the women's auxiliary of the G.I. Forum. She worked to increase Mexican American women's political involvement. To advance this cause she founded, with Ramona Morín, the California League of Mexican American Women (LMAW) in 1966, a precursor to the Comisión Femenil Mexicana Nacional (CFMN), founded in 1970 at the Mexican American National Issues Conference in Sacramento.[66] According to the Chicana historian Marisela Chávez, "After the 1970 conference, the Comisión established its base of operations in Los Angeles, building upon work already begun by LMAW."[67] Aware of the existing social and political climate for women of Mexican descent, Flores did not see a Chicana organization such as CFMN as a threat to the movimiento but rather as something that would strengthen it. Flores emphasized, "We expect that this great force of women power will give the movement one great *empuje* [push] to raise it one giant step higher in the drive for liberation."[68] The organization would grow to over twenty chapters nationwide by the late 1970s.[69] CFMN's main objectives were to formulate leadership among Chicanas so that they could become active leaders in their community, disseminate information relevant to Chicanas, develop methods of problem solving for Chicanas and Mexicanas, and network with other women's organizations and movements. In addition, beginning in 1971 Flores began to edit the *CFM Report*, the newsletter of the Comisión Femenil Mexicana. As the first president of CFMN and as the editor of several publications, Francisca Flores became one of the leading advocates for Chicana rights and an important voice of the Chicana movement. With the founding of the Chicana Service Action Center (CSAC), the tradition of the *CFM Report* continued in the *CSAC Newsletter*, which Flores began editing in 1973.

The founders of *Encuentro Femenil* formed alliances with Los Angeles Chicana leaders in order to document community issues and struggles and build greater political knowledge of these issues among a larger Chicana/o political community so that policies and institutions would be more responsive. For example, Corinne Sánchez, who has a long history of involvement and is currently the CEO of a multiservice community center in the San Fernando Valley called Proyecto del Barrio, worked with Flores to organize the CSAC, the first employment training center for Chicanas in East L.A. These rich links and the collaboration with the CSAC were documented in NietoGomez's article, "Chicanas in the Labor Force," which was published in *Encuentro Femenil*.[70] The article stated that 57 percent of Chicanas over the age of fourteen were in the labor force, but, "because the Chicana may suffer from sex discrimination as well as from racial discrimination, the Chicana's income is at the bottom of the economic ladder."[71] Finding that the median income of Chicanos was nearly three times higher than that of Chicanas, the article placed the work of the CSAC in context with national data finding that at the CSAC "53% of the Chicanas were found in low status, low paying jobs such as domestic workers, cleaning, laundry and food service, in addition to factory work." Further, the study found that "at the Chicana Service Action Center of Los Angeles, 50% of the Chicanas looking for work are unskilled and untrained women under the age of 30 years."[72]

The CSAC, founded in 1972 in the Boyle Heights neighborhood of East Los Angeles, was the result of a grant the Comisión Femenil Mexicana Nacional received from the Department of Labor.[73] The CSAC provided employment training, counseling, placement, and referral. That same year the CFMN incorporated with nonprofit status in order to receive moneys from the Department of Labor. The mission or goal of the CSAC was self-improvement and to organize and inform la mujer about her ability to become a leader in the community and and her rights as a worker and a woman. Eventually a rift developed between the CSAC and the national governing board of CFMN over the board's insistence on overseeing the operation of the CSAC and personal conflicts. These tensions ended in the CSAC becoming independently incorporated in 1975. Corinne Sánchez states:

> We had a newsletter and also developed a chapter of Latinas under Comisión [CFMN]. We split off from the main chapter; we were the East L.A. chapter. We organized apart from the Chicana Center, but we were all a part of the Chicana Center, many of us. A lot of us were Long Beach State people.[74]

During this process of growth, a rift had been growing between the CFMN governing board and the CSAC board and staff. After becoming an independent entity, the CSAC expanded its services to the Bell neighborhood, and the following year, 1976–1977, the CSAC was allocated more funds to permanently expand its program to Van Nuys and to establish a new training program for jobs traditionally held by men.

Movement work through publication and analysis was also carried out with the Mexican American Research Association (MARA), founded in 1970 as an advocacy and support group for women in the California Institute for Women (CIW) in Frontera, the only state prison for female felons, which housed one of the largest populations in the country.[75] MARA advocated for the Chicana, "through this association, [to] learn not only about Chicano pride and determination, but about herself and how she fits in the world outside. She knows that when she leaves the institution she is not alone, she has the support of the community and the group still inside."[76] The membership base of this association consisted of inmates, parolees, community members, and students. *Hijas de Cuauhtémoc* published an article discussing the situation of incarcerated Chicanas and those who had been released or were on emergency leave: "At this time there are currently no programs set up specifically to help Chicanas leaving the prison." For example, MARA gathered with other women at the COPA conference to discuss solutions to the lack of options for Chicanas on leaving prison. In "coordination with Mr. and Mrs. Valdez, sponsors of MARA in the California Institute for Women are working to develop an Emergency Fund and a house for La Chicana."[77] Through the technology of republication discussed earlier in this chapter, this *Hijas de Cuauhtémoc* article was reprinted in the 1971 Chicana special edition of *El Grito del Norte* in New Mexico. Later René Mares, who was the director of

Associated Studies at UCLA from 1972 to 1973 and a volunteer teacher for Chicanas at the CIW, wrote "La Pinta: The Myth of Rehabilitation," in *Encuentro Femenil*.[78]

Chicanas constituted 11 percent of the total population of CIW, and they fell into two categories: those charged with felonies or girls under the age of eighteen originally assigned to the California Youth Authority who had been transferred to the prison for "disruptive" behavior. The majority of the CIW population had been convicted of drug offenses, and about 85 percent of all Chicanas were "convicted for narcotics offenses or related drug offenses." MARA was dedicated to documenting issues incarcerated Chicanas faced, such as low attendance in vocational and educational classes because the materials were outdated and not relevant to the Chicano experience. In addition, no individual instruction was given and many Chicanas needed tutoring in order to pass the classes. This resulted in "Chicanas choosing to work in the kitchen, on the yard, in the laundry or in the garment factory." MARA also advocated for Chicana women with children in relation to placement and family care, in a context in which state agencies usually broke families up. They also helped secure rides for family members out to CIW, located forty miles from Los Angeles. They argued, "Pintas and Pintos alike are calling for a more humane and just revaluation of the present penal code. The primary focus has centered on the issues of 'indeterminate sentence.'" For example, a woman who was sentenced to serve one to ten years could be held indefinitely until the Women's Board of Terms and Parole determined the length of time to be served. A Chicana serving time in CIW explained the impact of MARA this way:

> When I first came here I was sad and lonely like so many women. . . . One of the most important things that has helped me is MARA. Before I came here I was not involved in any organization. MARA has really made me aware of my Raza and people.

Another inmate, Amelia Lopez, shared her experience:

> I'm a Chicana in prison. . . . Just to know that my Brown Sisters had a group and were interested in the same achievements, really sounded good to me. . . . You attended MARA, and you see what must be done, simply by what you hear. You hear your sisters saying don't walk alone, walk with us.[79]

Women were central to other Los Angeles Chicano movement organizations and the print cultures they generated. For example, approximately fifty women participated in the Los Angeles chapter of El Centro de Accion Social Autónomo (CASA), which was founded in 1968 as a mutual aid organization under the leadership of Bert Corona and Soledad Alatorre and became a Marxist-Leninist vanguard organization in 1975 after merging with the Committee to Free los Tres.[80] Marisela Chávez argues, "Marxism as a 'sex-blind' ideology, much as the ideology of Chicanismo which privileged race, class and ethnicity, merged together in CASA to engender a Marxist and nationalist vision that subsumed women and women's issues."[81] Laura Pulido attributes CASA's inability to incorporate women, with the exception of Magdalena Mora and Isabel H. Rodriguez, into the leadership to the emphasis on "study and theoretical work," as well as the existence of a gendered division of labor.[82]

Despite the fact that female members of CASA, including Isabel H. Rodriguez, Patricia Vellanoweth, Andrea Elizade, Margarita Ramírez, Evelina Márquez, Elsa Rivas, Evelina Fernández, Gilda Rodriguez, Maria Elena Durazo, Magdalena Mora, Jane Adkins, and Diane Factor, were committed to a class-based struggle, many of them did focus on women's issues in capitalist relations of power and organizational praxis. This is evidenced in print culture with the 1977 women's special edition of *Sin Fronteras*, edited by Evelina Márquez and Margarita Ramírez, which built on the socialist tradition of honoring International Women's Day. In addition, that same year a women's study group formed within the organization and produced a study guide to address "both gender inequities within CASA and to expand their general knowledge about women's roles in revolutions and how different theorists addressed the women's question."[83] In the end, the Chicana counterpublic constituted through print culture spread throughout and beyond the Chicano movement. Women's special issues—*Regeneración* (1971, 1975), *El Grito del Norte* (1971), *El Popo Femenil* (1972, 1973), *El Grito* (1973), *La Razón Mestiza* (1975), *Sin Fronteras* (1977), *ChismeArte* (1978), to name a few—flourished throughout the 1970s.

COLLECTIVE KNOWLEDGE PRODUCTION

In the era I am describing, Chicana poetry and prose were a politicized strategy of self-representation and knowledge production published in newspapers, articles, manifestos, open letters, and conference proceedings. Many contemporary Chicana intellectuals and writers got their training in the movement or through discursive traditions created by Chicana feminists who emerged from it. As forms and contents are dialectically related, new innovative forms of writing were imperative and indicative of new forms of political subjectivities. Outside of the realist conventions of political journalism, newsprint forms varied widely, from open letters to songs that introduced a new Chicana poetics and politically infused writing. The writing in the majority of the newsprint pieces appeared in a narrative format that mirrored the urgency of their words. The diverse forms Chicanas invented to "speak themselves" into poetic and political discourse testifies to a new sense of creative agency.[84] This kind of mixed-genre format would come to form the basis for a pedagogy of liberation among Chicanas themselves, as well as a coalitional strategy among women of color continuing with the profusion of women of color anthologizing in the 1970s and early 1980s embodied by collaborative projects such as the 1981 publication of *This Bridge Called my Back*.

In the early 1970s collective self-knowledge was often produced in a montage layout and mixed-genre format, serving as a precursor to women of color anthologizing. Developed out of an early women's course in La Raza studies, Dorinda Gladden Moreno's 1973 collection of poetry, prose, and artwork, *La mujer en pie de lucha*, is an early example of these practices. In 1970, while attending San Francisco State College, Dorinda Moreno and a group of Chicana women formed Concilio Mujeres as a support group for Chicanas in higher education. The group encouraged Raza women to enter higher education and pursue a profession.[85] Moreno, a single mother of three children, returned to school after being in the workforce. In 1973 their collection was published. In 1975 the organization used the 1973 book as the basis of a film that they went on to produce for public television. Citing this collection as a way to locate their own project, the editors of the first issue of *Encuentro Femenil* created intertextual conversations across disparate regions, social locations, and ideological differences, which was a widespread practice and part of the exchange created by the Chicana print community.

The same year Moreno published *La mujer en pie de lucha* Concilio Mujeres opened an office in the San Francisco Mission District in an effort to serve the Chicano community.[86] According to the sociologist Benita Roth, Moreno also served as director between 1974 and 1975 of a "library clearing house project" that involved collecting materials on Chicanas to inform "the broader movement . . . about the lives of Raza women."[87] Gathering and disseminating information on the Chicana was central to Concilio Mujeres as an organization. While Moreno was a graduate student at Stanford University, Concilio Mujeres began producing the newsletter *La Razón Mestiza*. In 1976 Concilio Mujeres produced a special edition on Chicanas in honor of International Women's Year titled *La Razón Mestiza II*.[88] Moreno also played a key role in creating a women's teatro group called Las Cucarachas. Moreno believed in the necessity of working with Chicano men and activism involving cultural and historical knowledge as vital to the liberation of both Chicanas and Chicanos.[89] By 1975 Concilio Mujeres ran into issues with funding and the participation of its membership, and between 1975 and 1980 the organization slowly ceased to exist.

These earlier forms of Chicana feminist print communities transformed both political discourse and the framework through which it was enunciated. Often portrayed as before their time, grassroots activist intellectuals like Betita Martinez, Mirta Vidal, and Enriqueta Longeaux y Vasquez were very much women *of* their time who created a Chicana/Latina essayist tradition that chronicled how their feminist convictions emerged out of this historical context, often in dialogue with one another. This political essayist tradition was carried on throughout the 1970s through NietoGomez's "la Feminista" and Cotera's two historical chronicles, *Diosa y Hembra* (1976) and *The Chicana Feminist* (1977). Historicizing, dialogue, and collaborative writing were trademarks of this early period.

PRINT CULTURES, ANTHOLOGIZING, AND AFFIRMATIVE COMMUNITIES IN PRODUCTION

The emergence of collections by U.S. third world women was preceded by anthologies published by women of color within their own racial and ethnic communities. Some examples are *The Black Woman: An Anthology*, edited by Toni Cade Bambara in 1970; *Asian Women*, edited by the Berkeley Asian Women's Study Group in 1971; and *La mujer en pie de lucha*, edited by Dorinda Moreno in 1973.[90] Anthologizing was a pedagogy of liberation that included using multiple genres such as testimonial, historical, and poetic treatments. Women of color anthologies provided the tools for consciousness raising and community building that forged a space for women within their respective movements and made women of color the subjects of knowledge rather than its objects. In many ways anthologizing was also a strategy of collective self-knowledge construction and played a critical pedagogical role for vastly different groups to learn about each other and themselves. A rise in anthology production and special journal issues dedicated to third world women at the end of the decade witnessed such publications as the special issue of *Heresies, Third World Women: The Politics of Being Other* (1979) and Dexter Fisher's *The Third Woman: Minority Women Writers in the U.S.* (1980).[91]

Anthologies by women of color have been an effective strategy for multiplying discursive arenas that help constitute counterpublics. The specific print technology of the anthology can be seen as producing discursive and public cultures where women of color could construct and learn the terms of their emerging coalitions or political projects. The anthology provided an avenue for discussing and negotiating conflict, contradiction, solidarity, understanding, and difference. In many ways this strategy forged the coalitional and tactical nature of women of color identities and made effective interventions into feminist scholarship and activism. Critically, there is also evidence that its circulation functioned to help constitute women of color as an interpretive and political community. Among women of color activists these texts were critically engaged, widely read, and collectively discussed and were often the impetus for the establishment of new groups as well as new political and cultural formations.[92]

The sheer number of collections published in the 1980s, as well as the diverse identities and struggles included, testifies to the power of this publishing strategy. Some of the anthologies produced in the 1980s include *Twice a Minority: Mexican American Women* (1980), edited by Margarita Melville; *But Some of Us Are Brave: Black Women's Studies*, (1982), edited by Gloria T. Hull, Patricia Bell Scott, and Barbara Smith; *Home Girls: A Black Feminist Anthology* (1983), edited by Barbara Smith; *Gathering Ground: New Writing and Art by Northwest Women of Color* (1984), edited by Jo Cochran, J. T. Stewart, and Mayumi Tsutakawa; *I Am Your Sister: Black Women Organizing across Sexualities* (1985), edited by Audre Lorde; *Women of Color: Perspectives on Feminism and Identity* (1985), edited by Audrey T. McCluskey; *Compañeras: Latina Lesbians: An Anthology* (1987), edited by Juanita Ramos; *Without Ceremony* (1988), edited by Asian Women United (New York); *Making Waves: An Anthology of Writings by and about Asian American Women* (1989), edited by Asian Women United of California; *The Forbidden Stitch: An Asian American Women's Anthology* (1988), edited by Shirley Geok-Lin Lim, Mayumi Tsutakawa, and Margarita Donnelly; *A Gathering of Spirit: A Collection by North American Indian Women* (1984), edited by Beth Brant; *Spider Woman's Granddaughters: Traditional Tales and Contemporary Writing by Native American Women* (1989), edited by Paula Gunn Allen; and *That's What She Said: Contemporary Poetry and Fiction by Native American Women* (1984), edited by Rayna Green.[93]

Women of color subaltern counterpublics were constituted largely through print communities produced by publications like *Triple Jeopardy: Imperialism, Sexism, Racism*, the newspaper of the Third World Women's Alliance, which had a national circulation from 1970 to 1975.[94] Both anthologies and movement newspapers served the vital role of multiplying the spaces in which these discursive communities operated, from big cities to smaller ones in Oregon, New Mexico, and Michigan. This strategy was not just about covering geographic terrain but about creating dialogues with different audiences in other ideological camps, sectors of organizing, and social movements. Other scholars who have studied these print communities have noted this critical function of republication. For example, Katie King states, "The complexity of interests, methods, and political possibilities the collection of working papers and polemics display, the reworking for different locations, and the envisioning of quite differing audiences, real and imagined, need to be kept in mind while we continue looking at anthologies."[95]

Crucial in mapping these poetic and political traditions are the writings of Chicana lesbian feminists of the 1970s who forged new forms of identity, community, and political consciousness. Often the most vibrant print cultures emerged due to marginalization and displacement from multiple movement spaces and discourses. This points to the tremendous poetic revolutions of lesbians of color who sought to make a new language and new genres to create new identities, desires, solidarities, and communities outside these displacements. The poetics of liberation were developed by such lesbian of color writers as Pat Parker, Cherríe Moraga, Toni Cade Bambara, Chrystos, Audre Lorde, Gloria Anzaldúa, Cheryl Clarke, Jewelle Gomez, Kitty Tsui, and Hattie Gossett, to name a few. It was often a survival strategy to turn to political poetry or creative writing to make feminist interventions. Much of this work went on to have transformative and lasting effects. I make this distinction because I do not want to "privilege" social movements as the site where "real" change happens but to shift our understanding of both social movements and alternative counterpublics that were formed in this era to challenge institutional and cultural forms of imperialism, sexism, homophobia, and racism. For example, the role of print production, distribution, and circulation in providing alternative spaces for the production of politicized subjectivities in the poetic revolutions of radical lesbians of color is marked by *This Bridge Called My Back*. Due to the multiple exclusions of lesbians and bisexuals and gender-nonconforming people of color within the Gay Liberation Front, the Chicano movement, Black Power, the New Left, the women's movement or the Asian American student movement, *This Bridge* epitomizes the ways in which a new space was crafted through writing and publishing as a coalitional venture. It is important to put these poetic revolutions in conversation with social movement practices and political struggles in order to forge a history of the formation of women of color feminist political projects.[96]

Even before *Bridge*, the critical importance of publishing and building print communities can be see in how lesbian of color activists worked together politically through counterpublics constituted through print communities and cultural production after being multiply marginalized and displaced in all the many movements in which they had been active. These alternative gendered print communities can also be traced through Chicana poetic revolutions that signaled desire and coalitional politics with other women of color as a space of resistance. These interconnections are explicit in the introduction to *Conditions: Five (The Black Women's Issue)*:

> We decided to use the work of Black women both as a political/cultural statement and also because we realized the limitations of our competence and/or experience as two Afro-American women to deal with the literary representation of other Third World women's lives. We feel strongly that all women of color need autonomous publications that encompass the experiences of all Third World women. AZALEA, a magazine by Third World lesbians, is a pioneering representative of this last category, along with the Third World women's issues of *HERESIES: A Feminist Publication on Art and Politics*.[97]

The formation of Kitchen Table: Women of Color Press exemplifies the process whereby lesbians of color made a home for their "displacement" and a political location from which to speak and write their own political visions.[98] Actors such as Barbara Smith and Lorrain Bethel played a role in facilitating this print community.[99] Third Woman Press, founded in 1979 by Norma Alarcón, also served as a critical site for the production of Chicana and women of color literatures and critical essays.[100]

These alternative gendered print communities can also be traced through Chicana poetic revolutions that signaled desire and coalitional politics with other women of color as a space of resistance. The historiography of this poetics is a crucial space of articulation in mapping Chicana feminisms because it is a significant strand in Chicana feminist genealogies, which is often elided as standing outside Chicano movement history. Movement print cultures provided a theoretical and historical basis for the formation of Chicana feminist scholarship, and they were used to rework the discursive frames of social struggle in order to craft new spaces for women within masculinist registers of nationalism, constituting a Chicana counterpublic.

INTERPRETIVE DILEMMAS, MULTIPLE MEANINGS: CONVERGENCE AND DISJUNCTURE AT THE 1971 CONFERENCIA DE MUJERES POR LA RAZA

The conference was a first.
A national meeting of Chicanas had never been organized before in the history of our movement.
We expected 150 women.
There were 550.
The women, mostly college age, started flowing in groups ranging from two to twenty coming in on chartered buses, cars, planes, even hitch hiking. About twenty-five states were represented . . . [and] there were complaints.
The one-dollar registration fee was too much.
The free cots were lousy.
The food that had been donated to the conference was not barrio food.
The people at the conference were not barrio people.
La Conferencia was trying to divide the movement.
Tempers flared.
Angry words were heard in the workshops.
Threats were heard in the general assemblies.
On Sunday there was a walkout by a minority of the participants.
ELMA BARRERA, "CHICANAS AND CHICANOS RADIO SHOW,"
HOUSTON, TEXAS, 1971

The influence and impact of the Houston Conference of Mujeres por la Raza may not be fully realized for many years to come.
FRANCISCA FLORES, "MEXICAN-AMERICAN WOMEN PONDER FUTURE ROLE OF THE CHICANA," 1971

THIS CHAPTER IS as much a history of the 1971 Conferencia de Mujeres por la Raza in Houston, Texas, as it is about the challenges of telling that history.

The interpretation and significance of the conference, as well as the meaning of feminismo, movimiento, and community, were highly contested in 1971. Nearly forty years later, the landscape of meaning remains contested—frozen in some places, fluid in others. Over the years I have talked with organizers and participants, read the editorials from both sides of the divide, and amassed an impressive amount of archival documents, retrieved from dusty files in official archives as well as activist archives in garages in California and Texas.[1] The documents detail how many participants attended and from which states and who sat on the fund-raising committee, but even after years of research the only certainty I have is that there are no easy answers. Despite this lack of certainty, la Conferencia de Mujeres por la Raza is a rich site from which to understand the political fault lines of early Chicana feminism. Many of the conflicts at the conference were the result of differences within regional political cultures, gendered movement discourses, and organizational tactics, which ultimately disrupted the emergence of a national Chicana movement during the early 1970s. This chapter, then, is another kind of contested history based on the impossibility (or perhaps futility) of what oral historians call interpretive authority. It draws attention to interpretive dilemmas and partial knowledges—my own and those of the attendees themselves—that are full of fraught (and sometimes faulty) memories. It includes reluctant narrators, painful tales, and some historical treasures.

The 1971 Conferencia de Mujeres por la Raza brought together Chicana organizations from diverse regions and social movement sectors. It brought together women from student organizations, unions, the Raza Unida Party, the land grant movement, and community organizers, among others. The conference signaled the growth of a national political movement and potential political unity among Chicanas at the height of the Chicano movement. The resolutions passed on issues of Chicana political leadership, sexuality, motherhood, economic justice, reproductive and educational rights, and the role of the Catholic Church in the oppression of Chicanas, as well as a condemnation of the Vietnam War, reflected the pinnacle and the possibility of early Chicana feminism. At the same time, the devastating walkout that occurred at the conference reflected the deep divisions, which challenged the articulation and mobilization of a Chicana feminist agenda within the Chicano movement.

By organizing this first national conference, the women from the Magnolia branch of the YWCA, in Houston's largest Mexican American neighborhood, issued a call to action to build a national movement. The response was enormous. Six hundred Chicanas came from more than twenty-three states to participate.[2] In Los Angeles several prominent local activists organized a regional meeting in preparation for the Houston conference at California State University, Los Angeles. Over 250 Chicanas came together with the hope of forging a united political agenda and even starting a national Chicana newspaper. Expecting only about one-fourth of all the participants who showed up, the Houston organizers scrambled to meet the needs of an additional 450 attendees. Gloria Guardiola, one of the Houston-based workshop organizers recalls:

> Women were coming from all over, spending the night in different people's homes. People from all over. We didn't expect it to be this huge thing. It was all by word of mouth. It just kept spreading . . . there were hundreds of people from Houston alone. It was kind of overwhelming. I had never seen that many Chicanas together in one place. It was there I realized that we had power, if we could get all of these women together. We were not anticipating fights, being called radical or whatever.[3]

This overwhelming response could have been seen as the positive need and desire for women in the Chicano movement to organize together. Instead, the conference came to represent the division among women.

Throughout the conference there were organizational problems. The workshops were overcrowded and could not accommodate everyone. And although the workshops were dynamic, participants were frustrated that they were poorly facilitated and some lacked microphones. Women had traveled with very few resources and needed housing. Some were told the Downtown Y housing would be $3 when instead it was $6.[4] On the third day a split developed. One group of women led a walkout to protest the racism of the YWCA, calling it a "missionary," white women's institution whose goal was to split the Chicano movement. The majority supported the reasons for the conference and stayed to continue the conversations regarding the numerous issues Chicanas confronted. The protesters argued it was selfish to discuss women's issues at a time when people participating in a farmworker protest march from Calexico to Delano were shot at and when Chicano men were coming home from Vietnam in body bags in increasing numbers. Those who walked out marched to nearby Zavala Park to hold their sessions in the "community," where they remained for a few hours before returning to the conference.

The split shaped the political terrain for years to come, exacerbating political divisions to such an extent that it disrupted the sense of a collective identity and political agenda. Some activists in women's groups continued to work together; other organizations fell apart. The reverberations of the 1971 Houston conference led Anna NietoGomez, a prominent theorist and activist of the day, to categorize the walkout as a conflict between Chicana feminists and loyalists. While clearly there were some regional tensions that emerged out of different traditions and styles of California/Tejana movement politics, the conference workshops and resolutions represented a vibrant, promising, and revolutionary critique of the institutional structures that oppressed Chicanas, even as they revealed the deep ideological disagreements over strategies. While many only remember this historical moment by the walkout—or women's inability to unite for a common national agenda in the Chicano movement—what this chapter intends to do is fill out the historical complexity, regional histories, and ideological cross currents in order to map the contested history of early Chicana feminism.

STRAINING TO HEAR: METHODOLOGICAL ISSUES

During 2002 and 2003 I traveled to Houston, looking for the organizers of the Conferencia de Mujeres por la Raza.[5] Over the thirteen years I had been conducting oral histories with early Chicana activists, all the women I interviewed spoke of the 1971 Houston conference as the pinnacle of possibility and a source of disappointment. There are a few secondary sources based on participants' reactions to the conference, but no one had written a historical account that takes the voices and perspective of the organizers into consideration to provide a better understanding of their view of what would become a notorious split in the history of early Chicana feminism.[6]

One methodological challenge, or source of richness, depending on how you look at it, is that people narrate their histories and the events they recollect in disparate ways, even when describing the same event. As much as the Chicano movement changed the lives of women who participated in positive ways, several women survived many devastating political battles and conflicts that opened up wounds that some still guard closely today. While some women have outright refused to be interviewed because of how painful their memories of the movement are, several others who agreed to speak with me carry visible traumas that shape the interviews and what can be captured through this process. Conflict, painful memories, and trauma shapes if and how narrators tell a story. Yet several narrators told me that sharing their stories often helps activists to integrate what happened, to have a fuller picture, and to move them toward healing the past. As I listened to the voices of the organizers I interviewed, I heard important stories of Chicana activism and the emergence of a homegrown Houston Chicana feminism coming to the surface. There were also many ruptures, gaps in understanding, and veiled memories caused by the trauma and confusion surrounding the walkout.

How narrators remember, come to voice, and weave their narratives shape the kinds of stories they construct, creating gaps or unexpected abundance in the archive, which in turn shapes the resources oral historians have to draw upon. While this is part of the joy and adventure of being an oral historian — experiencing the richness of memory, narrative structure, the sense of place, time, meaning, and ways of being that are invoked in the way a story is told — the different ways people tell stories can also be a methodological challenge. For example, in this story one narrative challenge for me was that those who walked out did not seem to remember the conference well, what it was like to be there, or the experience of the walkout. On the other hand, those who did not walk out tended to have vivid memories of the conference, what it was like to participate, the details of the walkout. While this is in part ideological and reflects how much significance the conference holds for the narrators themselves, it can lead to an unevenness: the "voice" of my story tends to favor those who stayed and vividly remember it. Like many oral historians, I met this challenge by also using the rich documentary evidence in the print materials of the movement, especially those written by the participants who walked out.

While key organizers of la conferencia include community and staff members of the Magnolia branch of the YWCA, Elma Barrera, a pioneering voice in broadcast journalism who was honored by the National Association of Hispanic Broadcasters, is often identified as the main organizer because she was the press contact for the conference and was involved in what she called the Chicano underground press. After our first interview, she felt bad about not remembering details; however, in our ongoing correspondence, she provided me with a gold mine of documentary evidence: sound recordings of the conference proceedings that I did not know existed. In one of her letters to me, she writes:

> So sorry I could not help you too much although since the interview, memories of the conference came rushing into my head. The hope we had of embracing these women and helping — the shame, the failure and the terrible emptiness that followed. There was so much confusion — what had we done wrong? Why did these women from California demand so much and why did they walk out? Today of course I know they were merely looking for a reason, a cause, against which to protest. They were young and trying very hard to be militant, even if they had to strike out against their own Hispanic (Chicana back then) sisters.[7]

During a follow-up phone call, Barrera told me about a tape of a radio show called "Chicanas and Chicanos" that she produced days after the conference. When I returned the next summer to do follow-up research, I visited Barrera to hear the tape, and she gave me this sonic treasure—a recording of her radio show that captured the only known existing sound footage of the conference, an excerpt of which opens this chapter. It has survived thirty years in a sweltering Houston garage and, by the looks of the tape, suffered some kind of water damage. Yet I hoped that despite its worse-for-wear appearance it might give me a glimpse into this turning point of early Chicana feminism. Listening to recordings she made, Barrera and numerous other activists I played the recording for, were captivated by the excitement that seems to emanate from the recording. As the recording played we heard the Chicano clap and the momentum building with a long litany of "Vivas!" All the activists commented on the power and potential generated by six hundred Chicanas gathering for the first time and the disappointment represented by the walkout.[8]

La conferencia serves as a map of fractures, tensions, and the various centers of gravity in the emergence of a political project of Chicana feminism. Listening to the difference in tone between the participants in 1971 and the contemporary narrators reveals how transitory meaning is. What it says about women who stayed or women who walked out, it is hard to say. Many of the women who walked out would not have defined themselves as Chicana feminists then. In fact, there was a strong critique of feminism by the walkout group in 1971, though many of them do understand themselves as feminists now. Others may not have called themselves feminists but came to see the need for such an agenda and even aligned themselves with it, sometimes within months or years after the 1971 meeting. This presents a challenge in representing that particular historical moment because along with the way ideologies and people's thinking about politics shifts; historical memory itself is not static.[9] That is, beyond the documentary evidence, oral history gives us the opportunity to understand the past and the narrators' changing relationships to their past selves.

CONFERENCIA DE MUJERES POR LA RAZA

It was unbelievable to see that many brown faces . . . all women together. It was beautiful to see Chicanas from every corner of the country, from every conceivable kind of organization.
ANNA NIETOGOMEZ, APRIL 22, 1991

In the epigraph above Anna NietoGomez describes what it felt like to walk the main conference hall, a gymnasium in the heart of a working-class Mexican American neighborhood where Chicanas had gathered for the first time to discuss their role in the Chicano movement, name the specificity of their issues, and strategize a common cause. Barrera recalls, "Well, to me it was . . . it was powerful, it was overwhelming," and yet she confesses that she could not fully feel the moment: "Because, you know, I had to go bake the beans, or I had to go look for blankets or go do whatever." She continues:

> Were we surprised? Absolutely we were surprised, because they started calling and I remember answering the phones at one point and it was a phone call from a woman saying that they wanted to register and they were renting a bus to come. I said, "No, you can't come anymore, we're filled, we don't have any more space," and she started crying. I felt so bad. She said, "But we have a bus and we have to come." We didn't have space, you know, because people just ended up sleeping in the gym; some of them slept in the gym and houses around the Y. So I went back to the phone and said, "OK, alright. Well, just come."[10]

The conference lasted three days, with two keynote addresses and three sets of workshops organized around the themes of identity, movement issues, and strategies. After the welcome on Friday, the first keynote address, "The Mexican American Women's Public and Self-Image," which emphasized a new "togetherness [that] can liberate Chicanas," was given on Friday night by Julie Ruiz, a professor from Arizona State University, and followed by a reception.[11] Saturday morning began with a general assembly at which the second keynote speech, "Machismo—What Are We Up Against," was delivered by Grace Gil Olivarez. Born to a working-class family in Arizona, Olivarez was the first woman to graduate from Notre Dame Law School in 1970.[12] Her keynote address elicited strong responses—both positive and negative—which were taken up in the workshops that followed. The workshop titles reveal an attempt to come to a shared Chicana analysis of institutions and sources of oppression, as well as to address real political differences and issues. The first round of workshops, on identity, were

"Sex and the Chicana: Noun and Verb"
"Choices for Chicanas: Education and Occupation"
"Marriage: Chicana-Style"
"Religion"

The second session of workshops, which began after lunch, focused on movimiento issues:

"Feminist Movement—Do We Have a Place in It?"
"Exploitation of Women—The Chicana Perspective"
"Women in Politics—Is Anyone There?"
"Militancy/Conservatism: Which Way Is Forward?"
"De Colores y Clases: Class and Ethnic Differences"

The workshops were led by community organizers such as Bertha Hernandez (advocate for poor women's rights from the Magnolia district), Raquel Orendaín (United Farmworkers of Texas), Sister Gloria Gallardo (Galveston-Houston Diocese), and María Jiménez (University of Houston MAYO chapter); and local feminist leaders such as Yolanda Garza Birdwell and Gloria Guardiola (both from the Houston community chapter of MAYO), Martha Cotera (a founder of Mujeres por la Raza, the women's caucus of the RUP), Anita Aleman (Jacinto-Treviño College, a Chicano school), Francisca Flores and Gracia Molina de Pick (Comisión Femenil Mexicana Nacional in California), and Enriqueta Longeaux y Vásquez (New Mexico's *El Grito del Norte*). After the workshops there was a general assembly where reports were given and resolutions drafted. Even on the first day, responses to Olivarez's speech began vigorous discussion on the role of feminism, the woman question, and challenges to openly criticizing men within the community and movimiento.[13]

ORGANIZING THE FIRST NATIONAL CONFERENCE: LOCAL ROOTS AND REGIONAL HISTORIES OF CHICANA MOBILIZATION

Magnolia Park, home to the women who organized the conference, is the largest and one of the oldest Latino neighborhoods in Houston. Mexican labor migration to the area is traced to the early decades of the twentieth century. Workers found jobs laying railroad tracks, on the docks loading cotton onto ships and railroad cars, and in the shipyard. Social organizations also have long roots in Houston. The Sociedad Mutualista Benito Juárez was founded in 1919. With migration from northern Mexico increasing during the 1920s, Mexican American businesses, a Mexican chamber of commerce, and Mexican social and recreation clubs flourished.[14] By 1930 Magnolia Park was the largest Mexican settlement in Houston. Its residents worked in factories, textile mills, industrial plants, and the ship channel. The Club Femenino-Chapultepec reflected the growing civic participation of women who organized social and recreational events and protested Houston's racial segregation. A branch of the League of United Latin American Citizens (LULAC) was founded in 1934, and the Ladies LULAC was founded in

1935. A wartime boom in jobs increased the Latino population throughout the Southwest. Magnolia Park grew so large that it eventually merged with El Segundo barrio and became known as the East End barrio. In the 1960s the Mexican American Youth Organization and La Raza Unida Party were active in the area. And *Papel Chicano*, a Houston movimiento newspaper, was based in Magnolia Park.[15]

At its national convention on April 15, 1970, in Houston, the YWCA passed a resolution "to thrust our collective power toward the elimination of racism wherever it exists and by any means necessary" by a unanimous vote.[16] The idea for the Conferencia de Mujeres por la Raza grew out of a group that formed at this national convention who resignified the abbreviation YWCA to stand for Young Women Committed to Action. Blanche Flores, a thirty-three-year old mother of three and the chairman of the Magnolia Park Branch of the YWCA said, "I saw there was not Mexican-American leadership."[17] She argued, "The Chicana has a problem with employment, her kids aren't getting the best education, and just look at the neighborhood—she's not getting what she's paying for. . . . We (Chicanas) have a lot of influence in our homes, but we've failed to carry it a step further to civic responsibility."[18] The group planned the conference as a response to the Y's campaign to eliminate racial prejudice.

According to mailers, meeting minutes, fund-raising letters, registration documents and rosters, Chicanas began to organize the conference in December 1970. To formalize their request they asked Mrs. Blanche Flores to take the proposal to the Y's board of directors, which unanimously approved the idea. In January 1971 the organizing committee formed. Mrs. Flores was named general chairman; Lucy Moreno, communications chairman; Ana Guerrero, finance; Elma Barrera, publicity; Stella Borrego and Connie Acosta, program; and Marie Bandin, Martha Moreno, and Sarah Bael, housing. The committee met weekly on Monday nights.

In the spirit of the new nationwide mission of the YWCA, organizers felt the conference provided a unique opportunity for Chicanas to "develop their mutual identity, to work toward a feeling of unity, to enhance their capacities to be meaningfully involved in their community."[19] The organizing plan, according to meeting notes, was to start "where we are with what we have—our two hands—and reach out to women locally" to define the issues of importance to them. In order to give everyone the opportunity to attend, the committee did extensive fund-raising. Internal documents stated, "Many of our women are poor, uneducated and not used to the luxury of thinking of their own needs." In addition to securing the facilities and speakers, the organizers were able to provide food for everyone for the entire conference, provide

FIGURE 5.1. Martha Lopez (far right center), Conferencia de Mujeres por la Raza, 1971. *Hijas de Cuauhtémoc*, unpublished issue. Courtesy of Sylvia Castillo.

free or low-cost housing, and give a limited number of travel scholarships for those who would be prevented from attending by lack of funds—all for a registration fee of $1.

Indeed, the final program illustrates an enormous community-based effort at fund-raising and sponsorship. Of the thirteen-page conference program, eleven were community sponsorships from local organizations and Mexican American–owned businesses, including a shoe repair shop, florist, tortilla factory, a barbershop, a beauty salon, a carnecería, a panadería, and a farmacia, as well as Amador's Taco Garden, a Mexicatessen, and other restaurants. Other sponsors were civic organizations, for example, the Magnolia Mothers Club, community leaders, and a city council candidate. The food for the conference

FIGURE 5.2. Group photo 1: Conferencia de Mujeres por la Raza, 1971. *Hijas de Cuauhtémoc*, unpublished issue. Courtesy of Sylvia Castillo.

was donated. Even the accommodations reflected true neighborhood-based organizing: a hotel, the YWCA Residence Hall, St. Mary's Seminary, and one hundred cots. These traditions of civic participation and community involvement came to represent contested ideals of community at the conference. With the diversity of participants—from Chicago, Michigan, New Mexico, Idaho, D.C., Kansas, Arizona, Colorado, California, and Texas (the last two states had the largest contingents)—came contested meanings of "culture" "feminism," and "community."[20] The debates reveal the tensions that became polarized around ideas such as "feminista vs. movimiento," "anglo vs. home-grown," and "California vs. Texas."

SEX AND THE CHICANA: NOUN AND VERB

The sexuality and religion workshops produced resolutions that were debated in the General Assembly and became two of the fault lines in the terrain of culture, change, and tradition over which women's rights were debated. The sexuality workshop produced a wide range of resolutions to "correct the many sexual hang-ups facing the Chicano community." The workshop was facilitated by Yolanda Birdwell, a Mexican immigrant and longtime activist and one of the first women active in Houston's MAYO chapter, and Gloria Guardiola, an educator and member of MAYO in Houston. In preparation for the workshop, Birdwell went door to door in Houston's Chicano neighborhoods asking women their views about sexuality and how sexuality could be adopted into the broader movement for Chicano liberation. The groundbreaking workshop was one of the first political spaces in which sexuality was discussed openly and addressed as part of the Chicano movement. The resolutions that were proposed put forth a wide-ranging agenda that included a shift in attitudes toward a more positive view of sexuality, the eradication of patriarchal values in relation to sexuality and the sexual double standard, a commitment to sex education, access to birth control and legal abortions, twenty-four-hour child care centers, and an end to the practice of sterilization and medical experimentation on Chicana women.

Birdwell and Guardiola researched and wrote a bilingual booklet titled *La Mujer, Destrucción de Mitos: Formación y Práctica del Pensamiento Libre (Woman, Destruction of Myths: Formation and Practice of Free Thinking)*. Although both women were active members of MAYO, they had very different perspectives on movement politics. Birdwell, who was married with a child and at least a decade older than the youth active in MAYO, found the organization to have relatively progressive politics around sexuality and gender, which she attributed to women's leadership and to progressive men such as MAYO leader Gregory Salazar. She recalls:

> I became part of the leadership of MAYO Mexican American Youth Organization in Houston, and that was the beginning of how I changed from what my life was in Mexico to what it became. [It shaped] my understanding of racism and my understanding of feminism to that point.[21]

FIGURE 5.3. Group photo 2: Conferencia de Mujeres por la Raza, 1971. Courtesy of Anna NietoGomez.

When I spoke with Guardiola, she felt the opposite: "I was already becoming disillusioned with the machismo of the Chicano movement. We were always there to help them out. It was the guys who took the credit." When I asked about women's participation in MAYO, she replied, "Actually the Houston MAYO had more women than guys, and we were very active. It was that way in general in the state of Texas . . . I'm talking mainly in South Texas." She and some of her activist friends became interested in the women's movement and feminism along with some other activist friends, but other women in her movement circles were reluctant.

> Porque decia que [Because they said], "Well, we got to help our men." I said, "Men, they help themselves." Have you noticed that as soon as they became very well known, what do they do? Go out with white women, you know, the hippie girls. So I said, "Don't you see? They're using us like the Anglos use the Mexicano for their labor; they use us for our labor." That's how I saw it. You empower a group, but you got to empower both sexes. That's when I became more critical. And eventually there *were* women in local leadership like Yolanda Birdwell and Josie Perez. Mainly it was the women who ran it after a while.[22]

Birdwell, a lifelong socialist activist, shared the process of how they came up with the idea of the pamphlet. They wanted analysis from the ground up, and the pamphlet called for the revolutionary overhaul of practices, thoughts, and structures that oppress women within the Chicano community, as well as a change in the larger structural elements in the dominant society. The tone was prescriptive and produced in the spirit of scientific socialism. It was a manifesto of sorts that circulated widely for many years beyond the conference.[23] When I asked Birdwell what they talked about in the workshop, she said:

> We talked about orgasms. We talked about masturbation. We talked about infidelity. We talked about virginity. We talked about . . . all these myths. So it was a very heated discussion. I remember not even having time before we went to lunch, you know, to answer all the questions with all the people raising their hands.

When I asked how people received these ideas, if they were scandalized, she smiled and said:

> Let me just say this to you . . . yes, there were some people who were scandalized, but it was good for them to be scandalized. They needed to hear a new

word. They needed to hear that they were not getting a good deal in bed. That is my position then, and it is my position now.

Attendees recall that that workshop was the first time in the movement that a group of mujeres openly talked about sex and sexuality among themselves. Anna NietoGomez recalls:

> We needed to talk about it. It was the first workshop that talked about the church and the impact of the church on women's identity and its control over her body, and her role in the church. It was heavy. It was great.
>
> Oh, the women were heavy. I mean, [the sexual politics] were real obvious, like it was no big secret. It was just finally stating what you could see but that no one would talk about. Every time you went to a conference your commitment at that conference was to go back and share the information with other people. So then the dudes back in L.A. started to trivialize the conference and say all we did was talk about sex, how we were endangering the family and that we ignored the political issues of the church as an oppressive institution. So I don't even know if anybody finally heard what we said.[24]

THE CATHOLIC CHURCH, CHICANA LIBERATION THEOLOGY, AND A CRITIQUE OF PATRIARCHY

Many participants recognized the revolutionary potential of Chicanos organizing within the Catholic Church, and the resolutions indicated a demand for greater responsiveness to the Chicano community and community needs. The religion workshop proposed resolutions to recognize the *Plan Espiritual de Aztlán* by taking over existing church resources in order to provide services to the Chicano community, to oppose institutionalized religion, and to demand that the Catholic Church become part of revolutionary change or "get out of the way."

Religion was vigorously debated. Several Chicana nuns, who were in the Chicana liberation theology movement that was just gaining steam, participated. Their new organization, Las Hermanas, cofounded by Gregoria Ortega of El Paso and Gloria Graciela Gallardo of San Antonio, had held its first conference in Houston one month earlier, in April.[25] The three-day conference was attended by fifty women, most of whom were Chicana, although Puerto Rican, Mexican, and Anglo sisters representing twenty religious congregations in eight states also attended. According to Lara Medina, Las Hermanas chose to confront the Catholic Church in an effort to change it from within.

Understanding their role as agents of change within the sanctified patriarchy led them to take an aggressive and proactive stance against the Church's exclusionary practices and teachings. Coming together in Houston at the first Las Hermanas meeting in April 1971 set in motion the process of bringing the Chicano movement and Chicana feminism into the U.S. Roman Catholic Church.[26]

While they argued for the revolutionary and even feminist potential of Catholicism, and would later challenge patriarchy within the Catholic Church and go on to develop a Chicana feminist theology, they were outvoted by young, vocal Chicana activists in the conferencia workshop. The final resolution of the religion workshop read, "We, as mujeres de la Raza, recognize the Catholic Church as an oppressive institution and do hereby resolve to break away and not go to it to bless our unions."

Other resolutions that came to the floor of the conference read: "[Be it resolved] That the National Chicana Conference go on record as recommending that every Chicano community promote and set up 24-hour day-care facilities and be it further resolved that these facilities will reflect the concept of La Raza as the united family, and on the basis of brotherhood (La Raza) so that men, women, young and old assume the responsibility for the love, care, education and orientation of all children of Aztlán."[27] In addition there were resolutions condemning the use of Chicanas for medical reproductive testing, calling for the release of political prisoners, speaking against the war in Vietnam, and demanding welfare reform. Not all workshops produced resolutions. In many cases it was the first time these issues were discussed, so there were a large variety of ideas and perspectives. In some of the larger workshops there were also problems with facilitation and acoustics.

Saturday ended with a dinner, a mariachi mass, and singing and dancing. During the dinner hour, a large group of women who were interested in creating a national network to facilitate discussion met in the auditorium. The group formed into three committees organized by task: a national newsletter, a newspaper, and a journal. *Hijas de Cuauhtémoc* was voted the national newspaper and a vehicle for Chicanas from different regions to learn about their issues. It had transitioned from a campus to a community newspaper, moving its office to the city of Hawaiian Gardens. Further, the national network formed at the 1971 Conferencia de Mujeres por la Raza planned for the second Chicana national conference to be held in July 1972.[28]

THE WALKOUT

Sisters, I am really disappointed in this conference because I have seen this disunity.

No, No. Don't walk out! Don't walk out.

Our enemy is not with the macho but the gavacho *[slang for "white man"].* CONFERENCE PARTICIPANTS

Instead of merely discussing the polarization at the conference and how each side justified its position, I want to see these conflicts as a discursive map that reveals how the emergent form of Chicana feminism collectively articulated at the conferencia was registered through a range of debates. These debates represented deep questions about the meaning of gender, culture, authenticity, and communty, which served as fault lines through which the argument for women's rights within Chicano culture was staged. At the conferencia these concerns were refracted through a series of issues ranging from the relationship to what were seen as Anglo institutions (the YWCA), Anglo culture (hot dogs), and the presence of white women at the conference. The individualism of Anglo culture was deemed "selfish" or self-centered and capable of undermining the collective demands of the Chicano movement and thereby of distancing (or worse, dividing) it from the real issues: racism, poverty, labor exploitation, and the Vietnam War. These fault lines are at the center of the walkout.

NietoGomez narrates her memory of how the walkout started by recalling, "[Betita Martinez], the editor of *El Grito* [*del Norte*] newspaper coming out of the Southwest, which was the best newspaper at that time, spoke [in front of the conference], and then she came and sat by me." A presentation of the community women from the Magnolia neighborhood followed. "Many of the women were on welfare. They broke their backs. . . . They had truly put forth everything that they had to give to this conference. They believed in it so much."[29]

During the Sunday morning General Assembly, a community member from the Magnolia barrio, Bertha Hernandez, was speaking when four women went onto the stage and took the microphone from her. Keta Miranda recalled:

The women from San Diego MEChA told me there was going to be a walkout. By the time the Plenary Session rolled around María Elena Gaitán took the mic, saying that we didn't need this conference organized by the YWCA and that a women's conference was counterproductive to the Chicano movement. She kept talking. The room buzzed.[30]

Those who called for the walkout argued "that Chicanas had no business holding the conference at the YWCA because it was run by gavachas." According to the coverage in movement papers, the walkout group argued, "[We should not be] talk[ing] about Chicanas as being oppressed by Chicanos. We should talk about movimiento issues. Our enemy is not with the macho but the gavacho."[31] Sound recordings of the conference include the following pleas by participants calling for the walkout:

> I'm disappointed because I didn't see any of my sister campesinas around here. I am very disappointed in that. I don't feel like I belong here because I am a campesina and I don't see any of my sisters.
> I just came from walking across the Imperial Valley . . . walking with César Chávez where people were being shot at—and then I come here and all you are talking about is me, me, me. . . . Poor me.[32]

In addition to the principal complaint that the conference was being held at the YWCA, the walkout group critiqued the lack of participation by women from the Houston barrios, the organizational problems at the conference, and the racism some experienced at the Y. Some felt that talking about a women's agenda was divisive to the movement, while others were disturbed by the presence of white women at the conference. The theme of machismo was taken up, and debates arose surrounding the idea that some women were "more concerned with recognition rather than self-determination."[33] Ultimately this led to some walkout participants characterizing these differences as "movimiento vs. feminism," while the position of those who stayed were characterized by NietoGomez as "feminista vs. loyalist."

Those who led the walkout were students from Cal State Los Angeles, several women from the UCLA MEChA chapter, and one member of the University of Houston MAYO chapter. One-fourth of the participants responded to their call and walked out of the gymnasium at the Magnolia Park Y and went down the block to hold an alternative meeting in deliberation "with the community" at nearby Zavala Park. They put forward an alternative set of resolutions and returned to the YWCA within a few hours. Since the final session at which resolutions were agreed on had broken down because of the walkout, the resolutions drafted in the workshops, and those proposed by the walkout group, were to be taken back to participants' communities for discussion, then brought back to the second Conferencia de Mujeres por la Raza. Amid the confusion participants engaged in quick caucusing and political back-and-forth. Keta Miranda recalled:

We watched Betita [Martinez] to see if she would join the walkout, and we caucused among ourselves. So I got together with the women from San Diego and San Fernando Valley—the Valley said they were going to walkout because the conference was organized by the Y. Others argued that the conference was not against the Chicano movement.[34]

While both Martinez and the San Diego group stayed, one of the people who walked out, Cecelia Quijano, explains that she attended the conference with fellow UCLA MEChA members. Their delegation had been organized by MEChA following a meeting of Southern California student movement leaders (MEChA Central) who met to discuss their opposition to the conference.

What I remember is that we met at UCLA, and I think that it was one of the MEChA meetings with all the MEChA presidents from all of Los Angeles. I remember that Cal State Northridge was there, or what used to be called the San Fernando College, and Cal State L.A., and others.

We came together at a meeting to talk about the conflict in Houston, and I remember that most of the dialogue around the idea of the conflict in Houston was really divisive, that it was separating Chicanas from Chicanos, and that, you know, our issues were really as a people, not as a gender.[35]

Quijano's narrative refers to the conference as a "conflict" even before it took place. The decision to send a delegation of Chicana student activists from Los Angeles was made at the MEChA meeting. Quijano recalls, "It was decided that we would go, that, you know, three or four women would go, and that MEChA would pay for our airfare to Houston, and that we would go to see what was going on and make it known that we were against the conference itself."[36]

Off tape Quijano shared with me that she's not sure they ever really gave the Houston conference a chance. I asked if she felt like she let the men at the meeting decide for them and if they knew prior to going to Houston that they would walk out. She replied:

To an extent. I felt like it was like a mission for us. That's not to say that I was not involved in the dialogue, because I was, and I did feel very strongly. I didn't want for the women to break us up, and . . . [I remember feeling] that it's a white thing, that's what white women do, and all this other stuff. I didn't know anything about feminism.[37]

Another member of MEChA at UCLA who attended as part of the delegation was Susan Racho. When we spoke about the conference, she said that she did not remember a meeting beforehand or how she decided to go to the conference. She said that her memories of the conference itself are a blur because at the time she was attending so many conferences. One thing she did remember is that their opposition to the conference was linked to the idea that infiltrators or people connected to the government had organized it.[38]

The conference was widely covered in the Chicano movement press, but most people who were not in attendance came to know of it through a pamphlet, *Chicanas Speak Out. Women: New Voice of La Raza*, written by Mirta Vidal, a Chilean exile, for the socialist Pathfinder Press. Chicanas of San Diego, a delegation of thirty-two student and community activists, produced one of the most thorough accounts of the conference and reported on both sides of the walkout. They argued that "the entire spectrum of the Chicano Movement was reflected at the conference. Therefore if there was confusion at the conference one must consider the number of women present, the diversity of ideas and the difficulty in organizing the 1st National Conference for Chicanas."[39] Many considered the conference a rather large showing of support for Chicana emancipation and an affirmation of a women's rights agenda and leadership within the Chicano movement. In addition to problems caused by the unexpectedly large attendance and the wide diversity of participants, the fact that the conference was not organized by a movement organization or established movement leaders was a source of conflict. Because the conferencia was organized by the Magnolia Branch of the YWCA, it may have been vulnerable to criticism challenging its legitimacy as an authentic Chicano movement event.

The first Denver Youth Liberation conference in 1969 had a thousand participants and can be seen as one of the first national gatherings of the movement. When two years later six hundred Chicanas gathered in Houston to map the contribution of women to the movement, it was no small feat. But instead of creating momentum and a shared blueprint for action, like *El Plan Espiritual de Aztlán* did at the Denver conference, activists left Houston confused and dejected, and the conflict at the conference set back a united national agenda for Chicanas for many years.

When I asked Leticia Hernández what she remembered most about the Houston conference, she said:

All the infighting, you know. I guess you go into things with rose-colored glasses, and you think, "Wow, we're going to do this, and we're going to do the other thing, and we're all going to come together and we're going to free ourselves; we're going to do great things for our people." And then you get somewhere, and we were boycotted. We had things to say that we believed in and people walked out on us [laughs].[40]

While there were regional variations and histories, as well as differences in opinion, ideological orientation, ideas about strategy in relation to reform and revolution, and experience with gendered oppression and movement organizing, to some participants it was clear that the leaders of the walkout were there "to divide and to sabotage the conference. They were there with clear purpose. They had a mission in mind, and that was to stop the conference or to divide it—sabotage it—because they thought it was wrong."[41] Francisca Flores argued, "The Women's Conference presented such force and potential for a breakthrough against existing stumbling blocks and obstacles in women's struggle for equality that persons who disagree with this direction urged and supported some women to form a flank within the groundswell in order to break it."[42]

MAKING MEANING OUT OF CONFLICT

The walkout eludes easy categorization or interpretive schema. Often in relation to debates over gender and sexuality there is a facile effort to reduce differences to class divisions or between women who were more professionally oriented versus community people. In this case, the organizers were by and large women from working-class neighborhoods who were active at their local YWCA and those who led the walkout were first-generation college students. A study of the class backgrounds of presenters, facilitators, and participants reveals that many were just beginning their careers in civil rights organizations or public institutions like the Y, and the great majority were students. Another cleavage that we could assume divided those who stayed from those who walked out is ideology, following the assumption that those who walked out were more oriented to a revolutionary agenda and those who stayed were more reformist. Yet this easy schema also falls apart under closer scrutiny.

On both sides of the walkout there was significant ideological diversity. Chicanas who worked within institutions such as education or the media, who were leaders and members of labor- and community-based organizations, or who participated in Socialist and Communist Party formations were among those who stayed as well as those who walked out. Some on both sides of the divide went on to be lifelong anti-imperialist and Marxist activists, community organizers; others spoke for reproductive justice throughout the 1970s. While there was a wide ideological spectrum on both sides of the walkout, one notable difference is that among those who stayed were several of Chicana feminism's earliest theorists, leaders, and writers, including Anna NietoGomez, Martha Cotera, Grace Olivarez, Betita Martinez, Yolanda Birdwell, Gloria Guardiola, and Francisca Flores. These early Chicana feminists followed one of two paths. One group, mostly those who came from California, remained or attempted to remain in the Chicano movement to develop their gendered, class, and race analysis from movement spaces. The other group may have stayed in movimiento organizations such as La Raza Unida Party, but they also joined feminist organizations such as the Women's Political Caucus or NOW by the late 1970s. This distinction does seem to be a regional variation as most of those of the latter path tended to be Tejanas. Of those who walked out, some eventually became feminists or developed a gendered critique, but several told me that they did not necessarily come to this until years after the conference. Some women came to these new forms of consciousness within Chicano movement organizations, and others discovered the importance of women's voice in labor organizations, mixed-gender community organizations, immigrant rights groups, or as political party leaders. Others went on to be professionals, artists, and filmmakers.

While there are no easy answers, it would be a missed opportunity to say that all meaning is elusive. If we reject the imperative for interpretive authority and make space for multiple meanings, we can see the myriad interpretations that participants and organizers gave la conferencia: some were confused, some were confident, and others were quite strident in their opinions. They reflect the un-unified field of early Chicana feminism and the ways in which ideas of community, culture, and loyalty were mobilized against the emergence of an independent Chicana political agenda or national organizational effort. There is much documentary evidence; the challenge is how to make sense of it. The different stances activists took reflect the contested nature of early Chicana feminism, the effort to create consensus on gendered critiques within women's experience of organizing in the Chicano movement, and the conflict of divergent agendas, some internal and others external.

Early Chicana feminism emerged out of an ideologically contested and un-unified social movement field where regional and historical differences came into play. Below I discuss the fault lines over which dense and contested meanings were signified and struggled over.

INSTITUTIONS AND CULTURAL AUTHENTICITY

Those who called for the walkout viewed the conference as a YWCA conference. A delegation from the UCLA MEChA reported, "The idea for planning this conference grew out of a meeting of Houston's YWCA (which incidentally has just initiated a program to Eliminate Racism on a Three-Year Plan). Plans, having begun in December of last year, provided sufficient publicity to draw more Chicanas than anticipated, as well as ones more knowledgeable, opinionated and outspoken than probably anticipated."[43]

Some organizers from Houston were devastated by the walkout, but others seemed to take it in stride. For example, Lucy Moreno said, "The walkout was not so much a critique of the organizers themselves as it was a criticism of the institution of the YWCA itself."[44] Keta Miranda said she was deeply appreciative of their ability to organize a national conference and pull together women from so many different organizations. Yet it was the inclusion of so many Mexican American social, civic, and community organizations that led to criticism of the conference. The community donated the food (hot dogs), which was criticized as Anglo in arguments that mobilized cultural authenticity and a Chicano nationalist perspective. Elma Barrera described how the argument was polarized around culture: "We had hot dogs; they wanted rice and beans. Bertha [the activist from Magnolia neighborhood who was speaking on stage when the walkout organizers took the mic] wasn't Chicana enough; *we* weren't Chicana enough. They were barrio people, they wanted barrio issues. They want you to know they were gung-ho on Chicano things and we weren't Chicano enough."[45]

REGIONAL DIFFERENCES

Although the majority of women from California organizations did not join the walkout, the walkout faction was led mostly by activists from Los Angeles, who came to be known as the "California Women." Yet any strictly regional understanding of what led to the walkout breaks down entirely because one of the key Houston activists, an ally to many of the organizers, also walked out. In addition, two other key organizers from the Houston MAYO chapter, Gloria Guardiola and Yolanda Birdwell, who facilitated the sexuality workshop, said that although they understood the criticisms of the conference, they chose not to walk out because they felt that it would be more productive to have a conversation. While attributing the walkout entirely to regional differences would be inaccurate, many organizers did perceive differences in region, and once real differences were articulated, they were read through already existing regional tensions.

Barrera recalled this about the conference: "It was exciting when they came in to register because we were just expecting a few and we had never seen women like that because they were different women. They looked different, they acted differently, and they talked different." "They were from California, and we were just from the barrio," she said as she laughed and explained, "It was different, you know, that's what people don't understand about us." I asked her what she meant. She responded:

> We weren't sophisticated in that way, but California women were sophisti-cated. We didn't have César Chávez, you know. Even though I had picked cotton—my parents had picked cotton and my dad and my brother. As a mat-ter of fact, they were going to California to pick food because we didn't have any money. We weren't in a movement; we were just cotton pickers. And the people here were just, you know, people from the Eastside. Marta [Moreno] is from there, you know, right there from the eastside down close to Navi-gation where the Y was, and we just didn't . . . have any college professors or college students doing research and running things.[46]

I pointed out that she was running programs for her community at the Y and organizing a national conference. She laughed and said, "I know, I know, but we didn't know that. It was defined in a different way for us. We were so sin-cere about things that we were doing. And we just wanted to make it better for maybe a future generation or for us because we were still young, and it needed to be better for us."[47] I understood her to mean that although there was a powerful Chicano organizing tradition in Texas and that many women were central to these organizations, she did not feel part of a broader move-ment with the powerful leadership and cohesive cultural symbolism gener-ated by Chávez and the UFW.

In this and many more ways we can see that there were different politi-cal cultures or political logics in different regions, and this influenced how women engaged in the political process of organizing. While there is great historical diversity among Chicanas and Latinas, in this context many of the differences in political organizing cultures can be linked to the segregation Te-janas faced as part of their historical experience living in the South.[48] In segre-gated communities many Tejanas worked to change school boards or institu-tions, but because they were institutions in largely Mexican-origin towns or Mexican barrios in larger towns they came to feel a certain ownership of these spaces that activists in other regions may have disavowed as "white." Much of Chicano politics in Texas aimed at transforming those institutions, as can be seen by La Raza Unida Party's success in changing school boards to be more representative of the communities they served.[49] In many movement circles California, especially Southern California, was seen by and large as a more cultural nationalist region, accustomed to privileging and celebrating Chicano and Mexican culture as an alternative way of being outside of the hegemonic culture and institutions. While the Blowouts of East Los Angeles and the early student movement were intended to demand that society's institutions be responsive to those who populate them, their strategic vision of the youth movement in California was influenced by a form of Chicano nationalism. Juan Gómez-Quiñones has commented on the tensions in the movement between a rhetorical commitment to radicalism or revolution while most organizational efforts focused on reforming existing institutions like churches, schools, and unions.[50]

Leticia Hernández recalls, "There was regionalism. We weren't [seen as] Chicanas but as the 'the Californians.' The Texans would say, 'You Californians think you know it all' and 'You just learned about la raza, [but] we've been fighting this all our lives.'" When I asked which particular groups pointed out these regional differences, she responded, "Just, well, everybody—the Texas people in particular. I guess I felt bad that all the women from California were not together. I mean there was infighting between the women who went from UCLA and Cal State L.A. versus the Long Beach women. Some people coalesced with us, and some people walked out on us."[51] On the other hand, some Tejana organizers characterized the leaders of the walkout as young, inexperienced women who just needed something to protest. Differing regional organizing cultures and histories converged and conflicted, pitting those dedicated to institutional change against each other. The majority of the six hundred women who attended participated not as a YWCA event but as the first national gathering of women of the Chicano movement, which happened to be held at that venue.

THE "F" WORD: CONTESTED IDEOLOGIES, CONTESTED FEMINISM

When we went to that conference we were told that we were being too radical, that we were being too feminist, that we wanted to be like white women and that our job was to work alongside our man and to work within the movement.
LETICIA HERNÁNDEZ, INTERVIEW, JULY 30, 1992

When I investigated the source of Chicana consciousness among the Houston organizers, many told me they were just homegrown feminists. There was no women's group that they were involved in, or any organized pres-

ence of women among Chicanas, but individually they held very strong beliefs. Many women in the movement who were forthright organizers and may
have had an implicit gender analysis did not publicly advocate Chicana feminism. Many strong movement organizers challenged gender imbalances by
their sheer presence but did not have a feminist consciousness at the time.
I asked Barrera, "So you were a feminist then?" she responded, "Yeah. I was
full-fledged." Yolanda Birdwell said that she came of age politically along with
many members of the Houston MAYO chapter who had a feminist consciousness. When I asked what motivated them to organize the conference, one
of the women said simply, "Well, it had never been done before." Barrera
reflected:

> I would like to believe that why we did it was because feminism was new to
> us. . . . It was about freedom, political ideas. It was like an explosion; it was
> like being in a dark room and the door opening and the sun coming in. It was
> wonderful to me to know that I had the power and that I could do whatever
> I wanted. Never mind that I had been taken out of school to go pick cotton;
> that I had to be where all the women were all the time and I wasn't allowed
> to do a lot of things; and that my parents had a second-grade education; that
> my brother and I still graduated from high school and still went to college;
> that he became a lawyer and I became a reporter and that I went to live in
> Mexico. Never mind that I had done all those things. I was still, you know,
> cooped up, mentally. I was still cooped up, and then it was like wonderful
> when feminism came to be.[52]

The Houston conference experience filtered the way that NietoGomez
conceptualized this field of feminist political positions and expedited a theory
of Chicana feminism. In an effort to make sense of why Chicana feministas differed from other "strong" movement women. In her 1974 article, "La
Femenista," [sic] she argued:

> Differences between the philosophies of the "loyalists" and the "femenistas"
> have indeed been controversial. The loyalists do not recognize sexism as a
> legitimate issue in the Chicano movement. Femenistas see sexism as an inte-
> grated part of the Chicana's struggle in conjunction with her fight against
> racism.[53]

While NietoGomez was naming a fissure along ideological lines, other
scholars have argued that she created a dichotomy between feminists and non-

feminists. In our oral history she said that she was trying to comprehend how Chicanas with similar backgrounds and roles in the movement would part ways on voicing a critique of sexism in organizations or using what Betita Martinez called the "F" word. She recalled:

> From my own individual experience, the women's leadership was broken into two camps. Those in the camp I was a part of would say, "You can't advocate for civil rights and yet deny civil rights among your own group." Those women who were advocating nationalism felt that civil rights for women was good, but it wasn't time; it just wasn't the right time. You know, first things first. [They] were very strong, independent women—the same kind of women as we were as far as independence, intelligence, vocal-ness, and organizational abilities.[54]

NietoGomez explained that she felt a sense of solidarity and shared purpose with these women whom she had organized with for years. She wrote the piece to try to understand the opposing views of her sisters in struggle. She continued:

> They really felt that advocating feminism was a betrayal to the movement, like betraying the family, so they felt very strongly about what that meant. It was kind of promoting the thing that the women come last. I think with the men being at war [in Vietnam] and everything they felt even more strongly about it.

While NietoGomez explained how Chicanas who may have felt like sisters in the struggle became divided over the issue of feminism, the story of Cecelia (Chicki) Quijano and Sylvia Castillo illustrates that the issues were so complex that they divided friend from friend.

Quijano was from the neighborhood of Florence and was a leader of the Huntington Park High School walkout, the only one that happened in South Los Angeles during the 1968 East Los Angeles Blowouts. Quijano started hanging out with kids from the eastside through her brother, who had been in prison and was one of the veteranos dedicated to improving community safety, running after-school programs, combating police brutality, and making sure the kids in the neighborhood got to school. Quijano's participation in the walkouts was one of the successes of the Chicano youth movement: the ability to link youth across sectors and bring together high school and college students with street youth and former prisoners (pintos). The walkouts in South

Los Angeles brought together a coalition of African American, Latino (Chicano and Cuban), and white students. Quijano was a good student with excellent grades, but she was expelled from high school for her role in the walkouts. She received her GED and describes her road to college.

> During that period of time I was just kind of hanging out with the people from Roosevelt High School who I knew from the walkout. We were kind of up and down [the street], you know, different places, agencies, and there was an office—I think it was close to Wabash, if I'm not mistaken—where they did recruitment for the universities. That was like their whole focus there, getting young Chicanos and Chicanas into the university. So as it turns out, a couple of the people who were involved in that project were also veteranos from Florence, which is the neighborhood I grew up in. I believe that they were alumni of UCLA. So I talked to some of the people there, and they were able to get me into the program at Cal State Long Beach for Upward Bound, and also helped me apply to UCLA.[55]

Attending Upward Bound together in summer 1970, Quijano and Sylvia Castillo became fast friends, despite being from different neighborhoods. Sylvia grew up in the shadows of the burgeoning aircraft industry in Lakewood. The two remained friends through the school year, even though Chicki went to UCLA and Sylvia attended Long Beach State.

> Well, we would see each other all the time because we all went to the same parties. We went to a lot of house parties, and then there was also a Chicano Center there in Long Beach back in the day. So after we met we spent a lot of time there. There was really a lot of competition and distrust between us, because we were all from really different backgrounds. Sylvia was one of the only Chicanas from suburbia, you know, suburban Lakewood. I had always lived in South Central since I moved to L.A. when I was three years old. And, of course, also in the movement at that time everybody wanted to prove *quien era mas Chicano* [who was most Chicano], you know.

I teased her by asking, "So you were the *mera, mera?*" She replied:

> I was the mera. Well, in that group I was. Certainly, at the UCLA group it would have been a different story, because it was the kids from the eastside. But Sylvia was really, was so not. You know, she wanted to make friends. She was so sweet. So when we finally got past that kind of competition, distrust, we became really good friends. And of course, Sylvia had a car, and she had a boyfriend on the eastside, so that was all right.[56]

Although they had met in the movement and have remained friends for nearly forty years, the only time Quijano and Castillo ever had a falling out was during la conferencia. Quijano, part of the walkout group, arrived at the conference to find that one of her poems had been published in the Hijas newspaper, even though she disagreed with their women's rights agenda at the time. Their fight resulted in not speaking to each other for years, and each woman talked out how difficult it was to feel that they had lost their friendship over ideological differences.

Most of the women I interviewed identified themselves as Chicana feminists. But, as the oral histories reveal, this was a contested term, underpinned by anxieties. NietoGomez recalled:

> Well, we called ourselves feministas. There were all different kinds of feminists. I think a lot of women across the United States called themselves feministas, but they were uncomfortable with that term because it meant that they would have to justify themselves as being legitimate and not being Anglicozed, you know, and not fighting for the wrong movement, a different movement, a movement that didn't represent their interests and had been in conflict with their economic interests.[57]

When I asked Corinne Sánchez, "Did you ever have problems with using the word *feminist* to describe what you were doing?" she replied, "Never, [it was] more natural than *Chicana*."[58]

In contrast, when I asked Leticia Hernández if the Hijas de Cuauhtémoc called themselves feminists, she replied:

> Oh no, in fact we were fighting that. We didn't want to be white women. We didn't want to be feminists. We wanted to be women—Chicanas in our own right given equal partnership, you know, but it is, it is a feminist line. It's very much the same feminist line that all feminists have; we want to be equal partners.

Others came to their critique of sexism later. Chicki Quijano, for example, told me that it was not until a few years later, when she was working in a community organization, that she realized how profoundly sexism and the sexual double standard shaped the organizational culture for women in the movement. When we talked about her experience at the Houston conference, I asked her if she already knew at the MEChA meeting in Los Angeles that she would participate in the walkout. She replied, "I think probably as a result of that meeting, that's probably when MEChA got together and decided that *tontas* [fools] would go." I asked, "Why do you say that?"

Because we didn't realize that, we didn't understand the issues that were involved between men and women. For me, we felt, like, you know, very powerful. We had a big mouth, you know. I was completely ignorant of what feminism was about, and I didn't really get the issues.

I stated, "But you had experienced sexual harassment or seen sexism before."

Yeah, if a guy harassed me in the neighborhood, I would just tell my brother. There was nothing advanced about that, that was the way life already was, you know. My cultural experience was one where women were mothers and women were homemakers, and women were the nurturers, and it seemed like a Mother Nature kind of thing. All of that was what was being brought out as part of the culture. I pictured myself in that role, you know, that was my real role.[59]

Perhaps one of the greatest ironies of these conflicts is that Chicanas were not organizing to separate themselves from the movement but to see how the project of Chicano liberation could be expanded to the whole community, how to increase the subjects of liberation.[60] They were coming together in Houston to discuss their experience as women in the movement and how to mobilize together. They did not see themselves as dividing the movement; they were strengthening it.

These responses illustrate the contested nature of early Chicana feminisms as well as a continuum of Chicana feminist thought and practice. In addition, they reveal the profound effects of the vendida logic, which portrayed Chicana feminists as traitors to the race (malinches), whitewashed (agringadas), or sexually deviant due to their challenge to patriarchy.[61] The emergence of early Chicana feminism was caught between those in the Chicano movement who viewed claims of women's equality and liberation as an "anglo bourgeoise trip" and those on in the women's liberation movement who failed to see race and class issues as "feminist" issues. Feminism in the United States is usually stereotyped and reduced to liberal feminism, which was quite blind to how gender was lived through race and class. But even radical and socialist feminists could fall short in their social analysis, leading often to the alienation of many women of color feminists. For example, Betita Martinez, who began organizing in 1959 with the civil rights movement and the Cuban solidarity movement, joined SNCC in 1961. She was a member of SNCC's women's group with Casey Hayden and Mary King and became the head of SNCC New York in 1964.[62] She describes this tension in her participation with New York Radical Women:

It made sense until the day that Martin Luther King was assassinated, and there was a meeting that night and nobody was even talking about Martin Luther King being assassinated. All white women. I said, "What is this? This is crazy. I'm not about to complain about my husband tonight or whatever, not doing the dishes." So I left, and I never went back, and that was the kind of experience that a number of women of color had in terms of a women's movement. So while that tension—the racism within the women's movement, the classism within the women's movement—were not unknown subjects, I guess unlike some other Chicanas I also felt that there were aspects of the women's movement that women of color had to pay attention to. We were connected in ways. There really *was* sexism. I saw the sexism in the Chicano movement. There were other issues the white women would talk about, too. There were concerns, clinics, and rape and wife beating. There were these issues that crossed color lines.

This impasse created a need for Chicana feminists to create a space of their own, grounded in their own political concerns and cultural and social worlds—a feminism that understood how gender was lived through class and race oppression—a third space feminism.[63]

While understanding the racial or class oppression that was named by both nationalists and Marxists in the movimiento, Chicana feminists began using what would later be called an intersectional analysis, one of the touchstones of women of color feminist theory. Like other sister formations, early Chicana feminists called attention to the ways that their experience of economic exploitation was both racial and gendered and, similarly, how racial hatred and discrimination were constructed along class, gender, and sexual dimensions. Chicana feminists began to point out how they experienced class exploitation vis-à-vis the marginalization of women's role in production and their exploitation in the reproduction of labor. While both white women and Chicano men faced labor market segmentation and economic discrimination, Chicanas showed how patriarchy, capitalism, and racism came together as overlapping systems of power to marginalize them.

Several members of the Hijas de Cuauhtémoc left politics after the conference, and the group ceased to exist in the same manifestation. Leticia Hernández explained:

For me, it made it really difficult to stay with it. I just said, "You know what? I can't deal with this anymore." There was a lot of infighting in our own group. When we came back home . . . it was a very stressful time going to Houston. It was stressful in the car. We had two station wagons, and we had eight women in each station wagon—all from Long Beach and L.A. It was a hard trip. I guess a disappointing trip, and then of course to be shut down that way. We were deflated.[64]

While some members of Hijas such as Anna NietoGomez and Corinne Sánchez graduated or moved on from Long Beach State, others continued with campus organizing over the following years at Cal State Long Beach. For example, during an orientation night in October 1972, Sylvia Castillo and Martha López served as spokeswomen for the Hijas de Cuauhtémoc at an event attended by thirty mujeres to discuss the issues Chicanas faced on campus and in the Chicano movement.[65] That year Castillo served as chair of the Hijas de Cuauhtémoc, and other organizational tasks rotated between her and other members of the *mesa directiva* that included Martha López, Norma Owen, and Cindy Honesto.[66] The core membership that year was approximately fifteen women. The group organized their own events, established counseling programs for Chicana students, formed a Chicana teatro group, and hosted self-defense classes. They also planned ways to stay in communication with MEChA's chairperson, Dolores Ramos, in order to advocate for Chicana students on campus.[67] They organized events off campus, including the seminar "La Mujer" in the city at Hawaiian Gardens, which included an educational seminar, discussion, a presentation by Teatro Carnalas Unidas, and a screening of *Salt of the Earth*, as well as pan dulce and café.

The fourth issue of *Hijas de Cuauhtémoc* was written and pasted up but never published. It contained a report on the Houston conference, an article on women's rights in Mexico, an article on Chicanas in education, and an exposé titled "Young Chicanas Speak Out," which addressed colorism and the European standard of beauty in the Chicano community, the sexual double standard, and sex education. Although no further issues were published after the 1971 Houston conference, the political project of the Hijas was continued in community-based organizing, the development of early Chicana Studies, and the publication of the first journal of Chicana scholarship, *Encuentro Femenil*, in 1973.

CONCLUSION

"By 1971 contact between Raza women had been sharply reduced because of pressures to close off communication by the nationalist movement."[68] This closing of communication was probably most dramatically illustrated by the walkout staged at the 1971 Conferencia de Mujeres por la Raza in Houston. Although many activists took things in stride and continued to orga-

nize, others experienced deep existential questions. Leticia Hernández recalled how her experiences in Houston led her to leave political organizing
and turn her attention to cultural work.

> [I realized] for as much as they wanted to talk about liberation of Chicanas
> they were still trying to please their men, and I couldn't comprehend that
> after we came back from the Houston conference. I was just so disillusioned
> with the whole thing that I said, "You know what? I don't need this shit," and
> I just backed away. I backed away from MEChA, I backed away from Hijas
> and the women's group. That's when I got involved with the Ballet Folk-
> lórico and I dedicated all my energies to that.[69]

The journey that led to this research was motivated by many questions:
What did the conference organizers have in mind when they put the event
together? What was at the root of the conflict? Why do people who (now) call
themselves feminist occupy both sides of this schism? What would the history
of Chicana feminism be like if a national movement had formed in 1971, as
the conference seemed to promise? How do we frame or understand the 1971
Houston conference? In the words of Elma Barrera, spoken just days after the
conference, "La Conferencia was a lot of things. It was anger, sisterhood, disunity; it was organizing for the future."[70]

CHAPTER SIX

CHICANAS IN MOVEMENT: ACTIVIST AND SCHOLARLY LEGACIES IN THE MAKING

FOLLOWING THE POLITICAL organizing trajectories of members of the Hijas de Cuauhtémoc throughout the 1970s, this chapter explores how many of the members became involved in community-based organizations, established early Chicana Studies, and participated in new forms of solidarity inspired by movements for decolonization and national liberation in the third world. Discovering new forms of internationalism and third world consciousness, many of the members traveled with women's delegations to China and the 1975 UN International Women's Year in Mexico City, as well coordinated national solidarity brigades to Cuba. This new consciousness coincided with their work building community organizations in the greater Los Angeles area around the issues of welfare, employment, education, health, and violence prevention.

The 1970s were a formative decade of struggle for Chicana Studies within the new field of Chicano Studies until more formal spaces became institutionalized with the founding of Mujeres Activas en Letras y Cambio Social (Women Active in Letters and Social Change, MALCS) in 1982 and the formation of the Chicana caucus in 1983, which formally became part of the National Association for Chicano Studies in 1986. The chapter concludes by reflecting on the contested terrain on which Chicana feminisms developed in the 1960s and 1970s and maps out the legacies on which Chicana and women of color feminist scholars and activists continue to build.

FROM NATIONALISM TO INTERNATIONALISM

The Hijas de Cuauhtémoc expanded and multiplied the subjects of liberation hailed within nationalism by grounding a different and political notion of historicity, memory, and political genealogy. However, this strategy of retrofitting nationalism ultimately became ineffective because the effort to use a historical material basis to link their political vision and activism to earlier revolutionary women activists was eventually overtaken by the use of over-determined signifiers of culture and national belonging by others. This is illustrated in the struggle of signification at the Houston conference, involving markers of culture and authenticity. Although many activists, ironically on both sides of the walkout, would later continue to push for gender equality and women's rights, the first national conference was seen as a pivotal moment—whether Chicanas could consolidate a national presence and share an agenda in the movement. The argument for walking out was staged through the sliding signifiers of culture, language, food, loyalty to men in times of war, and standing with the "community." Many activists tried, and sometimes succeeded, to retrofit nationalism, but eventually the majority of this political cohort moved out of the practices through which cultural nationalism had become a disciplining mechanism for women and went on to work with community-based and internationalist struggles.[1] This shift was not isolated to the Chicano movement. Max Elbaum's important study illustrates how sixties radicals, inspired by third world revolutions, turned increasingly toward internationalism and a third world brand of communism.[2] Within the feminist movement, there was a different and growing international vision inspired by the Decade of Women and the First International Women's Year. Many women of color feminists saw their frustrations echoed at the international conference, where the first world feminist focus on a liberal agenda of political rights was challenged by third world feminists who linked their agendas for women's rights with economic and cultural rights.[3]

The multiple feminist insurgencies of U.S. women of color emerged not just from an antisexist critique of nationalist movements or an antiracist critique of women's liberation, but from the kinds of coalitions between disparate groups of women of color that came together under the banner of third world solidarity. This internationalism and third world solidarity also generated new forms of consciousness among racially marginalized peoples, women in particular, that helped build cross-racial alliances and the political subjectivity "people of color" and U.S. third world women or "women of color."

Accordingly, the members of Hijas de Cuauhtémoc built new forms of internationalism and third world consciousness after the organization ceased to formally exist. Corinne Sánchez traveled to Mexico City in 1975 for the International Women's Year (IWY), along with other women from Long Beach who also worked for the CSAC.[4] In a 1997 interview Sánchez commented on the importance of this confluence:

It was exciting for women in general, but [for us] more of the minority issues were being given preference, and we became more involved with the women's free clinic. We got involved with a lot of health issues, women's conferences. It was mixed like International Women's Year. We took a whole group of women to International Women's Year.[5]

The Chicana historian Marisela Chávez also has written about Chicana activists from California and Texas who attended the IWY conference in Mexico City, the first conference of the three that would be held as part of the UN Decade of Women.[6] She argued that while their experiences changed neither their beliefs nor their organizing strategies, it did galvanize Chicanas "to act locally and nationally in light of their newfound international bonds."[7] According to Sánchez, as a result of the growing focus on the notion of third world liberation, she traveled to China in 1976.

> Mao was still alive. It was part of an educational group. A lot of the women were Marxist. We [traveled with] the People's Friendship Association, and we were more interested in how China struggled through the sexism and the racism, and all of those isms. We wanted to see it firsthand. We went more as a part of this women's group that developed out of the Chicano center. We were outgrowths. There were several of us who went after that.[8]

In 1977 NietoGomez received a scholarship from the China Friendship Association to travel to China as part of a women's solidarity trip. It gave her an opportunity to reflect on her then-recent battle at California State University, Northridge: "I learned women's history in China and really got a perspective of what I had gone through, what so many people have gone through, just a process of fighting for change."[9] Sylvia Castillo left Cal State Long Beach in 1972 and volunteered for a La Raza Unida Party campaign to incorporate East Los Angeles as a city. The RUP activists in California were trying to build a base that could extend the work of the Chicano third party started in Crystal City, Texas.[10] In 1976 Castillo traveled to Cuba with a delegation of North American youth to build apartments for textile workers. Inspired by the power of the Cuban and Angolan women leading the work brigades, she returned home and dedicated the next five years to the effort to end the U.S. economic blockade.[11] Keta Miranda also traveled to Cuba and continued to engage in community organizing, working for the California chapter of La Raza Unida Party, writing for *La Raza*, and later becoming an organizer for the Communist Party USA.

Throughout the 1970s U.S. women of color built coalitions around key issues such as prisoners' rights and violence against women of color. The latter included the cases of Joanne Little, who was charged with killing a prison guard who had repeatedly raped her, and Inéz Garcia, who was incarcerated for second degree murder for killing the man who held her down while another man raped her. Other shared political interests that forged a women of color political project included a call to end forced sterilization and the articulation of a broader reproductive health agenda for women of color, which had not been adequately taken up by the women's movement.[12] Various organizations started third world women's child care centers and collectives to address the need for child care that was attentive to linguistic and cultural differences. Other convergences occurred around labor rights, welfare rights, and access to education and affirmative action. For example, Corinne Sánchez went on to work at the Chicana Service Action Center (CSAC) in East Los Angeles, an economic development project of the Comisión Femenil Mexicana Nacional, and later became an attorney, serving as the executive director of the multiservice Chicano/Latino community center, El Proyecto del Barrio, in the San Fernando Valley. Anna NietoGomez worked closely with community organizations such as the CSAC, as well as the Chicana Welfare Rights Organization. Sylvia Castillo went on to work with the Community Coalition, a grassroots organization that helps "transform the social and economic conditions in South L.A. that foster addiction, crime, violence and poverty by building a community institution that involves thousands in creating, influencing and changing public policy."[13] NietoGomez told me that her feminism was inspired by the work of community women activists of the 1950s and early 1960s in the Community Service Organization and various election campaigns of Edward Roybal. In this way the roots of Chicana feminism emerged from the community, traveled through the university, and returned to community and cross-border visions of social change.

CHICANA STUDIES: SCHOLARSHIP ON THE FRONT LINES

The emergence of the field of Ethnic Studies was the result of decades of struggle on the part of movements for educational access, self-determination, and building collective knowledge outside of Eurocentric paradigms. The Third World Liberation Fronts at San Francisco State and UC Berkeley went on strike and achieved the institutionalization of these forms of knowledge production in the founding of Ethnic Studies departments in 1969.[14] While *El Plan de Santa Barbara: A Chicano Plan for Higher Education* adopted in April 1969 helped establish a vision for Chicano Studies, Chicana feminists have called attention to *El Plan*'s exclusion of women, leading Mary Pardo to label it a "man"-ifesto and others to rewrite it to encapsulate a feminist vision, renaming it "El Plan de Santa y Barbara."[15]

While the inclusion of women in Ethnic Studies is often historicized as part of the multiculturalism of the 1980s, it was in fact a struggle of early women of color feminists during the very founding Ethnic Studies programs. Hijas de Cuauhtémoc members Anna NietoGomez and Corinne Sánchez played a critical role in the formation of early Chicana Studies, both in institutionalizing spaces for the study of gender and sexuality in Chicano Studies and in creating new curricula. Building Chicana Studies was part of movement work and was often characterized as the intellectual arm of the movement. In 1970 at the San Diego Chicano Coordinating Council in Higher Education meeting, the organizational body that drafted *El Plan de Santa Barbara*, the Chicana caucus demanded that both curricula and affirmative action for Chicanas be developed just one year after *El Plan* was adopted.[16] These measures fought against the ways female activists were told that education would be wasted on women because it was assumed that "all" they would do after leaving the university was become mothers.

In May 1972 a Chicano Studies/MEChA conference was held at California State University, Northridge. A resolution was passed requiring all Chicano Studies majors to take at least one class on "la Mujer." It declared: "This proposal recognizes the need to lift the veil of the Virgin's face to show a real woman who is not exempt from the trials of life. In order to truly understand the needs and problems of La Raza, we must include the Chicana in our study."[17] The following year the Chicana Curriculum Workshop, organized at UCLA on June 18–22, brought together the leading Chicana thinkers and resulted in a groundbreaking Chicana curriculum for universities that could be adapted for high schools. It was published as a handbook titled *New Directions in Education: Estudios Femeniles de la Chicana*, edited by Anna NietoGomez and Corrine Sánchez.[18]

Tired of the faded yellow images of Azteca poster princesses that some in the movement held up to them as mirrors, Chicana activists played a formative role in seeking and producing new forms of knowledge. *Encuentro Femenil* discussed the need to move beyond women's symbolic value within Chicano Studies.

In 1969, there was a great eagerness to experience the first Chicano Studies classes. The women were very excited to learn about their heritage both as Chicanos and as mujeres. However, the women were very disappointed to discover that neither Chicano history, Mexican history, nor Chicano literature included any measurable material on the mujer. At best she would be referred to mystically as "la India," the bulwark of the family, or she would be referred to romantically as "la Adelita," "la Soldadera" of the movement.

La mujer either had a baby in her arms or a rifle in her hand or both. But few dealt with the identity of la mujer in the family, or even knew who "la Adelita" was. They were merely symbols for her to look towards, and if she was any Chicana at all, the spirit of either model was expected to appear instinctively.[19]

The Chicana print community created the space, knowledge production, publication, and circulation that proved vital for early Chicana studies as these periodicals and manifestos moved into the classroom and were assigned as required reading as scholarship was being developed. A sampling of early Chicana Studies syllabi in the years 1971–1974 include many articles from a women's special issue of *Regeneración*, volumes 1 and 2 of *Encuentro Femenil*, and the political pamphlet published by Pathfinder Press, *Chicanas Speak Out, Women: New Voice of la Raza*, which was written by Mirta Vidal and covered the 1971 Houston conference. Early Chicana studies courses also included articles on women from a wide array of newspapers from different sectors of the Chicano Movement across the Southwest, including *Hijas de Cuauhté-moc*, *El Grito del Norte*, *El Malcriado* (the UFW paper), MEChA newspapers, and *La Verdad* (from San Diego, California). Indeed, the need to classroom materials for burgeoning Chicana studies classes is what motivated Dorinda Moreno to compile *La mujer en pie de lucha* for a class at San Francisco State University. Other texts used at this time included *Third World Woman*, books on women's suffrage and participation in the Mexican Revolution, classic socialist readings on "the woman question," Frantz Fanon's *Dying Colonialism*, and women's movement's texts such as Celestine Ware's *Woman Power: The Movement for Women's Liberation* and Robin Morgan's *Sisterhood Is Powerful*.[20]

The emergence of a feminist intellectual and political tradition within Chicano Studies was not without conflict. The Chicana feminist historian Cynthia Orozco documented Chicana Studies and the ideological conflicts that hindered its early flourishing, finding, in short, that "feminism has been suppressed and feminists have been repressed."[21] The most notorious struggle over sexism within Chicano Studies in these early years occurred over the denial of tenure and termination of Anna NietoGomez at Cal State Northridge in 1976. While clearly personalities and personal conflicts were involved, the NietoGomez case at CSUN, which houses one of the largest and most historic Departments of Chicano Studies, was the canary in the coal mine signaling to Chicana feminista activists and writers alike the conditions in which they would have to fight in order to bring forth the vibrant field of Chicana Studies that thrives today.

"A CASE OF SEXISM": ANNA NIETOGOMEZ
AND THE FIGHT FOR TENURE

*History will reflect how the study of the Chicana created a political
controversy because it mirrored the contradiction between the rhetoric
of liberation and the practice of continued oppression.*
ANNA NIETOGOMEZ, LETTER OF RESIGNATION, SEPTEMBER 3, 1976

On February 27, 1976, the Personnel Review Committee of the Chicano
Studies Department voted to deny Anna NietoGomez tenure and recommend 1976 as her terminal year. While the chair of the department and the
dean of the division eventually agreed with this decision, many student and
community groups called it "a case of sexism."[22] On September 3, 1976, after
a very public fight over her tenure, Anna NietoGomez officially resigned from
her position at California State University, Northridge.[23]

NietoGomez began teaching in Chicano Studies at CSUN in 1971. While
this was definitely a demanding time in her life, NietoGomez described the
vibrancy of the period.

> It was my intention to do some more, but quite frankly when I look back at
> that time, I was a crazy woman. I mean, we put out two journals. I was in-
> volved in a welfare rights organization, an employment organization, and
> we were starting a new child care center in the Valley. I was teaching, and
> when you're teaching, I mean, you have to prep every night. I would start at
> eleven o'clock and go to bed at two or three. I was always reading and doing
> research and writing. We were always going out and speaking. It was a very
> prolific time. I had my baby. Milio [Emilio, her son] never slept more than
> four hours at a time, so you put him to bed at ten and around two o'clock he
> was ready to start the day. When he woke up he didn't wake up for a bottle;
> he woke up to start the day. I think I was so prolific because for the first time
> I felt so secure, so accepted. Everything I did had complete support.

Although NietoGomez had received excellent reviews up until 1975, the year
before she was to receive tenure, the Personnel Committee recommended that
she be granted another year "to balance her professional growth." The committee recommended that she focus on pursuing graduate study toward an advanced degree, get more involved in the development of the department, and
upgrade her instructional performance.[24] The following year, the Personnel
Review Committee, consisting of three faculty members and three students
(elected by the faculty and by MEChA) issued the official decision to deny

NietoGomez tenure and recommend 1976 as her terminal year. The basis of their decision was that "no satisfactory improvement [was] made on recommendations suggested by the review committee one year ago.[25]

On March 5, 1976, in an open meeting with the committee, NietoGomez spoke out against the decision and argued that sexism within the department resulted in the difficulty of teaching Chicana Studies and a double standard in faculty review. In attendance were sixty students, some of whom spoke about harassment they suffered as a result of being associated with Chicana feminists and taking Chicana classes.[26] To address the specific criticism that she had no graduate training, NietoGomez wrote, "It's true, I have not received a M.A., but as I understand it, neither has the present nor has the past chairperson of Chicano Studies. This is perfectly all right in the world of double standards."[27] NietoGomez and the support committee that formed to fight the decision had a hard time believing the department would deny her tenure on that basis, because, according to NietoGomez, "There were four men [in the department] with tenure who only had a B.A. Chicano Studies [at the time] had two roads you could take. You could either go the traditional road and publish, or you could go the nontraditional road and be involved in the community. Well, I chose being involved in the community, and I did publish."[28]

NietoGomez refuted the decision and presented further documentation of her publications, community-based research, and service to the university. Citing the Chicano Studies mission to bridge the academy and the community, NietoGomez argued that she acquired "professional growth" outside of the university through her extensive work with community organizations and institutions. In the documentation on her professional growth, NietoGomez wrote that her involvement with community organizations was the vehicle through which she collected data and published research on vital issues affecting Chicanas in such areas as child care, welfare, employment, and women's participation in the movement. She claimed, "Community organizations have been my source of training in Chicano Studies."[29]

The supplemental documents from her tenure file show that she had sixteen publications, most of which involved community-based research and the development of a Chicana studies curriculum. During her years at CSUN, NietoGomez also developed four courses, "Contemporary Issues of the Chicana," "History of the Chicana," "The Family," and "Third World Woman." She served as an adviser to several organizations, including Hermanas Unidas and the Chicano House child care co-op. She also played a pivotal role in developing resource material on the Chicana in both the Chicano Studies library and in the university library.

The charge of sexism by NietoGomez was refuted as slander and an effort "to discredit members of the Chicano Studies Personnel and Review Committee (four of whom are women)."[30] The faculty and students who supported NietoGomez's dismissal charged that she was "academically deficient" and "incompetent."[31] They argued that her lectures were disorganized, that she did not speak Spanish, and that the enrollment in her classes had been low. Further, they criticized her for not regularly attending departmental functions.

On March 10, 1976, NietoGomez attended an open MEChA meeting and she distributed her curriculum vitae and a description of her scholarly, teaching, and community work. Students asked questions about a leaflet condemning NietoGomez for initiating an appeals process. Some students accused NietoGomez of wanting to cause the downfall of Chicano Studies. Other students spoke out against the sexism in Chicano Studies. They were criticized for portraying Chicano Studies in a negative light and called provocateurs. Four female students read their statement, "Sexism Is Not the Issue," defending the vote to deny NietoGomez tenure. At the meeting she suggested that students vote to retain or terminate her themselves. However, MEChA officials reacted negatively, saying that this would violate the good faith that should be shown to the Personnel Review Committee.[32] Eventually, the meeting degenerated into a back and forth between those who supported NietoGomez and those who did not.

After a review of the additional materials she submitted, the Personnel Review Committee voted again to recommend termination on March 17. On March 26 NietoGomez received a letter from the chairperson of the Chicano Affairs Committee supporting the original decision of termination. Students across campus who were outraged at the treatment of NietoGomez formed a support committee that consisted of students, community members, and activists. In addition, CSUN students printed a newspaper, *Women Struggle*, that detailed NietoGomez's fight for tenure. Several other community and student publications ran editorials in support of NietoGomez, including the *CSAC NEWS*, *CSAC News & Letters*, and *La Gente* (see figure I.16), the Chicano student newspaper at UCLA.

Editorial staff from *La Gente* attended the open MEChA meeting and wrote an editorial in support of NietoGomez. As the movement to support Anna NietoGomez grew, students and community activists circulated petitions and wrote letters to the president of the university and the dean of the School of Humanities. Among her prominent supporters were Francisca Flores, director of the Chicana Service Action Center; Martha P. Cotera, librarian, writer, and La Raza Unida Party activist; Grace M. Davis, deputy mayor of Los Angeles; and actress and activist Jane Fonda. The Support Committee for Anna NietoGomez organized a rally on May 17, 1976, at CSUN to demand her reinstatement.

Dismayed that NietoGomez chose to challenge the decision, her opponents on campus accused her of trying to end Chicano Studies by taking the decision to the "white" administration. In addition to charging NietoGomez with purposely "creating anarchy," a tactic used by provocateurs, faculty statements accused her of "self-indulgent individualism" because she "placed herself above the collective" decision of the committee and "purposely escalated the situation into a major crisis."[33] The position paper read:

> Criticism must be kept within the group. In no case can it be permitted for members to take their case to the administration or to go to outside groups for support. When this occurs, the actions of that person or persons become self-indulgent and break down any collective strength that the group may have. An analysis of the facts clearly demonstrates that Anna wanted to provoke a crisis.[34]

The statement ended by declaring "that Anna's taking the issue outside of the body, to the administration and to the white feminists, is incorrect."[35] Playing on the common antifeminist themes of individualism, dividing/destroying the movement, and being agringadas and the vendida logic (in this case to the administration), the CSUN chapter of MEChA issued a statement declaring, "Be it known that the faculty and the Mecha [sic] Body of the Chicano Studies Department at CSUN unanimously support the action taken by its Personnel Review Committee." It further condemned NietoGomez because she "violated the precepts of this organization by seeking and obtaining aid as well as support outside the Chicano Studies Department."[36] The statement went on to condemn the tactics of *La Gente de Aztlán* of UCLA for publishing an editorial addressing what they saw "as an in-house issue to be decided upon by this body." Instead of announcing the fact that they were in attendance at the meeting, CSUN MEChA criticized "the publication's staff [for taking] it upon themselves in an unobjective gesture to state a position on a matter which did not concern them at all."[37] Claiming that "the issue of sexism in Chicano Studies is not an internal problem, it is an issue of the people, and that it is everyone's responsibility to take a stand against sexism," NietoGomez continued to speak out and meet with student organizations in Los Angeles. She met with *La Gente*'s staff to discuss censorship and criticism of their editorial, as well as with MEChA Central, which comprised the leadership of all MEChA chapters in the greater Los Angeles area.

NietoGomez eventually pursued the case with the Equal Employment Opportunity Commission, claiming sex discrimination or sexism and unequal promotion practices.[38] In addition, NietoGomez feared the committee members made their decision based on rumor and accusations of student harassment instead of adhering to her teaching and publication record.[39] The rumor that dismayed NietoGomez the most was that she had raped a male student, although no complaint was ever filed. She herself filed a grievance procedure to try to get to the bottom of the issue. No evidence was ever presented in the case. NietoGomez claimed that rumors were used to "confuse the issue as a personal one instead of looking into the political implications of exploiting the seniority and carnalismo system to protect the vested interests of a few."[40]

During the battle over her tenure at CSUN, NietoGomez received death threats and threatening letters at her faculty office. She recalled, "It was like, you know, these old movies about the witch-hunts and the hysteria in Salem? Just like that. Ayy, that was crazy. I was getting threatening phone calls at night. They vandalized my door." Her office door was defaced. The word "Puta [Whore]" was carved so deeply into it that it had to be replaced.

Students who supported NietoGomez were attacked and called "stupid, nonmovement, maricons [fags], and they were accused of being pigs [police]."[41] NietoGomez claimed that students were intimidated so that when fall quarter rolled around enrollments in her classes were very low. She explained:

> At that point I gave up and I quit. What was I doing here if they didn't want me? What was the point? What was I trying to prove? So I got even further depressed, and my mom—whom I had been estranged from because she never supported my being active in the civil rights movement—told me to come home.[42]

NietoGomez resigned on September 3, 1976. Clearly written under duress, her letter of resignation outlines the three reasons she felt she was terminated.

1) difference in ideology on feminism, sexism and cultural nationalism;
2) my involvement with independent Chicano Student activists;
3) my involvement with women and my continued differences with the immature Phd "feudal jefe" who maintains influence over students and faculty through chisme, intimidation, and macho hero-worship.

The last point is a reference to the ways in which the issues were not only polarized but also became a highly personalized battle between NietoGomez and the Chicano historian and personnel committee member Rodolfo Acuña. The letter concluded, "My record stands clear: I have worked in the community. I have published 16 articles in five years in a pioneer field. This is more than any other person with tenure in Chicano Studies can say."[43]

When discussing what happened, NietoGomez focused on the climate in which she worked and some defining moments or disjunctures when she realized that she and her colleagues did not share the same understanding of what was important. She recalled:

> We started the women's organization Las Hermanas. Marlene Sanchez (Mars for short), Rosa Dominguez, Tomas Zavala, Bernice Rincon, and other people like that who very curious about what was happening in the world so they formed an international students organization with other students from around the world. I became their adviser, and they would work out of my office. That was the beginning of the end for me at Northridge because it encouraged the students to look outside Chicano Studies. At first I didn't understand it, I mean, why wouldn't you want to know what's going on in Peru or in Chile, you know, [with what happened to] Salvador Allende. Why wasn't that important? I encouraged students to take classes in different departments. Later on I understood that it was seen as a threat to Chicano studies. Chicanos came to campus to learn, to find out about the world, but I realized that our activities were seen as taking students away from Chicano Studies.

Other sources of conflict included how to handle cases of apparent child abuse at the child care cooperative, as well as criticism of NietoGomez because several gay men came out and began to organize openly, which was attributed to her classes.

> They were very proud of who they were, and they were into their relationships, so that threatened a lot of males who were interested the Chicana movement who wanted to support it but didn't want to be called gay. So that was a very big threat to the strong sense of homophobia.

By end of the struggle, NietoGomez could not find a full-time teaching job and felt that she had been "blacklisted" from Chicano studies. "I lost all my friends, it appeared like, I felt like I was completely abandoned by the civil rights movement that I had worked so hard in—by the women—because they just kind of disappeared. It got so bad, it got so ugly, you know."[44] Nieto-Gomez was unemployed for several years. As a single mother with a small child, she felt the only way to survive was to move back home to San Bernardino, where she eventually found work as an affirmative action officer for the county. Her EEOC claim was ultimately denied because the department gave tenure to a female faculty member after NietoGomez's termination.[45]

While the struggle for Chicana Studies reemerged in the early 1980s, NietoGomez represents a generational gap of Chicana knowledge, scholarship, and activism as very few movement women remained to become founding faculty within Chicano Studies.[46] The struggle continued through the 1970s and early 1980s as embodied by the 1981 formation of Mujeres en Marcha, a group of Chicana scholars at UC Berkeley who published *Chicanas in the '80s: Unsettled Issues*.[47] At the eleventh annual NACS conference in Tempe, Arizona, in 1982, the group organized a panel to bring attention to gender inequality and create discussion about the struggle of Chicanas to be recognized as scholars within the organization and the field of Chicano Studies.[48] Powerfully using consciousness-raising techniques, they generated three proposals for the next NACS conference: (1) a plenary on gender oppression; (2) child care provisions; and (3) an antisexism session organized by men of the organization. While none of these changes was implemented at the 1983 NACS conference, the Chicana Caucus of NACS was formed that year, even though it was not formally incorporated into the organization until 1986.[49]

Some women who were active in the movimiento such as Adaljiza Sosa-Riddell went on to help establish Mujeres Activas en Letras y Cambio Social (Women Active in Letters and Social Change) (MALCS) in spring 1982 at a meeting of Chicana/Latina scholars and activists at UC Davis.[50] The organization was founded due to a sense of isolation and lack of acknowledgment of Chicana/Latina scholars. The MALCS declaration was written in 1983, and the first MALCS Summer Institute was held in 1985 at UC Davis. MALCS produced a newsletter beginning in 1984, which then became a working paper series titled *Trabajos Monográficos*. In 1991 the series became the journal *Chicana Studies*, which has now become the *Journal of Chicana/Latina Studies*. With its annual summer institutes designed to mentor Chicana/Latina scholars and generate scholarship and criticism, the organization continues to this day.

While early Chicana Studies proponents did not see immediate changes, the theme of the 1984 NACS conference was "Voces de la Mujer." Cynthia Orozco wrote, "Without a doubt, the greatest problem in Chicano Studies for women has been the suppression of feminism. In the final analysis, the possibility of feminism depends on the willingness of men to give up power and privilege. Thus far, men in Chicano Studies have not done so."[51] Acknowledging heterosexism and the interconnection of sexual, racial, class, and gender oppressions, in 1990 the Lesbian Caucus was incorporated into the NACS, despite resistance at the conference in Albuquerque, New Mexico.[52]

Although there have been great strides made in the field and gender and sexuality continue to be the most vibrant and fastest-growing areas of Chicana and Chicano Studies, some resistance has continued. For example, Ignacio Garcia's now-infamous 1996 essay, "Juncture in the Road: Chicano Studies since 'El Plan de Santa Barbara,'" draws the line between good Chicano Studies scholarship and what he calls "post-modern sectarianism—lesbian-feminism, neo-Marxism, and a militant form of Latinoism." He explains his view:

> Chicana Studies, as an extension or at times a competitor of Chicano Studies, has become possibly the major challenge to the field [of Chicano Studies]. Women scholars are searching for new paradigms, and in the process have debunked or critically assailed much of the early Chicano scholarship. . . . However, a small but influential number of Chicana scholars have taken on an adversarial role in their relations to Chicano Studies, and they are influencing the direction of Chicana scholarship. These gender nationalists find the lurking "macho" in every Chicano scholarly work.[53]

Finally, in 1995, at its twenty-fourth annual conference, NACS officially changed its name to the National Association of Chicana and Chicano Studies (NACCS) to reflect growing gender and feminist consciousness within the organization. However, many Chicana scholars and activists are still struggling against what Anna Sandoval observes as "an uncritical male-centered nationalism [that] is resurfacing in some settings," often, discouragingly, among younger male scholars who supposedly "know better."[54] On the other hand, many veteranos and veteranas have retooled and have a more holistic vision based on the lessons learned in early Chicana feminist scholarship and activism, and many more generations are building on this legacy.

EARLY CHICANA FEMINIST PRACTICES AND THEORIES: LEGACIES IN THE MAKING

This book is an archaeology of three layers of remembrance that illustrate how memory and representations of the past animate political subjectivities and have the potential to shift the horizon of political possibility. For emergent political subjects, retrofitted memory creates alternative registers of meaning and authority, both moral and political. The first instance of retrofitted memory is when women in Mexico organized to become political subjects and fight the dictatorship of Porfirio Díaz at the turn of the twentieth century. Naming themselves daughters of Cuauhtémoc situated them in the decolonizing legacy of the last Aztec emperor, who died fighting Spanish colonization, in their fight against Díaz's neocolonial efforts to sell Mexico's wealth to U.S. economic interests in the name of "modernity." It was from within this legacy that the activists waged their fight for women's suffrage and the right to education. The second remembrance is the way in which Chicanas active in the Chicano movement of the 1960 and 1970s claimed these feminist foremothers as a way to locate their struggle for social justice in dominant society and for women's rights in their own communities as part of a larger revolutionary struggle.

The third remembrance is our reclaiming of las Chicanas del movimiento and activists in the social movements of the 1960s and 1970s as part of a legacy for younger generations of women of color feminists who claim them as our own. This is a form of retrofitted memory because we claim them as part of our feminist legacy for their early insistence on the interconnectedness of our struggles for racial, gendered, sexual, and economic justice. We claim their anti-imperialist struggles and their view that we could not work for justice in our communities without attention to our interconnectedness to others. Their understanding of a common struggle in their challenge to capitalism, white supremacy, heterosexism, and patriarchy motivated me when I first heard these histories as an undergraduate woman of color activist and organizer. I claimed this legacy as a way to fight historical oblivion and the erasure of a history that we so vitally needed as we confronted some of the same challenges in our movements of the 1990s. Even more recently, those who follow behind my generation have claimed this legacy of Chicana feminism. In fact, at Cal State Long Beach in 2009 the Chicana feminist organization Conciencia Femenil was founded to combat what they call the cycle of zero or chronic erasure of Chicanas on campus by following in "the footsteps of their foremothers las Hijas de Cuauhtémoc." They organize under the slogan, "Looking back, moving forward, para que nunca más nos vuelvan a borrar [so that we will never again be erased]."[55] In spring 2010 they held their first conference and invited the women who had worked on *Hijas de Cuauhtémoc* and the first journal of Chicana scholarship founded in 1973, *Encuentro Femenil*, to be present on the keynote panel, which I moderated. We stayed all afternoon to participate in an intergenerational forum on Chicana feminist scholarship and activism that the students had organized. Unfortunately, the symbolic violence and intimidation in reaction to the organizing of Chicana students in the 1960s continues today. Conciencia Femenil was publicly attacked with homophobic and sexist threats to organizers of the conference and to presenters made on-line through the comments forum of the daily campus newspaper after they had published a story announcing the event.

Early Chicana feminist theories and practices are vibrant intellectual and political traditions that are alive in many contemporary community organizations and social movements and continue to nourish new generations of activists, scholars, and cultural workers. They are building on a foundation of Chicana feminisms in the movimiento years that was community-based, grounded in a materialist analysis, and engaged in cross-border and third world solidarity. In addition to these characteristics, Chicana feminism had a complex relationship to nation and an explicit critique of gender inequality and gender/sexual violence (specifically, in its racial and colonial forms). In its early years Chicana feminism was an un-unified field that reflected tensions between women while still building a shared "hermanidad." Chicana feminisms of this era were grounded in structures of belonging (community, family, and culture) that attempted to work in partnership with men in their communities and organizations and, when this was not possible, created autonomous organizations. Finally, Chicana feminists of the 1960s and 1970s helped to develop an intersectional analysis of oppressions that has not only created a political philosophy that embraces multiple identities and multi-issue organizing but also multiplies the "space and places" in which Chicana feminisms are practiced.[56] These practices have also led to new knowledge formations and analytic practices that insist that scholars see the interconnectivity of struggles for social justice and that not all feminisms are practiced within women's movements or even by those who label themselves feminist.

Nearly all Chicana feminists in this early period worked in mixed-gender organizations, and those who formed autonomous women's organizations did so because of negative experiences with their male counterparts. Chicanas positioned their feminism squarely in the movement and most often articulated the position that the problem was systemic and not individual. They emphasized the need to educate both men and women on how sexism and exclusion held back the movement and for the most part attempted to create equal partnership with men in their organizations, leaving only as a last resort. Even when Chicana activists formed women's organizations, many participated in double militancia in Chicano organizations and Chicana groups. Ultimately, Chicana feminists created a counterpublic—a parallel discursive arena and political spaces—through their organizing, artistic production, print communication, political vision, and community-making practices.

Then, as now, Chicana feminists did not share the same views and cannot be portrayed monolithically. In this period, specifically, feminism was a contested tradition and an insurgent form of thinking that represented the very tensions between women.[57] There was no unified field of feminism politically or ideologically; while many activists built solidarity among Chicanas, there were some actors who did not like each other; and there were tensions with those who opposed Chicana feminism ideologically. Within early Chicana feminism there were different ideologies that developed at different times or temporal logics within the life cycle of various organizations or within the consciousness of individuals, whether they were in mixed or single gender organizations. That is to say, different activists and organizations came to their own forms of Chicana feminisms at different times.

Like other women of color feminisms, Chicana feminism contributed to an understanding of the *interlocking nature of oppressions*, what has come to be known as intersectionality.[58] Chicana feminists developed an analysis of oppression that theorized the ways in which gender oppression was determined by processes of racialization, economic class, and sexuality. This understanding was first articulated as the double or triple oppression of women (or quadruple oppression of lesbians of color), but soon enough the limits of this formulation were explored and activists started to name how these oppressions were intersecting and often simultaneous and mutually constitutive. The 1974 article "La Femenista" by NietoGomez forges both an identity and a theory of Chicana feminismo and a concept of multiple oppressions, which is often ascribed to the academy but has roots firmly in social movements.[59]

> The Chicana feminist has been calling attention to her socioeconomic oppression as a Chicano and as a woman since 1968. The Chicana feminist has called attention to how racism, sexism, and sexist racism are used to maintain the Chicana woman's social and economic oppression. However, it can be truthfully said that she has been ignored. The Chicana feminist has had to struggle to develop and maintain her identity in spite of the paternal and maternal tendencies of two social movements to absorb her into their general movements for their own rank and file.[60]

Many early women of color and third world women feminists first named this problem as the "both/and" (instead of either/or) or "ampersand" problem, what Frances Beal famously called double jeopardy in 1969.[61] These multiple equations served as shorthand for how multiple systems of oppression such as colonialism, economic class, ethnicity/race, gender, and sexuality affected differently situated political actors. Orozco argued that during the Chicano movement "Chicana activists did not recognize patriarchy as a system separate in origins and in everyday life and quite distinct from racism and capital-ism. Chicanas struggled against the interconnectedness of this triple burden, but largely battled racism and capitalism on the ideological front."[62]

Feminism is part of a larger struggle for justice that historically has emerged in revolutionary and other struggles for freedom, for example, the antislavery, labor, and civil rights movements of the nineteenth and twentieth centuries. This evolving understanding of the interconnectedness of oppressions led to activists working across multiple struggles and across movements. Women of color and Chicana feminisms grounded their struggle in their community's pursuit of freedom and were committed to fighting multiple oppressions.[63] They developed a multiple oppressions framework after decades of being silenced by comrades who had determined that their issues were secondary or subsidiary to the primary oppression of class or race and that gender and sexual oppression would be resolved by overthrowing capitalism (racism, sex-ism, and homophobia were seen as part of capitalist patriarchy) or creating a Chicano homeland.

This intersectional analysis of crosscutting oppressions also created the context for social movement actors with multiple identities to be legitimated. The rise of these theories in women's studies have been credited to French feminism or poststructuralism. Yet it is crucial to understand the critical prac-tices and knowledge engendered by how the multiple identities of women of color organizers led to a critique of the unified subject and master narratives of liberation. This is not merely because of their "identities" but also because of the politics they built around them to empower themselves and their com-munities. Developing their own theories of the subject, this critique about the fiction of the individual self and failures of modernity emerged from grass-roots political theory and praxis. This was an uneven process. Activist claims could be critiquing the individual, rational, and unified subject of the En-lightenment by using a modernist claim, but almost always it was modified, retrofitted, or hybridized by narratives that named multiple oppressions and multi-identities. In navigating these social movement conditions and differ-ent forms of analysis, U.S. women of color activists developed what Chela Sandoval has theorized as "differential consciousness." This project aims to move us toward a historical framework that can register social actors that navigate multiple oppressions, multiple movements, and multiple identities, ultimately leading to a rich tradition of multisited struggle and multi-issue organizing—what I have called the multiple insurgencies of U.S. women of color.

Along with the commitment to community, Chicana feminists have dedi-cated themselves to improving the material conditions of their communities and have grounded Chicana feminism in a view of *economic justice*. Chicana feminism includes a spectrum of approaches, from a critique of capitalism and economic exploitation to a range of Marxist ideologies to guide their views of the world and their understandings of how to wage their struggle.[64] Like the Hijas de Cuauhtémoc, who linked their feminism to Mexico, Chicana feminism has a rich internationalist, cross-border, and transnational orientation. Drawing from the Mexican roots of Chicana feminism, as suggested by Ruiz and Pérez, Chicana feminism has historically had not just a border consciousness (Anzaldúa) but a cross-border consciousness that reflects Chicana feminist commitment to international solidarity. Originally emerging from solidarity with national liberation and decolonial movements of the third world, this form of consciousness helped form new coalitions among third world peoples in the United States. While early Chicana feminists were often grounded in a commitment to organize in their own communities in the United States, there was also a tradition of solidarity work that manifests as Chicanas became the key organizers in solidarity organizations with Cuba, Vietnam, Nicaragua, El Salvador, South Africa, and, most recently, the indigenous peoples of Chiapas and the growing national indigenous movement in Mexico. Inherent in this practice in an anti-imperialist critique and a worldview built on transnational national and multiracial solidarity.

Early Chicana feminisms had a complex continuum in relation to questions of nation and nationalism that varied from forms of feminism-in-nationalism to the retrofitting of nationalism to amplify the kinds of subjects included in the project of nation. Ultimately, after an early period of Chicana feminisms, many activists abandoned nationalist claims and nationalist imaginaries to create alternative ways of belonging between and beyond nationalist frames.[65] They imagined a way out of nationalism that crossed national and racial/ethnic divides, and their critiques signaled the coming of a postnationalist critique that resonated with many other feminist and queer activists. As Catrióna Esquibel argues, "Lesbians of color, such as Pat Parker, Hilda Hidalgo, and Audre Lorde, moved into the construction of postnationalist images in their critique of nationalist rhetoric that continues to be used against women, against gays and lesbians, and in service of male privilege."[66] They engaged in unpacking the complex ways in which women were figured into the process of colonization through the coupling of colonial violence and sexual violence or what would later be called "sexing the decolonial imaginary."[67]

Early Chicana feminism was characterized by an explicit challenge to gender hierarchy, sexual coercion, and violence. Chicana feminists challenged discrimination and power inequality based on gender (and often sexuality) inside as well as outside the Chicano community. While they share these views with other feminists, their approach and agenda differed in that they did not view gender as the primary source of oppression (a practice reserved for those privileged enough to see race as invisible or naturalized by their dominant social position). They critiqued male supremacy, sexual violence, and sexual objectification within their own communities and the ways they were enacted along racialized lines by dominant society. Chicanas began to reclaim their sexuality as their own, fight against the sexual double standard, and stand up against movement men who created divisions through sexual politics. Critically, this was also a time when a Latina reproductive rights agenda began to be articulated that included the right *not* to be sterilized, as well as the demand for birth control, sexual education, and abortion.[68]

While early Chicana feminism did not always develop an antidiscrimination stance toward non-normative sexualities and genders or link homophobia and sexism in its critique of patriarchy, it, like other early women of color feminisms, laid the foundation for other "intersectional" paradigms of gay, lesbian, bisexual, transgender, and queer to emerge.[69] The Chicana/o political analysis of homophobia and concepts like Queer Aztlán are linked to Chicana lesbian feminists who struggled to make these connections in political, poetic, and practical realms.[70] Part of this growing development includes how women of color feminisms, and Chicana feminisms in particular, began to develop a critique of heterosexism and heteronormativity to name new forms of racialized sexuality through the Chicana Sex Wars that occurred when the Chicana lesbian caucus pushed the sexual envelope in what was then called the National Association of Chicano Studies and MALCS, unsettling both male and heterosexual feminist colleagues throughout the 1980s and early 1990s.[71] While critics dismiss queer studies as an academic formulation, it is vital to note the community histories of third world, Latina, and Chicana lesbian feminist activism in Salsa Soul Sisters, Las Buenas Amigas, Lesbianas Unidas, and the mixed-gender organizations Gay Latino Alliance (GALA) and Gay and Lesbianas Unidas.[72] The legacy of this work can be seen in the vibrant queer Chicana cultural and political tradition that is carried on by the Lesbian, BiMujeres, and Trans Caucus of NACCS, Los Angeles-based Tongues, Butchlalis de Panochitlán, or groups such as the Austin Latina Latino Lesbian and Gay Organization (ALLGO).

The writings of Anna NietoGomez and the members of the Hijas de Cuauhtémoc are among the earliest feminist writings in the Chicano Movement. They are historically significant as a genealogy of early Chicana feminism and are a testament to the emergence of Chicana feminism within the movement, not, as many historians have suggested, after it. This book captures the tumultuous time when what it meant to be a woman and to be Mexican American shifted under the activism of Chicanas and Chicanos who ushered in this watershed moment in the social history of gender. This project has captured both the significant and the more subtle shifts in political identity and racial and gender consciousness documenting the emergence of a new historical subjectivity of Chicanas. While the 1960s and 1970s represent a historic shift in the construction of an empowered political subjectivity, la Chicana, it is also linked to a longer history of working-class Mexicana's and Chicana's strength and labor radicalism that is the bedrock of Chicana feminism. The roots of Chicana feminism can be traced to the beginning of the twentieth century with figures such as Sara Estela Ramírez, a Tejana labor organizer and socialist activist, and organizations like the Liga Femenil Mexicanista, founded at El Primer Congreso Mexicanista in 1911, and their newspaper, *La Mujer Moderna*, edited by Andrea and Teresa Villareal, or the debates about women's liberation in the Yucatan Feminist Congress or the Partido Liberal Mexicano.[73] Others have pointed to labor radicalism and how Chicana feminism has built on the historical legacy of the labor radicals Luisa Moreno, Josefina Fierro de Bright, Emma Tenayuca, Lucy Parsons, and Manuela Solis Sager.[74]

Opponents of a women's rights agenda within the Chicano movement claimed that feminists were dividing the movement. Yet the oral histories conducted for this book document the ways in which sexism, sexual harassment, the objectification of female activists, the exclusion of women from leadership and decision making, and the confinement of women to cooking and secretarial labor were the real issues dividing the movement. A unified Chicano Movement could not truly emerge without a transformative gender and sexual justice agenda. This book has told the story of a political movement and how its gendered contractions led to collective action by young Chicanas who came together out of necessity to confront the array of women's issues that were not being addressed in Chicano political organizing. Using an interdisciplinary approach, this project has employed oral histories, archival documents, and a rich visual culture to narrate how struggles over gender and sexuality were negotiated within the daily life of political organizing in the Chicano movement. Beyond a recuperative story, this is one that reclaims the roots of Chicana feminism and restores the voices of the participants whose narratives and analysis transform the way we understand the politics of history. More than a history project, this is also a memory project, one that re-members a critical political genealogy and one that interrogates the ways in which memory structures create subjugated historical knowledges about women of color within both Chicano Studies and hegemonic feminist histories.[75]

Chicana feminisms emerged from multiple sites and struggles, and the histories of these struggles are as diverse as their practices. Chicana feminist projects have emerged from the spaces of labor and union organizing, daily life, the experience of (in)migration, education, the kitchen table, the neighborhood, the environmental justice movement, economic justice, political organizing across racial, class, and sexual lines, HIV/AIDS activism, student organizing, and many other social justice struggles. While this legacy of Chicana feminism has been obscured and erased from official histories, it has lived on and been elaborated fearlessly by those who insist on fashioning a politics robust enough to address the simultaneity of oppressions: homophobia, sexism, classism, imperialism, colorism, citizenship status, militarism, and racism.

We can see how these ideas live on in the Latina Health Project and many community-based projects such as Mujeres Unidas or Proyecto contra SIDA por Vida of San Francisco, Fuerza Unida of San Antonio, and Hermanas en la Lucha of Denver. Campus organzations like Raza Womyn de UCLA and the proliferation of MALCS chapters at the University of Texas, San Antonio, the University of Utah, the University of Minnesota, UCLA, Cal State Los Angeles, and UC Berkeley also illustrate this fierce commitment to a politics of multiple insurgencies.

Critical coalitions continue to be built, such as INCITE: Women of Color against Violence, which links intimate violence to state violence, colonialism and war; and Sister Song, a women of color reproductive health collective. Chicanas continue to do border and cross-border work fighting for immigrant rights throughout the United States, especially where newly arrived migrants have settled, calling for workers' rights in the Maquilas, demanding justice for the women of Juárez, or helping to build solidarity with indigenous women throughout the hemisphere. Even for new generations of activists who have not had formal access to this history, the legacy lives on in their dreams and political work to bring about a new world to re-member and enact our own retrofitted memories.

ELMA BARRERA grew up in West Texas and graduated from the University of Houston with degrees in English and Spanish literature. She traveled to Mexico City, where she worked at the American embassy. On her return she worked for the Magnolia YWCA and was a key organizer in the Conferencia de Mujeres por la Raza in 1971. In 1977 Barerra was chosen by the White House to help organize the National Women's Conference in Houston in honor of the International Decade for Women. She became the first Latina broadcast journalist in Houston. While working at Channel 13 as a journalist she produced and anchored the first TV news show in Spanish and later was cofounder of the first Spanish-language TV station in the city and the Houston Association of Hispanic Journalists. Barrera has served on several advisory boards. In 2000 she was honored by the National Association of Hispanic Journalists for her lifelong achievement.

YOLANDA BIRDWELL was born in 1940, in the state of Tamaulipas, Mexico. She came to the United States at the age of eighteen as a student. She settled in Houston and lived with her grandmother. She began her activism with MAYO in Houston in 1968 and became part of the leadership. Birdwell organized the workshop on sexuality at the Conferencia de Mujeres por la Raza in Houston and coauthored, with Gloria Guardiola, the political pamphlet *La Mujer, destrucción de mitos*. She was also active in La Raza Unida and has been a lifelong anti-imperialist, socialist, and feminist activist.

SYLVIA CASTILLO was born in 1952. She grew up in Pico Rivera, California. She became an activist in the early 1960s because of her mother, a fair housing advocate and Democratic Party leader. Castillo attended Long Beach State University in 1970 and became active in the Hijas de Cuauhtémoc organization. She earned a bachelor's degree in political science from UCLA. Her international solidarity work includes activism to end apartheid in South Africa and promoting friendship with the people of Cuba and Central America. Castillo is a founding member of the Venceremos Brigade and has been honored by the Liberty Hill Foundation and the California Wellness Association for her outstanding violence prevention work with Latino and African American youth in South Los Angeles. Castillo is currently the senior adviser to California Assembly Speaker Emeritus Karen Bass.

GLORIA GUARDIOLA was born in San Antonio, Texas, and was raised by her grandfather and two aunts. She became a teacher. Guardiola organized the workshop on sexuality at the Conferencia de Mujeres por la Raza in Houston and coauthored, with Yolanda Birdwell, the political pamphlet *La Mujer, destrucción de mitos*. Guardiola went on to become a member of the National Organization of Women (NOW), was active in the Texas women's political caucus, and worked for the Association for the Advancement of Mexican Americans for nine years.

LETICIA HERNÁNDEZ was born in 1950 in Los Angeles and grew up in East Los Angeles. She enrolled at California State College, Long Beach, in 1969 through the EOP program and became involved on campus with UMAS, later MEChA, the Hijas de Cuauhtémoc, and

Ballet Folklórico. In 1978 she moved to Washington, D.C., and in 1983 began to work for the Honorable Esteban E. Torres, U.S. House representative for California's Thirty-fourth District. Hernández returned to California in 1985, where she continued to work for Representative Torres, first as a field representative and then as a district office director. In 1991 she began her career at the California State University Chancellor's Office, holding progressively more responsible positions that led to her current post as secretariat to the Board of Trustees.

ELIZABETH (BETITA) MARTINEZ was born in 1925, in Washington, D.C. She attended Swarthmore College in Philadelphia and after graduating went to New York to work at the United Nations. She became an editor at Simon and Schuster, then Books and Arts editor at the *Nation* magazine, before dedicating herself to the civil rights movement when she joined the Student Nonviolent Coordinating Committee (SNCC). After her time with SNCC, she moved to New Mexico where she coedited *El Grito del Norte*, a Chicano movement newspaper. During that time she traveled to then-North Vietnam with an international antiwar delegation. In her many years of work for social justice, organizing, teaching, and writing, she has edited and been the author of numerous books, including *Letters from Mississippi, The Youngest Revolution, A Personal Report on Cuba, 500 Years of Chicano History in Pictures, 500 years of Chicana Women's History*, and *De Colores Means All of Us*.

MARIE "KETA" MIRANDA grew up in the Florence neighborhood of South Los Angeles and attended Los Angeles City College and California State University, Los Angeles, where she was active in MEChA. She was a writer for *La Raza* magazine and an organizer for the Raza Unida Party of Los Angeles and later for the Community Party U.S.A. She returned to college and received her B.A. from the University of California, Irvine, and her Ph.D. in the History of Consciousness Program from UC Santa Cruz. She is currently an associate professor of Bicultural and Bilingual Studies at the University of Texas, San Antonio, and the author of *Homegirls in the Public Sphere*, a groundbreaking study of Chicana girls in gangs.

ANNA NIETOGOMEZ was born in 1946 in San Bernardino, California, where she also grew up. She began her education at the community college and transferred to California State University, Long Beach. While there she was one of the founders of UMAS/MEChA and later was a founder of the Hijas de Cuauhtémoc. She went on to coedit the first Chicana scholarly journal, *Encuentro Femenil*, and worked for the Chicana Service Action Center. NietoGomez is the author of dozens of articles and pamphlets on Chicana rights, labor, community organizing, education, and history, and was a pioneer of the Chicana Studies curriculum. She attended UCLA, studied ethnic cinematography, and taught at California State University, Northridge (CSUN), where she developed and taught classes on la Chicana and community organizing. After being denied tenure, she left CSUN and earned her M.S.W. at the University of Southern California. She is a licensed clinical social worker and worked for the state of California in the Departments of Health and Mental Health.

CECELIA QUIJANO was born in 1952, in San Antonio, Texas. She grew up in South Los Angeles in the Florence neighborhood. As a high school student she led a student walkout in response to the Blowouts in East L.A. and was expelled. She had been exposed at a young age to community organizing around the prisons and Católicos por la Raza. Quijano became active in UMAS in high school and went to UCLA after attending Upward Bound at California State University, Long Beach. At UCLA she became active in UMAS/MEChA and attended the 1971 Conferencia de Mujeres por la Raza with a delegation of women from the Los Angeles area.

CORINNE SÁNCHEZ, Esq., was born in 1947 and grew up in San Bernardino, California, where she attended San Bernardino City College from 1965 to 1968. She became active in the Chicano student movement in UMAS and later MEChA at California State University, Long Beach, attending, with some pauses, from 1968 to 1974. There she worked for EOP and taught Upward Bound courses. She went on to serve as deputy director at the Los Angeles Women's Center and the Chicana Service Action Center in East Los Angeles. She has been practicing law since 1993, with a focus on family law, working against domestic violence and advocating for children. Sánchez is one of nine founders and board member of the only Latina Lawyers Bar Association in the nation. She is currently president of El Proyecto del Barrio, Inc., a multiservice community center in Pacoima, California. Among many awards, she received the Mi Corazón Award from the Dolores Huerta Foundation in 2004 and was named Woman of the Year by the California State Assembly in 1987 and 2009.

1. I conducted oral history interviews with many of the remaining members of the Hijas de Cuauhtémoc and had telephone conversations and correspondence with others. Sadly, two of the original members had untimely deaths due to breast cancer before I began interviewing in 1991. To contextualize and round out the perspective of the group, I conducted oral history interviews with activists involved in regional organizing, as well as several Chicana activists from Texas and New Mexico who were active in the same era. In researching the 1971 Conferencia de Mujeres por la Raza, I interviewed organizers and participants. In addition, this project is based on extensive archival research that I gathered in California and Texas, including the Southern California Library and the special collections of the Benson Library, University of Texas at Austin; the Bancroft Library, University of California, Berkeley (UC Berkeley); and the libraries at California State University, Long Beach (CSULB), and Stanford University. I draw from numerous collections at UC Santa Barbara's Chicano Studies Library, UC Berkeley's Ethnic Studies Library, and the University of California, Los Angeles (UCLA), Chicano Studies Research Center (CSRC) Library, as well as smaller archives of political organizations and individual activists. When I first began this research there were no archived copies of the *Hijas de Cuauhtémoc* newspaper. I have been depositing both print and audio resources at the CSULB and UCLA CSRC archives. Some of the oral histories that appear in this book have been archived at the Los Angeles Women's Movements Oral History Collection at the Virtual Oral/Aural History Archive at CSULB: www .csulb.edu/voaha.

2. Anna NietoGomez's name also appears as Nieto-Gómez in documents of this era, but she has since made it clear that her last name is spelled without the hyphen and accent.

3. Robin D. G. Kelley, *Freedom Dreams: The Black Radical Imagination* (Boston: Beacon Press, 2002); Kimberly Springer, *Living for the Revolution: Black Feminist Organizations, 1968–1980* (Durham: Duke University Press, 2005); Linda Burnham, "The Wellspring of Black Feminist Theory" Working Paper Series, No. 1 (Oakland, CA: Women of Color Resource Center, 2001).

4. The spelling of Cuauhtémoc varied (e.g., Cuahtemoc, Guatemoc, Cuauhtemoc). I use the most common spelling. Because the group engaged in an innovative crafting of identity and historical consciousness, the mutable spellings of several words indicate that their endeavor was not stabilized but a shifting signifier in the production of Chicana feminist consciousness. All three editions of the newspaper came out in 1971 but were not dated. I refer to each issue in the order it was published and use volume and issue numbers for easier reference.

5. Tomás Ybarra-Frausto defines *rasquachismo* as "an underclass sensibility rooted in everyday linguistic practices and in artistic works put together out of whatever was at hand." "Interview with Tómas Ybarra-Frausto: The Chicano Movement in a Multicultural/ Multinational Society," in *On Edge: The Crisis of Contemporary Latin American Culture*, ed. George Yúdice, Jean Franco, and Juan Flores (Minneapolis: University of Minnesota Press, 1992), 208.

6. See, for example, Dionne Espinoza, "Pedagogies of Nationalism and Gender:

Cultural Resistance in Selected Representational Practices of Chicana/o Movement Activists, 1967–1972" (Ph.D. diss., Cornell University, 1996); Dolores Delgado Bernal, "Grassroots Leadership Reconceptualized: Chicana Oral Histories and the 1968 East Los Angeles School Blowouts," *Frontiers: A Journal of Women Studies* 19:2 (1998): 113–142; Vicki L. Ruiz, *From Out of the Shadows: Mexican Women in Twentieth-Century America* (New York: Oxford University Press, 1998); Marisela R. Chavez, "'We Lived and Breathed and Worked the Movement': The Contradictions and Rewards of Chicana/Mexicana Activism in el Centro de Acción Social Autónomo-Hermandad General de Trabajadores (CASA-HGT), Los Angeles, 1975–1978," in *Las Obreras: Chicanas Politics of Work and Family*, ed. Vicki L. Ruiz (Los Angeles: Chicano Studies Research Center, 2000); Maylei S. Blackwell, "Contested Histories: *Las Hijas de Cuauhtemoc*, Chicana Feminisms, and Print Culture in the Chicano Movement, 1968–1973," in *Chicana Feminisms: A Critical Reader*, ed. Gabriela Arredondo, Aida Hurtado, Norma Klahn, Olga Najera-Ramirez, and Patricia Zavella (Durham, NC: Duke University Press, 2003); Virginia R. Espino, "Women Sterilized as They Give Birth: Population Control, Eugenics and Social Protest in the Twentieth-Century United States" (Ph.D. diss., Arizona State University, 2007); Elena R. Gutiérrez, *Fertile Matters: The Politics of Mexican-Origin Women's Reproduction* (Austin: University of Texas Press, 2008); Yolanda Alaniz and Megan Cornish, *Viva La Raza: A History of Chicano Identity and Resistance* (Seattle: Red Letter Press, 2008).

7. Michel Foucault, "Nietzche, Geneaology, History," in *Language, Counter-Memory, Practice: Selected Essays and Interviews*, ed. D. F. Bouchard (Ithaca: Cornell University Press, 1977).

8. Michel-Rolph Trouillot, *Silencing the Past: Power and the Production of History* (Boston: Beacon Press, 1995), 24.

9. Ibid., 25.

10. I remained active in organizing and social justice work, and the interviews and continued conversation provided an important space of intergenerational dialogue.

11. For a history of Mexican Los Angeles, see George J. Sánchez, *Becoming Mexican American: Ethnicity, Culture, and Identity in Chicano Los Angeles, 1900–1945* (New York: Oxford University Press, 1995).

12. Lisa Lowe's work has inspired me to examine the intertwined process of remembering and forgetting in what she calls the "economy of affirmation and forgetting." Her analysis of the erased figure of the transatlantic Chinese coolie and what it reveals about "New World modernity" elucidates how absences can be critical instances in which to interrogate the politics of knowledge production. Lisa Lowe, "The Intimacies of Four Continents," in *Haunted by Empire: Geographies of Intimacies in North American History*, ed. Laura Stoler (Durham: Duke University Press, 2006): 191–212.

13. "Longo" is the Caló term for Long Beach.

14. For a discussion of the Los Angeles preparatory meetings, see the second issue of *Hijas de Cuauhtémoc* (1971); and "Chicana Regional Conference," *La Raza* 1:6 (1971): 43–44.

15. For a discussion of the Houston conference, see Francisca Flores, "Conference of Mexican Women: Un Remolino," *Regeneración* 1:10 (1979): 1; Gloria Guardiola and Yolanda Birdwell, "Conferencia de Mujeres por la Raza: Point of View," *Papel Chicano* (June 12, 1971): 2; Carmen Hernandez, "Conferencia de Mujeres: Carmen Speaks Out," *Papel Chicano* (June 12, 1971): 1; Rosa Marta Morales, "Conferencia de Mujeres por la Raza: Rosa en Español," *Papel Chicano* (June 12, 1971); "National Chicana Conference," *La Verdad*

(July-August 1971); Mirta Vidal, *Chicanas Speak Out: Women, New Voice of La Raza* (New York: Pathfinder Press, 1971). For a discussion by the women who walked out, see Suzan Racho, Gloria Meneses, Socorro Acosta, and Chicki Quijano, "Houston Chicana Conference," *La Gente* (May 31, 1971).

16. Anna NietoGomez, "La Femenista," *Encuentro Femenil* 1:2 (1974): 28–33.

17. Diana Taylor, *The Archive and the Repertoire: Performing Cultural Memory in the Americas* (Durham, NC: Duke University Press, 2007), xvii.

18. Ibid., 18.

19. Ibid., 19–20.

20. Gayatri Chakravorty Spivak, "Can the Subaltern Speak?" in *Marxism and the Interpretation of Culture*, ed. Cary Nelson and Lawrence Grossberg (Chicago: University of Illinois Press, 1988).

21. Taylor, *The Archive and the Repertoire*, 2007.

22. Kelley, *Freedom Dreams*; Perez, *The Decolonial Imaginary*.

23. Jaqui M. Alexander and Chandra Talpade Mohanty, eds., *Feminist Genealogies, Colonial Legacies, Democratic Futures* (New York: Routledge, 1997).

24. Other social movements have called attention to memory in cultural politics. See Issac Julien, *The Passion of Remembrance*, 95 min. 16mm, 1986; and the black British cultural scholars Kobena Mercer's *Welcome to the Jungle*, and Stuart Hall, "Cultural Identity and Diaspora."

25. Emma Pérez, *The Decolonial Imaginary: Writing Chicanas into History* (Bloomington: Indiana University Press, 1999), xvi.

26. Teresa de Lauretis, ed., *Feminist Studies/Critical Studies* (Bloomington: Indiana University Press, 1986).

27. Ignacio M. García, "Junctures in the Road: Chicano Studies since 'El Plan de Santa Barbara,'" in *Chicanas/Chicanos at the Crossroads*, ed. David R. Maciel and Isidro D. Ortiz (Tucson: University of Arizona Press, 1996).

28. Nancy Fraser, "Rethinking the Public Sphere: A Contribution to the Critique of Actually Exiting Democracy," in *Habermas and the Public Sphere*, ed. Craig Calhoun (Cambridge, MA: MIT Press, 1992), 109–142.

CHAPTER ONE

1. Foucault, "Nietzsche, Genealogy, History"; Pérez, *The Decolonial Imaginary*.

2. Hayden White, *The Content of Form: Narrative Discourse and Historical Representation* (Baltimore: Johns Hopkins University Press, 1987).

3. Michel Foucault, *Power/Knowledge: Selected Interviews and Other Writings, 1972–1977*, ed. Colin Gordon (New York: Pantheon, 1980).

4. In *Black Feminist Thought: Knowledge, Consciousness, and the Politics of Empowerment* (London: Harper Collins, 1990), Patricia Hill Collins supports her Fanonian analysis that knowledge can be a mode of domination by arguing that the knowledge gained by African American women at the "intersection of race, gender and class oppression provides a stimulus for crafting and passing on the subjugated knowledges of Black women's culture of resistance" (10). Her argument differs from Foucault's notion of subjugated knowledges, which he defines as "those blocks of historical knowledge which were present but disguised," namely, "a whole set of knowledges that have been disqualified[,] . . . naive knowledges, located low down on the hierarchy, beneath the required level of cognition or scientifically" (Foucault, *Power/Knowledge*, 82). Hill Collins suggests that black feminist thought is not

"naive knowledge" but "has been made or appear so by those controlling knowledge validation procedures" (18).

5. For an important work on how the telling of social movement history from the
bottom up, or how daily life transforms the "political," see Lalita K. et al., *We Were Making
History . . .": Life Histories in the Telangana People's Struggle* (London: Zed Books, 1990).

6. Becky Thompson, *A Promise and a Way of Life: White Antiracist Activism* (Minneapolis: University of Minnesota Press, 2001); Becky Thompson, "Multiracial Feminism:
Recasting the Chronology of Second Wave Feminism," *Feminist Studies* 28:2 (Summer
2002): 337–360; Benita Roth, *Separate Roads to Feminism: Black, Chicana, and White Feminist Movements in America's Second Wave* (New York: Cambridge University Press, 2004);
Winifred Breines, *The Trouble between Us: An Uneasy History of White and Black Women in
the Feminist Movement* (New York: Oxford University Press, 2006); Rosalyn Baxandall,
"Re-Visioning the Women's Liberation Movement's Narrative: Early Second Wave African American Feminists," *Feminist Studies* 27:1 (Spring 2001): 225–245; Belinda Robnett,
"African American Women in the Civil Rights Movement: Spontaneity and Emotion in Social Movement Theory," in *No Middle Ground: Women and Radical Protest*, ed. Kathleen M.
Blee (New York: New York University Press, 1998), 65–95; "African-American Women in
the Civil Rights Movement, 1954–1965: Gender, Leadership, and Micro-Mobilization,"
American Journal of Sociology 101:6 (May 1996): 1661–1693; Springer, *Living for the Revolution*, and *Still Lifting, Still Climbing*.

7. Sara Evans, "Visions of Women-Centered History," *Social Policy* 4 (Spring 1982):
46–49.

8. Much of our collective thinking has been documented in "Whose Feminism, Whose
History? Reflection on Excavating the History of (the) U.S. Women's Movement(s)," by
Sherna Berger Gluck in collaboration with Maylei Blackwell, Sharon Cotrell, and Karen S.
harper, in *Community Activism and Feminist Politics: Organizing across Race, Class and Gender*, ed. Nancy A. Naples (New York: Routledge, 1997), 31–56. Gluck interviewed Johnnie
Tillmon, founder of the 1961 welfare rights organization ANC Mothers Anonymous in
Watts (ANC stands for "Aid to Needy Children"), a self-defined poor women's movement
comprising mostly African American women and some Latina welfare recipients. harper
interviewed Asian American feminists active in the Los Angeles area in the late 1960s and
early 1970s who were organized under the name Asian Sisters, which founded the first Asian
Women's Center. Cotrell interviewed participants in American Indian women's organizations, focusing much of her research on WARN. We were the core members and remained in
contact, writing and presenting papers at conferences together and collaborating for a little
over six years. Other women who worked with us at various times include Chanzo Nettles,
Adrianne Carrier, and Rubi Fregoso, who interviewed black women in club movements, the
Daughters of Bilitis (an early lesbian organization), and other Chicana feminists respectively.

9. Sandoval, "U.S. Third World Feminism." This decentering has happened not only
in the women's movement but also within lesbian feminism. See Arlene Stein, "Sisters and
Queers: The Decentering of Lesbian Feminism," in *Cultural Politics and Social Movements*,
ed. Marcy Darnovsky, Barbara Epstein, and Richard Flacks (Philadelphia: Temple University Press, 1995), 133–153.

10. See Andrea Smith's critique of the call to "move beyond the black/white binary," in
"Heteropatriarchy and the Three Pillars of White Supremacy: Rethinking Women of Color
Organizing," in *Color of Violence: The INCITE! Anthology* (Boston: South End Press, 2006),
66–73. My critique of white supremacy within narratives of U.S. feminism does not attempt
to "go beyond" the distinct logic of racism experienced by blacks in the United States but

challenges the ways in which liberalism celebrates the gains of the civil rights movement as a way to dismiss other claims of racial segregation, hatred, and exclusion by claiming that structural racism is "over."

11. When attention is given to this historical fact, it is usually done in a tokenistic manner. One exception examines the interrelationship of the antilynching and antislavery movements and the rise of feminism, as well as black women's participation in first wave women's movements: see Angela Y. Davis, *Women, Race, and Class* (New York: Vintage Books, 1981). See also Ellen Carol DuBois, *Feminism and Suffrage: The Emergence of an Independent Women's Movement in America, 1848–1869* (Ithaca: Cornell University Press, 1978); and bell hooks, *Ain't I a Woman: Black Women and Feminism* (Boston: South End Press, 1981).

12. For a history of black women's club movement, see Paula Giddings, *When and Where I Enter: The Impact of Black Women on Race and Sex in America* (New York: William Morrow, 1983).

13. While these forms of feminist and womanist struggles predate "women of color" as a category, there remains a long history of multiple feminist insurgencies by women from diverse communities that have yet to be historicized because of the politics of periodization. For a history of women involved in LULAC, see Cynthia E. Orozco, "Alicia Dickerson Montemayor: The Feminist Challenge to the League of United Latin American Citizens, Family Ideology, and Mexican American Politics in Texas in the 1930s," in *Writing the Range: Race, Class, and Culture in the Women's West*, ed. Susan Armitage and Elizabeth Jameson (Norman: University of Oklahoma Press, 1997), 435–456; for a labor history, see Jacqueline Jones, *Labor of Love, Labor of Sorrow: Black Women, Work and Family from Slavery to the Present* (New York: Basic Books, 1985); and for an exploration of forms of black nationalist feminism in the Garveyite movement, see Karen S. Adler, "'Always Leading Our Men in Service and Sacrifice': Amy Jacques Garvey, Feminist Black Nationalist," in *Race, Class and Gender: Common Bonds, Different Voices*, ed. Esther Ngan-Ling Chow, Doris Wilkinson, and Maxine Baca Zinn (London: Sage, 1996). For other critiques of the wave model, see Kimberly Springer, *Living for the Revolution: Black Feminist Organizations, 1968–1980* (Durham, NC: Duke University Press, 2005), 8.

14. The most prominent examples of this are Sara Evans, *Personal Politics: The Roots of Women's Liberation in the Civil Rights Movement and the New Left* (New York: Knopf, 1979); and Rochelle Gatlin, *American Women since 1945* (Jackson: University of Mississippi Press, 1987). Shirley Jackson, in her article "Something about the Word: African American Women and Feminism," in Blee, *No Middle Ground*, 38–50, argues that African American women developed a "separate feminist identity" through organizations like the National Black Feminist Organization (NBFO) as a way to refuse singular understandings based on race *or* gender.

15. Helen Zia, "Women of Color in Leadership," *Social Policy* 23:4 (Summer 1993): 51–55.

16. Janet R. Jakobsen, *Working Alliances and the Politics of Difference: Diversity and Feminist Ethics* (Bloomington: Indiana University Press, 1998).

17. Gluck et al., "Whose Feminism?"; Baxandall, "Re-Visioning the Women's Liberation Movement's Narrative."

18. Ruth Rosen, *The World Split Open: How the Modern Women's Movement Changed America* (New York: Penguin, 2006); Breines, *The Trouble between Us*.

19. Springer, *Living for the Revolution*, 3.

20. Norma Alarcón, "The Theoretical Subjects of *This Bridge Called My Back* and Anglo

American Feminism," in *Making Face, Making Soul—Haciendo Caras: Creative and Critical Perspectives of Women of Color*, ed. Gloria E. Anzaldúa (San Francisco: Aunt Lute Foundation, 1990), 357; Cherríe Moraga and Gloria Anzaldúa, eds., *This Bridge Called My Back: Writings by Radical Women of Color*, 2nd ed. (New York: Kitchen Table: Women of Color Press, 1983).

21. Most texts focus on feminist consciousness-raising groups in New York, Boston, and Chicago, which excludes the majority of Chicana organizing and much of the Asian American feminisms that emerged on the West Coast or the American Indian women's struggles in the Midwest and on the West Coast. It should be noted that diverse regional perspectives in second wave historiography are not the sole factor in erasing the emergence of women of color feminisms as Puerto Rican, East Coast Latina feminisms, and a strong tradition of black radical feminism have also been excluded. See Alice Echols, *Daring to Be Bad: Radical Feminism in America, 1967–1975* (Minneapolis: University of Minnesota Press, 1989); Evans, *Personal Politics*; Gatlin, *American Women since 1945*.

22. Barbara Ransby, *Ella Baker and the Black Freedom Movement: A Radical Democratic Vision* (Chapel Hill: University of North Carolina Press, 2003); Belinda Robnett, *How Long? How Long? African Women in the Struggle for Civil Rights* (New York: Oxford University Press, 1997). The literature documenting women's participation and leadership in the civil rights movement includes Bernice McNair Barnett, "Invisible Southern Black Women Leaders in the Civil Rights Movement: The Triple Constraints of Gender, Race, and Class," in Chow, Wilkinson, and Baca Zinn, *Race, Class and Gender*; and Vicki L. Crawford, Jacqueline Anne Rouse, and Barbara Woods, eds., *Women in the Civil Rights Movement: Trailblazers and Torchbearers, 1941–1965* (Bloomington: Indiana University Press, 1993); Bettye Collier-Thomas and V. P. Franklin, *Sisters in Struggle: African American Women in the Civil Rights–Black Power Movement* (New York: New York University Press, 2001). For an important reconceptualization of leadership, see Robnett's concept of bridge women: "African-American Women in the Civil Rights Movement, 1954–1965"; and *How Long?*.

23. For critical histories of black feminism, see Kimberly Springer, ed., *Still Lifting, Still Climbing: African American Women's Contemporary Activism* (New York: New York University Press, 2005); E. Frances White, "Africa on My Mind: Gender, Counter Discourse, and African American Nationalism," in *Expanding the Boundaries of Women's History: Essays on Women in the Third World*, ed. Cheryl Johnson-Odim and Margaret Strobel (Bloomington: Indiana University Press, 1992).

24. Casey Hayden and Mary King, "Sex and Caste: A Kind of Memo," *Liberation* 1:1–2 (April 1966): 35–36.

25. Also absent in the analysis are the forms of feminism produced by the younger generation of black women they mentored, as illustrated by Springer, *Still Lifting*. For histories of the TWWA, see Maylei S. Blackwell, "Geographies of Difference: Mapping Multiple Feminist Insurgencies and Transnational Public Cultures in the Americas" (Ph.D. diss., University of California, Santa Cruz, 2000); Kristen Anderson-Bricker, "'Triple Jeopardy': Black Women and the Growth of Feminist Consciousness in SNCC, 1964–1975," in Springer, *Still Lifting*; Joon Pyo Lee, "The Third World Women's Alliance, 1970–1980: Women of Color Organizing in a Revolutionary Era" (M.A. thesis, Sarah Lawrence College, 2007).

26. For an important critique, see Katie King, *Theory in Its Feminist Travels: Conversations in U.S. Women's Movements* (Bloomington: Indiana University Press, 1994), who asks why Cellestine Ware, a founder of one of the four groups Echols uses to illustrate a history

of radical feminism (New York Radical Feminists), is left out of a history that argues that the efforts to generate a black feminism were "less than successful."

27. Echols, *Daring to Be Bad*, 129. For an important corrective, see Kelley, *Freedom Dreams*; and Springer, *Living for the Revolution*.

28. Rosen, *The World Split Open*, 276.

29. For contrary views, see Baxandall, "Re-Visioning the Women's Liberation Movement's Narrative"; Thompson, "Multiracial Feminism"; Springer, *Living for the Revolution*.

30. Elsa Barkley Brown, "What Has Happened Here: The Politics of Difference in Women's History and Feminist Politics," in *The Second Wave: A Reader in Feminist Theory*, ed. Linda Nicholson (New York: Routledge, 1997), 281.

31. New scholarship on lesbians of color organizing is emerging to help address this multisited emergence. See Alice Y. Hom, "Documenting Lesbian of Color Community Building in Los Angeles and New York, 1970s to 1990s" (Ph.D. diss., Claremont Graduate School, forthcoming).

32. Thompson, "Multiracial Feminism."

33. Roth, *Separate Roads to Feminism*, 3.

34. Blackwell, "Geographies of Difference."

35. Angel Y. Davis, *Blues Legacies and Black Feminism: Gertrude "Ma" Rainey, Bessie Smith and Billie Holiday* (New York: Pantheon Books, 1998), xiv.

36. See Lisa Lowe's comments in an interview she conducted titled "Angela Davis: Reflections on Race, Class and Gender in the USA," in *The Politics of Culture in the Shadow of Capital*, ed. Lisa Lowe and David Lloyd (Durham, NC: Duke University Press, 1997), 309.

37. Baxandall, "Re-Visioning the Women's Liberation Movement's Narrative"; Rosie Bermudez, "Recovering Histories: Alicia Escalante and the Chicana Welfare Rights Organization, 1967–1974" (M.A. thesis, California State University, Dominguez Hills, 2010).

38. Roque Ramirez, "Communities of Desire"; Claudia Salazar, "A Third World Woman's Text: Between the Politics of Criticism and Cultural Politics," in *Women's Words: The Feminist Practice of Oral History*, ed. Sherna Berger Gluck and Daphne Patai (New York: Routledge, 1991); Roth, *Separate Roads to Feminism*.

39. Barbara Noda, "Low Riding in the Women's Movement," in Moraga and Anzaldúa, *This Bridge Called My Back*. "Lowriding" is part of Chicano car culture and refers to modifying a car so that it has lower suspension and rides very close to the road; such cars are used for cruising slowly. The practice is not limited to Chicanos, but the historical Mexican American connection to the style and the development of this subculture cannot be denied. In this instance, Noda refers to lowriding as a different way of occupying space and a different way of being in the women's movement, just as lowriders occupy the space of the street differently.

40. See Springer, *Still Lifting*; Springer, *Living for the Revolution*; Maylei S. Blackwell, "Triple Jeopardy, 'Racism, Sexism, and Imperialism': Third World Women's Alliance and the Transnational Imaginary," forthcoming. Also see Lowe, "Angela Davis: Reflections on Race."

41. Max Elbaum, *Revolution in the Air: Sixties Radicals Turn to Lenin, Mao, and Che* (New York: Verso, 2002); Kelley, *Freedom Dreams*; Cynthia A. Young, *Soul Power: Culture, Radicalism, and the Making of a U.S. Third World Left* (Durham, NC: Duke University Press, 2006); Laura Pulido, *Black, Brown, Yellow, and Left: Radical Activism in Los Angeles* (Berkeley: University of California Press, 2006).

42. Chandra Talpade Mohanty, "Cartographies of Struggle: Third World Women and

the Politics of Feminism," in *Third World Women and the Politics of Feminism*, ed. Chandra Talpade Mohanty, Ann Russo, and Lourdes Torres (Indianapolis: Indiana University Press, 1991), 1–47.

43. The concept of hidden transcripts of resistance refers, of course, to James Scott's *Domination and the Arts of Resistance: Hidden Transcripts* (New Haven: Yale University Press, 1990); see Gluck et al., "Whose Feminism?"

44. See Antonio Gramsci, *Selections from the Prison Notebooks*, ed. and trans. Quintin Hoare and Geoffrey Nowell Smith (New York: International Publishers, 1971).

45. For more information on the American Indian women's movement, see Rayna Green's *Native American Women: A Contextual Bibliography* (Bloomington: Indiana University Press, 1983); and "American Indian Women: Diverse Leadership for Social Change," in *Bridges of Power: Women's Multicultural Alliances*, ed. Lisa Albrecht and Rose Brewer (Philadelphia: New Society Publishers, 1990), 61–73. See also Women of All Red Nations, "W.A.R.N. Report II" (Sioux Falls, SD: WARN, 1980); Ohoyo Resource Center, *Words of Today's American Indian Women (Ohoyo Makachi)* (Washington, DC: U.S. Department of Education, 1981); M. Annette Jaimes, with Theresa Halsey, "American Indian Women: At the Center of Indigenous Resistance in North America," in *The State of Native America: Genocide, Colonization and Resistance*, ed. M. Annette Jaimes (Boston: South End Press, 1992); M. Annette Jaimes Guerrero, "Civil Rights versus Sovereignty: Native American Women in Life and Land Struggles," in *Feminist Genealogies: Colonial Legacies and Democratic Futures*, ed. M. Jacqui Alexander and Chandra Talpade Mohanty (New York: Routledge, 1997); and "Savage Hegemony: From 'Endangered Species' to Feminist Indigeinism," in *Talking Visions: Multicultural Feminisms in a Transnational Age*, ed. Ella Shohat (Cambridge, MA: MIT Press, 1999); Elizabeth A. Castle, Madonna Thunder Hawk, Marcella Gilbert, and Lakota Harden, "'Keeping One Foot in the Community': Intergenerational Indigenous Women's Activism from the Local to the Global (and Back Again)," *American Indian Quarterly* 27:3–4 (Summer–Fall 2003): 840–861; Gluck et al., "Whose Feminism?"; Donna H. Langston, "American Indian Women's Activism in the 1960s and 1970s," *Hypatia: A Journal of Feminist Philosophy* 18:2 Special Issue, Indigenous Women in the Americas (Spring 2003): 114–132.

46. Donna J. Haraway, "Situated Knowledges: The Science Question and the Privilege of Partial Perspective," in *Simians, Cyborgs, and Women: The Reinvention of Nature* (New York: Routledge, 1991), 183–202.

47. See, e.g., Steve Stern, *The Secret History of Gender: Women, Men and Power in Late Colonial Mexico* (Chapel Hill: University of North Carolina Press, 1994); Lynn Stephen, *Women and Social Movements in Latin America: Power from Below* (Austin: University of Texas Press, 1997).

48. Davis, *Blues Legacies and Black Feminism*, xi, xv.

49. Several theorists of women of color activism have written about this idea. See, e.g., Aída Hurtado's essay, "Underground Feminisms: Inocencia's Story," in *Chicana Feminisms: A Critical Reader*, ed. Gabriela F. Arredondo et al. (Durham, NC: Duke University Press, 2003), 260–290.

50. Indeed, Linda Burnham argues for an adjustment of our historical understanding of these hallmarks of women of color feminist theory in her article, "The Wellspring of Black Feminist Theory," *Working Paper Series No. 1* (Oakland, CA: Women of Color Resource Center, 2001), and challenges academics and lawyers to understand this genealogy of intersectionality, which begins before Kimberlé Crenshaw's often-cited article, "Mapping the Mar-

gins: Intersectionality, Identity Politics and Violence against Women of Color," *Stanford Law Review* 43:6 (1991): 1241–1299.

51. Sandoval, "US Third World Feminism," 14.

52. Rosaura Sánchez, "The History of Chicanas: A Proposal for a Materialist Perspective," in *Between Borders: Essays on Mexicana/Chicana History*, ed. Adelaida R. Del Castillo (Encino, CA: Floricante Press, 1990), 1–29; Foucault, *Power/Knowledge*.

53. Yolanda Broyles-González, *El Teatro Campesino: Theater in the Chicano Movement* (Austin: University of Texas Press, 1994).

54. Arturo F. Rosales, *Chicano! The History of the Mexican American Civil Rights Movement* (Houston: Arte Público Press, 1996).

55. For a discussion of the unified subject, see Linda Martín Alcoff, *Visible Identities: Race, Gender, and the Self* (New York: Oxford University Press, 2006).

56. Gloria Anzaldúa, *Borderlands: The New Mestiza = La Frontera* (San Francisco: Consortium, 1999); Sonia Saldívar-Hull, *Feminism on the Border: Chicana Politics and Literature* (Berkeley: University of California Press, 2000).

57. For other studies on the Chicano student movement, see Juan Gómez-Quiñones, *Mexican Students por la Raza: The Chicano Student Movement in Southern California, 1966–1967* (Santa Barbara, CA: Editorial La Causa, 1978); and Ernesto Chávez, "Creating Aztlán: The Chicano Student Movement in Los Angeles, 1966–1978" (Ph.D. diss., University of California, Los Angeles, 1994). See also Juan Gómez-Quiñones, *Chicano Politics: Reality and Promise, 1940–1990* (Albuquerque: University of New Mexico Press, 1990). Gómez-Quiñones dedicated only a few sentences to women's participation in the Chicano movement, but at least he includes them in the narrative history of movement events; Carlos Muñoz Jr., *Youth, Identity, Power: The Chicano Movement* (London: Verso, 1989); Rodolfo Acuña, *Occupied America: A History of Chicanos*, 3rd ed. (New York: Harper and Row, 1988).

58. Muñoz, *Youth, Identity, Power*, 88. Two chapters later, when Muñoz discusses "The Struggle for Chicano Studies," he somewhat retroactively places Anna NietoGomez, a leader of the Hijas de Cuauhtémoc, back into the history of the Chicano student movement by characterizing her as "one of the first Chicana feminists to emerge from the ranks of the student movement." It is problematic that someone who contributed substantially to the student movement and published numerous articles is left out of this history, to be inserted and depicted only through the controversy over being denied tenure in 1976 at California State University, Northridge. There are literally two other places where "women" are discussed in the book: a two-paragraph discussion of women in the Raza Unida Party and at the end of the chapter "From Chicano to Hispanic" in a discussion of a "vibrant Chicana feminist politics and scholarship" that included NACS, *Third Woman* journal, and MALCS.

59. While some Chicana activists chose to form caucuses, others formed parallel women's organizations that continued the mission and spirit of the work with a gendered perspective. See Dionne Espinoza's important study of women in the Brown Berets, "'Revolutionary Sisters': Women's Solidarity and Collective Identification among Chicana Brown Berets in East Los Angeles, 1967–1970," *Aztlán: A Journal of Chicano Studies* 26:1 (Spring 2001). See also Lee Bebout, "Hero Making in El Movimiento: Reies López Tijerina and the Chicano Nationalist Imaginary," *Aztlán: A Journal of Chicano Studies* 32:2 (Fall 2007): 93–121. Usually female members continued in movement organizing and Chicana organizations.

60. Ramón A. Gutiérrez, "Chicano History: Paradigm Shifts and Shifting Boundaries," in *Voices of A New Chicana/o History*, ed. Refugio I. Rochín and Dennis N. Valdés (East Lans-

ing: Michigan State University Press, 2000), 100. While Gutiérrez locates the origins of Chicana Feminism falsely in "bourgeois feminism," his argument illustrates the "re-visioning" of Chicano history or what I call "retrofitted" history.

61. Sonia A. López, "The Role of the Chicana within the Student Movement," in *Essays on la Mujer Anthology*, No. 1, ed. Rosaura Sánchez and Rosa Martinez Cruz (Los Angeles: Chicano Studies Center Publications, UCLA, 1977); Patrícia Hernandez, "Lives of Chicana Activists: The Chicano Student Movement (A Case Study)," and Adelaida Del Castillo, "Mexican Women in Organization," in *Mexican Women in the United States: Struggles Past and Present*, ed. Magdalena Mora and Adelaida R. Del Castillo, Occasional Paper No. 2 (Los Angeles: Chicano Studies Research Center Publications, UCLA, 1980).

62. Hernandez, "Lives of Chicana Activists," 17.

63. In later years after Chicana feminist agendas emerged, there were interconnections such as the use of Black feminist texts such as Michelle Wallace's *Black Macho and the Myth of the Superwoman* (New York: Dial Press, 1978), as well as Chicanas who read women's liberation writings and even some who published in Robin Morgan's edited volume, *Sisterhood Is Powerful*. See Elizabeth (Betita) Martinez, "Colonized Women: The Chicana an Introduction"; and Enriqueta Longeaux y Vasquez, "The Mexican-American Woman," both in *Sisterhood Is Powerful: An Anthology of Writings from the Women's Liberation Movement*, ed. Robin Morgan (New York: Vintage Books, 1970), 376–378, 379–384. Other points of overlap are with women of La Raza Unida pushing the women's political caucus of Texas to be more inclusive. Martha Cotera, Interview by author, Santa Barbara, CA, August 8, 1994.

64. For some published engagements of this issue, see Cynthia Orozco, "Sexism in Chicano Studies and the Community," in *Chicana Voices: Intersections of Class, Race, and Gender*, ed. Teresa Córdova et al. (Austin: Center for Mexican American Studies Publications, 1986); Mujeres en Marcha, *Unsettled Issues: Chicanas in the 80s* (Berkeley: Chicano Studies Library Publications Unit, 1983); and Teresa Córdova, "Roots and Resistance: The Emergent Writings of Twenty Years of Chicana Feminist Struggle," in *Handbook of Hispanic Cultures in the United States: Sociology*, ed. Félix Padilla (Houston: Arte Público Press and Instituto de Cooperación Iberoamericana, 1994).

65. Even within these spaces debates have pushed all of us to be more inclusive of gender and sexual diversity in ways earlier generations had not imagined. This is evidenced in the long-debated name change of the Lesbian Caucus to the Lesbian, BiMujeres, and Trans Caucus. Luz Calvo and Catriona Esquibel, "Latina Lesbians, BiMujeres, and Trans Identities: Charting Courses in the Social Sciences," in *Latina/o Sexualities: Probing Powers, Passions, Practices, and Policies*, ed. Marysol Ascencio (New Brunswick: Rutgers University Press, 2010), 217–229.

66. García, "Junctures in the Road." In addition, Lorena Oropeza argues that Chicano scholars have largely focused on what the movement was not able to accomplish and that "the future vitality of Chicana and Chicano Studies depends upon an inclusive vision of the field and of whom may rightfully claim membership within it" (210). See Lorena Oropeza, "Making History: The Chicano Movement," in *Voices of a New Chicana/o History*, ed. Refugio I. Rochín and Dennis N. Valdés (East Lansing: Michigan State University Press, 2000), 197–230.

67. Ernesto Chavez, *"Mi Raza Primero!" Nationalism, Identity, and Insurgency in the Chicano Movement in Los Angeles, 1966–1978* (Berkeley: University of California Press, 2002), 5.

68. George Mariscal, *Brown-Eyed Children of the Sun: Lessons from the Chicano Movement, 1965–1975* (Albuquerque: University of New Mexico Press, 2005), 3.

69. Alma García, "The Development of Chicana Feminist Discourse, 1970–1980," in *Unequal Sisters: A Multicultural Reader in Women's History*, ed. Ellen Carol DuBois and Vicki L. Ruiz (New York: Routledge, 1990), 418–431; Vicki Ruiz, "La Nueva Chicana: Women and the Movement," in *From Out of the Shadows*, 99–126. There is also a newer generation of scholars recuperating Chicana genealogies within the movement. See, e.g., Dolores Delgado Bernal's incisive analysis of women in the Blowouts, "Grassroots Leadership Reconceptualized"; Dionne Espinoza's study of women in the Brown Berets, "'Revolutionary Sisters'"; and Marisela R. Chavez's dissertation, "Despierten Hermanas y Hermanos! Women, the Chicano Movement, and Chicana Feminisms in California, 1966–1981" (Ph.D. diss., Stanford University, 2004); M. Chavez, "'We Lived and Breathed and Worked the Movement'"; Espino, "Women Sterilized as They Give Birth"; Elena R. Gutiérrez, *Fertile Matters: The Politics of Mexican-Origen Women's Reproduction* (Austin: University of Texas Press, 2008).

70. See Antonia I. Castañeda: "'Presidarias y Pobladoras': The Journey North and Life in Frontier California," in *Chicana Critical Issues*, ed. Norma Alarcón, Rafaela Castro, Emma Pérez, Beatriz Pesquera, Adaljiza Sosa-Riddell, and Patricia Zavella (Berkeley: Third Woman Press, 1993), 73–95; "Gender, Race, and Culture: Spanish-American Women in the Historiography of Frontier California," *Frontiers: A Journal of Women's Studies* 11:1 (1990): 8–20; "The Political Economy of Nineteenth-Century Stereotypes of California," in Del Castillo, *Between Borders*, 213–236. See also Cynthia Orozco, "Beyond Machismo, La Familia and Ladies Auxiliaries: A Historiography of Mexican-Origin Women's Participation in Voluntary Associations in the United States, 1870–1990," in *Renato Rosaldo Lecture Series*, 10 (1992–1993): 37–77; Emma Pérez, "Speaking from the Margin: Uninvited Discourse on Sexuality and Power," in *Building with Our Hands: New Directions in Chicana Studies*, ed. Adela de la Torre and Beatríz Pesquera (Berkeley: University of California Press, 1993), 51–71; Emma Pérez, "'A la Mujer': A Critique of the Partido Liberal Mexicano's Gender Ideology on Women," in Del Castillo, *Between Borders*, 459–482; Deena J. González, "'It is my last wish that . . .': A Look at Colonial Nuevo Mexicanas through Their Testaments," in de la Torre and Pesquera, *Building with Our Hands* 91–108; Vicki L. Ruiz, *Cannery Women, Cannery Lives: Mexican Women, Unionization, and the California Food Processing Industry, 1950–1980* (Albuquerque: University of New Mexico Press, 1987); Elizabeth (Betita) Martinez, *500 Years of Chicano History in Pictures* (Albuquerque: SouthWest Organizing Project [SWOP], 1991); Martha P. Cotera, *The Chicana Feminist* (Austin: Information Systems Development, 1977); Martha Cotera, *Diosa y Hembra: The History and Heritage of Chicanas in the U.S.* (Austin: Information Systems Development, 1976); Martha Cotera, "Mexicano Feminism," *Magazín* 1:9 (1973): 30–32. Ruiz, *From Out of the Shadows*; Vicki L. Ruiz and Virginia Sánchez Korrol, *Latina Legacies: Identity, Biography, and Community* (New York: Oxford University Press, 2005); Yolanda Leyva, "Listening to the Silences in Latina/Chicana Lesbian History," in *Living Chicana Theory*, ed. Carla Trujillo (Berkeley: Third Woman Press, 1998), 429–433; Pérez, *The Decolonial Imaginary*.

71. Deena J. Gonzalez, *Refusing the Favor: The Spanish-Mexican Women of Santa Fe, 1820–1880* (New York: Oxford University Press, 1999).

72. For the West, see Antonia Castañeda, "Women of Color and the Rewriting of Western History: The Discourse, Politics, and Decolonization of History," *Pacific Historical*

Review 61:4 (1992): 501–533. For borderlands, see her *Gender on the Borderlands: The Frontiers Reader* (Lincoln: University of Nebraska Press, 2007); Ellen Carol DuBois and Vicki L. Ruiz, *Unequal Sisters: A Multi-Cultural Reader in U.S. Women's History* (New York: Routledge, 1990), xii.

73. Delgado Bernal, "Grassroots Leadership Reconceptualized," 125.

74. Broyles-González, "Introduction," in *El Teatro Campesino*, xii.

75. Dionne Espinoza, "Pedagogies of Nationalism"; "Revolutionary Sisters". Also see her forthcoming book, *Bronze Womanhood: Chicana Labor and Leadership in the Chicano Civil Rights Movement, 1965–1980*.

76. M. Chávez, "Despierten Hermanas y Hermanos!" See also her forthcoming book on Chicana organizing in Southern California.

77. Enriqueta Vásquez, *Enriqueta Vásquez and the Chicano Movement: Writings from "El Grito del Norte,"* ed. Lorena Oropeza and Dionne Espinoza (Houston: Arte Público Press, 2006).

78. José Angel Gutiérrez, Michelle Meléndez, and Sonia Adriana Noyola, *Chicanas in Charge: Texas Women in the Public Arena* (Lanham, MD: AltaMira Press, 2007).

79. Laura E. Garcia, Sandra M. Gutierrez, and Felicitas Nuñez, *Teatro Chicana: A Collective Memoir and Selected Plays* (Austin: University of Texas Press, 2008).

80. Alaniz and Cornish, *Viva La Raza*.

81. Moraga and Anzaldúa, *This Bridge Called My Back*; Anzaldúa, *Making Face, Making Soul—Haciendo Caras*; Carla Trujillo, *Chicana Lesbians: The Girls Our Mothers Warned Us About* (Berkeley: Third Woman Press, 1991); Deena J. Gonzalez, "Speaking Secrets: Living Chicana Theory," in Trujillo, *Living Chicana Theory*, 46–77; Latina Feminist Group, *Telling to Live: Latina Feminist Testimonios* (Durham, NC: Duke University Press, 2001); Delgado Bernal, "Grassroots Leadership Reconceptualized"; Saldívar-Hull, *Feminism on the Border*.

82. Rina Benmayor, Ana Juarbe, Celia Alvarez, and Blanca Vásquez (Oral History Task Force), *Stories to Live By: Continuity and Change in Three Generations of Puerto Rican Women*, Working Paper Series, Centro de Estudios Puertorriqueños (New York: Hunter College, CUNY, 1987); Sherna Berger Gluck and Daphne Patai, *Women's Words: The Feminist Practice of Oral History* (New York: Routledge, 1991); Claudia Salazar, "A Third World Woman's Text: Between the Politics of Criticism and Cultural Politics," in *Women's Words: The Feminist Practice of Oral History*, ed. Sherna Berger Gluck and Daphne Patai (New York: Routledge, 1991), 93–106; Gwendolyn Etter-Lewis and Michele Foster, eds., *Unrelated Kin: Race and Gender in Women's Personal Narratives* (New York: Routledge, 1996); Patricia Zavella, "The Politics of Race and Gender: Organizing Chicana Cannery Workers in Northern California," in Alarcón et al., *Chicana Critical Issues*; Judy Yung, *Unbound Feet: A Social History of Chinese Women in San Francisco* (Berkeley: University of California Press, 1995); Gluck and Patai, *Women's Words*; Debra J. Blake, "Reading Dynamics of Power through Mexican-Origin Women's Oral Histories," *Frontiers: A Journal of Women's Studies* 19:3 (1998): 24–41; Vicki L. Ruiz, "Situating Stories: The Surprising Consequences of Oral History," *Oral History Review* 25:1/2 (1998): 71–80; René Jara and Hernán Vidal, eds., *Testimonio y Literatura* (Minneapolis: Institute for the Study of Ideologies and Literature, 1986); Doris Sommer, "'Not Just a Personal Story': Women's Testimonios and the Plural Self," in *Life/Lines: Theorizing Women's Autobiography*, ed. Bella Brodzki and Celeste Schenck (Ithaca: Cornell University Press, 1988); George Yúdice, "Testimonio and Postmodernism," *Latin American Perspectives* 70 (Summer 1991): 15–31.

83. Michiko Tanaka, *Through Harsh Winters: The Life of a Japanese Immigrant Woman [as told to] Akemi Kikumura* (Novato, CA: Chandler and Sharp, 1981); Mary Paik Lee, *Quiet Odyssey: a Pioneer Korean Woman in America* (Seattle: University of Washington Press, 1990); María Elena Lucas, *Forged under the Sun: The Life of María Elena Lucas* (Ann Arbor: University of Michigan Press, 1993); Gary Soto, *Jessie de la Cruz: A Profile of a United Farm Worker* (New York: Persea Books, 2000); Yolanda Broyles-Gonzalez, *Lydia Mendoza's Life in Music: Norteño Tejano Legacies* (New York: Oxford University Press, 2001).

84. Angela Y. Davis, *If They Come in the Morning: Voices of Resistance* (New York: Third Press, 1971); Mary Brave Bird, Mary Crow Dog, and Richard Erdoes, *Lakota Woman* (New York: Grove Weidenfeld, 1990); Elaine Brown, *A Taste of Power: A Black Woman's Story* (New York: Anchor Books, 1994).

85. Mohanty, "Cartographies of Struggle."

86. Other oral historians have studied the tension between what Alessandro Portelli calls personal memories and public history. See his study, *The Battle of Valle Giulia: Oral History and the Art of Dialogue* (Madison: University of Wisconsin Press, 1997).

87. The historian Richard White has called memory the enemy in history in his book *Remembering Ahanagran: Storytelling in a Family's Past* (New York: Hill and Wang, 1998).

88. Catriona Rueda Esquibel, *With a Machete in Her Hand: Reading Chicana Lesbians* (Austin: University of Texas Press, 2006).

89. Leyva, "Listening to the Silences."

90. Carla Trujillo, "Chicana Lesbians: Fear and Loathing in the Chicano Community," in Alarcón et al., *Chicana Critical Issues*; Hill Collins, *Black Feminist Thought*; Foucault, *Power/Knowledge*.

91. See, e.g., Kamala Vieweswaren, *Fictions of Feminist Ethnography* (Minneapolis: University of Minnesota Press, 1994).

92. "Gayatri Spivak on the Politics of the Subaltern: Interview with Howard Winant," *Socialist Review* 20:3 (July–September 1990): 83.

93. Fernando Coronil, "Listening to the Subaltern: The Poetics of Neocolonial States," *Poetics Today* 15:4 (Winter 1994): 645. Special issue: Loci of Enunciation and Imaginary Constructions: The case of (Latin) America, I.

94. See Robert Carr, "Crossing the First World/Third World Divides: Testimonial, Transnational Feminisms, and the Postmodern Condition," in *Scattered Hegemonies: Postmodernity and Transnational Feminist Practices*, ed. Inderpal Grewal and Caren Kaplan (Minneapolis: University of Minnesota Press, 1994).

95. In "Can the Subaltern Speak?" Spivak argues that Deleuze and Guattari collapse in her critique of European postmodern theorists' unacknowledged subject positions within the global economic relations of power and production. See Gilles Deleuze and Félix Guattari, *Anti-Oedipus: Capitalism and Schizophrenia* (New York: Viking Press, 1977).

96. For an application of Spivak's intervention, see "Can the Subaltern Vote?" by Leerom Medovoi, Shankar Raman, and Benjamin Robinson, *Socialist Review* 20:3 (July–September 1990): 133–149.

97. Angie Chabram-Dernersesian's "Chicana/o Studies as Oppositional Ethnography," *Cultural Studies* 4:3 (October 1990): 228–247, theorizes the place of self-representation in the practice of critical ethnography.

98. Haraway, "Situated Knowledges."

99. Blackwell, "Geographies of Difference."

100. Robert Carr, "Crossing the First World/Third World Divides: Testimonial, Trans-

national Feminisms, and the Postmodern Condition," in Grewal and Kaplan, *Scattered Hegemonies*.

CHAPTER TWO

1. Corinne Sánchez, interview by author, San Fernando Valley, CA, September 3, 1997. In the Los Angeles Women's Movements Oral History Collection, the Virtual Oral/Aural History Archive, California State University, Long Beach, www.csulb.edu/voaha.

2. Sallie Radcliffe and Sarah Westwood discuss how the traditional study of politics and social movements focuses on the "externalities" of political protest. In contrast, one hallmark of studying women's social movements is the focus on the "internalities" of protest and, I would argue, power. See their introductory chapter, "Gender, Racism and the Politics of Identities in Latin America," in their edited volume, *"Viva": Women and Popular Protest in Latin America* (New York: Routledge, 1993), 1.

3. Springer, *Living for the Revolution*.

4. Based on the godparent system in Catholicism, comadrazgo has been transformed into an alternative model of kinship that scholars such as Rosa Linda Fregoso argue "developed historically as a women-centered alternative to the patriarchal kinship basis of familia," which has been central to women's survival. See *meXicana Encounters: The Making of Social Identities on the Borderlands* (Berkeley: University of California Press, 2003), 90. Other scholars, such as Vicki Ruiz (*From Out of the Shadows*), emphasize the ideas of female reciprocity among female family members and neighbors, or what Keta Miranda calls a form of feminine or Chicana solidarity. Miranda argues in the context of barrio life that the tradition of comadrazgo can serve as a kinship system "between younger women and older, compassionate and understanding women who have also resisted and survived la vida dura." See Marie "Keta" Miranda, *Homegirls in the Public Sphere* (Austin: University of Texas, 2003). See also Esquibel, *With Her Machete in Her Hand*; Catherine S. Ramirez, "Representing, Politics, and the Politics of Representation in Gang Studies," *American Quarterly* 56:4 (December 2004): 1135–1146.

5. Francisco Balderrama and Raymond Rodríguez, *Decade of Betrayal: Mexican Repatriation in the 1930's* (Albuquerque: University of New Mexico Press, 2006), 122.

6. Catherine S. Ramírez, *The Women in the Zoot Suit: Gender, Nationalism, and the Politics of Cultural Memory* (Durham, NC: Duke University Press, 2009).

7. See the important work of Gloria Holguín Cuádraz, "Chicanas and Higher Education: Three Decades of Literature and Thought," *Journal of Hispanic Higher Education* 4:3 (July 2005): 215–234, in which she also argues that "the passage of the National Defense Education Act of 1958 provided low-interest loans to individuals otherwise unable to finance a college education" (218).

8. Cynthia E. Orozco, *No Mexicans, Women, or Dogs Allowed: The Rise of the Mexican American Civil Rights Movement* (Austin: University of Texas Press, 2009).

9. For critical histories of Chicana and Mexican labor in the U.S. see Vicki L. Ruiz, *Working for Wages: Mexican Women in the Southwest, 1930–1980* (Tucson, AZ: Southwest Institute for Research on Women, 1984); Patricia Zavella, *Sunbelt Working Mothers: Reconciling Family and Factory* (Ithaca: Cornell University Press, 1993); and Denise Segura, "Chicanas and Triple Oppression in the Labor Force" in *Chicana Voices: Intersections of Class, Race, and Gender*, ed. Teresa Córdova et al. (Austin: Center for Mexican American Studies, University of Texas, 1986).

10. The Chicana sociologist Gloria Cuádraz describes how Title IV of the Higher Education Act provided "grants, loans, and work study for need-based financial aid students who otherwise would have been financially unable to attend 4-year colleges and universities across the country." Cuádraz, "Chicanas and Higher Education," 218.

11. This postwar sense of hope and social mobility is a stark contrast to the conditions of veteran's lives in the post-Vietnam era (one in four homeless men served in that war). See Sánchez, *Becoming Mexican American*, for a rich historical discussion of the social history of Mexicans and Mexican Americans in the pre-World War II era in Los Angeles, specifically, on educational aspirations. See also Jaime O. Cádenas, "Cousins of Caliban: Nation, Masculinity, and Latino Men in California, 1945 to the Mid-1960s" (Ph.D. diss., University of California, Los Angeles, 2000).

12. Patricia C. Gándara, *Over the Ivory Walls: The Educational Mobility of Low-Income Chicanos* (Albany: State University of New York Press, 1995).

13. Garcia, "The Development of Chicana Feminist Discourse, 1970–1980."

14. Adaljiza Sosa-Riddell, "Chicanas and el Movimineto," *Aztlán: A Journal of Chicano Studies* 5:1–2 (1974): 155–165; Maxine Baca Zinn, "Political Familism: Toward Sex Role Equality in Chicano Families," *Aztlán: A Journal of Chicano Studies* 6:1 (1975): 13–26; Richard T. Rodriguez, *Next of Kin: The Family in Chicano/a Cultural Politics* (Durham, NC: Duke University Press, 2009).

15. See Davis, *Black Feminism and Blues Legacies*.

16. Vicki L. Ruiz, "Claiming Public Space at Work, Church and Neighborhood," in *Las Obreras: Chicana Politics of Work and Family*, ed. Vicki L. Ruiz (Los Angeles: Chicano Studies Research Center Publications, UCLA, 2000), 23.

17. Carolyn Ashbaugh, *Lucy Parsons: American Revolutionary* (Chicago: Charles H. Kerr, 1976), 7. Three days later, during the Haymarket Riots, when a bomb was thrown at the police who were dispersing the crowd, Parsons's husband was arrested, convicted, and executed for killing a police officer, although there was never any evidence linking him to the killing.

18. In 1939, according to Elizabeth (Betita) Martinez, Parsons joined the Communist Party in an effort to help free the Scottsboro Boys and other black prisoners because she acknowledged the clear connections between racism, gender, and the larger class struggle. Elizabeth (Betita) Martinez, *500 Years of Chicana Women's History* (New Brunswick, NJ: Rutgers University Press, 2008), 44.

19. According to Ruiz, Luisa Moreno, "its driving force," drew on her connections with Latino labor unions, mutual aid societies, and other grassroots groups to ensure a truly national conference. Ruiz, *From Out of the Shadows*, 95. See also David G. Gutiérrez, *Walls and Mirrors: Mexican Americans, Mexican Immigrants, and the Politics of Ethnicity* (Berkeley: University of California Press, 1995).

20. Ruiz, *From Out of the Shadows*, 101. In 1941 Moreno, with other organizers such as Dorothy Ray Healy, came to Southern California to help organize cannery workers, and together they built the second largest UCAPAWA affiliate, Local 3. "Moreno encouraged cross-plant alliances and women's leadership" (82). After the war red baiting led to the collapse of the UCAPAWA and ultimately the deportation of Moreno due to her connections to the Communist Party. After her deportation Moreno traveled to Mexico and then to Cuba, "where she participated in the revolutions early years" (76).

21. Martinez, *500 Years of Chicana Women's History*, 77.

22. Ruiz, *From Out of the Shadows*, 96.

23. Martinez, *500 Years of Chicana Women's History*, 77. For a history of Fierro de Bright and the struggle against the Hollywood blacklist, see Marez, "Subaltern Soundtracks."

24. Orozco, *No Mexicans, Women, or Dogs Allowed*.

25. Roberto R. Calderón and Emilio Zamora, "Manuela Solis Sager and Emma Tenayuca: A Tribute," in Córdova et al., *Chicana Voices*, 33–39.

26. Martinez, *500 Years of Chicana Women's History*, 72.

27. Calderón and Zamora, "Manuela Solis Sager and Emma Tenayuca," 35.

28. Adaljiza Sosa-Riddell and Elisa Facio have been working on a book documenting Chicana participation on the left titled, *Chicana Rebellions: Chicana Feminisms and Socialist Legacies*. The historian Devra Weber is also completing a history on the Mexican left in the United States; see her forthcoming essay, "Keeping Community, Challenging Boundaries: Indigenous Migrants, Internationalist Workers, and Mexican Revolutionaries, 1900–1920," in *Mexico and Mexicans in the History and Culture of the United States*, ed. John Tutino (Austin: University of Texas Press, forthcoming). The most documented connection of the old and new left in Chicano organizing is the case of Bert Corona and Chole Alatorre and CASA. See Mario T. García, *Memories of Chicano History: The Life and Narrative of Bert Corona* (Berkeley: University of California Press, 1994); Chávez, *"Mi Raza Primero!"*; and M. Chavez, "Despierten Hermanas y Hermanos!" For important work on this question in relation to black feminism, see Erik S. McDuffie, "No Small Change Would Do: Esther Cooper Jackson and the Making of a Black Left Feminist,'" in *Want to Start a Revolution? Radical Women in the Black Freedom Struggle*, ed. Dayo F. Gore, Jeanne Theoharis, and Komozi Woodward (New York: New York University Press, 2009), 25–46.

29. While the Chicano movement has been defined by its break with the Mexican American political generation, Ernesto Chávez has also documented many key links between the two generations and challenged the idea of a complete break between the two, in *¡Mi Raza Primero!*

30. García, "The Development of Chicana Feminist Discourse."

31. Ibid.

32. Anna NietoGomez, interviews by author, Norwalk, CA, April 7, 18, and 22, 1991. In the Los Angeles Women's Movements Oral History Collection, the Virtual Oral/Aural History Archive, California State University, Long Beach, www.csulb.edu/voaha.

33. Sylvia Castillo, interview by author, Long Beach, CA, May 24, 1996.

34. López, "The Role of the Chicana within the Student Movement," 23.

35. Leticia Hernández, interviews by author, Long Beach, CA, July 28 and 30 and August 21, 1992. In the Los Angeles Women's Movements Oral History Collection, the Virtual Oral/Aural History Archive, California State University, Long Beach, www.csulb.edu/voaha.

36. Corinne Sánchez, interview by author, San Fernando Valley, CA, September 3, 1997.

37. NietoGomez, interview by author, April 22, 1991.

38. Hernández, interview, July 22, 1992; Denise Segura, "'In the Beginning He Wouldn't Lift Even a Spoon': The Division of Household Labor," in *Building with Our Hands: New Directions in Chicana Studies*, ed. Adela de la Torre and Beatriz M. Pesquera (Berkeley: University of California Press, 1993), 181–195.

39. Hernández, interview, July 28, 1992.

40. NietoGomez, interview, April 18, 1991.

41. Hernández, interview, July 28, 1992.

42. Cecilia Quijano, interviews by author, Downey and Long Beach, CA, February 9 and September 13, 2007.

43. Hernández, interview, July 18, 1992. Unfortunately, many Chicanas report still finding racialized, gendered, and sexual hostility on campuses, according to recent studies of undergraduate Chicana experiences conducted by leading Chicana feminist researchers. See, e.g., Aída Hurtado, *Voicing Chicana Feminisms: Young Women Speak Out on Sexuality and Identity* (New York: New York University Press, 2003); Alma M. García, *Narratives of Mexican American Women: Emergent Identities of the Second Generation* (Walnut Creek, CA: AltaMira Press, 2004).

44. See Muñoz, *Youth, Identity, Power*; Gómez-Quiñones, *Mexican American Students por la Raza*; and Michael Soldatenko, "Mexican Student Movements in Los Angeles and Mexico City, 1968," *Latino Studies* 1 (2003): 284–300.

45. By 1969 there were 22 chapters of UMAS in California with over 600 members. "What Is U.M.A.S.," California State University, Long Beach, Special Collections, UMAS file.

46. NietoGomez, interview, April 22, 1991.

47. Raymond Williams, *Marxism and Literature* (London: Oxford University Press, 1977).

48. See Carol Hardy-Fanta, "Latina Women and Political Leadership: Implications for Latino Community Empowerment," in *Latino Politics in Massachusetts: Struggles, Strategies, and Prospects*, ed. Carol Hardy-Fanta and Jeffrey N. Gerson (New York: Routledge, 2002), 193–212.

49. Armando Rodriguez and Keith Taylor, *From the Barrio to Washington: An Educator's Journey* (Albuquerque: University of New Mexico Press, 2007), 90.

50. "Introduction," *Encuentro Femenil* 1:2 (1974): 4.

51. Hernández, interview, July 28, 1992.

52. NietoGomez, interview, April 22, 1991. At that time many women sought illegal abortions in the United States or across the border in Tijuana, Mexico.

53. In 1973 a Mexicana went to the University of Southern California Medical Center in Los Angeles complaining of swollen feet due to her pregnancy. Because the doctors did not know what she was saying and because of the racist medical discourses affecting Latinas, they aborted her pregnancy and sterilized her. See Committee to Stop Forced Sterilization, "Stop Forced Sterilization Now!—Alto a esterilización forzada ¡hoy!" (Los Angeles, n.p.); and "Stop Forced Sterilization Now!" *La Raza* 2:4 (January 1975): 12–15; Gutiérrez, *Fertile Matters*; Elena R. Gutiérrez, "Policing 'Pregnant Pilgrims': Situating the Sterilization Abuse of Mexican-Origin women in Los Angeles County," in *Women, Health, and Nation: Canada and the United States since 1945*, ed. Georgina Feldberg, Molly Ladd-Taylor, Alison Li, and Kathryn McPherson (Montreal: McGill-Queen's University Press, 2003), 379–403; Espino, "Women Sterilized as They Give Birth"; Virginia Espino, "Women Sterilized as They Give Birth: Forced Sterilization and Chicana Resistance in the 1970s," in Ruiz, *Las Obreras*, 65–82.

54. *El Plan Espiritual de Aztlán*, reprinted in *Aztlán: An Anthology of Mexican American Literature*, ed. Luis Valdez and Stan Steiner (New York: Vintage Books, 1972), 402–406.

55. Hernández, interview, July 30, 1992.

56. In almost all the interviews I conducted, Hijas de Cuauhtémoc members referred to the male leadership as the "guys" or even the "dudes." I note this because it would be overly generalized to understand this to mean all guys; in the vernacular that they developed together, "the guys" refers to a specific group of people.

57. Hernández, interview, July 28, 1992.

58. D. Letticia Galindo, "Dispelling the Male-Only Myth: Chicanas and Caló," *Bilingual Review* 17:1 (1992); D. Letticia Galindo and María Dolores Gonzales, ed. *Speaking Chicana: Voice, Power, and Identity* (Tucson: University of Arizona Press, 1999).

59. NietoGomez, interview, April 22, 1991. Benita Roth also found a similar pattern of the strategic use of cussing and masculinized movement language. Roth, *Separate Roads to Feminism*.

60. "UMAS Special Elections," pamphlet, California State University, Long Beach, Special Collections, UMAS file. It is important to note that other UMAS women also held office, among them Mary Lou Hernandez, who was vice president in 1968–1969. The seven-member executive board comprised four women and three men. Women held the offices of corresponding and recording secretaries, treasurer, and vice president. Men were president, vice president, and historian.

61. Espinoza, "'Revolutionary Sisters."

62. Nancy Nieto, "Macho Attitudes," *Hijas de Cuauhtémoc*, issue 1 (1971).

63. Cherríe Moraga, *The Last Generation: Prose and Poetry* (Boston: South End Press, 1993), 158.

64. See López, "The Role of the Chicana within the Student Movement"; Del Castillo, "Mexican Women in Organization."

65. Hernández, interview, July 30, 1992.

66. Thanks to Gloria Cuádraz, whose rich conversations helped me think through this point. See Sergio de la Mora, *Cinemachismo: Masculinities and Sexuality in Mexican Film* (Austin: University of Texas Press, 2006), for a discussion of virile nationalism.

67. For a critique of movement sexual politics, see "Political Education Workshop," *Hijas de Cuauhtémoc* (1971).

68. Hernández, interview, July 30, 1992.

69. In the second issue of the *Hijas de Cuauhtémoc* an article titled "Political Education Workshop" discussed the problem of sexual/political initiation. During my interviews with Keta, she told me that she had authored the piece, but as was the practice in many Chicano magazines and movement papers her name did not appear on the by-line (to emphasize collective editorial practices rather than individuals). Marie (Keta) Miranda, interview by author, Santa Cruz, CA, May 22, 1996.

70. Sylvia Castillo, interview by author, Long Beach, CA, May 24, 1996.

71. Nieto, "Macho Attitudes."

72. Unfortunately, attacking women's sexuality has been a common strategy for opponents of women's organizing both globally and locally. See, e.g., Cynthia Rothschild, *Written Out: How Sexuality Is Used to Attack Women's Organizing*, a report of the International Gay and Lesbian Human Rights Commission and the Center for Women's Global Leadership (San Francisco: IGLHRC, 2000).

73. López, "Role of the Chicana within the Student Movement," 26–27.

74. Del Castillo, "Mexican Women in Organization," 9.

75. bell hooks, quoted in Elizabeth (Betita) Martinez, ed., *De Colores Means All of Us: Latina Views for a Multi-Colored Century* (Cambridge: South End Press, 1998), 175.

76. Elizabeth (Betita) Martinez, "Chingón Politics Die Hard," in Martinez, *De Colores Means All of Us*, 172–181.

77. Del Castillo, "Mexican Women in Organization," 8.

78. See Patricia Zavella, "Feminist Insider Dilemmas: Constructing Ethnic Identity

with Chicana Informants," in *Feminist Dilemmas in Fieldwork*, ed. Diane L. Wolf (Boulder, CO: Westview Press, 1996), 138–159.

79. Sánchez, interview, September 3, 1997; Sylvia Castillo, interview by author, Long Beach, CA, November 22, 2003; Hernández, interview, July 30, 1992.

80. NietoGomez, interview, April 22, 1991.

81. Note on language: in this context, "older" simply means upper-class status, women who were seniors and juniors from the perspective of freshman and sophomores. Hernández, interview, 1992.

82. Marie (Keta) Miranda, interview by author, Santa Cruz, CA, May 24, 1994.

83. Del Castillo, "Mexican Women in Organization," 9.

84. NietoGomez, interview, April 22, 1991; Hernández, interview, July 30, 1992.

85. NietoGomez, interview, April 22, 1991.

86. Miranda, interview, May 24, 1994.

87. Delgado Bernal, "Grassroots Leadership Reconceptualized."

88. Brodkin Sacks, cited in Delgado Bernal, "Grassroots Leadership Reconceptualized," 123.

89. Delgado Bernal, "Grassroots Leadership Reconceptualized," 124. By being specific about roles the women she interviewed identified with, Delgado Bernal was able to broaden the concept of leadership to more accurately examine grassroots leadership through Brodkin Sacks's paradigm of cooperative leadership. Karen Brodkin Sacks, *Caring by the Hour: Women, Work, and Organizing at Duke Medical Center* (Urbana: University of Illinois Press, 1988), and "Gender and Grassroots Leadership," in *Women and the Politics of Empowerment*, ed. Ann Bookman and Sandra Morgan (Philadelphia: Temple University Press, 1988), 77–94. For other studies of grassroots leadership, see Robnett, "African American Women and the Civil Rights Movement"; Nancy A. Naples, *Grassroots Warriors: Activist Mothering, Community Work, and the War on Poverty* (New York: Routledge, 1998); Mary Pardo, "Mexican American Women Grassroots Community Activists: 'Mothers of East Los Angeles,'" *Frontiers: A Journal of Women Studies* 11:1 (1990): 1–7.

90. Baca Zinn, "Political Familism," 17, 21–22.

91. Rodriguez, *Next of Kin*; Maylei Blackwell, "Lideres Campesinas: Nepantla Strategies and Grassroots Organizing at the Intersection of Gender and Globalization," *Aztlán: A Journal of Chicano Studies* 35:1 (2010): 13–47.

92. Fregoso, *meXicana Encounters*, 85.

93. NietoGomez, interview, April 22, 1991.

94. López, "The Role of the Chicana within the Student Movement," 26.

95. Sánchez, interview, September 3, 1997.

96. Castillo, interview, November 22, 2003.

97. Sylvia Castillo, interview by author, Oakland, CA, July 1, 2001.

98. Hernández, interview, July 30, 1992.

99. "Our Philosophy," *Hijas de Cuauhtémoc*, n.d., 1.

100. See Gema Matsuda, "La Chicana Organizes: The Comisión Femenil Mexicana in Perspective," *Regeneración* 2:3 (1974): 25–27, for a discussion of Chicana organizations on the Cal State Los Angeles campus such as VELA and the Chicana Forum.

101. "El Movimiento and the Chicana: What Else Could Break Down a Revolution but Women Who Do Not Understand True Equality," *La Raza* 1:6 (1971): 40–42. Keta Miranda is the uncredited author.

102. Matsuda, 25.

103. Ibid., 27.

104. Russo, "Chicanas Speak: Hijas Establish Goals."

105. Anna NietoGomez, speech delivered at Chicana Feminisms Conference, California State University, Long Beach, March 19, 2010.

106. Sonia E. Alvarez, *Engendering Democracy in Brazil: Women's Movements in Transition Politics* (Princeton: Princeton University Press, 1990); Norma S. Chinchilla, "Feminism, Revolution, and Democratic Transitions in Nicaragua," in *The Women's Movements in Latin America: Participation and Democracy*, 2nd ed., ed. Jane S. Jaquette (San Francisco: Westview Press, 1992), 37–51; Francesca Miller, *Latin American Women and the Search for Social Justice* (Hanover, NH: University Press of New England, 1991).

CHAPTER THREE

1. Homi K. Bhabha, "Introduction: Narrating the Nation," in *Nation and Narration*, ed. Homi K. Bhabha (New York: Routledge, 1990), 1–7; Espinoza, "Pedagogies of Nationalism."

2. See also the important essay by Laura E. Pérez that examines feminist representational practices and Chicano nationalism: "*El desorden*, Nationalism, and Chicana/o Aesthetics," in *Between Woman and Nation: Nationalisms, Transnational Feminism and the State*, ed. Caren Kaplan, Norma Alarcón, and Minoo Moallem (Berkeley: Third Woman Press, 1999), 19–46; and *Chicana Art: The Politics of Spiritual and Aesthetic Altarities* (Durham, NC: Duke University Press, 2007).

3. *El Plan Espiritual de Aztlán*.

4. Mariscal, *Brown-Eyed Children of the Sun*; Jason M. Ferreira, "All Power to the People: A Comparative History of Third World Radicalism in San Francisco, 1968–1974" (PhD diss., University of California, Berkeley, 2003).

5. For a larger analysis of Chicanas and cultural nationalism, see Beatriz Pesquera and Denise Segura, "There Is No Going Back: Chicanas and Feminism," in *Chicana Critical Issues*, ed. Editorial Board of Mujeres Activas en Letras y Cambio Social (Berkeley: Third Woman Press, 1993), 95–105; and Córdova, "Roots and Resistance."

6. García, "The Development of Chicana Feminist Discourse," 12.

7. "Cultural Nationalism: A Fight for Survival," *Chicano Student Movement* 2:2 (August 1969): 3.

8. The strange logics of the regulatory nature of these narratives is readily apparent in the ways in which Anna NietoGomez was dismissed as not Chicana because her maternal grandfather was Puerto Rican or as racially suspect because of her dark skin and curly hair.

9. Important exceptions include Ernesto Chávez, whose critique of nationalism involves a historical understanding of how the ideology was equated to male dominance in Chicano movement organizations, and Rodriguez's *Next of Kin*, which builds on the Chicana feminist critique to study the cultural history of la familia.

10. Fregoso, *meXicana Encounters*, 85.

11. Wahneema Lubiano, "Black Nationalism and Black Common Sense: Policing Ourselves and Others," in *The House That Race Built: Original Essays by Toni Morrison, Angela Y. Davis, Cornel West, and Others on Black Americans and Politics in America*, ed. Wahneema Lubiano (New York: Pantheon Books, 1997).

12. Ella Shohat, "Introduction," in *Talking Visions: Multicultural Feminism in a Transnational Age*, ed. Ella Shohat (Cambridge, MA: MIT Press, 1998), 20.

13. Inderpal Grewal and Caren Kaplan, "Introduction: Transnational Feminist Practices and Questions of Postmodernity," in *Scattered Hegemonies: Postmodernity and Transnational Feminist Practices*, ed. Inderpal Grewal and Caren Kaplan (Minneapolis: University of Minnesota Press, 1994), 2.

14. Mariscal, *Brown-Eyed Children of the Sun*.

15. Mary Pat Brady, *Extinct Lands, Temporal Geographies: Chicana Literature and the Urgency of Space* (Durham, NC: Duke University Press, 2002).

16. For an important discussion of the bind for women in national liberation movements surrounding the question of nationalism, see Kumari Jayawardena, *Feminism and Nationalism in the Third World* (New Delhi: Kali for Women; London: Zed Books; Totowa, NJ: Biblio Distribution Center, 1986); Jace Weaver, Craig S. Womack, and Robert A. Warrior, *American Indian Literary Nationalism* (Albuquerque: University of New Mexico Press, 2006). See also the Forum Native Feminisms without Apology in *American Quarterly* 60:2 (June 2008): 241–315.

17. See also Rudolfo Anaya, "Aztlán: A Homeland without Boundaries," in *Aztlán: Essays on the Chicano Homeland*, ed. Rudolfo A. Anaya and Francisco Lomeli (Albuquerque: University of New Mexico Press, 1991), 230–241. Since *El Plan* both Anaya and Alurista have revised their notions of Aztlán to be less essentialist and more inclusive.

18. Angie Chabram-Dernersesian, "'Chicana! Rican? No, Chicana-Riqueña!' Refashioning the Transnational Connection," in *Multiculturalism: A Critical Reader*, ed. David Theo Goldberg (Cambridge: Basil Blackwell, 1994), 269–295. Also see de Lauretis, *Feminist Studies/Critical Studies*.

19. Chávez, *"Mi Raza Primero!"*; Michael Omi and Howard Winant, *Racial Formation in the United States: From the 1960s to the 1980s* (New York: Routledge, 1986); Guillermo Bonfil Batalla, *México Profundo: Reclaiming a Civilization*, trans. Philip A. Dennis (Austin: University of Texas Press, 1996). Mexican nationalism was consolidated after the Mexican Revolution, and mestizaje became its racial project through the writings of the minister of education, José Vasconcelos, who reconceptualized Mexico as *la raza cósmica* (the cosmic race). While Chicano studies has often adopted a celebratory stance to his thinking, upon closer reading it should be noted that creating the so-called fifth race was not for the purposes of creating some kind of racial utopia where the world's races would come together through mixture but was a project of racial "whitening" of indigenous peoples with the explicit goal to "deindianize" them in the process of creating a mestizo nation. As Chávez uses Raymond Williams's notion of residual culture, this culturally celebratory form of genocide should be deeply problematized in Chicana/o studies as part of the residue of concepts of mestizaje. Raymond Williams, "Base and Superstructure in Marxist Cultural Theory," in *Problems in Materialism and Culture*, 2nd ed. (New York: Verso, 1997).

20. For critiques of sexism, see, e.g., Mujeres en Marcha, *Unsettled Issues: Chicanas in the 80s* (Berkeley, CA: Chicano Studies Library Publications Unit, 1983). See the corrido "The Female of Aztlán" by familia Dominguez, cited by Sosa-Riddell as a form of internalized stereotypes of masculinity; see José E. Limón, "Carne, Carnales, and the Carnivalesque: Bakhtinian Batos, Disorder, and Narrative Discourses," *American Ethnologist* 16:3 (1989): 471–486.

21. Américo Paredes, "The United States, Mexico, and Machismo," in *Folklore and Culture on the Texas Mexican Border*, ed. Richard Bauman (Austin: Center for Mexican American Studies, University of Texas, 1993), 215–234.

22. Mirandé, *The Chicano Experience*, 179.

23. Rendón, *Chicano Manifesto*, 104 cited in Mirandé, *The Chicano Experience*, 175.

24. As patron saint of Mexico, the Virgin of Guadalupe, who appeared to the indigenous peasant Juan Diego at Tepeyac (near Mexico City) in 1531, is said to be a syncretism between the Virgin Mother and the Mexican goddess Tonantzin; others believe she is a version of Coatlicue, the Aztec mother goddess. Malinche, synonymous with the word *traitor* in Mexico, was born of noble birth but after becoming enslaved was given among twenty slave girls to the conquistador Hernán Cortés. Fluent in Nahautl (the lingua franca of central Mexico) as well as Chontal and other Maya languages, Malintzín Tenépal was baptized Marina and served as a translator to Cortés, later bearing him children, who are often called the first mestizos.

25. Octavio Paz, *The Labyrinth of Solitude* (New York: Grove Weidenfeld, 1985); Adelaida R. Del Castillo, "Malintzín Tenépal: A Preliminary Look into a New Perspective," *Encuentro Femenil* 1:2 (1974): 58–78; Emma Pérez, "Sexuality and Discourse: Notes from a Chicana Survivor," in Trujillo, *Chicana Lesbians*; Norma Alarcón, "Traddutora, Traditora: A Paradigmatic Figure of Chicana Feminism," *Cultural Critique* 13 (1989): 57–87; Mary P. Brady, "Quotidian Warfare," *Signs* 28:1 (Autumn 2002): 446–447.

26. Norma Alarcón, "Chicana Feminism: In the Tracks of 'the' Native Woman," in Kaplan, Alarcón, and Moallem, *Woman and Nation*, 68.

27. Sosa-Riddell, "Chicanas and El Movimento," 156; Martha Cotera, "Feminism: The Chicana and Anglo Versions—A Historical Analysis," in *Twice a Minority: Mexican American Women*, ed. Margarita Melville (St. Louis: C. V. Mosby, 1980), 232.

28. NietoGomez, interview, April 22, 1991.

29. "Chicana Symposium," *La Raza* 2:10 (1969): 4.

30. Specifically, Frances Beal describes the emergence of the Third World Alliance as a reaction to the dual polemic in which black women were named the source of pathology in the black family in the *Moynihan Report* (1965) and also expected to walk two steps behind black men in black nationalist cultural politics. Frances Beal, interview by author, Oakland, CA, September 21, 1999.

31. See Palante, *Siempre Palante: The Young Lords*, DVD, dir. Iris Morales, P.O.V. PBS, October 15, 1996. For work on black nationalism, see Eddie S. Glaude Jr., *Is It Nation Time? Contemporary Essays on Black Power and Nationalism* (Chicago: University of Chicago Press, 2002); and on black feminism and nationalism, Patricia Hill Collins, *From Black Power to Hip Hop: Racism, Nationalism, and Feminism* (Philadelphia: Temple University Press, 2006).

32. Stuart Hall, "The Question of Cultural Identity," in *Modernity and Its Futures*, ed. Stuart Hall, David Held, and Tony McGrew (Cambridge: Polity Press, 1992), 274–316.

33. Ibid.

34. George Lipsitz, *Time Passages: Collective Memory and American Popular Culture* (Minneapolis: University of Minnesota Press, 1990), 213.

35. Ibid.

36. Alarcón, "Traddutora, Traditora," 281.

37. Combahee River Collective, "A Black Feminist Statement," in Hull, Scott, and Smith, *But Some of Us Are Brave*, 13–14. See also Kelley, *Freedom Dreams*.

38. Emma Pérez, "Feminism-in-Nationalism: The Gendered Subaltern at the Yucatán Feminist Congress of 1916," in Kaplan, Alarcón, and Moallem, *Woman and Nation*, 219–241.

39. Frederick C. Turner, *The Dynamic of Mexican Nationalism* (Chapel Hill: University of North Carolina Press, 1968).

40. NietoGomez, interview, April 22, 1991.

41. Ibid.

42. For an important discussion of women's participation and critique of the PLM's position on women, see Emma Pérez, "'A la Mujer': A Critique of the Partido Liberal Mexicano's Gender Ideology on Women," in *Between Borders: Essays on Mexicana/Chicana History*, ed. Adelaida R. Del Castillo (Encino, CA: Floricanto Press, 1990).

43. Manuel Gamio, *El imigrante mexicano: La historia de su vida* (México: Universidad Nacional Autónoma de México, 1969), 103–107.

44. Turner, *The Dynamic of Mexican Nationalism*, 192–193.

45. Quoted in Turner, *The Dynamic of Mexican Nationalism*, 193.

46. Ana Lau Javien, *La nueva ola del feminismo en México: Conciencia y acción de las mujeres* (México: Planeta, 1987), 28. Translation mine.

47. Shirlene Soto, *Emergence of the Modern Mexican Woman: Her Participation and Struggle for Equality, 1910-1940* (Denver: Arden Press, 1990), 34.

48. Ibid., 64.

49. Hernández Tovar, "Sara Estella Ramirez."

50. Ruiz and Sanchez Korrol, *Latina Legacies*, 608; Pérez, *The Decolonial Imaginary*, 67.

51. Teresa Palomo Acosta and Ruthe Winegarten, *Las Tejanas: 300 Years of History* (Austin: University of Texas Press, 2003), 74.

52. Shirlene Ann Soto, *The Mexican Woman: A Study of her Participation in the Revolution, 1910-1940* (Palo Alto: R&E Research Associates, 1979), 25.

53. Pérez, *The Decolonial Imaginary*, 68.

54. Palomo Acosta and Winegarten, *Las Tejanas*, 78.

55. Pérez, *The Decolonial Imaginary*.

56. Palomo Acosta and Winegarten, *Las Tejanas*, 78–79.

57. Juan Gómez-Quiñones, *Sembradoras: Ricardo Flores Magón y el Partido Liberal Mexicano: A Eulogy and Critique*, Monograph 5 (Los Angeles: University of California, Los Angeles Chicano Research Center, 1973), 76–77.

58. Benedict Anderson, *Imagined Communities: Reflections on the Origin and Spread of Nationalism*, rev. ed. (London: Verso, 1991).

59. The Chicana film scholar Rosa Linda Fregoso discusses the imaginative possibility of film, stating that "the Chicano nation [as] captured in these films represents an 'imagined community.' Far from fabricating or inventing a community, Chicana and Chicanos have re-invented (imagined anew) a 'community' of Chicanos and Chicanas." *The Bronze Screen: Chicana and Chicano Film Culture* (Minneapolis: University of Minnesota Press, 1993), xxiii; and Homi K. Bhabha, "DissemiNation: Time, Narrative, and the Margins of the Modern Nation," in *Nation and Narration*, 297.

60. Kobena Mercer, *Welcome to the Jungle: New Positions in Black Cultural Studies*, (London: Routledge, 1994), 64–65.

61. Gonzales, *I am Joaquín/Yo Soy Joaquín*.

62. For a discussion of the ways in which *Yo Soy Joaquín* functioned in the Chicano movement as a narrative of racial unity, see Angie Chabram Dernersesian, "'Chicana! Rican? No, Chicana-Riqueña!': Refashioning the Transnational Connection," in *Multiculturalism: A Critical Reader*, ed. David Theo Goldberg (Cambridge: Basil Blackwell, 1994), 269–295; and for a Chicano literary history reading of this text, see Rafael Pérez-Torres, *Movements in Chicano Poetry: Against Myths, Against Margins* (Cambridge: Cambridge University Press, 1995); Richard T. Rodríguez, *Next of Kin: The Family in Chicano/a Cultural Politics* (Durham, NC: Duke University Press, 2009).

63. Fregoso, *The Bronze Screen*, 6. See also Esquibel's reading of this text: *With Her Machete in Her Hand*.

64. Gonzales, *I Am Joaquín/Yo Soy Joaquín*, 64.

65. Several other images from Stan Steiner's classic *La Raza: The Mexican Americans* (New York: Harper & Row, 1969) depict the family as la raza or el movimiento as a prevalent visual trope that helped to produce expectations about leadership and power within the movement. The man in the image (Chávez) leads his people; the women, visually, follow. Another image combines both visual tropes by depicting the "revolutionary hero" as the patriarchal head of family.

66. See, for example, Sylvia Morales's film, *A Crushing Love*, which depicts Chicana activists who balance their social justice work and motherhood.

67. Rodríguez, *Next of Kin*, 7.

68. Anne McClintock, Aamir Mufti, and Ella Shohat, eds., *Dangerous Liaisons: Gender, Nation, and Postcolonial Perspectives* (Minneapolis: University of Minnesota Press, 1997), 7.

69. Maylei Blackwell, "Bearing Bandoleras: Transfigurative Liberation and the Iconography of la Nueva Chicana," in *Beyond the Frame: Women of Color and Visual Representations*, a Project of the Women of Color Research Cluster, ed. Angela Davis and Neferti Tadiar (Durham, NC: Duke University Press, 2005).

70. See Norma Cantú, "Women, Then and Now: An Analysis of the Adelita Image versus the Chicana as Political Writer and Philosopher," in Córdova et al., *Chicana Voices*, 8–10. Also, several Chicana and Mexicana scholars have done in-depth research on the role of women in the Mexican Revolution. See, e.g., Elizabeth Salas, *Soldaderas in the Mexican Military: Myth and History* (Austin: University of Texas Press, 1990); Ana Lau Jaiven and Carmen Ramos-Escandon, *Mujeres y revolución, 1900–1917* (México: Instituto Nacional de Estudios Históricos de la Revolución Mexicana, Instituto Nacional de Antropología e Historia, 1993).

71. Martha Lopez, "La Mexicana," *Hijas de Cuauhtémoc* 1 (n.d. [early 1971]).

72. For Vicki Ruiz's rich discussion, see "La Nueva Chicana: Women and the Movement," in *From Out of the Shadows*; pp. 111–112 specifically discuss the figure of la Soldadera.

73. See Alicia Arrizón, "*Soldaderas* and the Staging of the Mexican Revolution," *Drama Review* 42:1 (1998): 90–112; María Herrera-Sobek, "The Soldier Archetype," in *The Mexican Corrido: A Feminist Analysis*, ed. María Herrera-Sobek (Bloomington: Indiana University Press, 1990).

74. This form of eroticization may be linked to the fact that during the Mexican Revolution soldaderas were commonly vilified as prostitutes, according to Salas (*Soldaderas in the Mexican Military*), a practice echoed in the way women organizers are seen as indecent women or *mujeres de la calle* (women of the street).

75. See Mariscal, *Brown-Eyed Children of the Sun*, for a powerful reading of the image of Che.

76. See *Chicano Power! Latin Rock in the USA, 1968–1976*, 2 CD set and 40–page booklet (Soul Jazz Records CD 39, released 1999). For contemporary examples of how this image is being circulated in political art on T-shirts and stickers, see the politically conscious social justice art of Favianna Rodriguez at www.faviana.com/port_other/other1.php (accessed May 15, 2004).

77. "Introduction," *Encuentro Femenil* 1:2 (1974): 4.

78. Yvonne Yarbro-Bejarano, "The Lesbian Body in Latin Cultural Production," in *¿Entiendes? Queer Readings, Hispanic Writings*, ed. Emilie L. Bergmann and Paul Jullian Smith (Durham, NC: Duke University Press, 1995), 182.

79. Amalia Mesa-Baines, "El Mundo Femenino: Chicana Artists of the Movement—A Commentary on Development and Production," in *Chicano Art: Resistance and Affirmation* (Los Angeles: Wright Art Gallery, UCLA, 1991), 131–140.

80. Louis Althusser, "Ideology and Ideological State Apparatuses," in *Lenin and Philosophy and Other Essays* (New York: Monthly Review Press, 1971).

81. Pérez, *"El desorden*, Nationalism, and Chicana/o Aesthetics"; Luz Calvo, "Art Comes for the Archbishop: The Semiotics of Contemporary Chicana Feminism and the Work of Alma Lopez," *Meridians: Feminism, Race, Transnationalism* 5:1 (2004): 201–224. Alicia Gaspar de Alba and Alma López, eds., *Our Lady of Controversy: Alma López's "Irreverent Apparition"* (Austin: University of Texas Press, 2011); Pérez, *Chicana Art*.

82. Esquibel, *With Her Machete in Her Hand*, 148.

83. Blackwell, "Geographies of Difference."

84. Muñoz, *Disidentifications*, 4.

85. Print culture and its visual images were often the basis of early Chicano film. *Yo Soy Joaquín* was made into a film directed by Luis Valdez in 1969, and Anna NietoGomez's "Chicana Feminist Slide Show" was the basis for the 1976 film *La Chicana*, directed by Sylvia Morales, assisted by another Hijas de Cuauhtémoc member, Cindy Honesto. Fregoso has developed an incisive comparative rendering of these two films in her book, *Bronze Screen*.

86. Ybarro-Frausto, "Interview with Tomás Ybarro-Frausto."

87. According to Angela Y. Davis in her essay, "Black Nationalism: The Sixties and the Nineties," in *Black Popular Culture*, ed. Gina Dent (Seattle: Bay Press, 1992), 317–324, key among these suppressed moments is Huey Newton urging an end to verbal gay bashing and an examination of black male sexuality after Jean Genet's sojourn with the Black Panther Party.

CHAPTER FOUR

1. The analysis of interlocking or simultaneous oppressions is a contribution of women of color feminist interventions of the 1960s and 70s. The statement by the Combahee River Collective, active from 1974 to 1980 in Boston, is the classic example. See Combahee River Collective, "A Black Feminist Statement," in *But Some of Us Are Brave*.

2. Several other scholars have documented what I call Chicana print communities; see García, "The Development of Chicana Feminist Discourse"; Alarcón, "Chicana Feminism"; Roberta Fernández, "Abriendo Caminos in the Brotherland: Chicana Writers Respond to the Ideology of Literary Nationalism," *Frontiers: A Journal of Women Studies* 14:2 (1994): 23–50. See also Blackwell, "Geographies of Difference"; "Contested Histories: Las Hijas de Cuauhtemoc." Pearlita R. Dicochea also writes about *Regeneración* and *Encuentro Femenil* in her article, "Chicana Critical Rhetoric: Recrafting La Causa in Chicano Movement Discourse, 1970–1979," *Frontiers: A Journal of Women Studies* 25:1 (2004): 77–92.

3. Alarcón, "The Theoretical Subject(s)."

4. Blackwell, "Geographies of Difference."

5. Fraser, "Rethinking the Public Sphere," 123. See also Steven Gregory, "Race, Identity and Political Activism: The Shifting Contours of the African American Public Sphere," *Public Culture* 7 (1994): 147–164. For an important reworking of Fraser to understand Chicana girls in gangs, see Marie (Keta) Miranda, *Homegirls in the Public Sphere* (Austin: University of Texas Press, 2003).

6. Fraser, "Rethinking the Public Sphere," 116.

7. Ibid., 123.

8. The lasting impact of las Hijas de Cuauhtémoc can be measured in the sheer number of publications included in Alma Garcia's *Chicana Feminist Thought: The Basic Historical Writings*. Twenty-six percent, or a little over one-fourth, of all the writings included were from *Hijas de Cuauhtémoc* or the journal they helped to found in 1973, *Encuentro Femenil*. There are seventeen articles from women involved in *Hijas de Cuauhtémoc* or *Encuentro Femenil* that appear in the first half of the total collection of essays, numbering eighty-two; roughly half the articles in the first half of the book correspond roughly to the period the members were active.

9. Cotera, "Feminism: The Chicana and Anglo Versions," 231.

10. *El Grito* was based at the University of California, Berkeley, and its special edition on women was produced in 1973. *El Popo* was first published in 1970 by students at Cal State, Northridge; the newspaper took its name from El Popocatepetl volcano in Mexico.

11. The introduction to the first issue of *Encuentro Femenil* not only testifies to the formation of a gendered print community, but it is through that community that the journal locates its endeavor. See "Introduction," *Encuentro Femenil* 1:2 (1974): 3–4.

12. Vásquez, *Enriqueta Vásquez and the Chicano Movement*; Elizabeth (Betita) Martinez, interview by author, San Francisco, CA, September 21, 1999. According to Martinez, she and Vásquez and Beverly Axelrod (the attorney who defended Reies Tijerina) edited the paper, along with many other activists from the New Mexico land grant movement including Jose Madril and Baltazar Martinez, who were involved in the courthouse raid in Tierra Amarilla; the artist Rini Templeton; Valentina Valdez, who wrote often for the paper and was married to Anselmo Tijerina; Catherine Montague, who did typesetting; and others who wrote, including Fernanda Martinez, Nita Luna, and Adelita Medina.

13. The Sleepy Lagoon Defense Committee (first known as the Citizens' Committee for the Defense of Mexican American Youth) came together in October 1942 in response to the indictment of twenty-two young men for murder (all defendants but one were Mexican American) by the Grand Jury of Los Angeles County for the murder of José Diaz, whose death occurred at a party on the Williams ranch in the city of Los Angeles near a little pond called the Sleepy Lagoon. Two years later all charges were dropped.

14. Sandoval, "US Third World Feminism."

15. Pérez, *The Decolonial Imaginary*.

16. Anzaldúa, *Borderlands/La Frontera*.

17. Anderson, *Imagined Communities*; Mohanty, "Cartographies of Struggle"; Fernández, "*Abriendo Caminos* in the Brotherland," lays out Chicana writers' engagement with Chicano nationalism through textual sources without a larger contextual and historical analysis. While she deploys Anderson's theory in her reading of the 1973 women's issue of *El Grito*, the first Chicano journal (1968), my analysis differs in its focus on the function of print communities in the formation of new political subjectivities and as a space of Chicana political and cultural autonomy and moves beyond textual analysis to engage those who created a Chicana print community.

18. Partha Chatterjee, *The Nation and Its Fragments: Colonial and Postcolonial Histories* (Princeton: Princeton University Press, 1993).

19. There was also a school of thought within the Chicano movement that saw Chicano communities in the United States as internal colonies; see Mario Barrera, Carlos Muñoz, and Charles Ornelas, "The Barrio as Internal Colony," in *People and Politics in Urban Society*, ed. Harlam Hahn, Urban Affairs Annual Review, vol. 6 (Los Angeles: Sage, 1972): 465–498; Tomás Almaguer, "Toward the Study of Chicano Colonialism," *Aztlán: Chicana Journal of*

the Social Sciences and the Arts 2:1 (1971): 7–21; Robert Blauner, "Internal Colonialism and Ghetto Revolt," *Social Problems* 16 (Spring 1969): 393–408.

20. Rafael Pérez-Torres, *Movements in Chicano Poetry: Against Myths, Against Margins* (Cambridge: Cambridge University Press, 1995).

21. Pérez, *The Decolonial Imaginary*.

22. For a review of the early literature, see Judith Sweeny, "Chicana History: A Review of the Literature," in *Essays on La Mujer*, ed. Rosaura Sánchez and Rosa Martinez Cruz (Los Angeles: Chicano Studies Resource Center Publications, UCLA, 1977), 99–123. For an expansive review of Chicana writings over the past twenty years, see Córdova, "Roots and Resistance."

23. NietoGomez, interview, April 22, 1991.

24. Raul Ruiz, "The Chicanos and the Underground Press," *La Raza* 3:1 (1977): 8–10.

25. NietoGomez, interview, April 18, 1991.

26. López, "The Role of the Chicana."

27. Beatriz Pesquera, interview by author, Long Beach, CA, March 23, 1995.

28. Enriqueta Longeaux y Vasquez, "The Woman of La Raza," *El Grito del Norte* 2:9, 6 July 1969.

29. López, "The Role of the Chicana," 24.

30. *Chicano!* [videorecording]: *The History of the Mexican American Civil Rights Movement*, vol. 1: "Quest for a Homeland," coproduced by Galan Productions, Inc., and the National Latino Communications Center, in cooperation with KCET, Los Angeles, 1996.

31. Anna NietoGomez, "Chicanas Identify!" *Hijas de Cuauhtémoc* 1 (n.d.). Note: I quote at length here because access to these sources is difficult, and although the language may seem dated or polemical, I feel it is important to ground my analysis in the discourse of the time as well as illustrate the use of la Chicana, la Mexicana, el Macho, and la Mujer as unified subjects.

32. NietoGomez, "La Femenista," 39.

33. Cotera, *The Chicana Feminist*; and "Feminism: The Chicana and Anglo Versions."

34. Cotera, quoted in NietoGomez, "La Femenista," 39.

35. Arjun Appadurai, *Modernity at Large: Cultural dimensions of Globalization* (Minneapolis: University of Minnesota Press, 1996); and "The Production of Locality," in *Counterworks: Managing the Diversity of Knowledge*, ed. Richard Fardon (New York: Routledge, 1995).

36. Articles from Hijas de Cuauhtémoc by Jeanette Padilla, Leticia Hernández, and a report on the Houston Conference appeared in *The Women's Press*, Eugene, Oregon (1971). The Puerto Rican Young Lords left the Denver Youth Liberation Conference due to the rhetoric of Chicano nationalism that excluded them; however, they followed Chicana activism through republication (Iris Morales, pers. comm.). For a history of the Young Lords Party and women's involvement, see Morales's film, *¡Palante, Siempre Palante!* (1996).

37. Martha Cotera, interview by author, Santa Barbara, CA, August 8, 1994.

38. Zavella, "Feminist Insider Dilemas."

39. Pesquera and Segura, "There Is No Going Back," 102.

40. Palomo Acosta and Winegarten, *Las Tejanas*, 237; Handbook of Texas On-line, s.v. "Mujeres por la Raza," www.tshaonline.org/handbook/online/articles/MM/vimgh.html (accessed December 31, 2009).

41. Palomo Acosta and Winegarten, *Las Tejanas*, 237.

42. Evey Chapa, "Mujeres por la Raza Unida," *Caracol* 1 (September 1974): 3. See also

Dionne Espinoza's forthcoming book, which includes important research on women in La Raza Unida Party.

43. Miranda, interview, May 22, 1996.

44. "Chicana Symposium," *La Raza* 2:10 (1969): 4; "Corazón de Aztlán," *Daily Bruin*, November 25, 1969.

45. The facilitators were Lola Marquez and Sandra Ugarte, Philosophy of La Chicana Nueva; Carmen Delgado and Vicki Castro, Chicanas in Education; Linda Apodaca and Evy Alarcón, La Chicana y la Comunidad; Anna NietoGomez and Gema Matsuda, Chicana and Communication; Keta Miranda and Blanca Olivares, Political Education of La Chicana.

46. Miranda, interview, May 24, 1994; May 22, 1996.

47. Del Castillo, "Mexican Women in Organization," 7.

48. Anna NietoGomez, "Madres por Justicia!!" *Encuentro Femenil* 1:2 (1973): 12–18.

49. Robert Bauman, "The Black Power and Chicano Movements in the Poverty Wars in Los Angeles," *Journal of Urban History* 33:2 (2007): 277–295.

50. Chicana student organizing such as VELA, Chicana Forum, and Comisión Femenil is documented by Matsuda in "La Chicana Organizes." She describes the hostility Chicanas faced when trying to establish a Comisión chapter on campus by the leadership of MEChA at Cal State Los Angeles who felt that a women's organization would be a distraction.

51. Dorinda Moreno, ed., *La mujer en pie de lucha: y la hora es ya!* (San Francisco: Espina del Norte, 1973).

52. Alicia Escalante, "Canto de Alicia," *Encuentro Femenil* 1:1 (1973); Morales, *A Crushing Love*.

53. Escalante, "Canto de Alicia."

54. The ELAWRO (1968) also identified itself as the Chicana Welfare Rights Organization (CWRO) (1970).

55. Alicia Escalante, "The Los Angeles Chicana Welfare Rights Organization," speech delivered at Cal State University Northridge, spring 1974. Acquired from the personal archive of Anna NietoGomez.

56. Mark Toney, "Revisiting the National Welfare Rights Organization," *Colorlines*, www.colorlines.com/index.php, accessed July 23, 2008.

57. Tillmon not only led the local Los Angeles-based struggle for welfare rights, but went on to make coalitions with NOW, claiming that "welfare is a women's issue" in a 1972 *Ms.* magazine article and encouraged Martin Luther King Jr. to hold a march on Washington for poor people's rights. Tillmon went on to help found the National Welfare Rights Organization. Unfortunately, a potentially powerful alliance between black women and Chicanas broke down because of differences that they were not able to negotiate at the time. Their common agenda called for accountability at the welfare office, and they articulated a militant class-based program of poor people's liberation. Yet their differences involved the ways in which issues of race, language, and culture intersect with class and gender. The Chicanas demanded bilingual welfare services and culturally sensitive, bilingual, community control of child care. It was over these demands and their cultural and language differences that the group split, according to Tillmon. Alicia Escalante went on to form the East L.A. Welfare Rights Organization in 1967, citing the Chicano movement as her major political influence. Johnnie Tillmon, interview conducted by Sherna Berger Gluck, Oral History Collection, Long Beach State.

58. Alicia Escalante, "The Los Angeles Chicana Welfare Rights Organization," speech

delivered at California State University, Northridge, spring 1974, from the personal archive of Anna NietoGomez.

59. Escalante, "The Los Angeles Chicana Welfare Rights Organization."

60. Francisca Flores, "A Reaction to Discussions on the Talmadge Amendment to the Social Security Act," *Encuentro Femenil* 1:2 (1974): 13–14.

61. Alicia Escalante, "A Letter from the Chicana Welfare Rights Organization," *Encuentro Femenil* 1:2 (1974): 16.

62. Ibid., 18.

63. Bill Flores, "Francisca Flores," CSU Fresno, May 2, 1996. http://clnet.ucla.edu/research/francisca.html; accessed May 12, 2006.

64. Ibid.

65. Before June 1963 *Carta EDITORIAL* was titled *Carta Perales* and was edited by Leon Perales. Perales left his position as editor and was replaced by Francisca Flores and Delfino Verela, who served as associate editors. *Carta EDITORIAL: For the Informed—Interested in Mexican American Affairs* 1:6 (June 17, 1963): 1.

66. Flores, "Francisca Flores." Marcie Miranda-Arrizón, "Building Herman(a)dad: Chicana Feminism and Comisión Femenil Mexicana Nacional" (M.A. thesis, University of California, Santa Barbara, 1998).

67. M. Chávez, "Despierten Hermanas y Hermanos!"

68. Francisca Flores, "El Mundo Femenil Mexicana," *Regeneración* 1:10 (1971): 1.

69. Comisión Femenil de Los Angeles Papers, Chicano Studies Resource Center Library, University of California, Los Angeles; Comisión Femenil Mexicana National Archives, Department of Special Collections, Davidson Library, University of California, Santa Barbara.

70. The CSAC is listed as the author of "Chicanas in the Labor Force" in the table of contents, while NietoGomez's name appears on the by-line in *Encuentro Femenil* 1:2 (1974): 28–33. NietoGomez also produced a pamphlet, "Labor and Chicanas," published by the Chicana Service Action Center for Public Information in March 1980, which was reprinted from *Somos* (July–August) 1979.

71. "Chicanas in the Labor Force," *Encuentro Femenil* 1:2 (1974): 28.

72. Ibid., 29.

73. In March 1972 Francisca Flores along with other members attended a conference in Phoenix, Arizona, that was sponsored by the Women's Bureau, a division of the Department of Labor. They demanded an explanation as to why employment services were not being implemented specifically for Chicanas. The women of CFMN were offered some funding by the U.S. Department of Labor; however, to access those funds they needed to become incorporated as a nonprofit organization. As a result, in September 1972 a one-year grant was given to Comisión Femenil Mexicana Nacional to establish a center. According to Chávez, the CSAC continued to be funded by the Department of Labor until 1974, then from 1975 to 1976 the CSAC was funded by the city of Los Angeles's "county allotment of the comprehensive Employment and Training Act (CETA)." See M. Chávez, "Despierten Hermanas y Hermanos!"

74. Corinne Sánchez, interview by author, San Fernando Valley, CA, September 3, 1997.

75. CIW is known officially as the California Institution for Women and was technically in Corona, but residents of that city objected to the use of their city's name in the prison's title. In 2003 the facility was moved to Chino.

76. Mary Vangie, "Women at Frontera, Ca.," *Regeneración* 1:10 (1971): 8.

77. "COPA CONFERENCE," *Hijas de Cuauhtémoc* (1971).

78. René Mares, "La Pinta: The Myth of Rehabilitation," *Encuentro Femenil* 1:2 (1974): 20–27.

79. Ibid.

80. M. Chávez, 2004.

81. Ibid., 198.

82. Laura Pulido, *Black, Brown, Yellow & Left: Radical Activism in Los Angeles* (Berkeley: University of California Press, 2006), 199.

83. M. Chávez, "Despierten Hermanas y Hermanos!" 214.

84. For an analysis of poetry and poetic revolutions of Chicanas in this moment, see Angie Chabram Denersesian's "And, Yes . . . The Earth Did Part: On the Splitting of Chicana/o Subjectivity," in de la Torre and Pesquera, *Building with Our Hands*, 34–56.

85. Martinez, *500 Years of Chicana Women's History*; Roth, *Separate Roads to Feminism*.

86. Ibid.

87. Roth, *Separate Roads to Feminism*, 143.

88. Martinez, *500 Years of Chicana Women's History*; Roth, *Separate Roads to Feminism*.

89. Roth, *Separate Roads to Feminism*, 144.

90. Toni Cade, ed., *The Black Woman: An Anthology* (New York: New American Library, 1970); *Asian Women* (Berkeley: University of California Press, 1971); Moreno, *La mujer en pie de lucha*; Farah Jasmine Griffin, "Conflict and Chorus: Reconsidering Toni Cade's *The Black Woman: An Anthology*," in Glaude, *Is It Nation Time?* As far as audience and the role these particular anthologies played, they were used to create a space for women's voices within their respective movements. All of them served as foundational texts in the emergent Asian American women, black women and la Chicana courses that began to crop up in a larger ethnic studies field. On the other hand, other anthologies such as *This Bridge* were, according to that work's editors, "a reaction to the racism of white feminism soon became a positive affirmation of the commitment of women of color to our *own* feminisms" (xxiii; original emphasis).

91. Analyzing women's movement anthologies demarcates the multiple genealogies of U.S. feminism, especially in relationship to "difference," that speaks to their importance historically. See, e.g., Katie King's explication of diverse sites of theory production in *Theory in Its Feminist Travels* and Jakobsen's *Working Alliances and the Politics of Difference*.

92. Gloria Anzaldúa, interview conducted by author, Santa Cruz, CA, June 29 and September 24, 1999; Luz Calvo, interview by author, Santa Cruz, CA, September 1999. Calvo, a Chicana dyke activist, explained how *This Bridge* functioned with political organizing circles at the time, noting that when activists who were involved in various organizations met to discuss the publication it prompted new organizing and inspired the formation of new organizations among women of color.

93. I cut the list off at 1990, but for an exhaustive and methodical bibliographic listing with annotations, see Martha Ramírez and Judy Young, "Women of Color in Collaboration and Conflict: An Annotated Bibliography," in *Enunciating Our Terms: Women of Color in Collaboration and Conflict*, ed. María Ochoa and Teresía Teaiwa (Santa Cruz: University of California, Santa Cruz, Center for Cultural Studies, 1994), 141–155.

94. Maylei Blackwell, "Triple Jeopardy."

95. King is referring specifically to Pat Robinson's essay, "Poor Black Women," introducing "A Collective Statement: Black Sisters," produced and printed in Toni Cade's 1970

The Black Women: An Anthology, which went through multiple mutations as it was published in *Voices from Women's Liberation* and *Sisterhood Is Powerful* (both 1970), in contrast to Beal's article, "Double Jeopardy," which was also republished in numerous venues with very little variation. King, *Theory in Its Feminist Travels*, 16.

96. Part of the problem here is the rigid division between "politics" that are suitable for the study of history and the "poetic" realm, where many Chicana lesbians made their early interventions. It is perhaps telling that women who were marginalized in the movement took up poetic revolutions as the site of their activism, an effective strategy for changing consciousness. See Audre Lorde's thinking on this in her essay, "Poetry Is Not a Luxury," in *Sister Outsider: Essays and Speeches* (Trumansburg, NY: Crossing Press, 1984).

97. Lorraine Bethel and Barbara Smith, "Introduction," in *Conditions: The Black Women's Issue* (Brooklyn: Conditions, 1979). See also Hom, *Documenting Lesbian of Color Community Building*, for an analysis of AZALEA.

98. Barbara Smith, interview by author, Santa Barbara, CA, February 8, 2000.

99. Bethel and Smith, "Introduction."

100. The continuity of these strategies is well documented by tatiana de la tierra's work on activist Latina lesbian publishing between 1991 and 1996 that focuses specifically on *esto no tiene nombre* and *conmoción*. tatiana de la tierra, "Activist Latina Lesbian Publishing: *esto no tiene nombre* and *conmoción*," *Aztlán: A Journal of Chicano Studies* 27:1 (2002): 139–178.

CHAPTER FIVE

1. See Flores, "Conference of Mexican Women: Un Remolino," 1; Guardiola and Bird-well, "Conferencia de Mujeres por la Raza"; Hernandez, "Conferencia de Mujeres por la Raza: Carmen Speaks Out"; Rosa Marta Morales, "Conferencia de Mujeres por la Raza: Rosa en Español"; "National Chicana Conference"; Vidal, *Chicanas Speak Out*; "Chicanas—Houston," *El Young Lord*, July 7, 1971, 2; Tomasin Medal, "Chicana Conference," *El Tecolote* 1:20 (June 16, 1971): 8. For a discussion by the women who walked out, see Suzan Racho, Gloria Meneses, Socorro Acosta, and Chicki Quijano, "Houston Chicana Conference," *La Gente*, May 31, 1971.

2. López, "The Role of the Chicana within the Student Movement."

3. Gloria Guardiola, interview by author, Houston, TX, November 16, 2002.

4. Hernandez, "Conferencia de Mujeres de la Raza: Carmen Speaks Out."

5. When I met Elma Barrera for our first scheduled interview in November 2002, she told me that another key organizer, Martha Moreno, had died only two days before. Moreno was a lifetime community activist and prominent community member, serving the East End neighborhood of Houston. She was a social worker and an ardent advocate for Chicano/Hispanic and women's rights. Lucas Wall, "Martha Moreno Activist," *Houston Chronicle*, November 19, 2002.

6. Vidal, *Chicanas Speak Out*; Roth, *Separate Roads to Feminism*.

7. Elma Barrera, personal correspondence with author, January 20, 2003.

8. From Houston, I drove to San Antonio to share the tape with Keta Miranda, a professor at the University of Texas, San Antonio, and an activist who traveled with members of the Los Angeles delegation to the conference in her youth. When I returned home I played the recording for NietoGomez and Castillo.

9. Emily Honig, "Women at Farah Revisited: Political Mobilization and Its Aftermath among Chicana Workers in El Paso, Texas, 1972–1992," *Feminist Studies* 22:2 (Sum-

mer 1996): 425–452; Alessandro Portelli, *The Order Has Been Carried Out: History, Memory, and Meaning of a Nazi Massacre in Rome* (New York: Palgrave Macmillan, 2003); Alessandro Portelli, *The Death of Luigi Trastulli and Other Stories: Form and Meaning in Oral History* (Albany: State University of New York Press, 1991); Steve J. Stern, *Remembering Pinochet's Chile: On the Eve of London, 1998* (Durham, NC: Duke University Press, 2004); Pierre Nora, "Between Memory and History: Les Lieux de Memoire," *Representations* 26 (Spring 1989): 7–24.

10. Barrera, interview, November 15, 2002.

11. "La Conferencia de Mujeres por la Raza, Conference Report," Lucy R. Moreno Collection, Nettie Lee Benson Latin American Collection, Benson Library, University of Texas, Austin; "National Chicanas [*sic*] Conference."

12. Graciela (Grace) Olivarez (1928–1987) was a professor of law at the University of New Mexico from 1972 to 1975. Her career was dedicated to advocating for Mexican American/Latin American peoples, the elderly, the poor, youth, the unemployed, and women. She lectured on Mexican American culture, problems and concerns at numerous universities and appeared before several government hearings. She worked with several OEO programs and was appointed to the directorship of the Community Service Administration under President Jimmy Carter, becoming the third-highest-ranking woman official in federal government in 1977. Gayle J. Hardy, *American Women Civil Rights Activists: Biobibliographies of 68 Leaders, 1825–1992* (Jefferson, NC: McFarland, 1993). Olivarez is also sometimes spelled with an *s*; I chose to spell it with a *z* because that is how it appears in the program of the Conferencia de Mujeres por la Raza and also in her publications.

13. Ignacio García, "Mexican American Youth Organization Precursors of Change in Texas," *Working Paper Series* 8 (Tucson: Mexican American Studies and Research Center, 1987).

14. *Handbook of Texas Online*, s.v. "Magnolia Park, Texas," www.tsha.utexas.edu/hand book/online/articles/view/MM/hvm6.html (accessed May 4, 2004); Martha Liebrum, "Politics and the Woman: East End," *Houston Post*, March 1, 1972.

15. For a history of Houston leading up to the Chicano movement, see Emma Pérez, *The Decolonial Imaginary*, and Guadalupe San Miguel Jr., *Brown, not White: School Integration and the Chicano Movement in Houston* (College Station: Texas A&M University Press, 2001).

16. Barbara J. Nelson and Alissa Hummer, *Leadership and Diversity: A Case Book* (Los Angeles: University of California, Los Angeles, 2004).

17. Connie Lunnen, "La Conferencia, It's a Beginning, Say Chicanas," *Houston Chronicle*, May 17, 1971, F1.

18. Ibid.

19. "An Orientation to La Conferencia de Mujeres por la Raza," mailing from February 1971, Lucy R. Moreno Collection, Nettie Lee Benson Latin American Collection, Benson Library, University of Texas, Austin.

20. The following is a breakdown of the number of Chicanas who attended the conference and their sending states: Arizona: 6, Colorado: 11, California: 106, Illinois: 7, Michigan: 3, New Mexico: 9, Texas: 57, Washington, DC: 5, Idaho: 1, Kansas, 1. "Mujeres por la Raza (list of attendees)," Lucy R. Moreno Collection.

21. Yolanda Birdwell, interview by author, Houston, TX, August 8, 2003.

22. Gloria Guardiola, interview by author, Houston, TX, November 16, 2002.

23. I would like to thank Rosa Linda Fregoso for first bringing my attention to this pamphlet, which she generously gave to me. She had come across the pamphlet when she

was a young woman living in Houston, and as she tells it, it changed her life and the way she understood herself as a Chicana.

24. NietoGomez, interview, April 22, 1991.

25. See Lara Medina, *Las Hermanas: Chicana/Latina Religious-Political Activism in the U.S. Catholic Church* (Philadelphia: Temple University Press, 2005), for a rich history of this movement. Several scholars have commented that the founding conference of Las Hermanas in Houston in April 1971 is technically the first national Chicana feminist conference.

26. Medina, *Las Hermanas*, 45.

27. Vidal, *Chicanas Speak Out*.

28. "La Conferencia de Mujeres por la Raza, May 28–30, 1971, Conference Report, Houston, Texas," filed by the San Antonio Mental Health Field Program. Personal archives of Anna NietoGomez.

29. NietoGomez, interview, April 22, 1991.

30. Marie (Keta) Miranda, interview by author, Santa Cruz, CA, May 22, 1996.

31. "National Chicanas Conference." María Elena Gaitán, who was a student at Cal State Los Angeles at the time, was active in the UFW and CASA. In the 1990s she became a performance artist, using her art to advance social justice. Some of her one-woman shows were "Chola con Cello" (1992) and "The Adventures of Connie Chancla" (1999). Yolanda Broyles-González, "Performance Artist María Elena Gaitán: Mapping a Continent without Borders (Epics of Gente Atravesada, Traviesa y Entremetida)," *Frontiers: A Journal of Women Studies* 24:2–3 (2003): 87–103.

When I talked with Gaitán about the history of the conference, she told me that she had led the walkout and offered to do an interview. When I followed up on several occasions she said that she was not available because she was writing her memoirs.

32. Sound recording, "Chicanas and Chicanos" radio broadcast, Houston, Texas, June 1971. Barrera had attempted to donate this tape to a university collection specializing in Mexican American history in Houston, but no one returned her phone call. For this reason, she sent it with me and requested that it be archived as part of the Mujeres Initiative at the Chicano Studies Research Center library at UCLA, an archiving project I began with the late archivist Yolanda Retter.

33. Racho et al., "Houston Chicana Conference."

34. Marie (Keta) Miranda, interview by author, Santa Cruz, CA, May 24, 1994.

35. Cecilia Quijano, interviews by author, Downey and Long Beach, CA, February 9 and September 13, 2007.

36. Ibid., September 13, 2007.

37. Ibid.

38. Susan Racho, telephone interview by author, November 2007.

39. "National Chicana Conference."

40. Leticia Hernández, interviews by author, Long Beach, California, July 28 and 30 and August 21, 1992.

41. NietoGomez, interview, April 22, 1991.

42. Francisa Flores, "Successful Mujeres por la Raza Convention Held in Houston," *Mexican American Sun*, June 24, 1971, A1, A4.

43. Racho et al., "Houston Chicana Conference."

44. Lucy R. Moreno, in discussion with the author, August 8, 2003.

45. Barrera, interview, November 15, 2002.

46. Ibid.

47. Ibid. Barrera led a campaign in the neighborhood to promote girls' sports when she noticed that the Y did not provide gymnasium space for girls because it was assumed girls had to stay at home to help with chores while their brothers played sports.

48. Patricia Zavella, "Reflections on Diversity among Chicanas," *Frontiers: a Journal of Women's Studies* 13:2 (1991): 73–85; Palomo Acosta and Winegarten, *Las Tejanas*.

49. Cynthia Orozco's research on LULAC also points to a long history of civil rights strategies; see *No Mexicans, Women, or Dogs Allowed*.

50. Gómez-Quiñones, *Chicano Politics*.

51. Hernández, interview, July 30, 1992.

52. Barrera, interview, November 15, 2002.

53. NietoGomez, "La Feminista," 34–45.

54. NietoGomez, interview, April 22, 1991.

55. Quijano, interview, September 13, 2007.

56. Ibid.

57. NietoGomez, interview, April 22, 1991.

58. Corinne Sánchez, interview by author, San Fernando Valley, CA, September 3, 1997.

59. Quijano, interview, September 13, 200.

60. Kobena Mercer, *Welcome to the Jungle: New Positions in Black Cultural Studies* (New York: Routlege, 1994).

61. Cynthia Orozco also presented what she called four "sexist ideologies about feminism (and feminists) that emerged from the Chicano movement[.] (1) 'El problem es el gabacho no el macho.' (2) Feminism was Anglo, middle-class and bourgeois. (3) Feminism was a diversion from the 'real' and 'basic' issues, that is, racism and class exploitation. (4) Feminism sought to destroy 'la familia,' supposedly the based of Mexican culture and the basis for resistance to domination." Orozco, "Sexism in Chicano Studies and the Community," 12.

62. In an oral history with Martinez, she noted that third world solidarity also forged links between the Chicano and Black Power movements when Stokely Carmichael met with César Chávez in 1965. Based on her work in the Cuban solidarity movement, she stated that third world alliances were in a period of growth between 1966 and 1968, despite the tension between nationalists and internationalists in SNCC. Betita went on to work in the Chicano movement and became coeditor of *El Grito del Norte*. Elizabeth (Betita) Martinez, interview by author, San Francisco, CA, September 20, 1999.

63. Pérez, *The Decolonial Imaginary*.

64. Hernández, interview, July 30, 1992.

65. Russo, "Chicanas Speak, Hijas Establish Goals."

66. "Hijas de Cuauhtémoc Mesa Directiva Minutes, October 18, 1972," from the personal archives of Sylvia Castillo.

67. "Membership Hijas de Cuauhtémoc," document from the personal archives of Sylvia Castillo [in the author's possession]. Russo, "Chicanas Speak, Hijas Establish Goals."

68. NietoGomez, interview, April 29, 1991.

69. Leticia Hernández, interview, Long Beach, CA, July 28 and 30 and August 21, 1992.

70. "Chicanas and Chicanos," Houston radio show sound recording.

CHAPTER SIX

1. Vásquez, *Enriqueta Vásquez and the Chicano Movement*.

2. Max Elbaum, *Revolution in the Air: Sixties Radicals turn to Lenin, Mao and Che* (New York: Verso, 2002).

3. For further discussion of this debate within U.S. and Latin American feminisms, see Blackwell, "Geographies of Difference."

4. In several conversations, the feminist historian Sherna Gluck argued that it was the IWY national preparatory conference in Houston that expanded the women's liberation agenda to include more women of color and working-class and lesbian women.

5. Sánchez, interview, September 3, 1997.

6. Marisela R. Chávez, "Pilgrimage to the Homeland: California Chicanas and International Women's Year, Mexico City, 1975," in *Memories and Migrations: Mapping Boricua and Chicana Histories*, ed. Vicki L. Ruiz and John R. Chávez (Chicago: University of Illinois Press, 2008). See also *Las Mujeres de la Caucas Chicana*, DVD, dir. Linda Garcia Merchant, Voces Primeras, September 1, 2007.

7. Chávez, "Pilgrimage to the Homeland," 174.

8. Sánchez, interview, September 3, 1997.

9. NietoGomez, interview, April 29, 1991.

10. Sylvia Castillo, interview by author, Long Beach, CA, May 24, 1996. See Chávez, *Mi Raza Primero!* for a history of the RUP in Los Angeles; and Armando Navarro, *Raza Unida Party: A Chicano Challenge to the U.S. Two-Party Dictatorship* (Philadelphia: Temple University Press, 2000), for a history of the party. Castillo told me she worked there because Cecilia Quijano asked her to, and it was an effort at reconciliation after their friendship had become strained by being on different sides of the walkout in Houston. They have remained friends for nearly forty years.

11. Sylvia Castillo, interview by author, Long Beach, CA, September 2, 2007.

12. Espino, "Women Sterilized as They Give Birth"; Gutiérrez, *Fertile Matters*; and Elena R. Gutiérrez et al., *Undivided Rights: Women of Color Organize for Reproductive Justice* (Cambridge, MA: South End Press, 2004).

13. "Community Coaliton Mission Statement," www.cocosouthla.org/ (accessed January 10, 2010).

14. See Muñoz, *Youth, Identity, Power*, for an analysis of the role Mexican American students played in these strikes, specifically at UC Berkeley (69–70).

15. Mary Pardo, "A Selective Evaluation of El Plan de Santa Barbara," *La Gente* (March–April 1984): 14–15; Orozco, "Sexism in Chicano Studies."

16. Castillo, "CCHE Conference." See also Anna NietoGomez, "Un propósito para Estudios Femeniles de la Chicana," *Regeneración* 2:4 (1975): 30–32.

17. Anna NietoGómez, "Estudios de la mujer Chicana," *Encuentro Femenil* 1:1 (Spring 1973): 59.

18. Anna NietoGomez and Corinne Sánchez, eds., *New Directions in Education: Estudios Femeniles de la Chicana* (Los Angeles: University of California, Los Angeles, Extension Program and Montal Educational Associates, 1974). During July and August of that year, Sánchez headed the Institute to Prepare Chicanas in Administration in Washington, D.C., to discuss issues of Chicanas in education and the recently developed Chicana Studies curriculum with people throughout the nation.

19. "Introduction," *Encuentro Femenil* 1:2 (1974): 4.

20. Moreno, *La mujer en pie de lucha*; Third World Communications, *Third World Women* (San Francisco: Third World Communications, 1972); Frantz Fanon, *Dying Colonialism* (New York: Grove Press, 1965); Cellestine Ware, *Woman Power: The Movement for Women's Liberation* (New York: Tower Publications, 1970); Morgan, *Sisterhood Is Powerful*.

21. Orozco, "Sexism in Chicano Studies," 13.

22. "A Case of Sexism," *CSAC News* 24 (February-March 1976), a publication of the Chicana Service Action Center.

23. Anna NietoGomez, "Letter of Resignation," September 3, 1976, personal archive of Anna NietoGomez.

24. CSUN Memorandum to Dean Richfield, February 27, 1975, personal archive of Anna NietoGomez.

25. CSUN Memorandum to Dean Richfield, March 2, 1976, personal archive of Anna NietoGomez.

26. *Women Struggle*, CSUN, 1976, newspaper issued by the Support Committee for Anna NietoGomez.

27. NietoGomez, "Letter of Resignation." NietoGomez challenged the good faith nature of the 1975 recommendations that she pursue an advanced degree because she stated she was never informed that her tenure relied on it. While that may be the case at the departmental level, the original job offer letter from the administration states, "Normally, initial recommendations for tenure and promotion are contingent upon completion of the acceptable terminal degree." Letter from President of San Fernando Valley State College, dated September 27, 1971, personal archive of Anna NietoGomez.

28. NietoGomez, interview, April 29, 1991.

29. She listed the following organizations as part of the research and training she had received: Chicana Service Action Center, the Chicana Welfare Rights Organization, Mujeres Unidas, the Van Nuys Community Center, Montal Educational Associates, publisher and editor of *Encuentro Femenil*. "Professional Growth," document from NietoGomez's personnel file, personal archive of Anna NietoGomez.

30. "Unsigned Letter in defense of the departmental committee's decision," personal archive of Anna NietoGomez.

31. Statement on Anna Nieto-Gomez, MEChA CSUN; "A Case of Sexism," *CSAC News*. Personal archive of Anna NietoGomez.

32. *Women Struggle*, CSUN, 1976.

33. Rodolfo Acuña, "An Analysis of the Anna Nieto-Gomez [Case]," n.d. Personal archive of Anna NietoGomez.

34. Ibid.

35. Ibid.

36. "Statement on Anna Nieto-Gomez," MEChA CSUN. Personal archive of Anna NietoGomez.

37. Ibid.

38. Anna NietoGomez, Document from personal archive of Anna NietoGomez, p. 1, n.d.

39. *Women Struggle*, CSUN, 1976, p. 3.

40. "Letter of Resignation," September 3, 1976. Personal archive of Anna NietoGomez.

41. Ibid.

42. NietoGomez, interview, April 29, 1991.

43. "Letter of Resignation," 1976.

44. NietoGomez, interview, April 29, 1991.

45. Years later she returned to school and received her master's degree in social work. She went on to work as a licensed clinical social worker.

46. Critically, several Chicana activists made the transition from the movimiento to the university and have continued to shape Chicana and Chicano Studies today: Beatriz Pesquera, Adelaida Del Castillo, Adaljiza Sosa-Riddell, Ines Hernández-Ávila, to name a few.

47. Mujeres en Marcha, *Chicanas in the 80's.*

48. Ibid.

49. Cynthia Orozco, "The Struggle for Chicana Studies," *La Gente* 13:5 (May 1983).

50. Adaljiza Sosa-Riddell, "History of MALCS," in *Readers Companion to U.S. Women's History*, ed. Wilma Mankiller et al. (New York: Houghton Mifflin, 1998), 386.

51. Orozco, "The Struggle for Chicana Studies."

52. Resistance included the notorious comment that if there was a Lesbian caucus "there should be a marijuanero caucus."

53. García, "Juncture in the Road."

54. Anna Marie Sandoval, *Toward a Latina Feminism of the Americas: Repression and Resistance in Chicana and Mexicana Literature* (Austin: University of Texas Press, 2008), 91–92.

55. Chicana Feminisms Conference Program, March 18–20, 2010, California State University, Long Beach. As one of the keynote panels of the conference, Conciencia Femenil invited Anna NietoGomez, Leticia Hernández, Adelaida Del Castillo, and me to speak about the genealogy of Chicana feminist activism. We engaged in intergenerational dialogue on feminist student activism, during which current students shared their challenges and visions for the future.

56. Sonia E. Alvarez, "Translating the Global Effects of Transnational Organizing on Local Feminist Discourses and Practices," *Meridians: feminism, race, transnationalism* 1:1 (2000): 29–67.

57. In fact, Vicki Ruiz argues that the period could be characterized by tensions between women. Ruiz, *From Out of the Shadows.*

58. Burnham, "The Wellspring of Black Feminism"; Kimberlé Crenshaw, "Demarginalizing the Intersection of Race and Sex: A Black Feminist Critique of Antidiscrimination Doctrine, Feminist Theory, and Antiracist Politics," *University of Chicago Legal Forum* (1989).

59. "La Femenista," *Encuentro Femenil* 1:2 (1974): 34–47.

60. Ibid., 34.

61. Frances M. Beal, "Double Jeopardy: To Be Black and Female," *Triple Jeopardy: Racism, Imperialism, Sexism*, New York, 1969; Combahee River Collective, "A Black Feminist Statement"; Deborah K. King, "Multiple Jeopardy, Multiple Consciousness: The Context of a Black Feminist Ideology," *Signs* 14:1 (Autumn 1988): 42–72.

62. Orozco, "Sexism in Chicano Studies," 11; See also Cherríe Moraga, "From a Long Line of Vendidas," in *Loving in the War Years: lo que nunca pasó pos sus labios* (Boston: South End Press, 1983), 52.

63. The analysis of the simultaneity of oppressions is a contribution of U.S. third world feminist interventions. For critical histories of how intersectionality was developed by black feminists, see King, "Multiple Jeopardy, Multiple Consciousness"; and Springer, *Living for the Revolution.*

64. Alaniz and Cornish, *Viva La Raza.*

65. Maylei S. Blackwell, "Las Hijas de Cuauhtémoc: Chicana Feminist Historical Subjectivities between and beyond Nationalist Imaginaries," in *Las nuevas fronteras de siglo XXI: Dimensiones culturales, políticas y socioeconómicas de las relaciones México-Estados Unidos*, ed. Norma Klahn, Pedro Castillo, Alejandro Alvarez, and Federico Manchon (México: UNAM, 2000), 783–818. The limits of nationalism were felt widely across many social movements, including third world women and women of color. See Mohanty, "Cartographies of Struggle"; Jayawardena, *Feminism and Nationalism in the Third World*.

66. Esquibel, *With Her Machete in Her Hand*, 148.

67. Pérez, *The Decolonial Imaginary*.

68. Gutiérrez et al., *Undivided Rights*; Gutiérrez, "Policing 'Pregnant Pilgrims'"; Espino, "Women Sterilized as They Give Birth," in Ruiz, *Las Obreras*. This agenda is being forged by many organizations, among them Sister Song and Women of Color Reproductive Health Collective.

69. Queer Studies critiques cite women of color feminist influences such as Muñoz's *Disidentifications*, or what Roderick Ferguson calls "queer of color critique," in *Aberrations in Black: Toward a Queer of Color Critique* (Minneapolis: University of Minnesota Press, 2004).

70. Moraga, *The Last Generation*; Anzaldúa, *Borderlands/La Frontera*; Trujillo *Chicana Lesbians*.

71. This history is narrated by Deena Gonzalez in "Telling Secrets, Living Chicana Theory." Many of these pioneering activists were committed, for the most part, to a version of Chicana lesbian separatism (although they did not "separate" from the Chicano organization, in distinction to lesbian separatism of the 1970s from their white counterparts). Interestingly, many of this generation fought aggressively against the inclusion of other sexual minorities like bisexual women, queer activist identities, and gender queer or gender nonconforming people and transpeople into the lesbian caucus. It was not until the Miami NACCS that a decade-long debate was resolved (with great conflict and acrimony among the few remaining lesbian separatists). The lesbian caucus name was changed to recognize the lesbian, bisexual, and queer experience of 1980s and 1990s and the increasing awareness of gender nonconforming or gender deviant politics. Nonetheless, throughout the 1980s the work of out Chicana lesbian activists such as Emma Pérez, Deena Gonzalez, Rusty Barcelo, Carla Trujillo, Deborah Vargas, Charlene Pendleton Jimenez, Lydia Otero, Sandra Soto, Yvonne Yarbro-Bejarano, and Yolanda Leyva throughout the 1980s politicized the space of NACS creating queer, specifically Chicana lesbian spaces, in both NACCS and MALCS.

72. Horacio N. Roque Ramírez, "Communities of Desire: Queer Latina/o History and Memory, San Francisco Bay Area, 1960s-1990s" (Ph.D. diss., University of California, Berkeley, 2001); "Claiming Queer Cultural Citizenship: Gay Latino (Im)migrant Acts in San Francisco," in *Queer Migrations: Sexuality, U.S. Citizenship, and Border Crossings*, ed. Eithne Luibhéid and Lionel Cantú Jr. (Minneapolis: University of Minnesota Press, 2005); "'That's *My* Place!': Negotiating Racial, Sexual, and Gender Politics in San Francisco's Gay Latino Alliance, 1975–1983," *Journal of the History of Sexuality* 12:2 (April 2003): 224–258; Hom, "Documenting Lesbian of Color Community Building"; Retter, "On the Side of Angels."

73. See Hernández Tovar, "Sara Estella Ramírez"; Ruiz, *From Out of the Shadows*; Pérez, "'A la Mujer.'"

74. Ruiz, *From Out of the Shadows*; Ruiz, *Las Obreras*.

75. Jaqui M. Alexander, *Pedagogies of Crossing: Meditations on Feminism, Sexual Politics, Memory, and the Sacred* (Durham, NC: Duke University Press, 2006).

BIBLIOGRAPHY

PRIMARY SOURCES

ARCHIVES

Nettie Lee Benson Latin American Collection, University of Texas at Austin
    Lucy Moreno Papers
    La Raza Unida Papers
    League of United Latin American Citizens (LULAC) Archives
The Bancroft Library Latin Americana Collection, University of California, Berkeley, Silvestre Terrazas Papers
Elma Barrera, Personal Archive, Houston, Texas
Yolanda Birdwell, Personal Archive, Houston, Texas
Sylvia Castillo, Personal Archive, Long Beach, California
Chicano Resource Center, County of Los Angeles Public Library, East Los Angeles Library
Chicano Studies Library and Ethnic Studies Library, University of California, Berkeley
Chicano Studies Research Center Library, University of California, Los Angeles
Collección Tloque Nahuaque and Department of Special Collections, Davidson Library, University of California, Santa Barbara
La Fototeca Nacional del Instituto Nacional de Antropología e Historia de México
Anna NietoGomez, Personal Archive, Lakewood, California
Southern California Library for Social Sciences and Research, Los Angeles
Special Collections and University Archives, California State University, Long Beach
Stanford University Library, Department of Special Collections
    Centro de Accíon Social Autónomo Collection
University of California, Santa Barbara Davidson Library, Department of Special Collections
    California Ethnic and Multicultural Archives
    Comisión Femenil Mexicana Nacional Archives

NEWSPAPERS, NEWSLETTERS, AND PERIODICALS

El Alacrán
Black Scholar
Caracol
Carta Editorial
CFM Report
CSAC News
Chicano Student Movement
Chicano Student News
Con Safos
Daily Bruin
Daily Forty-Niner
De Colores
Eastside Journal
Eastside Sun

Encuentro Femenil
La Gente
El Grito
El Grito del Norte
Hijas de Cuauhtémoc
Houston Post
Houston Chronicle
Magazín
Militant
Mexican American Sun
Ms. Magazine
Papel Chicano
El Popo
El Popo Femenil

La Raza (newspaper)
La Raza Magazine
Regeneración
Sin Fronteras
SOMOS
Sundial

Scene Magazine
El Tecolote
La Verdad
Women Struggle
Wyvernwood Chronicle
El Young Lord

ORAL HISTORIES AND AUDIO SOURCES

Anzaldúa, Gloria. Interview by author. June 29 and September 24, 1999, Santa Cruz, California.

Barrera, Elma. Interview by author. November 15, 2002, Houston, Texas.

Beal, Frances. Interview by author. September 21, 1999, Oakland, California.

Birdwell, Yolanda. Interview by author. August 8, 2003, Houston, Texas.

Castillo, Sylvia. Interview by author. May 24, 1996, Long Beach, California.

———. Interview by author. July 1, 2001, Oakland, California.

———. Interview by author. November 22, 2003, Long Beach, California.

———. Interview by author. September 2, 2006, Long Beach, California.

Calvo, Luz. Interview by author. Santa Cruz, California, September 1999.

"Chicanas and Chicanos." Radio broadcast. Houston, Texas, 1971.

Cotera, Martha. Interview by author. August 8, 1994, Santa Barbara, California.

Guardiola, Gloria. Interview by author. November 16, 2002, Houston, Texas.

Hernández, Leticia. Interview by author. July 28 and 30 and August 21, 1992, Long Beach, California. In Los Angeles Women's Movements Oral History Collection, Virtual Oral/Aural History Archive, California State University, Long Beach. www.csulb.edu/voaha.

Martinez, Elizabeth (Betita). Interview by author. September 21, 1999, San Francisco, California.

———. Interview by author. April 1995, Spokane, Washington.

Miranda, Marie (Keta). Interview by author. May 24, 1994, Santa Cruz, California.

———. Interview by author. May 22, 1996, Santa Cruz, California.

Moreno, Lucy R. Telephone interview by author. August 8, 2003.

NietoGomez, Anna. Interview by author. April 7, 18, 22, and 29, 1991, Norwalk, California. In Los Angeles Women's Movements Oral History Collection, Virtual Oral/Aural History Archive, California State University, Long Beach. www.csulb.edu/voaha.

———. Interview by author. March 26, 1995, Long Beach, California. In Los Angeles Women's Movements Oral History Collection, Virtual Oral/Aural History Archive, California State University, Long Beach. www.csulb.edu/voaha.

Quijano, Cecilia. Interview by author. February 9 and September 13, 2007, Downey and Long Beach, California.

Pesquera, Beatriz. Interview by author. March 23, 1995, Long Beach, California.

Racho, Susan. Interview by author. Fall 2007, Los Angeles, California.

Sánchez, Corinne. Interview by author. September 3, 1997, and January 2, 1998, San Fernando Valley, California.

Smith, Barbara. Interview by author, Santa Barbara, CA, February 8, 2000.

Tillmon, Johnnie. Interview by Sherna Berger Gluck. February 1984 and 1991, Los Angeles, California. Virtual Oral/Aural History Archive, California State University, Long Beach. www.csulb.edu/voaha.

VISUAL MEDIA

A Crushing Love: Chicanas, Motherhood and Activism. DVD. Directed by Sylvia Morales. 58 min. Women Make Films, 2009.

Chicano! The History of the Mexican American Civil Rights Movement. Vol. 1: *Quest for a Homeland* [videorecording]. Coproduced by Galan Productions, Inc., and the National Latino Communications Center, in cooperation with KCET, Los Angeles, 1996.

Las Mujeres de la Caucas Chicana, DVD, dir. Linda Garcia Merchant, Voces Primeras, September 1, 2007.

¡Palante, Siempre Palante!: The Young Lords. DVD. Directed by Iris Morales. 1996. P.O.V. PBS, October 15, 1996.

The Passion of Remembrance. DVD. Directed by Issac Julien and Maureen Blackwood. 80 min. Sankofa Film and Video, U.K., 1986.

PRINT SOURCES

"A Case of Sexism." *CSAC News* 24 (February-March 1976).

Asian Women. Berkeley: University of California Press, 1971.

Barrera, Elma, and Anna NietoGómez. "Chicana Encounter." *Regeneración* 2:4 (1975): 49–51.

Beal, Frances M. "Slave of a Slave No More: Black Women in Struggle." *Black Scholar* 6:6 (March 1975): 2–10.

Birdwell, Yolanda, and Gloria Guardiola. *La Mujer, Destrucción de Mitos: Formación y Practica del Pensamiento Libre*. Political Pamphlet, Houston, TX.

Briegel, Kaye. "'Our Culture Hell!' Feminism in Aztlán." Paper presented at the Pacific Coast Council on Latin American Studies Conference, October 26–28, 1972.

Carta EDITORIAL: For the Informed—Interested in Mexican American Affairs 1:6 (June 17, 1963): 1.

Castillo, Sylvia. "CCHE Conference." *Hijas de Cuauhtémoc* 1 (n.d.): 8.

Chapa, Evey. "Mujeres por la Raza Unida." *Caracol* 1 (September 1974): 3.

Chavez, Marta. "Chicana on Campus." *Hijas de Cuauhtémoc* 1 (n.d.): n.p.

"Chicana Regional Conference." *La Raza* 1:6 (1971): 43–44.

Chicana Service Action Center. *Chicana Service Action Center News*, no. 24 (February-March 1976).

"Chicana Service Action Center: Proyecto de La Comisión Femenil Mexicana Nacional, Inc." *Regeneración* 2:3 (1973): 6.

"Chicanas—Houston." *El Young Lord* (July 7, 1971): 2.

"Chicanas Take Wrong Direction." *El Popo Femenil* (CSUN), May 1973. Special ed.

Chicano Coordinating Council on Higher Education. "El Plan de Santa Barbara." *La Raza* 1:1 (1969): 46.

Committee to Stop Forced Sterilization. "Stop Forced Sterilization Now!" Los Angeles, n.d.

"La Conferencia de Mujeres por la Raza, May 28–30, 1971, Conference Report, Houston, Texas." Filed by San Antonio Mental Health Field Program. Personal archives of Anna NietoGomez.

"COPA Conference." *Hijas de Cuauhtémoc* (1971): n.p.

Cotera, Martha P. "Chicana Caucus." *Magazin* 1:6 (August 1972): 24–26.

———. *The Chicana Feminist*. Austin: Information Systems Development, 1977.

———. *Diosa y Hembra: The History and Heritage of Chicanas in the U.S.* Austin: Information Systems Development, 1976.

———. "Mexicano Feminism." *Magazin* 1:9 (September 1973): 30–32.

———. "When Women Speak." *Event* (January 1974).

"The Cuaahtemoc [*sic*] Feminine League." Manifesto published in *Under the Mexican Flag: The Mexican Struggle Outlined*, by Col. C. J. Velarde. Los Angeles: Southland Publishing House, 1926. 306–308.

"Cultural Nationalism: A Fight for Survival." *Chicano Student Movement* 2:2 (1969): 3.

"Dolores Huerta Talks about Republicans, Cesar, Children and her Home Town." *Regeneración* 2:4 (1975): 20–24.

Del Castillo, Adelaida R. "Malintzín Tenépal: A Preliminary Look into a New Perspective." *Encuentro Femenil* 1:2 (1974): 58–78.

Delgado, Sylvia. "Chicana: The Forgotten Women." *Regeneración* 2:1 (1971): 2–4.

———. "Young Chicana Speaks up on Problems Faced by Young Girls." *Regeneración* 1:10 (1971): 5–7.

Editorial. *La Gente* 6:4 (March 1976): 2.

"Encuentro Femenil: La visión Chicana" [interview with Adelaida del Castillo]. *Regeneración* 2:4 (1975): 46–48.

Escalante, Alicia. "A Letter from the Chicana Welfare Rights Organization." *Encuentro Femenil* 1:2 (1973): 15–19.

———. "Canto de Alicia." *Encuentro Femenil* 1:1 (1973).

———. "The Los Angeles Chicana Welfare Rights Organization." Speech delivered at California State University, Northridge, spring 1974. Personal archive of Anna NietoGomez.

Flores, Francisca. "Comisión Femenil Mexicana." *Regeneración* 2:1 (1971): 6.

———. "Conference of Mexican Women: Un Remolino." *Regeneración* 1:10 (1971): 1.

———. "Equality." *Regeneración* 2:3 (1973): 16–18.

———. "El Mundo Femenil Mexicana." *Regeneración* 1:10 (1971): 1.

———. "A Reaction to Discussions on the Talmadge Amendment to the Social Security Act." *Encuentro Femenil* 1:2 (1974): 13–14.

Flores, Francisca. "Guidelines on Fair Employment Practices in California: Chicana Status and Concerns." Chicana Service Action Center, 1974.

———. "Successful Mujeres por la Raza Convention Held in Houston." *Mexican American Sun*, June 24, 1971, A1, A4.

———. "Mexican-American women ponder future role of the Chicana." *Wyvernwood Chronicle*, July 1, 1971.

Flores, Maria. "La visión Chicana." *La Gente* 6:4 (March 1976): 23.

Gonzales, Rodolfo. *I Am Joaquín/Yo Soy Joaquín: An Epic Poem*. New York: Bantam Books, 1972.

Guardiola, Gloria, and Yolanda Birdwell. "Conferencia de Mujeres por la Raza: Point of View." *Papel Chicano*, no. 17 (June 12, 1971).

Hayden, Casey and Mary King. "Sex and Caste: A Kind of Memo," *Liberation* 1:1–2 (April 1966): 35–36.

Hernandez, Carmen. "Conferencia de Mujeres por la Raza: Carmen Speaks Out." *Papel Chicano*, no. 17 (June 12, 1971): 8.

Hernández, Leticia. "A Letter from Leticia." *Hijas de Cuauhtémoc* 1 (n.d.): n.p.

———. "Hijas de Cuauhtémoc." *Regeneración* 1:10 (1971): 9.

"Hijas de Cuauhtémoc Mesa Directiva Minutes, October 18, 1972." Personal archive of Sylvia Castillo.

Honesto, Cindy. "Chicana on Campus." *Hijas de Cuauhtémoc* 2:4 (n.d.): n.p.

———. "Introduction." *Encuentro Femenil* 1:2 (1974): 3–7.

Liebrum, Martha. "Politics and the Woman: East End." *Houston Post*, March 1, 1972.

Longeaux y Vasquez, Enriqueta. "La Chicana." *Magazín* 1:4 (April 1972): 66–68.

———. "Soy Chicana Primero." *El Grito del Norte* (April 26, 1971).

———. "The Woman of la Raza." *Regeneración* 2:4 (1974): 34–36.

Lopez, Martha. "La Mexicana." *Hijas de Cuauhtémoc* 1 (n.d.): n.p.

Lorenzana, Noemi. "La Chicana: Transcending the Old and Carving out a New Life and Self-Image." *De Colores* 2:3 (1975): 6–14.

Lunnen, Connie. "La Conferencia, It's a Beginning, Say Chicanas." *Houston Chronicle* (May 17, 1971), F1.

Martinez, Elizabeth (Betita). "La Chicana." *Ideal* (September 5–20, 1972): 1–2.

———. "La Chicana: A Socialist View." Paper written in response to 1975 Socialist Feminist Conference, Yellow Springs, OH.

Matsuda, Gema. "La Chicana Organizes: The Comisión Femenil Mexicana in Perspective." *Regeneración* 2:4 (1975): 25–27.

"Membership Hijas de Cuauhtémoc." Personal archives of Sylvia Castillo.

"Minority Students Academically Qualified." *El Alacran*, no. 5 (March 1971): 1.

Molina de Pick, Gracia. "Reflexiones sobre el feminismo y la Raza." *Regeneración* 2:4 (1975): 33.

Morales, Rosa Marta. "Conferencia de Mujeres por la Raza: Rosa en Español." *Papel Chicano*, no. 17 (June 12, 1971).

Morales, Rosita. "La mujer todavía impotente." *Hijas de Cuauhtémoc* (n.d.): n.p.

Moreno, Dorinda, ed. *La mujer en pie de lucha: y la hora es ya!* México: Espina del Norte, 1973.

Moreno, Maria. "I'm Talking for Justice." *Regeneración* 1:10 (1971): 12–13.

"El Movimiento and the Chicana: What Else Could Break Down a Revolution but Women Who Do Not Understand True Equality." *La Raza* 1:6 (1971): 40–42.

Mujeres en Marcha. *Unsettled Issues: Chicanas in the '80s.* Berkeley, CA: Chicano Studies Library Publications Unit, 1983.

"National Chicana Conference." *La Verdad* (July-August 1971): 15–17.

Nava, Yolanda M. "The Chicana and Employment: Needs Analysis and Recommendations for Legislation." *Regeneración* 2:3 (1973): 7–9.

———. "Employment Counseling and the Chicana." *Encuentro Femenil* 1:1 (1973): 34–61.

Navar, Isabelle. "Chicana: An Image of Strength." *Regeneración* 2:4 (1974): 4–6.

———. "Como Chicana mi madre." *Encuentro Femenil* 1:2 (1974): 8–12.

Nieto, Nancy. "Macho Attitudes." *Hijas de Cuauhtémoc* 1 (n.d.): n.p.

NietoGomez, Anna. "Chicana Feminism, Plática de Anna Nieto-Gómez." *Caracol* 2:5 (January 1976): 3–5.

———. "Chicanas: Perspective for Education." *Encuentro Femenil* 1:1 (1973): 34–61.

———. *Chicanas and Labor.* Chicana Service Action Center Public Information Pamphlet, March 1980.

———. "Chicanas Identify." *Regeneración* 1:10 (1971): 10. Also published in *Hijas de Cuauhtémoc* 1.

———. "Chicanas in the Labor Force." *Encuentro Femenil* 1:2 (1974): 28–33.

———. "Estudios de la Mujer Chicana." *Encuentro Femenil* 1:2 (1974): 19–20.

———. "La Femenista." *Encuentro Femenil* 1:2 (1974): 34–47.

———. "Heritage of la Hembra." In *Female Psychology: The Emerging Self*, ed. Sue Cox. Chicago: Science Research Associates, 1976: 226–235.

———. "History of Chicanas at CSUN." *SUNDIAL* [CSUN student newspaper] (1975).

———. "Letter of Resignation." September 3, 1976. Personal archive of Anna NietoGomez.

———. "Labor and Chicanas." *SOMOS* (July-August 1979).

———. "Madres por Justicia!!" *Encuentro Femenil* 1:2 (1973): 12–18.

———. "Male Tokenism." *La Raza* 2:1 (December 1969): 5.

———. "Sexism in the Movement." *La Gente* 6:4 (1976): 10.

———. "Somos Chicanas de Aztlan!" *La Raza* 2:9 (November 1969).

———. Speech delivered at Chicana Feminisms Conference, California State University, Long Beach, March 19, 2010.

———. "The Suffering Chicana." *SCENE Magazine* 8:1 (Fall 1975).

———. "Un propósito para estudios femeniles de la Chicana." *Regeneración* 2:4 (1975): 30–32.

———. "What Is the Talmadge Amendment?" *Regeneración* 2:3 (1973): 14–16.

———. "Women in Colonial Mexico." *Regeneración* 2:3 (1975): 14–15.

———. "Youth I Mirror." *La Raza* 2:1 (1969).

NietoGómez, Anna, and Corinne Sánchez, eds. *New Directions in Education: Estudios femeniles de la Chicana*. Los Angeles: University of California Extension Program and Montal Educational Associates, 1974.

Orozco, Cynthia. "The Struggle for Chicana Studies." *La Gente* 8:5 (1983): 11.

Pardo, Mary. "A Selective Evaluation of 'El Plan de Santa Bárbara.'" *La Gente* (March–April 1984): 14–15.

El Plan de Santa Barbara. Reprinted in Carlos Muñoz Jr., *Youth, Identity Power: The Chicano Movement*. London: Verso, 1989.

El Plan Espiritual de Aztlán. Reprinted in Luis Valdez and Stan Steiner, eds., *Aztlán: An Anthology of Mexican American Literature*. New York: Vintage Books, 1972.

"Political Education Workshop." *Hijas de Cuauhtémoc* 3 (n.d.): n.p.

El Popo Femenil (Special ed.). Contributions made by Anna NietoGómez's Chicana Class. MEChA/Chicano Studies, CSUN. Spring 1973.

"Preface." *Encuentro Femenil* 1:1 (1973): 1.

Racho, Suzan, Gloria Meneses, Socorro Acosta, and Chicki Quijano. "Houston Chicana Conference." *La Gente* 6 (May 31, 1971).

Regeneración 2:4 (1975). Special Women's Ed.

Rincón, Bernice. "Chicanas, Her Role in the Past and Her Search for a New Role in the Future." *Regeneración* 2:4 (1975): 36–39.

Rodarte, Irene. "Machismo vs. Revolution." In *La mujer en pie de lucha: y la hora es ya!* ed. Dorinda Moreno. México: Espina del Norte, 1973.

Ruiz, Raul. "The Chicanos and the Underground Press." *La Raza* 3:1 (1977): 8–10.

Russo, Anthony. "Chicanas Speak, Hijas Establish Goals." *Daily Forty-Niner* (October 13, 1972): 3.

Sánchez, Corinne. "Higher Education y la Chicana?" *Encuentro Femenil* 1, no. 1 (1973): 27–33.

Sosa-Riddell, Adaljiza. "Chicanas and el Movimiento." *Aztlán: A Journal of Chicano Studies* 5:1–2 (1974): 155–165.

"Stop Forced Sterilization Now!" *La Raza* 2:4 (January 1975): 12–15.

"Student Services." *Hijas de Cuauhtémoc* 2 (n.d.): 4.

Triple Jeopardy (Racism, Imperialism, Sexism). Newspaper published by the Third World Women's Alliance, New York, (1971–1976).

Tullos, Mary, and Dolores Hernandez. "Talmadge Amendment: Welfare Continues to Exploit the Poor." *La Raza* 1:7 (January 1972): 10–11.

"UMAS Special Elections." Pamphlet, California State University, Long Beach, Special Collections, UMAS file.

Vangie, Mary. "Women at Frontera, Ca." *Regeneración* 1:10 (1971): 8.

Vidal, Mirta. *Chicanas Speak Out: Women, New Voice of La Raza*. New York: Pathfinder Press, 1971.

Wall, Lucas. "Martha Moreno Activist." *Houston Chronicle*, November 19, 2002.

"What Is U.M.A.S?" California State University, Long Beach, Special Collections, UMAS files.

Williams, Maxine. "Why Women's Liberation Is Important to Black Women." In *Feminism and Socialism*, ed. Linda Jenness. New York: Pathfinder, 1972.

Women of All Red Nations. "W.A.R.N. Report II." Sioux Falls, SD, 1980.

"Women of 'La Raza' Unite!" *Ms. Magazine* 1:6 (December 1972): 128–129.

Women Struggle (Support Anna NietoGómez). Published by the Support Committee for Anna NietoGómez Staff.

"Women's Caucus Makes History." *Regeneración* 2:3 (1973): 32.

SECONDARY SOURCES

Acuña, Rodolfo. *Occupied America: A History of Chicanos*. 3rd ed. New York: HarperCollins, 1988.

Adler, Karen S. "Always Leading Our Men in Service and Sacrifice: Amy Jacques Garvey, Feminist Black Nationalist." In *Race, Class, and Gender: Common Bonds, Different Voices*, ed. Esther Ngan-Ling Chow, Doris Wilkinson, and Maxine Baca Zinn. London: Sage, 1996.

Alaniz, Yolanda, and Megan Cornish. *Viva la Raza: A History of Chicano Identity and Resistance*. Seattle: Red Letter Press, 2008.

Alarcón, Norma. "Chicana Feminism: In the Tracks of 'the' Native Woman." In *Woman and Nation: Nationalisms, Transnational Feminisms, and the State*, ed. Caren Kaplan, Norma Alarcón, and Minoo Moallem. Durham, NC: Duke University Press, 1999: 63–71.

———. "The Theoretical Subject(s) of *This Bridge Called My Back* and Anglo American Feminism." In *Making Face, Making Soul—Haciendo Caras: Creative and Critical Perspective by Women of Color*, ed. Gloria Anzaldúa. San Francisco: Aunt Lute Foundation, 1990: 356–69.

———. "Traddutora, Traditora: A Paradigmatic Figure of Chicana Feminism." *Cultural Critique* 13 (Fall 1989): 57–87.

Alarcón, Norma, Rafaela Castro, Emma Pérez, Beatriz Pesquera, Adaljiza Sosa-Riddell, and Patricia Zavella. *Chicana Critical Issues*. Berkeley: Third Woman Press, 1993.

Alarcón, Norma, and Caren Kaplan, eds. *Between Woman and Nation: Nationalisms, Transnational Feminisms, and the State*. Durham, NC: Duke University Press, 1999.

Alexander, Jaqui M., and Chandra Talpade Mohanty, eds. *Feminist Genealogies, Colonial Legacies, Democratic Futures*. New York: Routledge, 1997.

———. *Pedagogies of Crossing: Meditations on Feminism, Sexual Politics, Memory, and the Sacred*. Durham, NC: Duke University Press, 2006.

Almaguer, Tomás. "Ideological Distortions in Recent Chicano Historiography: The Internal Colonial Model and Chicano Historical Interpretation." *Aztlán: A Journal of Chicano Studies* 18 (Spring 1987): 7–28.

———. "Toward the Study of Chicano Colonialism." *Aztlán: A Journal of Chicano Studies* 2:1 (Spring 1971): 7–21.

Alvarez, Sonia E. *Engendering Democracy in Brazil: Women's Movements in Transition Politics.* Princeton: Princeton University Press, 1990.

———. "Translating the Global Effects of Transnational Organizing on Local Feminist Discourses and Practices." *Meridians: feminism, race, transnationalism* 1:1 (2000): 29–67.

Anaya, Rudolfo. "Aztlán: A Homeland without Boundaries." In *Aztlán: Essays on the Chicano Homeland*, ed. Rudolfo A. Anaya and Francisco Lomeli. Albuquerque: University of New Mexico Press, 1991: 230–241.

Anderson, Benedict. *Imagined Communities: Reflections on the Origin and Spread of Nationalism.* Rev. ed. London: Verso, 1991.

Anderson-Bricker, Kristin. "'Triple Jeopardy': Black Women and the Growth of Feminist Consciousness in SNCC, 1964–1975." In *Still Lifting, Still Climbing: Contemporary African American Women's Activism*, ed. Kimberley Springer. New York: New York University Press, 1999: 46–69.

Anzaldúa, Gloria. *Borderlands/La Frontera: The New Mestiza.* San Francisco: Spinster/Aunt Lute, 1987.

———, ed. *Making Face, Making Soul—Haciendo Caras: Creative and Critical Perspective by Women of Color.* San Francisco: Spinster/Aunt Lute, 1990.

Appadurai, Arjun. *Modernity at Large: Cultural dimensions of Globalization.* Minneapolis: University of Minnesota Press, 1996.

———. "The Production of Locality." In *Counterworks: Managing the Diversity of Knowledge*, ed. Richard Fardon. New York: Routledge, 1995: 208–229.

Arrizón, Alicia. "*Soldaderas* and the Staging of the Mexican Revolution." *Drama Review* 42:1 (Spring 1998): 90–112.

Ashbaugh, Carolyn. *Lucy Parsons: American Revolutionary.* Chicago: Charles H. Kerr, 1976.

Baca Zinn, Maxine. "Political Familism: Toward Sex Role Equality in Chicano Families." *Aztlán: International Journal of Chicano Research* 6:1 (1975): 13–26.

Balderrama, Francisco, and Raymond Rodriguez. *Decade of Betrayal: Mexican Repatriation in the 1930's.* Albuquerque: University of New Mexico Press, 2006.

Barkley Brown, Elsa. "What Has Happened Here: The Politics of Difference in Women's History and Feminist Politics." In *The Second Wave: A Reader in Feminist Theory*, ed. Linda Nicholson. New York: Routledge, 1997.

Barrera, Mario, Carlos Muñoz, and Charles Ornelas. "The Barrio as Internal Colony." In *People and Politics in Urban Society*, ed. Harlan H. Hahn. Los Angeles: Sage, 1972: 465–498.

Barry, Naomi, M. "Women's Participation in the Chicano Movement." *Latino Studies Journal* 8:1 (Winter 1997): 47–81.

Bauman, Robert. "The Black Power and Chicano Movements in the Poverty Wars in Los Angeles." *Journal of Urban History* 33:2 (January 2007): 277–295.

Baxandall, Rosalyn. "Re-Visioning the Women's Liberation Movement's Narrative: Early Second Wave African American Feminists." *Feminist Studies* 27:1 (Spring 2001): 225–245.

Beal, Frances. "Double Jeopardy: To Be Black and Female." *Triple Jeopardy: Racism, Imperialism, Sexism* (New York, 1969).

———. "Slave of a Slave No More: Black Women in the Struggle." *Black Scholar* 16:6 (March 1975): 2–10.

Behar, Ruth, and Deborah Gordon, eds. *Women Writing Culture.* Berkeley: University of California Press, 1995.

Benmayor, Rina, Ana Juarbe, Celia Alvarez, and Blanca Vásquez (Oral History Task Force). *Stories to Live By: Continuity and Change in Three Generations of Puerto Rican Women.* Working Paper Series, Centro de Estudios Puertorriqueños. New York: Hunter College, CUNY, 1987.

Bethel, Lorraine, and Barbara Smith. "Introduction." In *Conditions: The Black Women's Issue.* Brooklyn: Conditions, 1979.

Bermudez, Rosie. "Recovering Histories: Alicia Escalante and the Chicana Welfare Rights organization, 1967–1974." M.A. thesis, California State University, Dominguez Hills, 2010.

Bhabha, Homi K.,ed. "DissemiNation: Time, Narrative, and the Margins of the Modern Nation." In *Nation and Narration*, ed. Homi K. Bhabha. New York: Routledge, 1990: 291–322.

———. "Introduction: Narrating the Nation." In *Nation and Narration*, ed. Homi K. Bhabha. New York: Routledge, 1990.

———, ed. *Nation and Narration.* New York: Routledge, 1990.

Blackwell, Maylei S. "Bearing Bandoleras: Transfigurative Liberation and the Iconography of la Nueva Chicana." In *Beyond the Frame*, a Project of the Women of Color Research Cluster, ed. Neferti X. M. Tadiar and Angela Y. Davis. Durham, NC: Duke University Press, 2005: 171–195.

———. "Contested Histories: Las Hijas de Cuauhtemoc, Chicana Feminisms, and Print Culture in the Chicano Movement, 1968–1973." In *Chicana Feminisms: A Critical Reader*, ed. Gabriela Arredondo, Aida Hurtado, Norma Klahn, Olga Najera-Ramirez, and Patricia Zavella. Durham, NC: Duke University Press, 2003: 59–89.

———. "Geographies of Difference: Mapping Multiple Feminist Insurgencies and Transnational Public Cultures in the Americas." Ph.D. diss., University of California, Santa Cruz, 2000.

———. "Las Hijas de Cuauhtémoc: Chicana Feminist Historical Subjectivities between and beyond Nationalist Imaginaries." In *Las nuevas fronteras de siglo XXI: Dimensiones culturales, políticas y socioeconómicas de las relaciones México-Estados Unidos*, ed. Norma Klahn, Pedro Castillo, Alejandro Alvarez, and Federico Manchon. México: UNAM, 2000: 783–818.

———. "Líderes Campesinas: Nepantla Strategies and Grassroots Organizing at the Intersection of Gender and Globalization." *Aztlán: A Journal of Chicano Studies* 35:1 (Spring 2010): 13–47.

———. "Triple Jeopardy, Racism, Sexism, and Imperialism: Third World Women's Alliance and the Transnational Imaginary." Forthcoming.

Blake, Debra J. "Reading Dynamics of Power through Mexican-Origin Women's Oral Histories." In *Frontiers: A Journal of Women's Studies* 19:3 (1998): 24–41.

Blauner, Robert. "Internal Colonialism and Ghetto Revolt." *Social Problems* 16 (Spring 1969): 393–408.

Blea, Irene I. *U.S. Chicanas and Latinas within a Global Context: Women of Color at the Fourth World Women's Conference*. Westport, CT: Praeger, 1997.

Bonfil Batalla, Guillermo. *México Profundo: Reclaiming a Civilization*. Trans. Philip A. Dennis. Austin: University of Texas Press, 1996.

Brady, Mary P. *Extinct Lands, Temporal Geographies: Chicana Literature and the Urgency of Space*. Durham, NC: Duke University Press, 2002.

———. "Quotidian Warfare." *Signs: Journal of Women in Culture and Society* 28:1 (Autumn 2002): 446–447.

Breines, Winifred. *The Trouble between Us: An Uneasy History of White and Black Women in the Feminist Movement*. New York: Oxford University Press, 2006.

Brodkin Sacks, Karen. *Caring by the Hour: Women, Work, and Organizing at Duke Medical Center*. Urbana: University of Illinois Press, 1988.

———. "Gender and Grassroots Leadership." In *Women and the Politics of Empowerment*, ed. Ann Bookman and Sandra Morgan. Philadelphia: Temple University Press, 1988: 77–94.

Brown, Elaine. *A Taste of Power: A Black Woman's Story*. New York: Anchor Books, 1994.

Broyles-González, Yolanda. *Lydia Mendoza's Life in Music: Norteño Tejano Legacies*. New York: Oxford University Press, 2001.

———. "Performance Artist María Elena Gaitán: Mapping a Continent without Borders (Epics of Gente Atravesada, Traviesa y Entremetida)." *Frontiers: A Journal of Women Studies* 24:2–3 (2003): 87–103.

———. *El Teatro Campesino: Theater in the Chicano Movement*. Austin: University of Texas Press, 1994.

———. "Toward a Re-Vision of Chicana/o Theater History: The Roles of Women in El Teatro Campesino." In *El Teatro Campesino: Theater in the Chicano Movement*. Austin: University of Texas Press, 1994: 129–164.

Burnham, Linda. "The Wellspring of Black Feminist Theory." Working Paper Series 1. Women of Color Resource Center, Oakland, CA, 2001.

Cade, Toni, ed. *The Black Woman: An Anthology*. New York: Penguin, 1970.

Calderón, Roberto R., and Emilio Zamora. "Manuela Solis Sager and Emma Tenayuca: A Tribute." In *Chicana Voices: Intersections of Class, Race, and Gender*, ed. Teresa Cordova et al. Albuquerque: University of New Mexico Press, 1990: 38–39.

Calvo, Luz. "Art Comes for the Archbishop: The Semiotics of Contemporary Chicana Feminism and the Work of Alma Lopez." *Meridians: feminism, race, transnationalism* 5:1 (2004): 201–224.

Calvo, Luz, and Catriona Esquibel. "Latina Lesbianas, BiMujeres, and Trans Identities: Charting Courses in the Social Sciences." In *Latina/o Sexualities: Probing Powers, Passions, Practices, and Policies*, ed. Marysol Ascencio. New Brunswick: Rutgers University Press, 2010: 217–229.

Candelaria, Cordelia. "La Malinche, Feminist Prototype." *Frontiers: A Journal of Women Studies* 5:2 (1980): 1–6.

Cantú, Norma. "Women, Then and Now: An Analysis of the Adelita Image versus the Chicana as Political Writer and Philosopher." In *Chicana Voices: Intersections of Class, Race, and Gender*, ed. Teresa Córdova et al. Austin: Center for Mexican American Studies (CMAS), University of Texas, 1986: 8–10.

Cárdenas, Jaime O. "Cousins of Caliban: Nation, Masculinity, and Latino Men in California, 1945 to the mid-1960s." Ph.D. diss., University of California, Los Angeles, 2000.

Carr, Robert. "Crossing the First World/Third World Divides: Testimonial, Transnational Feminisms, and the Postmodern Condition." In *Scattered Hegemonies Postmodernity and Transnational Feminist Practices*, ed. Inderpal Grewal and Caren Kaplan. Minneapolis: University of Minnesota Press, 1994: 153–172.

Castañeda, Antonia I. *Gender on the Borderlands: The Frontiers Reader*. Lincoln: University of Nebraska Press, 2007.

———. "Gender, Race, and Culture: Spanish-Mexican Women in the Historiography of Frontier California." *Frontiers: A Journal of Women Studies* 11:1 (1990): 8–20.

———. "The Political Economy of Nineteenth-Century Stereotypes of Californians." In *Between Borders: Essays on Mexicana/Chicana History*, ed. Adelaida R. Del Castillo. Encino, CA: Floricanto Press, 1990: 213–252.

———. "'Presidarias y Pobladoras': The Journey North and Life in Frontier California." In *Chicana Critical Issues*, ed. Norma Alarcón, Rafaela Castro, Emma Pérez, Beatriz Pesquera, Adaljiza Sosa-Riddell, and Patricia Zavella. Berkeley: Third Woman Press, 1993: 73–94.

———. "Women of Color and the Rewriting of Western History: The Discourse, Politics, and Decolonization of History." *Pacific Historical Review* 61:4 (1992): 501–533.

Castillo, Ana. *Goddess of the Americas: Writings on the Virgin of Guadalupe*. New York: Riverhead Books, 1996.

———. *Massacre of the Dreamers: Essays on Xicanisma*. Albuquerque: University of New Mexico Press, 1994.

Castle, Elizabeth A., Madonna Thunder Hawk, Marcella Gilbert, and Lakota Harden. "'Keeping One Foot in the Community': Intergenerational Indigenous Women's Activism from the Local to the Global (and Back Again)." *American Indian Quarterly* 27:3–4 (Summer–Fall 2003): 840–861.

Certeau, Michel de. *The Practice of Everyday Life*. Berkeley: University of California Press, 1988.

———. *The Writing of History*. Trans. Tom Conley. New York: Columbia University Press, 1988.

Chabram Dernersesian, Angie. "And, Yes . . . The Earth Did Part: On the Splitting of Chicana/o Subjectivity." In *Building with Our Hands: New Directions in Chicana Studies*, ed. Adela de la Torre and Beatríz M. Pesquera. Berkeley: University of California Press, 1993: 34–56.

———. "'Chicana! Rican? No, Chicana-Riqueña!' Refashioning the Transnational Connection." In *Multiculturalism: A Critical Reader*, ed. David Theo Goldberg. Cambridge: Basil Blackwell, 1994: 269–295.

———. "Chicana/o Studies as Oppositional Ethnography." *Cultural Studies* 4:3 (October 1990): 228–247.

———. "I Throw Punches for My Race, but I Don't Want to Be a Man: Writing Us— Chica-nos (Girl, Us)/Chicanas—into the Movement Script." In *Cultural Studies*, ed. Lawrence Grossberg, Cary Nelson, and Paula A. Treichler. New York: Routledge, 1992: 81–111.

Chapa, Evey, and Sally Andrade. *La Mujer Chicana: An Annotated Bibliography*. Austin: Chicana Research and Learning Center, 1976.

Chatterjee, Partha. *The Nation and Its Fragments: Colonial and Postcolonial Histories*. Princeton: Princeton University Press, 1993.

Chávez, Ernesto. "Creating Aztlán: The Chicano Student Movement in Los Angeles, 1966–1978." Ph.D. diss., University of California, Los Angeles, 1994.

———. "Culture, Identity, and Community: Musings on Chicano Historiography at the End of the Millennium." *Estudios Mexicanos* 14:1 (Winter 1998): 213–235.

———. *"Mi Raza Primero!" Nationalism, Identity, and Insurgency in the Chicano Movement in Los Angeles, 1966–1978*. Berkeley: University of California Press, 2002.

Chávez, Marisela R. "Despierten Hermanas y Hermanos! Women, the Chicano Movement, and Chicana Feminisms in California, 1966–1981." Ph.D diss., Stanford University, 2004.

———. "Pilgrimage to the Homeland: California Chicanas and International Women's Year, Mexico City, 1975." In *Memories and Migrations: Mapping Boricua and Chicana Histories*, ed. Vicki L. Ruiz and John R. Chavez. Chicago: University of Illinois Press, 2008: 170–195.

———. "'We Lived and Breathed and Worked the Movement': The Contradictions and Rewards of Chicana/Mexicana Activism in el Centro de Acción Social Autónomo-Hermandad General de Trabajadores (CASA-HGT), Los Angeles, 1975–1978." In *Las Obreras: Chicana Politics of Work and Family*, ed. Vicki L. Ruiz. Los Angeles: Chicano Studies Research Center, UCLA, 2000: 83–104.

Chinchilla, Norma S. "Feminism, Revolution, and Democratic Transitions in Nicaragua." In *The Women's Movements in Latin America: Participation and Democracy*, 2nd ed., ed. Jane S. Jaquette. Boulder, CO: Westview Press, 1992: 37–51.

Clayborne, Carson. *In Struggle: SNCC and the Black Awakening of the 1960s*. Cambridge, MA: Harvard University Press, 1981.

Collier-Thomas, Bettye, and V. P. Franklin. *Sisters in the Struggle: African American Women in the Civil Rights—Black Power Movement*. New York: New York University Press, 2001.

Collins, Patricia Hill. *Black Feminist Thought: Knowledge, Consciousness, and the Politics of Empowerment*. London: HarperCollins, 1990.

———. *From Black Power to Hip Hop: Racism, Nationalism, and Feminism*. Philadelphia: Temple University Press, 2006.

Combahee River Collective. "A Black Feminist Statement." In *All the Women are White, All the Blacks are Men, But Some of Us Are Brave: Black Women's Studies*, ed. Gloria T. Hull, Patricia Bell Scott, and Barbara Smith. Old Westbury, NY: Feminist Press, 1982: 13–22.

Córdova, Teresa. "Roots and Resistance: The Emergent Writings of Twenty Years of Chicana Feminist Struggle." In *Handbook of Hispanic Cultures in the United States: Sociology*, ed. Félix Padilla. Houston: Arte Público Press and Instituto de Cooperación Iberoamericana, 1994: 175–202.

Córdova, Teresa, et al., eds. *Chicana Voices: Intersections of Class, Race, and Gender*. Austin: Center for Mexican American Studies Publications, 1986.

Coronil, Fernando. "Listening to the Subaltern: The Poetics of Neocolonial States," *Poetics Today* 15:4 (Winter 1994): 643–658. Special issue: Loci of Enunciation and Imaginary Constructions: The Case of (Latin) America, I.

Cotera, Martha. "Feminism: The Chicana and Anglo Versions—A Historical Analysis." In *Twice a Minority: Mexican American Women*, ed. Margarita Melville. St. Louis: C. V. Mosby, 1980: 217–234.

Crawford, Vicki L., Jacqueline Anne Rouse, and Barbara Woods. *Women in the Civil Rights Movement: Trailblazers and Torchbearers, 1941–1965*. Indianapolis: Indiana University Press, 1993.

Crenshaw, Kimberlé. "Demarginalizing the Intersection of Race and Sex: A Black Feminist Critique of Antidiscrimination Doctrine, Feminist Theory, and Antiracist Politics." *University of Chicago Legal Forum* (1989): 139–168.

———. "Mapping the Margins: Intersectionality, Identity Politics and Violence against Women of Color." *Stanford Law Review* 43:6 (1991): 1241–1299.

Crow Dog, Mary, and Richard Erdoes. *Lakota Woman*. New York: Grove Weidenfeld, 1990.

Cuádraz, Gloria Holguín. "Chicanas and Higher Education: Three Decades of Literature and Thought." *Journal of Hispanic Higher Education* 4:3 (July 2005): 215–234.

Cuadriello, Jaime, Beatriz B. Mariscal, and Carmen de Monserrat Robledo Galv. *La Reina de las Américas: Pieza de arte del museo de la Basílica de Guadalupe*. Albuquerque: University of New Mexico Press, 1997.

Darnovsky, Marcy, Barbara Epstein, and Richard Flacks, eds. *Cultural Politics and Social Movements*. Philadelphia: Temple University, 1995.

Davis, Angela Y. "Black Nationalism: The Sixties and the Nineties." In *Black Popular Culture*, ed. Gina Dent. Seattle: Bay Press, 1992.

———. *Blues Legacies and Black Feminism: Gertrude "Ma" Rainey, Bessie Smith and Billie Holiday*. New York: Pantheon Books, 1998.

———. *If They Come in the Morning: Voices of Resistance*. New York: Third Press, 1971.

———. "Reflection of the Black Woman's Role in the Community of Slaves." *Black Scholar* 3 (December 1971): 2–16.

———. *Women, Race, and Class*. New York: Random House, 1981.

de la Mora, Sergio. *Cinemachismo: Masculinities and Sexuality in Mexican Film*. Austin: University of Texas Press, 2006.

de la tierra, tatiana. "Activist Latina Lesbian Publishing: Esto no tiene nombre and conmoción." *Aztlán: A Journal of Chicano Studies* 27:1 (2002): 139–178.

De la Torre, Adela, and Beatriz M. Pesquera, eds. *Building with Our Hands: New Directions in Chicana Studies*. Berkeley: University of California Press, 1993.

De Lauretis, Teresa, ed. *Feminist Studies/Critical Studies*. Bloomington: Indiana University Press, 1986.

Del Castillo, Adelaida R. "Mexican Women in Organization." In *Mexican Women in the United States: Struggles Past and Present*, ed. Adelaida R. Del Castillo and Magdalena Mora. Los Angeles: Chicano Studies Research Center Publications, UCLA, 1980: 7–16.

Deleuze, Gilles, and Félix Guattari. *Anti-Oedipus: Capitalism and Schizophrenia*. New York: Viking Press, 1977.

Delgado Bernal, Dolores. "Grassroots Leadership Reconceptualized: Chicana Oral Histories and the 1968 East Los Angeles Blowouts." *Frontiers: A Journal of Women Studies* 19:2 (1998): 113–142.

———. "Learning and Living Pedagogies of the Home: The Mestiza Consciousness of Chicana Students." *International Journal of Qualitative Studies in Education* 14:5 (2001): 623–639.

Dicochea, Pearlita R. "Chicana Critical Rhetoric: Recrafting La Causa in Chicano Movement Discourse, 1970–1979." *Frontiers: A Journal of Women Studies* 25:1 (2004): 77–92.

DuBois, Ellen Carol. *Feminism and Suffrage: the emergence of an independent women's movement in America, 1848–1869*. Ithaca: Cornell University Press, 1978.

DuBois, Ellen Carol, and Vicki L. Ruiz, ed. *Unequal Sisters: A Multi-Cultural Reader in U.S. Women's History*. New York: Routledge, 1990.

Echols, Alice. *Daring to Be Bad: Radical Feminism in America, 1967–1975*. Minneapolis: University of Minnesota Press, 1989.

Elbaum, Max. *Revolution in the Air: Sixties Radicals Turn to Lenin, Mao and Che*. New York: Verso, 2002.

Epstein, Barbara. "Is That All There Is? Reappraising Social Movements." *Socialist Review* 20:1 (January-March 1990): 35–66.

Espino, Virginia. "Women Sterilized as They Give Birth: Forced Sterilization and Chicana Resistance in the 1970s." In *Las Obreras: Chicana Politics of Work and Family*, ed. Vicki L. Ruiz. Los Angeles: Chicano Studies Research Center, UCLA, 2000: 65–81.

———. "Women Sterilized as They Give Birth: Population Control, Eugenics, and Social Protest in Twentieth-Century United States." Ph.D. diss., Arizona State University, 2007.

Espinoza, Dionne. *Bronze Womanhood: Chicana Labor and Leadership in the Chicano Civil Rights Movement, 1965–1980*. Forthcoming.

———. "Pedagogies of Nationalism and Gender: Cultural Resistance in Selected Representational Practices of Chicana/o Movement Activists, 1967–1972." Ph.D. diss., Cornell University, 1996.

———. "'Revolutionary Sisters': Women's Solidarity and Collective Identification among Chicana Brown Berets in East Los Angeles, 1967–1970." *Aztlán: A Journal of Chicano Studies* (Spring 2001): 15–58.

Esquibel, Catriόna R. *With Her Machete in Her Hand: Reading Chicana Lesbians*. Austin: University of Texas Press, 2006, 148.

Etter-Lewis, Gwendolyn, and Michele Foster, eds. *Unrelated Kin: Race and Gender in Women's Personal Narratives*. New York: Routledge, 1996.

Evans, Sara. *Personal Politics: The Roots of Women's Liberation in the Civil Rights Movement and the New Left*. New York: Knopf, 1979.

———. "Visions of Women-Centered History." *Social Policy* 4 (Spring 1982): 46–49.

Fanon, Frantz. *Dying Colonialism*. New York: Grove Press, 1965.

Ferguson, Roderick. *Aberrations in Black: Toward a Queer of Color Critique*. Minneapolis: University of Minnesota Press, 2004.

Fernández, Roberta. "*Abriendo Caminos* in the Brotherland: Chicana Writers Respond to the Ideology of Literary Nationalism." *Frontiers: A Journal of Women's Studies* 14, no. 2 (1994): 23–50.

Ferreira, Jason M. "All Power to the People: A Comparative History of Third World Radicalism in San Francisco, 1968–1974." Ph.D. diss., University of California, Berkeley, 2003.

Flores, Bill. "Francisca Flores." CSU Fresno, May 2, 1996. http://clnet.ucle.edu/research/francisca.html. Accessed May 12, 2006.

Foucault, Michel. "Nietzsche, Genealogy, History." In *Language, Counter-Memory, Practice*, ed. Donald Bouchard. Ithaca: Cornell University Press, 1977.

———. *Power/Knowledge: Selected Interviews and Other Writings, 1972–1977*, ed. Colin Gordon. New York: Pantheon, 1980.

Fraser, Nancy. "Rethinking the Public Sphere: A Contribution to the Critique of Actually Existing Democracy." In *Habermas and the Public Sphere*, ed. Craig Calhoun. Cambridge, MA: MIT Press, 1992: 109–142.

———. *Unruly Practices: Power, Discourse, and Gender in Contemporary Social Theory*. Minneapolis: University of Minnesota Press, 1989.

Fregoso, Rosa Linda. *The Bronze Screen: Chicana and Chicano Film Culture*. Minneapolis: University of Minnesota Press, 1993.

———. *meXicana Encounters: The Making of Social Identities on the Borderlands*. Berkeley: University of California Press, 2003.

Frisch, Michael H. *A Shared Authority: Essays on the Craft and Meaning of Oral and Public History*. Albany: State University of New York Press, 1990.

Galindo, D. Letticia. "Dispelling the Male-Only Myth: Chicanas and Caló." *Bilingual Review* 17:1 (1992): 3–36.

Galindo, D. Letticia, and María Dolores Gonzales, eds. *Speaking Chicana: Voice, Power, and Identity*. Tucson: University of Arizona Press, 1999.

Gamio, Manuel. *El imigrante mexicano: La historia de su vida*. México: Universidad Nacional Autónoma de México, 1969.

Gándara, Patricia C. *Over the Ivory Walls: The Educational Mobility of Low-Income Chicanos*. Albany: State University of New York Press, 1995.

García, Alma M. *Chicana Feminist Thought: The Basic Historical Writings*. New York: Routledge, 1997.

———. "The Development of Chicana Feminist Discourse, 1970–1980." In *Unequal Sisters: A Multicultural Reader in US Women's History*, ed. Ellen Carol DuBois and Vicki L. Ruiz. New York: Routledge, 1990: 418–431.

———. *Narratives of Mexican American Women: Emergent Identities of the Second Generation*. Walnut Creek, CA: AltaMira Press, 2004.

García, Ignacio M. *CHICANISMO: The Forging of a Militant Ethos among Mexican Americans*. Tucson: University of Arizona Press, 1997.

———. "Junctures in the Road: Chicano Studies since 'El Plan de Santa Barbara.'" In *Chicanas/Chicanos at the Crossroads*, ed. David R. Maciel and Isidro D. Ortiz. Tucson: University of Arizona Press, 1996: 181–206.

———. "Mexican American Youth Organization Precursors of Change in Texas." Working Paper Series, no. 8. Mexican American Studies and Research Center, Tucson, AZ, 1987.

Garcia, Laura E., Sandra M. Gutierrez, and Felicitas Nuñez. *Teatro Chicana: A Collective Memoir and Selected Plays*. Austin: University of Texas Press, 2008.

García, Mario T. *Memories of Chicano History: The Life and Narrative of Bert Corona*. Berkeley: University of California Press, 1994.

———. *Mexican Americans: Leadership Ideology, and Identity, 1930–1960*. New Haven: Yale University Press, 1989.

Gaspar de Alba, Alicia, and Alma Lopez, eds. *Our Lady of Controversy: Alma Lopez's "Irreverent Apparition."* Austin: University of Texas Press, 2011.

Gatlin, Rochelle. *American Women since 1945*. Jackson: University of Mississippi Press, 1987.

Giddings, Paula. *When and Where I Enter: The Impact of Black Women on Race and Sex in America*. New York: William Morrow, 1983.

Giroux, Henry. "Insurgent Multiculturalism and the Promise of Pedagogy." In *Multiculturalism: A Critical Reader*, ed. David Theo Goldberg. Cambridge: Basil Blackwell, 1994: 325–343.

Gitlan, Todd. *The Twilight of Common Dreams: Why America Is Wracked by Culture Wars*. New York: Metropolitan Books, 1995.

Glaude, Eddie S., Jr. *Is It Nation Time? Contemporary Essays on Black Power and Nationalism*. Chicago: University of Chicago Press, 2002.

Gluck, Sherna Berger. "What's So Special about Women? Women's Oral History." *Frontiers: A Journal of Women Studies* 2:2 (1977): 3–17.

Gluck, Sherna Berger, in collaboration with Maylei Blackwell, Sharon Cotrell, and Karen harper. "Whose Feminism, Whose History? Reflections on Excavating the History of (the) U.S. Women's Movement(s)." In *Community Activism and Feminist Politics: Organizing across Race, Class, and Gender*, ed. Nancy A. Naples. New York: Routledge, 1997: 31–56.

Gluck, Sherna Berger, and Daphne Patai. *Women's Words: The Feminist Practice of Oral History*. New York: Routledge, 1991.

Goldberg, David Theo, ed. *Multiculturalism: A Critical Reader*. Cambridge: Basil Blackwell, 1994.

Gómez-Quiñones, Juan. *Chicano Politics: Reality and Promise, 1940–1990*. Albuquerque: University of New Mexico Press, 1990.

———. *Mexican American Students por la Raza: The Chicano Student Movement in Southern California, 1966–1967*. Santa Barbara: Editorial La Causa, 1978.

———. *On Culture*. Popular Series No. 1. Los Angeles: Chicano Studies Center Publications, UCLA, 1977.

———. *Sembradoras: Ricardo Flores Magón y El Partido Liberal Mexicano: A Eulogy and Critique*. Monograph, no. 5. Los Angeles: University of California, Los Angeles, Chicano Research Center, 1973.

———. "Toward a Perspective on Chicano History." *Aztlán: A Journal of Chicano Studies* 2:2 (Fall 1971): 124–132.

———. "Plan de San Diego Reviewed." *Aztlán: Chicano Journal of the Social Sciences* 2:1 (Spring 1970).

Gonzalez, Deena J. *Refusing the Favor: The Spanish-Mexican Women of Santa Fe, 1820–1880*. New York: Oxford University Press, 1999.

———. "'It is my last wish that . . .': A Look at Colonial Nuevo Mexicanas through Their Testaments." In *Building with Our Hands: New Directions in Chicana Studies*, ed. Adela de la Torre and Beatriz M. Pesquera. Berkeley: University of California Press, 1993: 91–108.

———. "Speaking Secrets: Living Chicana Theory." In *Living Chicana Theory*, ed. Carla Trujillo. Berkley: Third Woman Press, 1998: 46–77.

Gramsci, Antonio. *Selections from the Prison Notebooks*. Trans. Quintin Hoarse and Geoffrey Nowell-Smith. New York: International Publishers, 1971.

Green, Rayna. "American Indian Women: Diverse Leadership for Social Change." In *Bridges of Power: Women's Multicultural Alliances*, ed. Lisa Albrecht and Rose Brewer. Philadelphia: New Society, 1990: 61–73.

———. *Native American Women: A Contextual Bibliography*. Bloomington: Indiana University Press, 1983.

Gregory, Steven. "Race, Identity and Political Activism: The Shifting Contours of the African American Public Sphere." *Public Culture* 7 (1994): 147–164.

Grewal, Inderpal. "On the New Global Feminism and the Family of Nations: Dilemmas of Transnational Feminist Practices." In *Talking Visions: Multicultural Feminism in a Transnational Age*, ed. Ella Shohat. New York: New Museum of Contemporary Art, 1999: 501–505.

Grewal, Inderpal, and Caren Kaplan. "Introduction: Transnational Feminist Practices and Questions of Postmodernity." In *Scattered Hegemonies: Postmodernity and Transnational*

Feminist Practices, ed. Inderpal Grewal and Caren Kaplan. Minneapolis: University of Minnesota Press, 1994: 1–36.

―――, eds. *Scattered Hegemonies: Postmodernity and Transnational Feminist Practices*. Minneapolis: University of Minnesota Press, 1994.

Griffin, Farah Jasmine. "Conflict and Chorus: Reconsidering Toni Cade's *The Black Woman: An Anthology*." In *Is It Nation Time? Contemporary Essays on Black Power and Black Nationalism*, ed. Eddie S. Glaude Jr. Chicago: University of Chicago Press, 2002: 113–129.

Gutiérrez, David. *Walls and Mirrors: Mexican Americans, Mexican Immigrants, and the Politics of Ethnicity*. Berkeley: University of California Press, 1995.

Gutiérrez, Elena R. *Fertile Matters: The Politics of Mexican-Origin Women's Reproduction*. Austin: University of Texas Press, 2008.

―――. "Policing 'Pregnant Pilgrims': Situating the Sterilization Abuse of Mexican-Origin Women in Los Angeles County." In *Women, Health, and Nation: Canada and the United States since 1945*, ed. Georgina Feldberg, Molly Ladd-Taylor, Alison Li, and Kathryn McPherson. Montreal: McGill-Queen's University Press, 2003: 379–403.

Gutiérrez, Elena R., Jael Silliman, Marlene Gerber Fried, and Loretta Ross. *Undivided Rights: Women of Color Organize for Reproductive Justice*. Cambridge, MA: South End Press, 2004.

Gutiérrez, José Angel, Michelle Meléndez, and Sonia Adriana Noyola. *Chicanas in Charge: Texas Women in the Public Arena*. Lanham, MD: AltaMira Press, 2007.

Gutiérrez, Ramón A. "Chicano History: Paradigm Shifts and Shifting Boundaries." In *Voices of a New Chicana/o History*, ed. Refugio I. Rochín and Dennis N. Valdés. East Lansing: Michigan State University Press, 2000: 91–114.

―――. "Community, Patriarchy, and Individualism: The Politics of Chicano History and the Dream of Equality." *American Quarterly* 45:1 (1993): 44–72.

Hall, Stuart. "Cultural Identity and Diaspora." *Framework* 36 (1988): 222–237.

―――. "New Ethnicities." In *Black Film/British Cinema*, ed. Kobena Mercer. ICA Document 7. London: Institute of Contemporary Arts, 1988: 27–30.

―――. "The Question of Cultural Identity." In *Modernity and Its Futures*, ed. Stuart Hall, David Held, Tony McGrew. Cambridge, MA: Polity Press, 1992: 273–326.

Haraway, Donna J. "Situated Knowledges: The Science Question in Feminism and the Privilege of Partial Perspective." In *Simians, Cyborgs, and Women: The Reinvention of Nature*. London: Free Association Books, 1991: 183–202.

Hardy, Gayle J. *American Women Civil Rights Activists: Biobibliographies of 68 Leaders, 1825–1992*. Jefferson, NC: McFarland, 1993.

Hardy-Fanta, Carol. "Latina Women and Political Leadership: Implications for Latino Community Empowerment." In *Latino Politics in Massachusetts: Struggles, Strategies, and Prospects*, ed. Carol Hardy-Fanta and Jeffrey N. Gerson. New York: Routledge, 2002: 193–212.

Harvey, David. *The Condition of Postmodernity: An Enquiry into the Origins of Cultural Change*. Cambridge: Blackwell, 1990.

Hernandez, Patricia. "Lives of Chicana Activists: The Chicano Student Movement (A Case Study)." In *Mexican Women in the United States: Struggles Past and Present*, ed. Magdalena Mora and Adelaida R. Del Castillo. Occasional Paper 2. Los Angeles: Chicano Studies Research Center Publications, UCLA, 1980: 17–26.

Hernández Tovar, Inés. "Sara Estela Ramírez: The Early Twentieth Century Texas-Mexican Poet." Ph.D. diss., University of Houston, 1984.

Herrera-Sobek, María. "The Soldier Archetype." In *The Mexican Corrido: A Feminist Analysis*, ed. María Herrera-Sobek. Bloomington: Indiana University Press, 1990.

Hom, Alice Y. "Documenting Lesbian of Color Community Building in Los Angeles and New York, 1970s to 1990s." Ph.D. diss., Claremont Graduate School, forthcoming.

Honig, Emily. "Women at Farah Revisited: Political Mobilization and Its Aftermath among Chicana Workers in El Paso, Texas, 1972–1992." *Feminist Studies* 22:2 (Summer 1996): 425–452.

Honig, Emily, Laurie Coyle, and Gail Hershatter. *Women at Farah: An Unfinished Story*. El Paso: REFORMA, 1979.

hooks, bell. *Ain't I a Woman? Black Women and Feminism*. Boston: South End Press, 1981.

———. *Feminist Theory from Margin to Center*. Boston: South End Press, 1984.

———. *Talking Back: Thinking Feminist, Thinking Black*. Boston: South End Press, 1989.

Hull, Gloria T., Patricia Bell Scott and Barbara Smith, eds. *But Some of Us Are Brave: All the Women Are White, All the Blacks Are Men*. Old Westbury NY: Feminist Press, 1982.

Hurtado, Aída. "Underground Feminisms: Inocencia's Story." In *Chicana Feminisms: A Critical Reader*, ed. Gabriela F. Arredondo et al. Durham: Duke University Press, 2003: 260–290.

———. *Voicing Chicana Feminisms: Young Women Speak Out on Sexuality and Identity*. New York: New York University Press, 2003.

Jackson, Shirley. "Something about the Word: African American Women and Feminism." In *No Middle Ground: Women and Radical Protest*, ed. Kathleen M. Blee. New York: New York University Press, 1998: 38–50.

Jaggar, Alison M. *Feminist Politics and Human Nature*. Totowa, NJ: Rowman and Allenheld, 1983.

———. "Globalizing Feminist Ethics." *Hypatia: A Journal of Feminist Philosophy* 13:2 (Summer 1998): 17–25.

Jaimes, M. Annette, with Theresa Halsey. "American Indian Women: At the Center of Indigenous Resistance in North America." In *The State of Native America: Genocide, Colonization and Resistance*, ed. M. Annette Jaimes. Boston: South End Press, 1992: 311–344.

Jaimes Guerrero, M. Annette. "Civil Rights versus Sovereignty: Native American Women in Life and Land Struggles." In *Feminist Genealogies: Colonial Legacies and Democratic Futures*, ed. Jacqui M. Alexander and Chandra Talpade Mohanty. New York: Routledge, 1997: 101–124.

———. "Savage Hegemony: From 'Endangered Species' to Feminist Indigenism." In *Talking Visions: Multicultural Feminisms in a Transnational Age*, ed. Ella Shohat. Cambridge, MA: MIT Press, 1999: 413–430.

Jakobsen, Janet R. *Working Alliances and the Politics of Difference: Diversity and Feminist Ethics*. Bloomington: Indiana University Press, 1998.

Jara, René, and Hernán Vidal, eds. *Testimonio y literatura*. Minneapolis: Institute for the Study of Ideologies and Literature, 1986.

Jayawardena, Kumari. *Feminism and Nationalism in the Third World*. New Delhi: Kali for Women; London: Zed Books; Totowa, NJ: UBiblio Distribution Center, 1986.

Johnson-Odim, Cheryl. "Common Themes, Different Contexts, Third World Women, and Feminism." In *Third World Women and the Politics of Feminism*, ed. Chandra Talpade Mohanty, Ann Russo, and Lourdes Torres. Indianapolis: Indiana University Press, 1991: 314–327.

Johnson-Odim, Cheryl, and Margaret Strobel, eds. *Expanding the Boundaries of Women's History: Essays on Women in the Third World*. Bloomington: Indiana University Press, 1992.

Jones, Jacqueline. *Labor of Love, Labor of Sorrow: Black Women, Work and the Family From Slavery to the Present*. New York: Basic, 1985.

K., Lalita, et al. *"We Were Making History . . . ": Life Histories of the Telangana People's Struggle*. London: Zed Books, 1990.

Kaplan, Caren. "The Politics of Location as Transnational Feminist Practice." In *Scattered Hegemonies: Postmodernity and Transnational Feminist Practices*, ed. Inderpal Grewal and Caren Kaplan. Minneapolis: University of Minnesota Press, 1994: 137–153.

———. "Resisting Autobiography: Outlaw Genres and Transnational Feminist Subjects." In *De/Colonizing the Subject: Politics and Gender Women's Autobiographical Practice*, ed. Julia Watson and Sidonie Smith. Minneapolis: University of Minnesota Press, 1992: 115–138.

Kelley, Robin D. G. *Freedom Dreams: The Black Radical Imagination*. Boston: Beacon Press, 2002.

King, Deborah K. "Multiple Jeopardy, Multiple Consciousnesses: The Context of a Black Feminist Ideology." *Signs: Journal of Women in Culture and Society* 14:1 (1988): 42–72.

King, Katie. *Theory in Its Feminist Travels: Conversations in U.S. Women's Movements*. Indianapolis: Indiana University Press, 1994.

Kleiner, Diana J. "Magnolia Park, Texas." In *The Handbook of Texas Online* (University of Texas, Austin). www.tsha.utexas.edu/handbook/online/articles/view/MM/hvm6.html. Accessed May 4, 2004.

Laclau, Ernesto, and Chantal Mouffe. *Hegemony and Socialist Strategy: Towards a Radical Democratic Politics*. London: Verso, 1985.

Langston, Donna H. "American Indian Women's Activism in the 1960s and 1970s." *Hypatia: A Journal of Feminist Philosophy* 18:2 (Spring 2003): 114–132.

Latina Feminist Group. *Telling to Live: Latina Feminist Testimonios*. Durham, NC: Duke University Press, 2001.

Lau Jaiven, Ana, and Carmen Ramos-Escandón. *Mujeres y revolución, 1900–1917*. México: Instituto Nacional de Estudios Históricos de la Revolución Mexicana, Instituto Nacional de Antropología e Historia, 1993.

Lau Jaiven, Ana. *La nueva ola del feminismo en México: Conciencia y acción de lucha de las mujeres*. México: Planeta, 1987.

Lee, Joon P. "The Third World Women's Alliance, 1970–1980: Women of Color Organizing in a Revolutionary Era." M.A. thesis, Sarah Lawrence College, 2007.

Lerner, Gerda, ed. *Black Women in White America: A Documentary History*. New York: Vintage, 1973.

Leyva, Yolanda. "Listening to the Silences in Latina/Chicana Lesbian History." In *Living Chicana Theory*, ed. Carla Trujillo. Berkeley: Third Woman Press, 1998: 429–433.

Limón, José. "Carne, Carnales, and Carnivalesque: Bakhtinian Batos, Disorder and Narrative Discourses." *American Ethnologist* 16:3 (August 1989): 471–486.

Lipsitz, George. *Time Passages: Collective Memory and American Popular Culture*. Minneapolis: University of Minnesota Press, 1990.

Longeaux y Vásquez, "The Mexican-American Woman." In *Sisterhood Is Powerful: An Anthology of Writings from the Women's Liberation Movement*, ed. Robin Morgan. New York: Random House, 1970: 379–384.

López, Sonia A. "The Role of the Chicana within the Student Movement." In *Essays on la Mujer*, no. 1, ed. Rosaura Sanchez and Rosa Martinez Cruz. Los Angeles: Chicano Studies Center Publications, UCLA, 1977: 16–29.

Lorde, Audre. "Poetry Is Not a Luxury." In *Sister Outsider: Essays and Speeches.* Trumansburg, NY: Crossing Press, 1984: 36–39.

Lowe, Lisa. "Angela Davis: Reflections on Race, Class and Gender in the USA." In *The Politics of Culture in the Shadow of Capital*, ed. Lisa Lowe and David Lloyd. Durham, NC: Duke University Press, 1997: 303–323.

———. "The Intimacies of Four Continents." In *Haunted by Empire: Geographies of Intimacies in North American History*, ed. Laura Stoler. Durham, NC: Duke University Press, 2006: 191–212.

Lowe, Lisa, and David Lloyd, eds. *The Politics of Culture in the Shadow of Capital*. Durham, NC: Duke University Press, 1997.

Lubiano, Wahneema. "Black Nationalism and Black Common Sense: Policing Ourselves and Others." In *The House That Race Built: Original Essays by Toni Morrison, Angel Y. Davis, Cornel West, and Others on Black Americans and Politics in America Today*, ed. Wahneema Lubiano. New York: Pantheon Books, 1997.

Lucas, María Elena. *Forged under the Sun: The Life of María Elena Lucas*. Ann Arbor: University of Michigan Press, 1993.

Marez, Curtis. "Subaltern Soundtracks: Mexican Immigrants and the Making of Hollywood Cinema," *Aztlán* 29:1 (2004): 57–82.

Martín Alcoff, Linda. *Visible Identities: Race, Gender, and the Self*. New York: Oxford University Press, 2006.

Martinez, Elizabeth (Betita). "Chingón Politics Die Hard." In *De Colores Means All of Us: Latina Views for a Multi-Colored Century*. Cambridge, MA: South End Press, 1998: 172–181.

———. "Colonized Women: The Chicana an Introduction." In *Sisterhood Is Powerful: An Anthology of Writings from the Women's Liberation Movement*, ed. Robin Morgan. New York: Random House, 1970, 376–79.

———. *500 Years of Chicana Women's History*. New Brunswick: Rutgers University Press, 2008.

———. *500 Years of Chicano History in Pictures*. Albuquerque: SouthWest Organizing Project (SWOP), 1991.

———. "Listen Up, Anglo Sisters." In *De Colores Means All of Us: Latina Views for a Multi-Colored Century*. Cambridge, MA: South End Press, 1998: 182–189.

Martinez, Elizabeth (Betita), and Angela Y. Davis. "Coalition Building among People of Color." In *Enunciating Our Terms: Women of Color in Collaboration and Conflict*, ed. María Ochoa and Teresia Teaiwa. Inscriptions 7. Santa Cruz: Center for Cultural Studies, UCSC, 1994: 42–53.

Mariscal, George, ed. *Aztlán and Viet Nam: Chicano and Chicana Experiences of the War*. Berkeley: University of California Press, 1999.

———. *Brown-Eyed Children of the Sun: Lessons from the Chicano Movement, 1965–1975*. Albuquerque: University of New Mexico Press, 2005.

Matsumoto, Valerie. "Reflection on Oral History: Research in a Japanese American Community." In *Feminist Dilemmas in Fieldwork*, ed. Diane L. Wolf. Boulder, CO: Westview Press, 1996: 160–169.

McClintock, Anne, Aamir Mufti, and Ella Shohat, eds. *Dangerous Liaisons: Gender, Nation and Postcolonial Perspectives*. Minneapolis: University of Minnesota Press, 1997.

McDuffie, Erik S. "No Small Change Would Do: Esther Cooper Jackson and the Making of a Black Left Feminist." In *Want to Start a Revolution? Radical Women in the Black Freedom Struggle*, ed. Dayo F. Gore, Jeanne Theoharis, and Komozi Woodward. New York: New York University Press, 2009: 25–46.

McNair Barnett, Bernice. "Invisible Southern Black Women Leaders in the Civil Rights Movement: The Triple Constraints of Gender, Race, and Class." In *Race, Class, and Gender: Common Bonds, Different Voices*, ed. Esther Ngan-Ling Chow, Doris Wilkinson, and Maxine Baca Zinn. London: Sage, 1996: 265–287.

Medina, Lara. *Las Hermanas: Chicana/Latina Religious-Political Activism in the U.S. Catholic Church*. Philadelphia: Temple University Press, 2005.

Medovoi, Leerom, Shankar Raman, and Benjamin Robinson. "Can the Subaltern Vote?" *Socialist Review* 20:3 (July-September 1990): 133–149.

Mercer, Kobena, ed. *Black Film/British Cinema*. ICA Document 7. London: Institute of Contemporary Arts, 1988.

———. *Welcome to the Jungle: New Positions in Black Cultural Studies*. London: Routledge, 1994.

Mesa-Baines, Amalia. "El Mundo Femenino: Chicana Artists of the Movement—A Commentary on Development and Production." In *Chicano Art: Resistance and Affirmation, 1965–1985*, ed. Richard Griswold del Castillo et al. Los Angeles: Wright Art Gallery, UCLA, 1991: 131–140.

Miller, Francesca. *Latin American Women and the Search for Social Justice*. Hanover, NH: University Press of New England, 1991.

Miranda, Marie (Keta). *Homegirls in the Public Sphere*. Austin: University of Texas Press, 2003.

———. "Subversive Geographies: From Representations of Girls in Gangs to Self-Presentation as Civil Subjects." Ph.D. diss., University of California, Santa Cruz, 2000.

Miranda-Arrizón, Marcie. "Building Herman(a)dad: Chicana Feminism and Comisión Femenil Mexicana Nacional." M.A. thesis, University of California, Santa Barbara, 1998.

Mirandé, Alfredo. *The Chicano Experience: An Alternative Perspective*. Notre Dame: University of Notre Dame Press, 1985.

———. *Hombres y Machos: Masculinity and Latino Culture*. Boulder, CO: Westview Press, 1997.

Mirandé, Alfredo, and Evangelina Enriquez. *La Chicana: The Mexican American Woman*. Chicago: University of Chicago Press, 1979.

Mohanty, Chandra Talpade. "Cartographies of Struggle: Third World Women and the Politics of Feminism." In *Third World Women and the Politics of Feminism*, ed. Chandra Talpade Mohanty, Ann Russo, and Lourdes Torres. Indianapolis: Indiana University Press, 1991: 1–47.

Mohanty, Chandra Talpade, Ann Russo, and Lourdes Torres, eds. *Third World Women and the Politics of Feminism*. Indianapolis: Indiana University Press, 1991.

Mora, Magdalena, and Adelaida R. Del Castillo, ed. *Mexican Women in the United States: Struggles Past and Present*. Occasional Paper No. 2. Los Angeles: Chicano Studies Research Center Publications, UCLA, 1980.

Moraga, Cherríe. "From a Long Line of Vendidas." In *Loving in the War Years: lo que nunca pasó pos sus labios*. Boston: South End Press, 1983: 29–30.

———. "La Güera." In *This Bridge Called My Back: Writings by Radical Women of Color*, 2nd ed., ed. Gloria Anzaldúa and Cherríe Moraga. New York: Kitchen Table: Women of Color Press, 1983: 27–34.

———. *The Last Generation: Prose and Poetry*. Boston: South End Press, 1993.

———. *Loving in the War Years: lo que nunca pasó por sus labios*. Boston: South End Press, 1983.

Moraga, Cherríe, and Gloria Anzaldúa, eds. *This Bridge Called My Back: Writings by Radical Women of Color*. 2nd ed. New York: Kitchen Table: Women of Color Press, 1983.

Morgan, Robin, ed. *Sisterhood Is Powerful: An Anthology of Writings from the Women's Liberation Movement*. New York: Random House, 1970.

Mujeres en Marcha. *Unsettled Issues: Chicanas in the 80s*. Berkeley: Chicano Studies Library Publications Unit, 1983.

Muñoz, Carlos, Jr. *Youth, Identity, Power: The Chicano Movement*. London: Verso, 1989.

Muñoz, Jose E. *Disidentifications: Queers of Color and the Performance of Politics*. Minneapolis: University of Minnesota Press, 2004.

Naples, Nancy A. *Grassroots Warriors: Activist Mothering, Community Work, and the War on Poverty*. New York: Routledge, 1998.

Navarro, Armando. *Raza Unida Party: A Chicano Challenge to the U.S. Two-Party Dictatorship*. Philadelphia: Temple University Press, 2000.

Navarro, Sharon, Ann. "Las Mujeres Invisible! The Invisible Women." In *Women's Activism and Globalization: Linking Local Struggles and Transnational Politics*, ed. Nancy A. Naples and Manisha Desai. New York: Routledge, 2002: 83–98.

Nelson, Barbara J., and Alissa Hummer. *Leadership and Diversity: A Case Book*. Los Angeles: University of California, Los Angeles, 2004.

Nieto, Consuelo. "The Chicana and the Women's Rights Movement: A Perspective." *Civil Rights Digest* 6:3 (Spring 1974): 36–42.

———. *Chicana Identity: Interaction of Culture and Sex Roles*. Denver: Conference on Educational and Occupational Needs of Hispanic Women, 1976.

Noda, Barbara. "Low Riding in the Women's Movement." In *This Bridge Called My Back: Writings by Radical Women of Color*, 2nd ed., ed. Cherríe Moraga and Gloria E. Anzaldúa. New York: Kitchen Table: Women of Color Press, 1983: 138–139.

Nora, Pierre. "Between Memory and History: Les Lieux de Memoire." *Representations* 26 (Spring 1989): 7–24.

Ochoa, María, and Teresía Teaiwa, eds. "Enunciating Our Terms: Women of Color in Collaboration and Conflict." *Inscriptions* 7 (1994).

Ohoyo Resource Center. *Words of Today's American Indian Women: (Ohoyo Makachi)*. Washington, DC: U.S. Department of Education, 1981.

Omi, Michael, and Howard Winant. *Racial Formation in the United States: From the 1960s to the 1990s*. London: Routledge, 1994.

Oropeza, Lorena. "Antiwar Aztlán: The Chicano Movement Opposes U.S. Intervention in Vietnam." In *Window of Freedom: Race, Civil Rights, and Foreign Affairs, 1945–1988*, ed. Brenda Gayle Plummer. Chapel Hill: University of North Carolina Press, 2003: 201–220.

———. "Making History: The Chicano Movement." In *Voices of a New Chicana/o History*, ed. Refugio I Rochín and Dennis Valdés. East Lansing: Michigan State University Press, 2000: 197–230.

———. *¡Raza Si! ¡Guerra No! Chicano Protest and Patriotism during the Vietnam War Era*. Berkeley: University of California Press, 2005.

Orozco, Cynthia. "Alicia Dickerson Montemayor: The Feminist Challenge to the League of United Latin American Citizens, Family Ideology and Mexican American Politics in Texas in the 1930s." In *Writing the Range: Race, Class, and Culture in the Women's West*, ed. Susan Hodge Armitage and Elizabeth Jameson. Norman: University of Oklahoma Press, 1997: 435–456.

———. "Beyond Machismo, La Familia, and Ladies Auxiliaries: A Historiography of Mexican-Origin Women's Participation in Voluntary Associations in the United States, 1870–1990." *Renato Rosaldo Lecture Series.* Monograph 10 (1992–1993): 37–77.

———. *No Mexicans, Women, or Dogs Allowed: The Rise of the Mexican American Civil Rights Movement.* Austin: University of Texas Press, 2009.

———. "Sexism in Chicano Studies and the Community." In *Chicana Voices: Intersections of Class, Race, and Gender*, ed. Teresa Córdova et al. Austin: Center for Mexican American Studies Publications, 1986: 11–18.

Paik Lee, Mary. *Quiet Odyssey: A Pioneer Korean Woman in America.* Seattle: University of Washington Press, 1990.

Palomo Acosta, Teresa, and Ruth Winegarten. *Las Tejanas: 300 Years of History.* Austin: University of Texas Press, 2003.

Pardo, Mary. "A Selective Evaluation of *El Plan de Santa Barbara.*" *La Gente* (March/April 1984): 14–15.

———. "Mexican American Women Grassroots Community Activists: Mothers of East Los Angeles." *Frontiers: A Journal of Women Studies* 11:1 (1990): 1–7.

Paredes, Américo. "The United States, Mexico, and Machismo." In *Folklore and Culture on the Texas Mexican Border*, ed. Richard Bauman. Austin: Center for Mexican American Studies, University of Texas, 1993: 215–234.

Paz, Octavio. *The Labyrinth of Solitude.* New York: Weidenfeld, 1985.

Pérez, Emma. "'A la Mujer': A Critique of the Partido Liberal Mexicano's Gender Ideology on Women." In *Between Borders: Essays on Mexicana/Chicana History*, ed. Adelaida Del Castillo. Encino, CA: Floricanto Press, 1990: 459–482.

———. *The Decolonial Imaginary: Writing Chicanas into History.* Indianapolis: Indiana University Press, 1999.

———. "Feminism-in-Nationalism: The Gendered Subaltern at the Yucatán Feminist Congress of 1916." In *Woman and Nation: Nationalisms, Transnational Feminisms, and the State*, ed. Caren Kaplan, Norma Alarcón, and Minoo Moallem. Durham, NC: Duke University Press, 1999: 219–241.

———. "Irigaray's Female Symbolic in the Making of Chicana Lesbian Sitios y Lenguas." In *Living Chicana Theory*, ed. Carla Trujillo. Berkeley: Third Woman Press, 1998: 87–101.

———. "Sexuality and Discourse: Notes From a Chicana Survivor." In *Chicana Lesbians: The Girls Our Mothers Warned Us About*, ed. Carla Trujillo. Berkeley: Third Women Press, 1991: 159–184.

———. "Speaking from the Margin: Uninvited Discourse on Sexuality and Power." In *Building with Our Hands: New Directions in Chicana Studies*, ed. Adela de la Torre and Beatríz Pesquera. Berkeley: University of California Press, 1993: 57–74.

Pérez, Laura E. *Chicana Art: The Politics of Spiritual and Aesthetic Altarities.* Durham: Duke University Press, 2007.

———. "*El desorden*, Nationalism, and Chicana/o Aesthetics." In *Between Woman and National: Nationalisms, Transnational Feminisms and the State*, ed. Caren Kaplan, Norma Alarcón, and Minoo Moallem. Berkeley: Third Woman Press, 1999: 19–46.

Pérez-Torres, Rafael. *Movements in Chicano Poetry: Against Myths, against Margins.* Cambridge: Cambridge University Press, 1995.

Personal Narratives Group, ed. *Interpreting Women's Lives: Feminist Theory and Personal Narratives.* Bloomington: Indiana University Press, 1989.

Pesquera, Beatriz, and Denise Segura. "Beyond Indifference and Antipathy: The Chicana Movement and Chicana Feminist Discourse." *Aztlán: A Journal of Chicano Studies* 19:2 (1992): 69–93.

———. "There Is No Going Back: Chicanas and Feminism." In *Chicana Critical Issues*, ed. Norma Alarcón, Rafaela Castro, Emma Pérez, Beatriz Pesquera, Adaljiza Sosa-Riddell, and Patricia Zavella. Berkeley: Third Woman Press, 1993: 95–105.

Portelli, Alessandro. *The Death of Luigi Trastulli, and Other Stories: Form and Meaning in Oral History.* Albany: State University of New York Press, 1991.

———. *The Battle of Valle Giulia: Oral History and the Art of Dialogue.* Madison: University of Wisconsin, 1997.

———. *The Order Has Been Carried Out: History, Memory, and Meaning of a Nazi Massacre in Rome.* New York: Palgrave Macmillan, 2003.

Pulido, Laura. *Black, Brown, Yellow, and Left: Radical Activism in Los Angeles.* Berkeley: University of California Press, 2006.

Quintana, Alvin E. *Home Girls: Chicana Literary Voices.* Philadelphia: Temple University Press, 1996.

Radcliffe, Sarah, and Sallie Westwood. "Gender, Racism and the Politics of Identities in Latin America." In *"Viva": Women and Popular Protest in Latin America.* New York: Routledge, 1993: 1–29.

Ramírez, Catherine S. "Representing, Politics, and the Politics of Representation in Gang Studies." *American Quarterly* 56:4 (December 2004): 1135–1146.

———. *The Women in the Zoot Suit: Gender, Nationalism, and the Politics of Cultural Memory.* Durham, NC: Duke University Press, 2009.

Ramirez, Martha, and Judy Young. "Women of Color in Collaboration and Conflict: An Annotated Bibliography." *Inscriptions* 7 (1994): 141–155. Special issue: Enunciating Our Terms: Women of Color in Collaboration and Conflict, ed. María Ochoa and Teresía Teaiwa.

Ramos, Juanita, ed. *Compañeras: Latina Lesbians.* New York: Latina Lesbian History Project, the Print Center, 1987.

Ransby, Barbara. *Ella Baker and the Black Freedom Movement: A Radical Democratic Vision.* Chapel Hill: University of North Carolina Press, 2003

Rendón, Armando B. *Chicano Manifesto.* New York: Macmillan, 1971.

Robnett, Belinda. "African American Women in the Civil Rights Movement: Spontaneity and Emotion in Social Movement Theory." In *No Middle Ground: Women and Radical Protest*, ed. Kathleen M. Blee. New York: New York University Press, 1998: 65–95.

———. "African-American Women in the Civil Rights Movement, 1954–1965: Gender, Leadership, and Micro mobilization." *American Journal of Sociology* 101:6 (May 1996): 1661–1693.

———. *How Long? How Long? African American Women in the Struggle for Civil Rights.* New York: Oxford University Press, 1997.

Rochin, Refugio I., and Dennis N. Valdes, eds. *Voices of a New Chicana/o History.* East Lansing: Michigan State University Press, 2000.

Rodriguez, Armando, and Keith Taylor. *From the Barrio to Washington: An Educator's Journey*. Albuquerque: University of New Mexico Press, 2007.

Rodriguez, Lilia. "Barrio Women: Between the Urban and Feminist Movement." *Latin American Perspectives* 21:3 (Spring 1994): 32–48. Special issue: Social Movements and Political Change in Latin America, Part 2.

Rodriguez, Richard T. *Next of Kin: The Family in Chicano/a Cultural Politics*. Durham, NC: Duke University Press, 2009.

———. "The Verse of the Godfather: Signifying Family and Nationalism in Chicano Rap and Hip-Hop Culture." In *VELVET BARRIOS: Popular Culture and Chicana/o Sexualities*, ed. Alicia Gaspar de Alba. New York: Palgrave Macmillan, 2003: 107–124.

Roque Ramirez, Horacio N. "Communities of Desire: Queer Latina/o History and Memory, San Francisco Bay Area, 1960s-1990s." Ph.D. diss., University of California, Berkeley, 2001.

———. "'That's *My* Place!': Negotiating Racial, Sexual, and Gender Politics in San Francisco's Gay Latino Alliance, 1975–1983." *Journal of the History of Sexuality* 12:2 (April 2003): 224–258.

———. "Claiming Queer Cultural Citizenship: Gay Latino (Im)migrant Acts in San Francisco." In *Queer Migrations: Sexuality, U.S. Citizenship, and Border Crossings*, ed. Eithne Luibhéid and Lionel Cantú Jr. Minneapolis: University of Minnesota Press, 2005.

Rosaldo, Renato. *Culture and Truth: The Remaking of Social Analysis*. Boston: Beacon Press, 1993.

Rosales, Arturo F. *Chicano! The History of the Mexican American Civil Rights Movement*. Houston: Arte Público Press, 1996.

Rosen, Ruth. *The World Split Open: How the Modern Women's Movement Changed America*. New York: Penguin, 2006.

Rosenbloom, Rachel, ed. *Unspoken Rules: Sexual Orientation and Women's Human Rights*. London: Cassell, 1996.

Roth, Benita. "A Dialogical View of the Emergence of Chicana Feminist Discourse." *Critical Sociology* 33 (2007): 709–733.

———. *Separate Roads to Feminism: Black, Chicana, and White Feminist Movements in America's Second Wave*. New York: Cambridge University Press, 2004.

Rothschild, Cynthia. *Written Out: How Sexuality Is Used to Attack Women's Organizing*. A Report of the International Gay and Lesbian Human Rights Commission and the Center for Women's Global Leadership. San Francisco: IGLHRC, 2000.

Rubio-Goldsmith, Raquel. "Oral History: Considerations and the Problems for Its Use in the History of Mexicanas in the United States." In *Between Borders: Essays on Mexicana/Chicana History*, ed. Adelaida R. Del Castillo. Encino, CA: Floricanto Press, 1990: 161–173.

Ruiz, Vicki L. *Cannery Women, Cannery Lives: Mexican Women, Unionization, and the California Food Processing Industry, 1950-1980*. Albuquerque: University of New Mexico Press, 1987.

———. "Claiming Public Space at Work, Church and Neighborhood." In *Las Obreras: Chicana Politics of Work and Family*. Los Angeles: Chicano Studies Research Center, UCLA, 2000: 13–39.

———. *From Out of the Shadows: Mexican Women in Twentieth-Century America*. New York: Oxford University Press, 1998.

———. "La Nueva Chicana: Women and the Movement." In *From Out of the Shadows: Mexican Women in Twentieth-Century America*. New York: Oxford University Press, 1998: 99–126.

———. "Situating Stories: The Surprising Consequences of Oral History." *Oral History Review* 25:1–2 (1998): 71–80.

———. *Working for Wages: Mexican Women in the Southwest, 1930–1980*. Tucson: Southwest Institute for Research on Women, 1984.

———, ed. *Las Obreras: Chicana Politics of Work and Family*. Los Angeles: Chicano Studies Research Center, UCLA, 2000.

Ruiz, Vicki L., and Virginia Sánchez Korrol. *Latina Legacies: Identity, Biography, and Community*. New York: Oxford University Press, 2005.

Russo, Anthony. "Chicanas Speak: Hijas Establish Goals." *Daily Forty-Niner*, October 13, 1972, p. 3.

Salas, Elizabeth. *Soldaderas in the Mexican Military: Myth and History*. Austin: University of Texas Press, 1990.

Salazar, Claudia. "A Third World Woman's Text: Between the Politics of Criticism and Cultural Politics." In *Women's Words: The Feminist Practice of Oral History*, ed. Sherna Berger Gluck and Daphne Patai. New York: Routledge, 1991: 93–106.

Saldívar-Hull, Sonia. *Feminism on the Border: Chicana Politics and Literature*. Berkeley: University of California Press, 2000.

Sampaio, Ana. "Transnational Feminisms in a Global Matrix." *International Feminist Journal of Politics* 6:2 (2004): 181–206.

Sánchez, George J. *Becoming Mexican American: Ethnicity, Culture, and Identity in Chicano Los Angeles, 1900–1945*. Oxford: Oxford University Press, 1993.

Sánchez, Rosaura. "The History of Chicanas: A proposal for a materialist perspective." In *Between Borders: Essays on Mexicana/Chicana History*, ed. Adelaida R. Del Castillo. Encino, CA: Floricanto Press, 1990: 1–29.

Sánchez, Rosaura, and Rosa Martinez Cruz, ed. *Essays on la Mujer*. Los Angeles: Chicano Studies Center Publications, UCLA, 1977.

Sandoval, Anna Marie. *Toward a Latina Feminism of the Americas: Repression and Resistance in Chicana and Mexicana Literature*. Austin: University of Texas Press, 2008.

Sandoval, Chela. "Feminism and Racism: A Report on the 1981 National Women's Studies Association Conference." In *Making Face, Making Soul—Haciendo Caras: Creative and Critical Perspective by Women of Color*, ed. Gloria Anzaldúa. San Francisco: Aunt Lute Foundation, 1990: 55–71.

———. *Methodology of the Oppressed*. Minneapolis: University of Minesota Press, 2000.

———. "US Third World Feminism: The Theory and Method of Oppositional Consciousness in the Postmodern World." *Genders* 10 (Spring 1991): 1–24.

San Miguel Jr., Guadalupe. *Brown, not White: School Integration and the Chicano Movement in Houston*. College Station: Texas A&M University Press, 2001.

Scott, James. *Domination and the Arts of Resistance: Hidden Transcripts*. New Haven: Yale University Press, 1990.

Scott, Joan W., Cora Kaplan, and Debra Keates, eds. *Transitions, Environments, Translations: Feminisms in International Politics*. New York: Routledge: 1997.

Segura, Denise. "Chicanas and Triple Oppression in the Labor Force." In *Chicana Voices: Intersections of Class, Race, and Gender*, ed. Teresa Córdova et al. Austin: Center for Mexican American Studies, University of Texas, 1986: 47–65.

——. "'In the Beginning He Wouldn't Lift Even a Spoon': The Division of Household Labor." In *Building with Our Hands: New Directions in Chicana Studies*, ed. Adela de la Torre and Beatriz M. Pesquera. Berkeley: University of California Press, 1993: 181–195.

Shohat, Ella. "Introduction." In *Talking Visions: Multicultural Feminism in a Transnational Age*, ed. Ella Shohat. Cambridge: MIT Press, 1998: 1–62.

——, ed. *Talking Visions: Multicultural Feminism in a Transnational Age*. New York: New Museum of Contemporary Art, 1999.

Sievers, Sharon. "Six (or More) Feminists in Search of a Historian." In *Expanding The Boundaries of Women's History: Essays on Women in the Third World*, ed. Cheryl Johnson-Odim and Margaret Strobel. Bloomington: Indiana University Press, 1992: 319–330.

Simons, Margaret A. "Racism and Feminism: A Schism in the Sisterhood." *Feminist Studies* 5 (1979): 384–401.

Sinha, Mrinalini, Donna Guy, and Angela Woollacoff, eds. *Feminisms and Internationalism*. Oxford: Blackwell, 1999.

Smith, Andrea. *Conquest: Sexual Violence and American Indian Genocide*. Cambridge, MA: South End Press, 2005.

——. "Heteropatriarchy and the Three Pillars of White Supremacy: Rethinking Women of Color Organizing." In *Color of Violence: The INCITE! Anthology*, ed. Incite! Women of Color against Violence. Cambridge: South End Press, 2006: 66–73.

Smith, Barbara, ed. *Home Girls: A Black Feminist Anthology*. New York: Kitchen Table Press, 1983.

——. "Notes for Yet Another Paper on Black Feminism, or Will the Real Enemy Please Stand Up." *Conditions: Five* 2:2 (Autumn 1979): 123–127.

——. *The Truth That Never Hurts: Writings on Race, Gender and Freedom*. New Brunswick: Rutgers University Press, 1998.

Soldatenko, Michael. "Mexican Student Movements in Los Angeles and Mexico City, 1968." *Latino Studies* 1 (2003): 284–300.

Sommer, Doris. "'Not Just a Personal Story': Women's Testimonios and the Plural Self." In *Life/Lines: Theorizing Women's Autobiography*, ed. Bella Brodzki and Celeste Schenck. Ithaca: Cornell University Press, 1988: 107–130.

Sosa-Riddell, Adaljiza. "History of MALCS." In *Reader's Companion to U.S. Women's History*, ed. Wilma Mankiller et al. New York: Houghton Mifflin, 1998: 386.

Sosa-Riddell, Adaljiza, and Elisa Facio. *Chicana Rebellions: Chicana Feminisms and Socialist Legacies*. Forthcoming.

Soto, Gary. *Jessie de la Cruz: A Profile of a United Farm Worker*. New York: Persea Books, 2000.

Soto, Shirlene. *Emergence of the Modern Mexican Woman: Her Participation in Revolution and Struggle for Equality, 1910–1940*. Denver: Arden Press, 1990.

Spivak, Gayatri Chakravorty. "Can the Subaltern Speak?" In *Marxism and the Interpretation of Culture*, ed. Cary Nelson and Lawrence Grossberg. Chicago: University of Illinois Press, 1988: 271–315.

——. "Subaltern Studies: Deconstructing Historiography." In *In Other Worlds: Essays in Cultural Politics*. New York: Methuen, 1987: 197–221.

Springer, Kimberly. *Living for the Revolution: Black Feminist Organizations, 1968–1980*. Durham, NC: Duke University Press, 2005.

——, ed. *Still Lifting, Still Climbing: African American Women's Contemporary Activism*. New York: New York University Press, 1999.

Stein, Arlene. "Sisters and Queers: The Decentering of Lesbian Feminism." In *Cultural Politics and Social Movements*, ed. Marcy Darnovsky, Barbara Epstein, and Richard Flacks. Philadelphia: Temple University Press, 1995: 133–153.

Steiner, Stan. *La Raza: The Mexican Americans*. New York: Harper & Row, 1969.

Stephen, Lynn. *Women and Social Movements in Latin America: Power from Below*. Austin: University of Texas, 1997.

Stern, Steve J. *Remembering Pinochet's Chile: On the Eve of London 1998*. Durham, NC: Duke University Press, 2004.

———. *The Secret History of Gender: Women, Men and Power in Late Colonial Mexico*. Chapel Hill: University of North Carolina Press, 1994.

Stevenson, Linda S. "Las mujeres políticas y la izquierda en México: Reclamo de un nuevo espacio en la política institucional." In *Género y cultura en América latina: Cultura y participación política*, vol. 1, ed. Maria Luisa Tarrés Barraza. México: Colegio de México, 1998: 193–215.

Sweeney, Judith. "Chicana History: A Review of the Literature." In *Essays on La Mujer*, ed. Rosaura Sanchez and Rosa Martinez Cruz. Los Angeles: Chicano Studies Center Publications, UCLA, 1977: 99–123.

Tanaka, Michiko. *Through Harsh Winters: The Life of a Japanese Immigrant Woman / [as told to] Akemi Kikumura*. Novato, CA: Chandler and Sharp, 1981.

Taylor, Diana. *The Archive and the Repertoire: Performing Cultural Memory in the Americas*. Durham, NC: Duke University Press, 2007.

Terkel, Studs, et al. *Envelopes of Sound: Six Practitioners Discuss the Method, Theory, and Practice of Oral History and Oral Testimony*, ed. Ronald J. Grele. Chicago: Precedent Publishers, 1975.

Third World Communications. *Third World Women*. San Francisco: Third World Communications, 1972.

Thompson, Becky. *A Promise and a Way of Life: White Antiracist Activism*. Minneapolis: University of Minnesota Press, 2001.

———. "Multiracial Feminism: Recasting the Chronology of Second Wave Feminism." *Feminist Studies* 28:2 (Summer 2002): 337–360.

Thorton Dill, Bonnie. "The Dialectics of Black Womanhood." *Signs: Journal of Women in Culture and Society* 4 (1979): 543–555.

Toney, Mark. "Revisiting the National Welfare Rights Organization." *Colorlines*. www.colorlines.com/index.php. Accessed July 23, 2008.

Torres, Gerald, and Katie Pace. "Understanding Patriarchy as an Expression of Whiteness: Insights from the Chicana Movement." *Washington University Journal of Law and Policy* 18 (2005): 129–172.

Trouillot, Michel-Rolph. *Silencing the Past: Power the Production of History*. Boston: Beacon Press, 1995.

Trujillo, Carla. *Chicana Lesbians: The Girls Our Mothers Warned Us About*. Berkeley: Third Women Press, 1991.

———. "Chicana Lesbians: Fear and Loathing in the Chicano Community." In *Chicana Critical Issues*, ed. Norma Alarcón, Rafaela Castro, Emma Pérez, Beatriz Pesquera, Adaljiza Sosa-Riddell, and Patricia Zavella. Berkeley: Third Woman Press, 1993: 117–125.

Turner, Frederick C. *The Dynamic of Mexican Nationalism*. Chapel Hill: University of North Carolina Press, 1968.

———. "Los Efectos de la participación femenina en la Revolución de 1910." *Historia Mexicana* 16:4 (abril-junio 1967): 601–620.

Vargas, Zaragoza. "Chicanos and the Shaping of the Left." *Science and Society* 65:1 (Spring 2001): 131–136.

Vasquez, Carlos. "Women in the Chicano Movement." In *Mexican Women in the United States: Struggles Past and Present*, ed. Adelaida R. Del Castillo and Magdalena Mora. Los Angeles: Chicano Studies Research Publications, UCLA, 1980.

Vásquez, Enriqueta. *Enriqueta Vásquez and the Chicano Movement: Writings from "El Grito del Norte,"* ed. Lorena Oropeza and Dionne Espinoza. Houston: Arte Público Press, 2006.

Velez-I., Carlos G. "The Nonconsenting Sterilization of Mexican Women in Los Angeles." In *Twice a Minority: Mexican American Women*, ed. Margarita Melville. St. Louis: C. V. Mosby, 1980: 235–244.

Vieweswaren, Kamala. *Fictions of Feminist Ethnography*. Minneapolis: University of Minnesota Press, 1994.

Wallace, Michele. *Black Macho and the Myth of the Super Woman*. New York: Dial Press, 1978.

Ware, Cellestine. *Woman Power: the Movement for Women's Liberation*. New York: Tower Publications, 1970.

Weaver, Jace, Craig S. Womack, and Robert A. Warrior. *American Indian Literary Nationalism*. Albuquerque: University of New Mexico Press, 2006.

Weber, Devra. "Keeping Community, Challenging Boundaries: Indigenous Migrants, Internationalist Workers, and Mexican Revolutionaries, 1900–1920." In *Mexico and Mexicans in the History and Culture of the United States*, ed. John Tutino. Austin: University of Texas Press, forthcoming.

———. "Mexican Women on Strike: Memory, History, and Oral Narrative." In *Between Borders: Essays on Mexicana/Chicana History*, ed. Adelaida R. Del Castillo. Encino, CA: Floricanto Press, 1990: 175–200.

White, E. Frances. "Africa on My Mind: Gender, Counter Discourse, and African-American Nationalism." In *Expanding The Boundaries of Women's History: Essays on Women in the Third World*, ed. Cheryl Johnson-Odim and Margaret Strobel. Bloomington: Indiana University Press, 1992: 57–73.

White, Hayden. *The Content of the Form: Narrative Discourse and Historical Representation*. Baltimore: Johns Hopkins University Press, 1987.

White, Richard. *Remembering Ahanagran: Storytelling in a Family's Past*. New York: Hill and Wang, 1998.

Williams, Raymond. "Base and Superstructure in Marxist Cultural Theory." In *Problems in Materialism and Culture*. 2nd ed. New York: Verso, 1997: 31–49.

———. *Marxism and Literature*. London: Oxford University Press, 1977.

Wolf, Diane L. *Feminist Dilemmas in Fieldwork*. Boulder, CO:: Westview Press, 1996.

Yarbro-Bejarano, Yvonne. "The Lesbian Body in Latin Cultural Production." In *¿Entiendes? Queer Readings, Hispanic Writings*, ed. Emile L. Bergmann and Paul Jullian Smith. Durham, NC: Duke University Press, 1995: 181–200.

———. "Primer encuentro de lesbianas feministas latinoamericanas y caribeñas." In *Third Woman: The Sexuality of Latinas*, ed. Norma Alarcón, Ana Castillo, and Cherríe Moraga 4 (1989): 143–146.

Ybarra-Frausto, Tómas. "Interview with Tómas Ybarra-Frausto: The Chicano Movement in a Multicultural/Multinational Society." In *On Edge: The Crisis of Contemporary Latin*

American Culture, ed. George Yúdice, Jean Franco, and Juan Flores. Minneapolis: University of Minnesota Press, 1992: 207–216.

Young, Cynthia A. *Soul Power: Culture, Radicalism, and the Making of a U.S. Third World Left.* Durham, NC: Duke University Press, 2006.

Yúdice, George. "Testimonio and Postmodernism." *Latin American Review* 70 (Summer 1991): 15–31.

Yung, Judy. *Unbound Feet: A Social History of Chinese Women in San Francisco.* Berkeley: University of California Press, 1995.

Zavella, Patricia. "Feminist Insider Dilemmas: Constructing Ethnic Identity with Chicana Informants." In *Feminist Dilemmas in Fieldwork*, ed. Diane L. Wolf. Boulder, CO: Westview Press, 1996: 138–159.

———. "Playing with Fire: The Gendered Construction of Chicana/Mexicana Sexuality." In *The Gender/Sexuality Reader: Culture, History, Political Economy*, ed. Roger Lancaster and Micaela di Leonardo. New York: Routledge, 1997: 392–409.

———. "The Politics of Race and Gender: Organizing Chicana Cannery Workers in Northern California." In *Chicana Critical Issues*, ed. Norma Alarcón, Rafaela Castro, Emma Pérez, Beatriz Pesquera, Adaljiza Sosa-Riddell, and Patricia Zavella. Berkeley: Third Woman Press, 1993: 127–153.

———. "The Problematic Relationship of Feminism and Chicana Studies." *Women's Studies* 17:1–2 (1989): 23–34.

———. "Reflections on Diversity among Chicanas." *Frontiers: A Journal of Women Studies* 13:2 (1991): 73–85.

———. *Sunbelt Working Mothers: Reconciling Family and Factory.* Ithaca: Cornell University Press, 1993.

———. *Women's Work and Chicano Families: Cannery Workers of the Santa Clara Valley.* Ithaca: Cornell University Press, 1987.

Zia, Helen. "Women of Color in Leadership." *Social Policy* 23:4 (Summer 1993): 51–55.

Page numbers in italics refer to photographs and other illustrations.